RELIGION AND ADAPTATION

To Frannie —
With love from the author
Bill Adam

RELIGION
AND
ADAPTATION

WILLIAM Y. ADAMS

CSLI Publications
STANFORD

Copyright © 2005
CSLI Publications
Center for the Study of Language and Information
Leland Stanford Junior University
Printed in the United States
09 08 07 06 05   1 2 3 4 5

Library of Congress Cataloging-in-Publication Data

Adams, William Yewdale, 1927–
Religion and adaptation / by William Y. Adams.

p. cm.

Includes bibliographical references and index.

ISBN 1-57586-475-4 (hardcover : alk. paper)
ISBN 1-57586-476-2 (pbk. : alk. paper)

1. Religion. I. Title.

BL48.A33 2004
200–dc22   2004007978
CIP

∞ The acid-free paper used in this book meets the minimum requirements of
the American National Standard for Information Sciences—Permanence of
Paper for Printed Library Materials, ANSI Z39.48-1984.

CSLI was founded in 1983 by researchers from Stanford University, SRI International,
and Xerox PARC to further the research and development of integrated theories of
language, information, and computation. CSLI headquarters and CSLI Publications are
located on the campus of Stanford University.

CSLI Publications reports new developments in the study of language,
information, and computation. Please visit our web site at
http://cslipublications.stanford.edu/
for comments on this and other titles, as well as for changes
and corrections by the author and publisher.

To the Navajo and Nubian peoples
who taught me to appreciate religion

CONTENTS

Preface and Acknowledgments

This is a book of ideas, as much philosophical as anthropological, and more speculative than scholarly. I am not, and will never be, an expert on the subject of religion, and have up to now written very little about it. But for half a century, off and on, I've been thinking, reading, and teaching about it, and I feel the urge now to put some of my ideas on paper, before I forget them. In preparing the book I've done a certain amount of additional reading, but not nearly as much as I could or, probably, should have. The book covers only as much of the domain of religion as my experience and my thought has reached, which is a lot less than the total subject.

Readers are therefore warned not to expect more than is here. My aim is only to bring conceptual clarity to one particular field of human experience—that of religion—not to follow up on the larger philosophical issues that are suggested at many points. I'm also not attempting to develop a general theory of religion, for my studies have convinced me that no such thing is possible. Religion, like culture itself, is simply too complex and diverse a phenomenon to fit under the umbrella of any one theory. My hope is simply to enhance *understanding*, which is not the same thing as theory.

I have to make it clear at the outset that I'm an unabashed Baconian empiricist. In that tradition I have sought to understand religion not by reading what others have said about it, but by a comparative study of actual religions, living and dead. My qualification to write the book, insofar as I have one, is not a thorough knowledge of theoretical literature but a thorough knowledge of ethnographic and historical literature. My study, as I present it in these pages, has essentially three empirical bases:

1) A detailed first-hand experience of a few religions, supplemented by much additional reading about them. This is true above all in regard to

the religions of Navajo Indians, Arab villagers, and American Protestants, among all of whom I have lived for many years. It is true to a lesser extent in regard to Pueblo Indians, European Catholics, scriptural Islam, with which I have some first-hand as well as literary familiarity. This information, specifically that regarding Navajos and Arab villagers, forms the basis of Part 1 of my book.

2) Extensive reading about a great many other religions, past and present, in both ethnographic and historical literature. This information figures prominently in Part 3 of the book.

3) A fairly wide experience of human nature, gained through three quarters of a century of living, traveling, working, and interacting with people in more than forty countries, in a very wide variety of cultural circumstances, and in half a dozen languages. The insights thus gained come into play especially in Part 2 of the book.

I like to think that one of the virtues, or at least the novelties, of my work is that I have not taken Christianity as a yardstick or a norm for the study of religion, as many writers have consciously or unconsciously done. The simple reason is that virtually no one is able to be wholly objective in thinking about Christianity; its influence in our lives, either positive or negative, has simply been too powerful and pervasive. Writers who take Christianity as a model almost invariably end—if they don't begin—by making invidious comparisons, either favorable or unfavorable, between it and other religions. Such an approach would defeat my purpose at the outset, for my hope is that readers will approach the subject of religion with completely open minds, as any proper ethnographer should. Toward that end, I have begun the book with extended descriptions of two religions, outside the ambit of Christianity, that will serve as my principal models, and that I hope readers will find as interesting and appealing as I do.

As a characterization of my approach, I can hardly do better than to quote the words written by Emile Durkheim almost a century ago:

> Leaving aside all conceptions of religion in general, let us consider the various religions in their concrete reality, and attempt to disengage that which they have in common; for religion cannot be defined except by the characteristics which are found wherever religion itself is found. In this comparison, then, we shall make use of all the religious systems which we can know, those of the present and those of the past, the most primitive and simple as well as the most recent and refined; for we have neither

the right nor the logical means of excluding some and retaining others (Durkheim 1915: 24).

Another feature which may perhaps distinguish my work from that of predecessors is my lack of certainty on many points. I have the impression that most if not all the earlier scholars grew up in religious households, or at least religious environments. They began their inquiries and their writing with a confident assumption that they knew what religion was, and perhaps also what it wasn't, because they had experienced it at first hand. As a result their books about religion nearly always 'start in the middle,' rather then at the beginning—they tend to assume that readers have the same foreknowledge and the same presuppositions that they have. The either skip over altogether the all-important question of definition, or treat it in a very off-hand manner, as I will suggest at length in Chapter 8.

My own experience has been very different, for I grew up neither in a religious household nor, by and large, in a religious environment. I therefore began my studies with a frank recognition that I did not know what religion was and wasn't. This book is the culmination of my efforts to find out, and to a considerable extent it is part of a still ongoing inquiry.

To all intents and purposes, my approach is that of a visitor from another planet. I'm trying in the first instance to acquire an understanding of religion, mainly through empirical observation and through the testimony of the votaries. Then, in this book, I'm trying to pass on my understanding to other visitors from the alien planet, with the assumption that their minds at the outset were as blank as mine. I have therefore necessarily begun at what should properly always be the beginning point—with an attempt to define religion as well as the many terms that we use in trying to describe it.

Readers will find that my approach to religion, coming at it in this way, is a good deal more analytical, or perhaps I should say componential, than is that of most other writers. That is, I believe that the religions not only of individual peoples, but the subject of religion as a whole, can only be understood as the sum of all its parts, without any apriori assumption that some of them are unimportant. From that perspective I have devoted a great deal of space, in the chapters that follow, to beliefs and practices that are either ignored or dismissed as mere 'superstition,' by other writers, but which are in fact a very large part of the daily religious life of many peoples.

Why now?   My friend and colleague Lee Elioseff is responsible for the insight that the life of a scholar is like a continually rising balloon. The higher you get, the more territory you can see over, and the more you begin to see overall patterns that aren't evident at ground level. But as you rise further you begin to lose sight of the details, until you may reach a height at which you see only the grand patterns. It becomes easy to forget then that the big picture is made up of scores of little ones. Ideally, books should be written when you reach an optimum altitude, where you can see as much as possible of the big picture without losing sight of the small ones.

That is the altitude that I've been hoping to reach for some years, before writing a book about religion. I've had it in mind for a long time, but have put it off from year to year while seeking for more information, and greater insight. But I find now that more information does not bring more insight, and so I've about decided that I won't gain anything from further altitude. In other words, I think I've reached the optimum altitude *for me.* Some critics will perhaps suggest that I should get a better telescope, and keep going up, but at age seventy-six I have to face actuarial facts.

Readers need to be clear that my intention most of the time is not didactic. I'm not absolutely certain about a lot of the things that I've said in these pages, and I'm not sure at all in some cases. During most of my adult life I've been trying to explain religion to myself, not to others, and this book represents the sum of my efforts to date. So in these pages I am just thinking out loud, not lecturing. My book will not resolve any controversies; at best I hope that it may bring a measure of clarity to what is all too often a murky debate.

And if my purpose is not didactic, it assuredly is not evangelical. That is, I'm not trying to win anybody over to my particular point of view, which happens to be that of a freethinker. But I think that religious unbelief, no less than belief, is a highly personal matter, and should be respected as such. I've heard that the Sri Lankan constitution specifies that no person may try to change the religion of another person. If true, that strikes me as one of the most enlightened, sensible, and humane provisions of law that has ever been enacted. How much bloodshed and suffering would have been spared if all the world adhered to it!

*Why the
title?*   The book's title is meant to convey, in shorthand form, my particular approach to religion. I regard culture, in its totality, as humanity's basic adaptive mechanism in coping with its environment, and I regard reli-

gion, a major component of nearly all culture, as the principal mechanism by which people cope with one particular part of their environment—the part consisting of powerful but mostly unseen forces. The sub-title is meant to suggest every people's religion is a logical and a reasonable way of coping with the unseen environment *as they perceive it.*

The content of the book

Readers will soon discover that this is something of a hybrid work, part ethnographic and part philosophical, reflecting my dual interests. Rather than mix the two up, however, I have sought to keep them largely separate. The second and third parts, which are the book I set out to write, are couched at a highly abstract and more or less philosophical level. But a good anthropologist (which I hope I am) cannot generalize or philosophize without starting from a sound empirical data base, and in my case that begins with a familiarity with Navajo Indian religion and with Arab village religion.

The further I proceeded in writing Parts 2 and 3, the more evident it became that a highly abstract discourse could not be sustained without presenting at least an outline of the data on which it is based. Accordingly I have opened the book with capsule descriptions of the two religions with which I am most familiar, and a chapter making specific comparisons between the two. These are written in traditional ethnographic style, with a lot of particularized detail and without much philosophical interpretation. This, then, is the platform from which I dive into the murky waters of philosophical speculation. The data presented in Part 1 will be cited repeatedly, by way of exemplification, in Parts 2 and 3.

There is, consequently, a certain 'disconnect' between the first and the later parts of the book, in terms of the levels of discourse involved. One is highly specific, the others highly abstract. I am fully aware of this, but I don't think it can be avoided. If I would be at once ethnographer and philosopher, I have necessarily to speak in two separate languages, and at different levels. I have, consequently, opened each of the first and second parts with an introductory chapter, setting forth my qualifications and/or my motivation to write that part.

Sources and influences

The ideas expressed in these pages are my own, except in those cases where an external source is specifically acknowledged. That does not for a moment mean that I think they're original; I'm sure most of them are not. Religion being the endlessly fascinating and controversial subject that it is, it's probably not possible to say anything very profound about it that hasn't been said before. I mean only that these ideas have occurred to me without the benefit of external stimulation—as they probably have to scores of other thinking persons. But since this is my book containing my ideas, I haven't gone out of my way to identify other authors who may have said the same things, or those who have disagreed with them. I expect that reviewers will have a field day doing that.

Where I have cited the work or the influence of others, it is much of the time a summation of their ideas developed over a lifetime of work, as I have come to understand them—sometimes in their own words and sometimes as refracted through the lens of later scholars. For that reason I have largely dispensed with the usual scholarly apparatus, except where necessary to identify the sources of direct quotes or of unfamiliar material. Throughout I refer repeatedly to the work of thinkers like Tylor, Durkheim, Weber, Marx, and Freud, but usually without citing particular books and pages. The relevant works of each person thus named are listed in the Bibliography at the end of the book.

Acknowledg-
ments

I am grateful to my brother, Ernest Adams, and to an anonymous reviewer, both of whom read the manuscript in its entirety and made many insightful suggestions. I have not followed all of them, but that is because of legitimate differences of perception that I have now acknowledged in the text. With reference to Part 1, I have also to give very special thanks to David Brugge and to Edward Reeves—two of the outstanding authorities respectively on the Navajos and on Arab villagers. Both have read over my text in detail and have offered a great many valuable suggestions and corrections.

PART 1

THE ETHNOGRAPHY OF RELIGION

1

INTRODUCTION TO PART 1

My qualifications to write the next three chapters are those of a traditional, professionally trained ethnographer, in the dominant tradition of the mid-twentieth century. Although I have, from force of circumstances, spent most of my field career doing archaeology, my earliest interest was in living peoples rather than dead ones, and my first major published work is a study of a Navajo Indian community (Adams 1963). I have actually had a lot more formal training in ethnography than I have in archaeology, although I don't set a great deal of store by either. A good ethnographer, as viewed in the middle years of the last century, was not someone armed with a theoretically profound research problem or a battery of sophisticated analytical procedures. He or she was someone who lived for an extended period among another people, learned to understand their thoughts as well as their actions, partly through a command of the language, and who kept his/her eyes, ears, and mind open. It was not always necessary to have a narrowly focused topic of study; the overriding objective was to get to know the people, and to see the world through their eyes. Appropriate methods of study as well as specific topics of interest suggested themselves within the context of each particular field study situation. (The nature and the objectives of twentieth-century ethnography will be considered more fully in the Introduction to Parts 2 and 3.)

For what they are worth, I have met the above-mentioned criteria among both Navajo Indians and village Arabs, the former in the American Southwest and the latter in the northern Sudan and in Egypt. Before detailing my experiences among either, however, I should explain that in neither case was I, most of the time, doing overt ethnographic investigation. I lived and worked among the Navajos for over a decade in a number of different capacities, but most importantly as the operator of a trading post. My work among village Arabs for more than two decades was almost entirely as an archaeologist. But my interest and my sense of identity as an ethnographer was never extinguished; I kept my eyes and ears open, learned the languages after a fashion, and asked such questions as I could about cultural matters. Most importantly though I was in daily interaction with both peoples, on their home ground and much of the time on their terms. Most of the time, as trader and as archaeologist, I was a non-intrusive investigator; an onlooker and a participant without any overt research agenda. I was free simply to watch and listen and learn, without imposing myself as inquirer. I am convinced that, when one is in search first and foremost of understanding, this is the most advantageous role.

The Navajo experience

I spent a considerable part of my youth on the Navajo Reservation, where my mother was an official of the Bureau if Indian Affairs. In my 20s and early 30s I myself worked among the Navajos in a number of different capacities, most significantly for three years as the operator of a trading post (see Adams 1963). I was also more overtly an ethnographer on two occasions, once when investigating the Navajos' experiences in off-reservation employment, and once when investigating their perceptions of Public Health Service medical facilities. Like many Bilagáana (the Navajo word for White people) on the reservation I attended quite a few 'squaw dances,'[1] and I have observed portions of other ceremonies as well. I became, of necessity, fluent in the 'trader Navajo' pidgin, but it is not a language that permits of any amount of abstract discourse. I was never, in any overt sense, an investigator of Navajo religion. Apart from observing at first hand its pervasive influence in Navajo thought and action, nearly all of what I know about its specific content has come from reading. Nevertheless, I have had the opportunity to observe the ways Navajos think and act over a long period of time and in a wide variety of circumstances, and that has provided me with a window through which to view the Navajo world and its human and non-human inhabitants.

The interest generated by my personal experiences naturally led to a great deal of follow-up reading. As all anthropologists know, the literature on Navajo religion is immense, and I have not by any means read all of it. I have however read all of the major works and many of the more particularized ones, and I think that that, combined with years of first-hand contact, has given me a deeper insight into the religion of the

---

[1]This term, through now considered politically incorrect, is still universally employed by Navajos themselves as a designation for Enemy Way ceremonies.

Navajos than of any other people except the Nubians. I will be drawing on it extensively in the chapters that follow.

What I have said about the Navajos is true to a lesser extent as regards the religion of their Pueblo Indian neighbors, which I will also cite from time to time. I have known several Hopis fairly well, and have also observed ceremonies at Hopi, Zuni, and Santo Domingo. Again, however, my knowledge of the specific content of Pueblo religion has come mainly from extensive reading.

The Arab experience

My experience among Arabs has been chiefly though not exclusively with Nubians. They are a people of African origin, found today only in the far northern Sudan and southern Egypt. Their indigenous language belongs to a central African family, although all males and most females also speak Arabic. There are a few other distinctive features in Nubian culture, not found among neighboring peoples, but this is not true in the case of religion. The religious beliefs and practices of Nubian villagers are different in no important respect from those of other, purely Arabic-speakers to the north and south of them, from Khartoum to Cairo and Alexandria. For purposes of describing their religion I will therefore speak of the Nubians simply as Arabs, although in other contexts they insist on a separate identity.

I lived and worked off and on among Nubians, and to a lesser extent among other Arabs, for twenty-five years. The most salient experience however was the five continuous years that I spent directing archaeological excavations in the area that was to be flooded by the Aswan High Dam. During much of that time I lived in small villages, in which my only neighbors were Nubians, and nearly all interaction with them was in colloquial Arabic—another language that I had to learn out of pure necessity. In those circumstances I lived in much more intimate and more continuous contact with Nubians than I had ever done with Navajos; I had them as my immediate, next-door neighbors. Once again, of course, I was not conducting an ethnographic study of religion; I simply learned whatever I learned by incidental, daily observation and a small amount of inquiry.

The particular version of Islam that I encountered in the villages of the Sudan (and later also in Egypt) was not the canonical Islam of scripture, but the folk religion of peasant villagers. Its main focus is not on a distant and unapproachable Allah but on the scores of saints who are living presences, dwelling within the literally hundreds of local shrines scattered about the country. This has been of proportionately more interest to me than is scriptural Islam, partly because of my first-hand experience of it, but also because of the proletarian bias that I share with most anthropologists. Since neither I nor the villagers can read Classical Arabic, Islamic folk religion is much more accessible than is scriptural Islam, both to me and to them. Fortunately it too is the subject of a lot of excellent descriptive literature, much of which I've read. Once again, the descriptive matter presented in Chapter 3 is drawn as much or more from that literature as from my personal experience.

I have in addition a pretty considerable knowledge of orthodox (scriptural) Islam, which, as I will show in Chapter 3, is almost a separate religion from village Islam. I cannot read the scriptures in their original, Classical Arabic,[2] but I have read the Quran and many other works in translation, and have read a great deal about Islam written by both Muslims and Christians. In Khartoum I have lived among practicing, orthodox Muslims as well as among followers of the heterodox sects.

I have one advantage, vis-à-vis the Nubians and other Arabs, that I could never enjoy with Navajos. For them, as for all Near Eastern peoples, religion is not only a defined category of thought and action, but a hot topic. Serious discussions, as opposed to gossip, very often end up on the subject either of religion or politics, or frequently both. And I had, and still have, a great many intellectual Nubian and other Arab friends, with whom I could freely discuss questions of religion.

Other
ethnographic
experience

My other major cross-cultural experiences have been chiefly in Mexico, where I have traveled many times; in China, where I have traveled several times, and taught for five months (and witnessed at first hand the Tien An Men demonstrations of 1989); Egypt, where I worked off and on for a decade; England, where I spent two sabbatical years at Cambridge; and in France, where I have also traveled extensively and often. In all those countries I speak the native language after a fashion: fluently in the case of Spanish and French, colloquially in the case of Arabic, and haltingly in the case of Chinese. I include that information because of my conviction that no religion can be fully accessed without reference to the language in which it is embedded. At some levels, religion *is* language.

Purely as a tourist I have traveled in more than forty countries, and of course have visited an enormous number of religious sites, standing

---

[2]I speak Sudanese colloquial Arabic, which is essentially a separate language.

or in ruins. I say 'of course' because it's nearly unavoidable. An extraordinarily high proportion of the world's touristic attractions are religious
sites—further proof, if any were needed, of the importance that religion
has had everywhere and at all times. I have witnessed, and occasionally
been very moved by, major ceremonies in Guatemala, France, Egypt, the
Sudan, and Tibet, although I had at the time little insight into what they
meant for the participants or the onlookers.

I should add further that I have such knowledge of Christianity, and
more particularly of Protestant Christianity, as comes more or less automatically when growing up in America, surrounded by Protestant neighbors. I've attended a fair number of church services, as a courtesy to
friends or relatives, and I've read the Bible as well as several books about
it. I've also read up on certain areas of church doctrine, because they are
relevant to my special studies of medieval Nubian Christianity, on which
I'm considered something of an expert.

Apart from the Navajo and Arab cases, my ethnographic reading on
the subject of religion has been extensive but spotty. I've read several
of the classics, like Elsie Clews Parsons' *Pueblo Indian Religion* (1939),
Reichel-Dolmatoff's *Amazonian Cosmos* (1971), Evans-Pritchard's *Nuer
Religion* (1956), Geertz's *The Religion of Java* (1960), and Malinowski's
Coral Gardens and their Magic (1935), as well as several works on religion in China. In addition to ethnographic studies, I have read a great
many theoretical works on religion by anthropologists, and a few of the
classic ones by sociologists, but relatively few by followers of other disciplines. Persons with a more extensive knowledge of the theoretical literature will probably find many gaps in my knowledge, and as a result
may find much of my discussion naive.

Readers will recognize, then, that by far my most complete first-
hand knowledge of religion comes from three sources: American Protestantism, the Navajos, and Arab villagers. In Chapters 2 and 3 I will offer
capsule descriptions of the Navajo and the Arab village religions, partly
because they are the basis of much of my own understanding, and partly
because the differences between the two faiths, which at first glance
would seem nearly total, nicely frame the problem of how to understand religion more generally. I will consider those differences as well as
similarities in Chapter 4.

I have tried in Part 1 to present portraits of the Navajo and Arab religions as I came to know them at first hand, as well as through a great deal
of related literature. But those experiences and that literature belong to an

earlier time, not to today. Notwithstanding the best efforts of fundamentalists, no religion is immune to the forces of change, and those forces have been especially powerful in the turbulent half century we have just undergone. Visitors to the Navajo or the Arab worlds today will therefore not encounter precisely the beliefs or the practices I have described; my descriptions are snapshots of an earlier moment in time. I nevertheless describe them throughout these pages in the present tense, to underscore the fact that they were, when I and other scholars came to know them, living and vital religions, not merely remembrances of a vanished time.

Every religion has the two complementary aspects of belief and behavior, sometimes glossed by anthropologists as 'myth' and 'ritual.' In the treatment of Navajo and Arab village religion I have sought to describe both, but I have placed considerably more emphasis on the dimension of belief. This reflects my personal conviction that every religion is first and foremost a cognitive system, and only secondarily a system of behavior. People's religiosity, to my mind, is not measured by the frequency with which they say prayers or attend church; it is measured by the extent to which they rely on religious doctrines to understand the world in which they live. It is a theme that I will develop further in Part 2.

2

NAVAJO INDIAN RELIGION

The Navajos are by far the largest group of Indians in North America, in any cultural sense.[3] They number well over 200,000 persons today—a tenfold increase since a century ago. Their main reservation occupies an enormous contiguous area of high desert and mountains in Arizona, New Mexico, and Utah, but there are also three outlying, smaller reservations, and Navajos in addition occupy large areas of public land adjacent to the reservations. The total area of their occupancy is at least twenty million acres, an area as large as the New England states combined, with the exception of Maine.

Navajo religion has been an endless source of fascination for anthropologists for over a hundred years, and remains so today. The number of published titles runs into the hundreds, with more appearing every year. It may not be the most complex of all tribal religions, but it is surely the most complex one that has ever been recorded with any degree of completeness. (The religion of the neighboring Pueblo peoples is by all accounts still more complex, but large parts of it remain jealously guarded secrets, and will never be recorded.) By contrast there has always been a kind of mutual affinity between Navajos and anthropologists—the Navajos historically have been willing and even eager to explain their beliefs and practices to those who would make an effort to understand. And not only anthropologists, but virtually all Bilagáana[4] (the Navajo term for Anglos) have been charmed by the incredibly rich expressiveness both of the Navajo myths and of the accompanying ceremonies.

---

[3] In the census of 1990 the Cherokees, Choctaws, and Apaches were credited with higher numbers than the Navajos, but those figures represent self-reported data, much of it from persons having only a small quantum of Indian blood, and no vestiges of Indian culture. The combined enrolled membership of the various Cherokee, Choctaw, and Apache groups is well below the total Navajo figure.

[4] Corrupted from Spanish 'Americano.'

Linguistic as well as archaeological evidence makes it clear that the Navajos, with their close cousins the Apaches, migrated to their present habitat within the last thousand years, from someplace in northwestern Canada. Both groups are speakers of Athabascan languages, which otherwise are found almost entirely in the western sub-Arctic region of North America. Within that homeland their ancestors were nomadic foragers, but after arrival in the Southwest they became primarily sedentary farmers. After the immemorial fashion of nomads who settle down, they adopted most of the culture and lifestyle of their previously settled neighbors—in this case the various Pueblo groups. For four hundred years Navajos and Pueblos lived in close and almost symbiotic proximity, in which there was continual intermarriage, and a great deal of cultural borrowing. Much and perhaps most of the content of Navajo religion can be traced to this source, though there has been much reinterpretation, reflecting the creativity of the Navajo borrowers.

The first Spanish explorers arrived within Navajo territory in 1539, but there was no permanent settlement by Nakai (the generic term for all Spanish-speakers) until the end of the sixteenth century. Their arrival was by no means a disaster for the Navajos and Apaches, as it was for so many native groups; on the contrary it brought all kinds of new opportunities. The newcomers, in addition to new crops, brought sheep, goats, cattle, and horses, and these before very long became mainstays of the Navajo and Apache economies. Sheep and goats, and to some extent horses, became major food sources, but in addition horses transformed the formerly rather weak and scattered Athabascan groups into accomplished warriors and raiders. For more than three hundred years, intermittent raiding of the Spanish as well as the Pueblo settlements in New Mexico was an important feature of both Navajo and Apache life. The raids yielded mainly livestock, but also considerable numbers of human captives who were incorporated into the tribe, and further enriched its culture. As a consequence of their raiding economy, and the repeated Spanish attempts at reprisal, the Athabascan groups became somewhat more nomadic than in immediate preconquest days. Thanks to that propensity, as well as their warlike abilities, the Spanish rulers were never able to conquer and subjugate the Navajos and Apaches, despite three centuries of intermittent efforts. It was not until the coming of American rule in the Southwest, in 1846, that the groups were finally subjugated and confined to reservations, mostly between 1860 and 1885.

The Navajos' early experiences under American rule were advantageous, for the original U.S. policy, unlike Spanish and Mexican policy, did not aim at the total disarming and assimilation of all Indian groups. At first the Navajos and Apaches were subjected to considerably less military pressure than they had been under Mexican rule. During the Civil War, when most American troops were withdrawn for service elsewhere, the Athabascans had a veritable field day in raiding the settlements along the Rio Grande Valley. This however proved to be their undoing, for eventually it provoked a massive punitive expedition, led by Kit Carson and made up of a combined force of Anglo-Americans, Mexicans, Pueblo Indians, and even some 'Enemy Navajos' who had become allied with the Pueblos and Mexicans. The expedition of 1863 succeeded in rounding up some 8,000 men, women, and children—probably somewhat under half the total Navajo population—and marched them off to a rather miserable reservation on the high plains of eastern New Mexico. This was soon recognized as the hopeless expedient it was, and within a year Navajos began drifting away without hindrance. Four years later the whole enterprise was abandoned, and a treaty was signed under which the people were allowed to return to a part of their original homeland, on a reservation straddling the Arizona-New Mexico border.

The subsequent story of Navajo life under American rule was one of continual expansion, and continual success. The numbers both of people and of livestock increased so rapidly that the original reservation was enlarged again and again, until in the end it was over five times as large as the original, treaty reservation. In the process the Navajos and their sheep overran large tracts of territory that had been the traditional habitat of Hopis, Zunis, Paiutes, and even to some extent of Mormon and Mexican ranchers, without any serious interference from Uncle Sam. Navajo expansionism represents the single most conspicuous example we possess of successful Indian adaptation to the circumstances of Anglo-American rule.

At the time of their first return to the reservation the Navajos remained fairly nomadic, ranging far and wide in search of the best pastures. Before long however increasing population pressure forced them to become transhumant rather than nomadic. Most family groups moved back and forth between two or three fixed residences, in summer and winter pasture and farming areas, and this pattern persisted until about a generation ago, when the Navajos' primary dependence on livestock ended.

During the years between 1868 and World War II, the Navajos developed a fairly stable lifeway that made the best of both the traditional and the Anglo worlds. They continued to farm (mainly corn), raised ever-larger flocks of sheep and goats, and also kept very large numbers of horses, both for practical transport and for prestige. At isolated trading posts throughout the reservation they sold wool in the spring and surplus lambs in the fall, along with the famous Navajo blankets woven by the women, in exchange for a wide variety of American manufactured goods. The women developed a very distinctive and colorful style of dress, modeled on the dresses worn by American army wives in the later nineteenth century, but with the addition of great quantities of silver jewelry.

The traditional Navajo social organization and religion were left virtually undisturbed. During the raiding and warrior years the people of necessity had been organized into large bands under powerful, charismatic leaders, but those disappeared with the end of warfare and raiding. There was no government above the level of local communities, which were made up of widely scattered family residence groups, since the Navajos never gathered into nucleated settlements. Social authority was exercised within an established framework of clans, lineages, and smaller residential groups, in which social rights and obligations were clearly spelled out by kinship relationships. Outside the domain of kinship, local authority when necessary rested in the hands of especially respected persons, usually referred to as headman, but they had only persuasive, not coercive power. Beyond the level of the community, there was no over-arching tribal organization until the first Tribal Council was formed (at the behest of the Bureau of Indian Affairs) in 1924. As late as the 1950s however it was still seen as something foreign and intrusive by traditional Navajos.

Schooling in boarding schools, provided by the Bureau of Indian Affairs, was nominally compulsory after 1880, but only a minority of Navajos were actually forced to attend, and few attended for long enough to derive much benefit from it. The great majority of Navajo parents were strongly opposed to it, and refused to send their children voluntarily, while the widely scattered and remote homesteads could not be canvassed in any systematic way by the roundup patrols. There were in any case not nearly enough schools to accommodate all of the Navajo children; another reason why the Indian Bureau did not attempt to enforce the school policy with any consistency. It was still true in the 1940s that only a minority of Navajos had any English, and the proportion who were literate was minuscule. As of 1950, only one Navajo had completed a college education.

Christian missionary organizations were allowed to work on the reservation beginning in the 1880s, but they had extremely limited success for nearly a century. The Navajos simply 'had it too good' as they were, relying on their indigenous religion which continued to bring them satisfaction. There was never a serious government attempt to suppress the Navajo ceremonies, as there was among their Pueblo neighbors. Indeed some aspects of Navajo ceremonialism, and in particular the famous sand-paintings, seem to have reached their fullest florescence in the stable and relatively prosperous reservation years. At the same time, an interesting syncretism of functions took place. There had traditionally been distinct ceremonies for war, for hunting, and for curing, but after war was prohibited and nearly all the wild game were displaced by sheep and goats, all of the former war and hunting ceremonies were either lost, or more often were reinterpreted as curing ceremonies. Since disease remains today the primary area of uncertainty in Navajo life, its prevention or cure is the focus of nearly all major Navajo ceremonies.

As of the 1950s there had been almost no urbanization. As their livestock industry demanded, people lived in small family residential clusters, widely scattered over the vast and unfenced open range. The typical residential group consisted of about 15 people; most commonly an older couple, one or two of their married children, and grandchildren. They occupied two or three hogans (log structures covered with earth), which were never side by side, but 'within shouting distance,' as Navajos liked to say. Beyond that tightly interacting and interdependent group, they were surrounded not by other people but by wide open spaces and the big sky—a natural world on which they depended daily for grazing, for water, and for firewood.

Traditional Navajos as I knew them were a robust people, full of vitality and, in good times, an evident joy of living. Pleasure found expression very readily in laughter, in song (often completely spontaneous), and above all in good talk, which was highly prized. But bad times (due most often to drought or to illness) were as inevitable as good times; they were part of the ordained human condition. At such times people very largely kept their feelings to themselves, and became silent and withdrawn, for the overt expression of bad feelings is upsetting to the supernaturals. Drunkenness, when it occurred, very often ended in quarrels and fights, for it unleashed feelings for which traditional culture allowed no outlet. Life was very active for everyone, and frequently strenuous, but people in good health enjoyed that aspect of it. Everyone rode horses (which meant first of all rounding them up on the open range); everyone handled livestock; everyone cut firewood and hauled water.

There was of course a continual process of cultural erosion around the fringes of the reservation, where there was close and continuous contact with Anglo-Americans. In those areas there were many alternative opportunities to the traditional Navajo way of life, in the form of wage-paying jobs and town life. There was also ready access to alcohol, which was banned on the reservation but was readily had 'on the outside,' although it was nominally illegal there as well. Alcoholism had a very disruptive effect on traditional Navajo social life, as well as religion, around the reservation fringes, but much less so in the interior districts.

Such was the Navajo world as I knew it in the 1930s, 1940s, and 1950s; particularly during the time when I was trading at Shonto—one of the most isolated communities on the reservation. The trading post was 30 miles from the nearest post office, 55 miles from the nearest government center and hospital, 70 miles from the nearest paved road, and 132 miles from the nearest town, which was Flagstaff, Arizona. The Navajo religion that I describe in the pages that follow was the religion of Shonto, as I knew it half a century ago.

Navajo religion

Emile Durkheim, one of the great pioneers in the study of comparative religion, defined religion as 'a unified system of beliefs and practices ...' (Durkheim 1915: 47). As I will suggest in later pages, this is not often the case in the real world. The religion of most peoples is a highly disparate set of beliefs and practices; so much so that the appropriateness of the term 'system' may be questioned. But Navajo religion really does satisfy Durkheim's criteria. There is one central myth, which embodies among other things the whole history of the people, and from it other myths 'branch off' which explain the reason for particular ceremonies. Thus every ceremony is connected with the body of myth in a logical and coherent way.

It is a fascinating paradox that Navajo religion, despite its lack of a written component, is more nearly a 'scriptural' religion than is the Islam of Arab peasants, to be described in the next chapter. This is of course not true in a literal sense, since 'scripture' literally means writing. But almost the whole content of Navajo religion is embodied within a mass of highly complex and highly formal mythology, without which no understanding is possible. It is, far more than village Islam, a system of knowledge that absolutely requires the presence of learned practitioners (conventionally known as singers), who are the recognized repositories of myth. It is mythology alone that names the various supernatural powers, and tells as much as can be known about them. And since the mythology is far from precise, and like all mythology contains a good many seeming contradictions, so also religious knowledge can never be wholly precise or consistent.

Christians and Muslims of course faced the same problem, and they dealt with it by designating a formal class of theologians, whose duty it was to decide officially the meaning of scripture. Debates were supposedly resolved by learned conclaves which, while they did not really end the debates, reduced them to a certain number of defined positions. Among Navajos the singers are in a very real sense theologians, but until recently they never met in formal convocations, although there was a good deal of informal sharing of knowledge. In consequence, every man could have his own interpretation of myth. And even the most learned of singers will sometimes express bafflement, and say, 'All we know is what the words tell us.' Readers will therefore note, in the discussion that follows, a good deal of uncertainty and lack of specificity. Some of it may reflect my own limited knowledge of Navajo mythology, but much of it is in the heads of the Navajos themselves.

*The super-
naturals*

The Navajo language divides most if not all animate beings into two classes, called *Dighinii* and *Diné*.[5] The *Dighinii* is the class of supernatural beings, and *Diné* is the class of everything else, animal as well as human. The two classes are mutually exclusive, but they are not quite exhaustive; there seem to be some supernaturals that aren't considered *Dighinii* but are also certainly not *Diné*. The two terms are traditionally translated as Holy People and Earth Surface People, but neither translation is wholly satisfactory. The 'Holy People' are all possessed of supernatural power of one sort or another, but they certainly aren't all holy in any moral sense. 'Earth Surface People' is a bit misleading because some of the *Dighinii,* like the wind gods, also live on the earth surface.

Within the class of *Dighinii* there are subsets called *Yei* and *Hashch'ee*. Navajos disagree as to the precise boundaries of these sets, and whether or not they are mutually exclusive. As nearly as I can understand, the

---

[5]This word in its more usual context designates specifically the Navajo, and differentiates them from Hopis, Zunis, and other peoples who go by different names. As it occurs in myth, however, it may designate 'all creatures great and small' *within the Navajo world.* Since humans other than Navajos were not included within that world for a long time, they are generally not included under *Diné.*

Hashch'ee are a class of mostly good deities, to whom most of the lesser Navajo ceremonies are addressed. The *Yei* in some contexts are comparable to the *Katcina* of the Pueblo peoples; they are the visitor gods that come to earth and take part in ceremonies. There are nevertheless some Yei who never come to earth, and some who are evil.

At the center of the cosmic system is a powerful set of mostly anthropomorphic deities, some mostly good, some mostly bad, and some in between. They are heavily involved in human affairs but dwell elsewhere. They are the main focus of ceremonial activity. This is the component of Navajo religion that is most clearly of Pueblo Indian derivation, and many of the Navajo gods can be specifically identified with Pueblo gods. Surrounding them are a great many animal deities and spirits that are mostly helpers and intermediaries of the anthropomorphic deities. They may possibly represent the Athabascan substratum in Navajo religion, carried to the Southwest from the original homeland far to the north. There are also many powers that are neither human nor animal in form, and some that have no form at all. They play an important role in myth, but are usually not invoked in ceremony.

No Navajo has attempted a total enumeration of the supernaturals, let alone tried to classify them. There is also no clear conception of a hierarchical ranking among them. The relative importance or unimportance of particular deities is something judged by us, not by Navajos themselves, based on the frequency of their appearance in myth, and above all by the frequency with which they are invoked in ceremony.

Gladys Reichard (1963: 381–505) attempted to enumerate all the Navajo deities, based on a study of all mythology available to her, and came up with a list of 132 supernatural powers of one sort or another. The following is a very brief synopsis, based almost entirely on her work.

The central deities. At the heart of Navajo mythology is a small group of deities who appear over and over again. They are the male Sun, his consort Changing Woman (he also has many other consorts), and the Hero Twins to whom Changing Woman gave birth. They and most of the other major deities form a single kinship network, a circumstance which mirrors the most salient feature of Navajo social organization. Although there is no formal hierarchical ranking among the Navajo supernaturals, it seems apparent that these gods are the most powerful. They have the lead roles in the great saga that we call the Emergence Myth (summarized below), while most of the other deities are 'walk-ons.' However, they are not all addressed in major ceremonies; the Sun for example is too powerful to be disturbed. But Changing Woman (often also called Spider Woman), the quintessential Earth Mother, is the single deity nearest the hearts of Navajos, and is invoked again and again in prayers and ritual. She is the nearest thing to a wholly benevolent being in the Navajo pantheon. Also important is White Shell Woman, whom some Navajos identify as a twin sister of Changing Woman, while others insist she is simply Changing Woman under another name.

The earliest *Dighinii,* including the Sun, existed since the beginning of time, and they were the collective First Cause. However, many of the beings they created became creators in their own turn. For example, the original *Dighinii* created First Man and First Woman (who are *Dighinii* and not *Diné*), but it was they in turn who gave to the people many of the gifts that they currently enjoy, as well as some of the plagues.

Anthropomorphic deities. According to my count (derived from a reading of Reichard) there are 45 anthropomorphic deities, comprising 31 adult males, 9 adult females, including Changing Woman, and 9 children, including the Hero Twins.

Monsters. The monsters have highly variable forms, some human, some animal, some a combination of the two. The monsters were all slain by the Hero Twins long ago, but at least twelve of them are nevertheless still around, and must be propitiated. It is a characteristic of gods, familiar in Christian theology, that they can be simultaneously alive and dead.

Animal spirits. The 41 animal spirits include eleven mammals, of whom the bear and the coyote are the most important. Reverence for the bear is probably a legacy from the Navajos' original homeland in the far northwest, where 'bear ceremonialism' is a recurring feature throughout the Arctic and sub-Arctic regions. The name of the bear (*shash*) is invoked in oaths in the same way that Christians invoke the name of God. Coyote is the trickster, familiar as such to nearly all western American Indians. There are also fifteen bird spirits, of whom raven seems most important; seven reptiles and amphibians, and eight insects, of whom grasshopper is most important.

Plant spirits. Yucca and two kinds of cactus have a specially powerful indwelling spirit that can be helpful or harmful to man.

Natural phenomena. These play a very large role in Navajo mythology. Earth and geologic phenomena (especially cliffs and mountains); aspects of wind, weather, and the water; aspects of light and darkness; and celestial phenomena (sun, moon, and some planets) are all endued with sentient power, which provides the explanation for much in the observable world. According to Reichard's analysis there are at least 24 such deified forces.

Abstract concepts. Hunger, cold, sleep, poverty, old age, and death are sentient powers, without form, that beset humans. The Hero Twins set out to kill all of them, but each was able to convince the Twins that it was necessary for human well-being.

*Properties of
the deities*

Good and evil. Ideas about good (*zhon*) and evil (*chon*) are very important in Navajo thought. However, these terms are applied much more commonly to situations, to intentions, to acts, and to things than they are to persons. Good and evil, like love and anger, are potentials that exist within all humans and all supernaturals; there is no absolutely pure embodiment of either. Both are implicit in the possession of power itself. Among deities the Sun is highly benevolent, yet it was he who impregnated women with the Monsters that his sons then had to slay. Changing Woman is by all odds the kindliest of the Navajo deities, but she is also sexy, and therefore mischievous at times. I think the absence of a wholly benevolent deity within the pantheon reflects a clear recognition that, as Lord Acton put it, 'all power corrupts.'

Most overt religious activity is practical in character, and man-focused. That is, it aims at the achievement of quite specific conditions or goals within the human community. Consequently, Navajos tend to judge their deities in pragmatic terms; not as absolutely good or bad but as well-intentioned or ill-intentioned toward the *Diné*. From that perspective, Reichard (1963: 63–75) proposed a classification of the deities into the following categories:

Persuadable deities. These are the powers most often invoked in ceremonies, because their intentions are known to be good. They are not by any means incapable of evil; like many *Diné* they are simply well inclined. They include the Sun, Changing Woman, and most of the *Hashch'ee*, as well as many others.

Undependable deities. This is a rather large category of beings who are mean or mischievous by nature. They will sometimes give help when asked, but one can never count on it; sometimes they will bring harm instead. First Man and First Woman are in this category; they are responsible for witchcraft, and are the cause of a lot of disease.

Unpersuadable deities. These are the monsters, whose intentions toward man are always evil. They cannot be persuaded to help, but their harm can be averted by proper ritual. Hence, they are the subjects of a great deal of it.

Beings between good and evil. These are the disembodied powers like Hunger, Cold, and Death that were spared by the Hero Twins because they were able to argue their usefulness to man. The Twins' mother explained to them that these powers were good and bad in just about equal proportion. They figure in myth, but are not invoked in ceremonies.

Helpers of deities and man. These are creatures that, like the angels in Christian mythology, have no independent will of their own. They do the bidding of the higher powers, by bringing their messages or their good will or ill will to the Earth Surface People. Most of the animal spirits fall into this category, as also do the wind gods. They are said to be present at all ceremonies.

The relationship between *Dighinii* and *Diné* is a very unequal one, with the *Dighinii* having far more power. They created the *Diné* to do their bidding, and yet the *Diné* want favors from them, while at the same time fearing their wrath. Survival in the dangerous world they have created involves a delicate balancing act between invoking the good feelings of the *Dighinii,* and keeping the bad ones at bay.

The essential core of all Navajo religious belief and practice is embodied in the term *hozhoni*,[6] continually reiterated in prayers and chants. It is traditionally translated as 'beauty,' but even in its widest sense this word captures only a part of the meaning of *hozhoni*. Navajos have a great love of beauty in all its forms, and when *hozhoni* prevails life is indeed beautiful. But *hozhoni* covers everything that is embraced in the Christian conception of Good, when it is used in contrast to Evil.

Hozhoni is a state of harmonic balance, when everything human and superhuman is in its proper place, and behaving as it should. 'God's in

---

[6]In the spelling of Navajo words I have not employed the system of strictly phonetic spelling favored by anthropologists, because it requires so many diacritics that it can be confusing to persons not familiar with the system. I spell the words so as to approximate the way non-Navajos pronounce them.

his heaven; all's right with the world,' as Christians would say. But for Navajos it is a delicate balance. The supernaturals are not by any means always 'in their heaven' (i.e. where they belong), and when they are not, all is not right with the world. Active steps have to be taken to correct the situation.

The whole substantive meaning of *hozhoni* is contained within the stem syllable *zhon*.[7] It cannot be captured in English by a word, a page, or perhaps even a whole book. Nor can it in Navajo, for it is one of the few pure abstractions in a language otherwise famous for its specificity. Like many religious concepts in other languages, its meaning can only be adduced by the equivalent of 'discourse analysis;' that is, by studying its many different occurrences in myth and ceremony. Navajos themselves disagree as to what it covers in concrete terms. I think that everyone has his or her own vision of the best of all possible worlds, which defines *zhon* for him or her.

Toward the end of every prayer (as well as at many earlier points), the phrase *hozhonigo* is several times repeated. It is traditionally translated as 'walk in beauty.' The translation has great poetic appeal (and is dear to the hearts of New-Agers), but it involves a good deal of poetic license. First, as I have already suggested, *zhon* embraces much more than beauty, even broadly defined. Much more importantly, though, 'walk in beauty' sounds like an injunction to a specific individual. *Hozhonigo* is not an injunction to an individual, it is a wish and a command for the cosmos at large. *Zhon* is not a state of grace in any personal sense. 'Let harmony prevail' is a much more literal, though less poetic, translation of *hozhonigo*.[8]

I think the best way I can convey, not the precise meaning but the deep emotional yearning expressed in *hozhonigo,* is to liken it to the oft-expressed Christian prayer, 'Let there be peace on earth.' It is the heartfelt wish of everyone, and yet, because of human frailty, something very difficult to attain and to maintain, easily disturbed, and after disturbance hard to restore. As Navajos acknowledge and Christian usage implies, it cannot be attained without God's (or the gods') help. In the Navajo con-

---

[7]When this syllable stands alone, the final *n* is not audible. The pronunciation then approximates the French pronunciation of 'Jean.'

[8]The term is actually made up of four components: *ho,* which designates a state of prevailing condition; *zhon,* the core concept of harmony; the location marker *i,* which makes any statement place-specific, and *go,* a suffix which connotes movement in the direction of the thing just named. Thus, 'movement in the direction of prevailing harmony here.'

ception however peace must prevail not only on earth, but everywhere above and below it; throughout the cosmos.

The *Diné* are just as the gods created them—for better and worse. Collectively, they are neither better nor worse than the *Dighinii* themselves; they are just a lot less powerful. The sense of relative weakness, in relation to the gods, is the single most salient aspect of Navajo self-perception. *The human condition*

Within the human sphere, identity is defined by kinship. Kinfolk are 'we;' everyone else is 'they.' Kinfolk are those we trust, those we share with, those we help, and those from whom we ask help, as a matter of course. Others we don't entirely trust, because they are not 'our folks,' and there is always the possibility that they may be witches. And to ask help from non-kin is something of a disgrace, akin to begging.

Sexuality is the single most basic feature of the human condition, as of everything else in nature. 'Everything exists in two parts, the male and the female, which belong together and complete each other,' as Kluckhohn and Leighton (1946: 230) have phrased it. Women are somewhat weaker than men both in physical strength and in ritual power, but they are not in any sense inferior beings. However, the same authors have noted the curious 'Madonna-whore' paradox that is found in other cultures. 'Man is fickle—but is never thought to be otherwise. Woman is the one who is either all bad or all good. She gives all or denies all' (ibid: 138).

The good life is prosperous, quiet and orderly, not noisy and busy. Leisure time is highly valued. Cities, with their throngs and their noise, are unfriendly and threatening.

Navajo mythology is a body of enormously detailed tradition, which for centuries was carried only in the heads of those learned practitioners whom both we and the Navajos call singers (*hatathli*). Each singer had learned everything he knew through years of study with other singers. No one singer knew more than a portion of the complete body of mythology; that part relating to the particular ceremonies that he had learned to perform. To the extent that we can contemplate Navajo mythology today as something like a corpus, it is thanks to the work of a small number of diligent Bilagáana recorders and compilers, beginning with a dedicated army doctor (Washington Matthews) in the late nineteenth century. Recorded versions of Navajo myth fill several hundred pages, but there are certainly large areas that are still unrecorded. *Mythology*

Navajos like things well and logically ordered, and this is reflected throughout their religion. The whole corpus of their mythology forms much more nearly an integrated, coherent complex than is the case with most tribal peoples. It is also much more closely and coherently integrated with ritual than is usually the case. At its center is the Emergence Myth, which is essentially the history of the people, and from this stem all the other myths branch off, to explain the origin of all the different ceremonies. Nearly all the myths, except the Emergence Myth, are integrated with one or more specific rituals.

Navajo mythology must be appreciated not only as religion, but also as nearly the whole literature of a creative people who delight in well chosen and well spoken words. Myths are often recited in the evenings purely for entertainment. As Kluckhohn and Leighton (1946: 133) have observed, 'Most of the plots are familiar from other North American Indian tribes, but the style, the phrasing, the embroidery of incidents have their own local color and special Navaho quality. Throughout there is humor, a delight in puns, tremendous interest in places and place names, and great imaginative power.' There is, I should add, a pervading interest in sex, just as there is in modern American vernacular culture. It is not a reflection of sexual neuroses, as Freudians would have it; it is just something that is fun to think and to talk and to speculate about, as well as to do.

It seems evident that mythology has been an outlet for the creativity of individual singers. There is, as a result, no absolutely canonical form of any myth. Many of the more important ones have been recorded from several different singers, each of whom has given a somewhat different version. There is on the other hand something close to a canonical form for many of the prayers that occur within the myths, for these are formulas that will not work unless they are precisely repeated. Most if not all of the prayers are in a kind of verse.

The Emergence Myth. The Emergence Myth is the 'Bible' of the Navajos, for it embodies the whole of their history, as well as cosmology, science, and theology. Its main outline is known to all adults, and most people have quite specific knowledge of dramatic events like the slaying of the monsters and the quarrel of men and women, because they have heard them recited again and again. Its content has been thus encapsulated by Kluckhohn and Leighton (1946: 123):

... the Holy People lived first below the surface of the earth. They moved from one lower world to another because of witchcraft practiced by one of them. In the last of the twelve lower worlds the sexes were separated because of a quarrel, and monsters were born from the female Holy People. Finally a great flood drove the Holy People to ascend to the present world through a reed. Natural objects were created. Then came the first death among the Holy People. About this time too, Changing Woman, the principal figure among them, was created. After she reached puberty, she was magically impregnated by the rays of the sun and by water from a waterfall, and bore twin sons. These Hero Twins journeyed to the house of their father, the Sun, encountering many adventures and slaying most of the monsters.

In the course of all these events, the Holy People developed ways of doing things which were partly practical and partly magical. When they decided to leave for permanent homes at the east, south, west, north, the zenith, and the nadir, they had a great meeting at which they created the Earth Surface people, the ancestors of the Navahos, and taught them all the methods they had developed ....[9]

Rite myths. Among the most important things taught to the *Diné* by the departing *Dighinii* were at least 26 major rituals, mostly designed to deal with specific problem situations. Each of the rituals has its own mythology, which explains not only why it exists but how to perform it. These myths 'branch off' from the Emergence Myth at various points along the way.

Folk wisdom

As I will suggest in Chapter 13, every religion includes a great deal of shared knowledge about the supernaturals, that is nevertheless not embodied in any formal mythology, and is never recited. Much though not all of it is knowledge about evil things, and how to avoid them. Navajo beliefs about witchcraft, about ghosts, and about the afterlife fall into this category; they are usually spoken of only in whispers.

Witchcraft. Witchcraft might be regarded as the 'ugly underside' of Navajo religion. The origin of witchcraft is explained in the Emergence Myth, and other myths prescribe specific ways of dealing with it. There is however an extremely detailed body of folk wisdom about witches and their activities that lies outside the corpus of mythology. It has been difficult to elicit this information, because people are reluctant to talk about evil things, and nobody in his right mind admits to being a witch.[10]

---

[9] According to most versions, the *Diné* were present in the last four worlds.

[10] I know of at least one obviously deranged man who claimed to be a witch.

However, Clyde Kluckhohn (1944) was able collect a rather substantial body of witch-lore in one Navajo community.

Kluckhohn found a belief in four different kinds of witches: those who make and use corpse-poison; those who cause the intrusion of a foreign object into the bodies of their victims; those who bewitch their victims at a distance, using special songs and spells; and those who cause frenzy by introducing drugs into their victims. The great majority of witches are male; not because men are inherently more ill-intentioned than women, but because they possess more inherent power over supernatural forces. By day they are ordinary Navajos (or occasionally members of other groups), but at night they are likely to turn themselves into wolves, although they are capable of assuming many other forms as well. They are usually known in Navajo as 'human wolves' (*ma'ii diné*). They are believed to practice incest with their sisters, to eat corpses, and to indulge in other abominable behaviors. They are regarded as one of the most common causes of disease and death, and there are, as a result, a great many very specific rituals intended to avert or to exorcise their evil influence.

Ghosts (*ch'indi*) are another category of dangerous beings, about whom there are quite specific ideas, although they are not mentioned at all in mythology. When a person dies, the evil that was contained in him or her is released in the form a ghost. Ghosts go initially to live far to the north (an evil place in Navajo belief), but after four days they can and do return to earth as malevolent influences. They always appear in some concrete form, most commonly that of an animal. They are the causes of sickness and also of dire misfortunes. The fear of ghosts is extreme, and it accounts for the Navajos' almost pathological fear of contact with a corpse or anything remotely connected with it, for the ghost is either still in it or nearby. Those who are forced to bury the dead must undergo elaborate purification afterward.

The afterlife. Almost all Navajos profess some belief in an afterlife, but ideas about it are extremely vague and variable from person to person. As in the case of witches and ghosts, it is not something people like to talk or to think about. Reichard (1963: 42) denied that there was any individual afterlife; only a kind of Buddha-like reunion with the cosmos. However, Leland Wyman and his colleagues (1942) were able to collect a number of traditions about an afterworld peopled by individuals. All informants agreed that it was a place far to the north, and also below the earth surface. Many but not all believed that the afterlife involved a return to the last of the previous worlds occupied by the people, before their emergence into this one. The afterworld was conceived to be much like this world, with people living in hogans, growing corn, and raising sheep. Some thought it would be a happier place than this world, some thought it would be less happy; many thought it would be just about the same. Many thought that, as it was underground, the afterworld would be dark all the time, though people would nevertheless be able to see.

No one had any conception that the afterworld was a place of rewards and punishments, or that there was any way to prepare for it. Indeed, ideas about it seem to be wholly unconnected with any ideas about the deities, or with traditional mythology. Under the circumstances it might even be questioned whether Navajo eschatological beliefs should be considered as an aspect of religion. This issue will be more broadly considered in Chapter 13.

Ritual

Ritual is the business end of Navajo religion, 'the cutting edge of the tool,' as Anthony Wallace (1966: 102) called it. Even the greatest of the ceremonies is quintessentially practical. No ritual is performed purely or even primarily as an act of worship of the gods, and psalms in praise of them are few. Rituals are performed to secure the aid of the deities in achieving specific conditions or objectives within the human sphere.

As in Tibetan Buddhism, for example, ritual practice is overwhelmingly mechanistic. The gods are not responsive to words as such, unless they are embodied in continually repeated formulas and songs. In these performances the deities are not so much supplicated as compelled, through rituals to which, if they are properly performed, the *Dighinii* cannot fail to respond. But the rituals must be performed with absolute precision; if a mistake is made, the whole performance must be repeated from the beginning. Every ceremony involves large amounts of imitative magic, in which the gods are compelled by force of suggestion. For example, blowing tobacco smoke imitates the clouds, in which the gods will travel to earth.

The body of Navajo ritual is as complex as the mythology with which it is closely intertwined. At one time it included at least sixty collectively performed ceremonies ('sings'), and a nearly infinite number of individual observances. Kluckhohn and Leighton (1946: 160) estimated that an adult Navajo man might spend as much of one third of his waking hours in some form of ritual activity.

The major ceremonies. All Navajo collective ceremonies are called *zhi,* a word that we usually translate as 'ways.' Alternatively, both Navajos and Anglos often refer to them as 'sings.' They are roads to be traveled in order to maintain or restore *hozhoni.* In the traditional Navajo world there were separate ceremonies for hunting, for war, for curing, and for blessing, but the hunting ceremonies are no longer practiced, and the war ceremonies have been reinterpreted as curing ceremonies. Consequently, nearly all Navajo ceremonialism today focuses in one way or another on disease, the largest major threat that still hangs over the people. Blessingway ceremonies (*hozhonzhi*) are largely for its prevention (though they confer a more general well-being), while all other ceremonies are for its cure.

This results in an interesting paradox. All the 'ways' are collective performances, requiring the participation of many persons, and participation brings benefit to all, and yet each sing is necessarily focused on an individual 'patient.' Unlike Pueblo ceremonies, which they resemble in other respects, the sings are held situationally, as need arises, though some can only be held during winter months. In the best of times there would theoretically be few ceremonies, because nobody would be sick, and yet at the same time there is a feeling that frequent ceremonies are necessary for the well-being of the people as a whole. Consequently a wealthy family will sometimes sponsor a large and elaborate ceremony for a patient who is not very sick, for the sake of the prestige that it brings. Very occasionally a 'co-patient' is treated along with the main patient.

In 1938 Leland Wyman and Clyde Kluckhohn attempted an enumeration and classification of Navajo ceremonies; something that, as in the case of mythology, the people themselves have not been concerned to do. They recorded the names of 58 'ways' that were still clearly remembered, although only about 40 were being regularly performed. From fragments of tradition, they were able to deduce that there had been still others, of which most details and even the names had been lost. They estimated that there might have been between 65 and 70 Navajo ceremonies at the beginning of the twentieth century.

The classification devised by Wyman and Kluckhohn (1938) is a highly complex one, with four major categories and two levels of subcategories. In the major categories are 4 Blessingways, performed to bring well-being and protection; 22 Holy Ways, performed to cure illnesses brought on by the patient's own transgressions; 6 Life Ways, performed to heal the injuries caused by accidents; and 10 Evil Ways or Ghost Ways, performed to exorcise the illness caused by witchcraft. In the latter group are the three Enemy Way ceremonies, formerly war dances, that are performed to exorcise the evil caused by contact with non-Navajos, including Bilagáana.[11]

Every major ceremony has shorter and longer versions, and may be performed over a period of two, three, or five days and nights. The Holy Ways also have a nine-day version, which is always their preferred form. The number of days for the ceremony is agreed on in advance between the singer and the sponsoring family; it will depend on what the singer recommends and what the family can afford. The seriousness of the patient's illness will play some part in this decision, but families who can afford it like to sponsor the nine-day ceremonies anyway, as a kind of gift to the community.

Every ceremony is comprised of a sequence of many individual rituals, which must be performed in the prescribed order. To begin with there is always a ritual consecration of the hogan, which for the duration of the ceremony becomes a holy place. Recurring subsequent elements include the purification of the singer, patient, and other participants every morning before sunup; setting out prayer-sticks, painted and adorned with feathers, every morning; ritual bathing of the patient; eating of ritually prepared corn meal; ritual smoking of cigarettes; an invocation to the *Yei* gods to come and be present; and the making of a sand-painting on the hogan floor.[12] These are the main daytime activities. In the evening there is a short outdoor singing and drumming, by all of the male attendees who know the songs, and there is all-night singing on the last night. Masked dancers also perform on the last night of some ceremonies. All ceremonies are then concluded by a short Blessingway, held at dawn.

Every ceremony is conducted by a singer who has been hired by the patient's family, and he is in effect the sole 'doctor in charge.' He will in turn, for the larger ceremonies, recruit assistants to help with sand-painting and other specific ritual activities, and for the Holy Ways he may recruit a team of masked dancers who impersonate the gods (i.e. the *Yei*). All members of the resident family, as well as other attendees, will help out as they can, and may be assigned specific tasks by the lead singer. The more participants, the greater is the prospect of success for the ceremony, for their actions and intentions serve to focus goodwill

---

[11]They are colloquially known to both Navajos and Bilagaana as 'squaw dances,' because women have a leading role in them.

[12]Often called a dry-painting, to underscore the fact that it is executed without liquid.

on the patient. The patient, and sometimes also other participants, must undergo purification by sweat-bathing and purgation.

Rites of passage. There are many observances, by both parents, before, during, and after the birth of a child. When the survival of the baby is assured, a singer will be called in to conduct a naming ceremony. He will give the infant a so-called 'war name,' which for the rest of his life will be a closely guarded secret, never used as a term of address. Misuse of the 'war name' will cause harm to the individual who bears it. It is however the name by which he is known to the supernaturals.

At around the age of seven, both boys and girls are initiated into full ceremonial life, by a special initiation ceremony held on the next-to-last night of a Holy Way sing. Thereafter they may be present in the hogan during ceremonies, and may participate in some of the activities, like setting out prayer sticks. For girls the next rite of passage is the puberty ceremony, for which a special kind of Blessingway is held. It is a joyful event, and a public affair to which guests are invited. Marriage is also celebrated with a small version of Blessingway, but this is essentially a private affair within the family.

Death is not marked by any overt ritual; the one consideration is to get the body away and underground as quickly as possible. However there are all kinds of taboos and restrictions imposed on those who bury the corpse, and they must undergo a long purification, including Blessingway, afterward. It was once a common practice to bury a man's jewelry, saddle, and other personal possessions along with him, and yet, curiously, this was not connected with any belief about the need for them in the next world. Rather, they were buried to get them out of the way, because a man's personal possessions may become *ch'indi* when he dies. As a practical matter, this practice also avoided quarrels over inheritance.

Personal ritual. The most essential personal ritual is sweat-bathing, which should be undertaken from time to time just to maintain personal well-being. It is performed in a small, specially consecrated sweat-house, and is accompanied by various songs and other ritual observances. There are numerous other rituals to protect against witchcraft, and there are also personal rituals to bring success in weaving, in farming, in trading, in hunting, and in any kind of travel. Many and perhaps most of these involve special songs, which are enormously important both in the secular and in the religious life of Navajos. Some songs are retained as the private property of individual families, passed on by inheritance but not taught to outsiders. More will be said on this subject under the heading *Religion in everyday life*.

In the Navajo medico-religious system there are two wholly different kinds of practitioners.

Diagnosticians are the people you go to first when you are taken ill, or suffer bad luck, to find out 'where you went wrong' and what to do about it. By a combination of inquiry and divinatory magic, the diagnostician will pinpoint the source of your trouble, and on that basis can recommend an appropriate sing. For example, if you are afflicted with shoulder pain because you have eaten fish (one of many forbidden foods) you will need one of the Holy Way ceremonies; if your eyes are infected because of contact with bad Hopis, you will need one of the Evil Way ceremonies. If your pain is due to falling off a horse, you probably won't need a diagnostician to tell you that, but he or she can decide which is the proper Life Way ceremony for you. Symptoms play only a small part in these diagnoses, because there is no necessary connection between any evil influence and any particular symptom. A witch or a ghost or one of the supernaturals can cause any condition.

Diagnosticians, unlike singers, can be of either sex. Their practice is wholly shamanistic; it has come as a gift from the gods rather than through study. Divinatory techniques include stargazing, and the interpretation of natural phenomena such as cloud patterns and the flight of birds. One of the most common techniques nowadays is hand-trembling, in which the shoulder and arm muscles are tensed to such an extent that the extended hand begins to shake uncontrollably; the pattern of shaking and the direction in which the hand moves are then interpreted. When a diagnosis has been given and a cure recommended, it is then up to the patient's family to seek out a singer who can perform the recommended ceremony.

Singers. The major ritual performers are always called singers (*hatathli*), reflecting the fact that songs carry enormous ritual power. At the same time they are only one part of the practitioner's repertoire, which must include the ability to oversee and to personally conduct all the different aspects of one or more complex ceremonies, including in most cases the ability to make sand-paintings. The singer is in most respects a priest rather than a shaman, in that his power has been acquired purely through prolonged study, and not through any divine calling. At the same time his practice, in some ceremonies, involves a certain number of shamanistic, sleight-of-hand tricks. The singer's practice also includes a considerable amount of *materia medica,* administered as food or drink or poultices to the patient.

All properly qualified singers can conduct Blessingway, one or more of the Enemy Ways, and at least one of the Holy Ways or Life Ways. The most learned of singers can do several of these, but no one has mastered more than a fraction of the total corpus of ceremonies. Singers are, of necessity, specialists, and are recognized as such. They are of course also doctors, and like other doctors they work for hire only.

Some writers have made a distinction between singers, who know a lot of mythology and can conduct whole ceremonies, and 'curers' who know only parts of ceremonies (cf. Morgan 1936). However, this distinction was not made by the people at Shonto. All the ritual practitioners were called singers, but the extent of their knowledge and abilities ranged over a very wide spectrum, and this was well understood within the community. At the lower end of the scale were several individuals with limited knowledge, who nevertheless received a considerable trade because their fees were not high. They were however not much respected; the community regarded them essentially like dropouts from medical school. At the upper end was the only individual at Shonto who could perform a complete Holy Way ceremony. He was the single most respected man in the community, and was often consulted for advice, or for the mediation of disputes, having nothing directly to do with religion.

Herbalists. The curing system also includes herbalists, who may be of either sex. They are not, strictly speaking, ritual practitioners, but rather helpers. They have specialized knowledge about the magical as well as the material power of plants, and it often they who provide the herbs used by the singer in ceremonies.

Holy places   All the Pueblo villages have specially constructed holy rooms (*kivas*), which are usually though not always round, and usually though not always underground. The Navajos, who are not village dwellers, have nothing comparable. Instead, the hogan of the patient is converted into a holy place, the equivalent of a kiva, by a consecration ritual at the start of each ceremony. Navajo ceremonial space must be round, simulating the shape of the earth, and the traditional hogan, either round or octagonal, was ideally suited. But the mobile homes or other rectangular buildings, into which so many Navajos are now moving, cannot be used as ceremonial space. Instead, most families retain one of the older hogans, alongside their new homes, or else they have round structures specially built alongside their new homes.

Holiness (i.e. indwelling power) is associated with many features of the physical landscape, and above all with the so-called Four Sacred Peaks that define the limits of the Navajo world.[13] They are, among other things, the dwelling places of the powerful Wind Gods. There are also various rock formations as well as canyons and springs that are sacred to the whole Navajo people, and others that are particular to certain clans on smaller kin groups. These are not exactly places of pilgrimage, but they are places where prayers may be said and offerings left as people pass by.

*Holy and
unholy things*

Material things play a large role in Navajo religious belief, both in a positive and in a negative sense. There are many things that have beneficial power, and many others that must not be touched. The holiest of holy things is the sand-painting, executed on the hogan floor in the course of every major ceremony. Different colored sands are carefully poured from the singer's hand to produce complex designs, involving stylized representations of the gods and of animals, birds, and natural phenomena. At the conclusion of the ceremony the patient sits on the 'painting' while the singer applies sand from different parts of it to different parts of the body, thus transferring the power that the painting has captured into the patient's body, through physical contact. The sands are then very carefully and ritually disposed of.

Specially prepared corn meal is the most ritually efficacious of foods, and is eaten as part of every ceremony. Prayer sticks, made from wood painted with colored designs, and with feathers and beads attached, should be set out in front of the hogan, and sometimes in each of the four cardinal directions around it, when a sing is in progress. They may also be used at other times and in other contexts, to attract the gods. Quartz crystals, white shells, turquoise, and many other objects confer blessing on people or things with which they are in contact. 'A tanner places a turquoise or white shell bead on his pole in order to protect his joints from becoming stiff. A squirrel's tail should be tied to a baby's

---

[13] People in different parts of the reservation have different definitions of the Four Sacred Peaks. Everyone's list includes Mt. Humphreys (Arizona) at the west and Mt. Taylor (New Mexico) at the south, but various peaks in the Colorado Rockies and in Utah are identified as the northern and eastern peaks.

cradle so that the child will be protected in case of a fall' (Kluckhohn and Leighton 1946: 141–2).

Every singer possesses a 'medicine bundle' (*jish*) which contains a large number of ritually powerful objects, that are needed to make prayer sticks, to prepare the sand for sand-paintings, and for other activities connected with the sing. The *jish* may not contain any object of Bilagáana manufacture. Some singers also possess small carved stone 'fetishes' (small anthropomorphic figurines of the gods), which have enormous power.

The number of forbidden things, as well as of forbidden acts, is nearly endless. The most hideously dangerous of all things are corpses, and anything that has been in contact with them. A hogan in which a person has died was traditionally abandoned, and for a long time Navajos would not go to Government hospitals, because of the knowledge that persons had died there.[14] Anything that has been struck by lightning is also dangerous in the extreme. Forbidden foods include almost anything aquatic, whether animal, bird, or fish, as well as bears, coyotes, and snakes. The skin of a bear or coyote is highly dangerous, because it causes offense to a very powerful animal deity.

Iconography and symbolism

Most religions are rich in symbolism, and Navajo religion is exceptionally so—one reason for its tremendous appeal to artistically-minded Bilagáana. Its supreme expression is surely found in the colorful sand-paintings, with their elaborate but formally symmetrical arrangement of sacred beings and things, symbolizing the harmonic balance of earth and sky. Iconic symbolism is also found in the masked *Yei* dancers, and verbal symbolism in the poetic prayers. All the symbolism is meant to have its compelling influence on the supernaturals, and as such it reflects the essentially mechanistic nature of Navajo religious practice. The supernaturals are much more subject to influence through formulaic symbolism than they are through direct verbal appeals. The so-called prayers, highly poetic in form, are neither supplications, like Christian prayers, nor psalms of praise, like Islamic prayers. They are formulas to make something happen.

World-view

According to the Navajos' mythology this is the fourth and, hopefully, the last of their worlds, the previous ones having been destroyed by calamities. When *hozhoni* prevails this is the best of all possible worlds,

---

[14] This avoidance has almost wholly disappeared since the end of World War II.

and life is good. But the best of all possible worlds is nevertheless very far from a perfect world, given the nature both of the gods and of man. The world is full of dangers from both, and always will be, for it will not improve with time. In each of the four worlds, things were ordained to be as they were.

A Navajo in the best of times goes cheerfully rather than confidently through a world in which dangers are always close at hand, and can never be ignored. Thus, the traditional Navajo self-image is at once proud and humble: proud in relation to other peoples, and humble in relation to the gods. There is certainly no sense of human mastery over the world.

So far as the individual life course is concerned, however, the Navajo world-view is a somewhat degenerationist one. Childhood, before heavy responsibilities set in, is the best of times, for children are prized and loved, and receive a great deal of attention and affection. Adulthood is also a good time as long as strength and health hold out, but as those powers begin to fade, so also does the attraction of life. In a world where regular daily activities require a considerable amount of strength and health, the old become increasingly a burden to the kin who have to support them, and may be treated as such. There is no veneration of the old as such, for in a non-literate society the opportunities to acquire increasing wisdom with advancing age are limited. Singers are a partial exception, and are the only individuals who are likely to be respected in old age.

There is however an external dimension to the Navajo world-view. Theirs is, or was, quintessentially a tribal world, in which every people is part of the natural order and has its place. Every people has its own gods, and deals with them in its own way. There is a common feeling that the Pueblo gods are somewhat stronger than those of the Navajos, or at least that the Pueblo peoples are better able to control them, and they are as a result credited with superior ritual knowledge. Partly for that reason, Navajos always enjoy attending Pueblo village ceremonies.

Within the tribal world there were traditionally friendly tribes and enemy tribes; people to trade with, people to raid, and people from whom to expect raids. From about 1600 onward the most important enemy tribe, most of the time, were the Nakai (Spanish/Mexicans). Unlike other enemy tribes it was their intention permanently to defeat and subdue the Navajos, but they never succeeded. They were feared and to a considerable degree hated, but they were not resented, for enemy tribes are a part of the natural order.

Up to 1863 the Navajos had always been masters of their world, insofar as it could be mastered, and there is still a strong historical conscious-ness of this today. But into that tribal world we, the Bilagáana, came as an unnatural intrusion; something outside the natural order. Because we seem to be all over the whole world, with no identifiable homeland, we do not fit the model of an enemy tribe, and since we disarmed the Navajos in 1863 there has been no further war with us. We are simply oppressors in a greater or lesser degree, in that we have made the Navajos subject to external controls they had never previously experienced. As a result, despite the people's conspicuous success under Anglo-American rule, most Navajos feel toward us some measure of resentment. For them, it is historically a new feeling.

Resentment varies enormously from person to person, depending mostly on how well or how poorly they have fared in the reservation era. It is felt most keenly by those persons who have tried and failed to make their way in the Bilagáana world, and least by people who have either succeeded or have not tried. The latter was almost wholly true of the Navajos at Shonto as I knew them. But at least a latent resentment is present in everyone, as it is in all colonized people who are subject to any degree of control by outsiders. At the same time it is not at all accom-panied by feelings of inferiority. In fact most of the neighboring tribes think the Navajos have a superiority complex, and in some contexts they are right.

Religion in
everyday life

The modern secularizing world represents a distinct historical anomaly. People are offered, for the first time, two quite different ways of under-standing the universe, through religion or through science, without hav-ing to choose either one exclusively. As a result, individuals vary widely in the extent of their religious faith, depending on how much of how little of its explanatory function they concede to science. There are very few people, however, who put their faith exclusively in one or the other.

No such alternatives exist for traditional Navajos. In the domain of faith, just about everyone is a true and convinced believer in the myths and the deities, to the extent that they explain the phenomena of exis-tence, for there is no other way to make sense of the experienced world. There is at the same time a great deal in myth that doesn't explain any-thing, or doesn't explain it satisfactorily, and people may vary in the ex-tent to which they do or do not believe that part of the corpus. As in all human societies, some Navajos are natural skeptics and others natural believers, but no one questions altogether the existence of the gods, and their role in human affairs.

Much less unanimity exists in the domain of practice. People vary in the extent of their faith in particular ceremonies and other practices, depending partly on personal experience and partly on whether they have a natural bent toward acceptance or skepticism. Just as in the case of Christians, people are apt to be diligent or neglectful of religious practices to the extent that they are or are not god-fearing.

The single most important point to make about religion in Navajo everyday life is that it is not compartmentalized, as it is among Americans. It is interwoven through just about all the acts of daily life, in such a way that it is not readily recognizable to outsiders. There are songs to be sung, observances to be followed, and offerings to be made in the course of farming, of weaving, of tanning, of silversmithing, of traveling, and even of gambling. Navajos do not think of the farming songs, for example, as something separate from hoeing and weeding; both are equally parts of the basic agricultural technology. The crops will not come up if the seeds are not planted, but they will also not come up if the seeds are not subjected to ritual treatment beforehand.

The closest thing to a daily ritual, not connected with any specific activity or need, is the prayer that should be offered to the sun at sunrise, by a person standing outside the hogan door. There is also a sunset prayer, though it is not as regularly performed.

Much of the religious behavior of Navajos is also not apparent to outsiders because it consists first and foremost of avoidances: of substances, or persons, of words and of actions. These are adhered to by just about everyone, day in and day out, and they are as automatic as not touching a hot stove or a live electric wire. A long list of the traditional prohibitions was provided by Kluckhohn and Leighton (1946: 139–40):

> A very high proportion of the acts which arise out of convictions about beings and powers are negative in character. Thus lightning-struck trees must be avoided. Coyotes, bears, snakes, and some kinds of birds must never be killed. The eating of fish and of most water birds and animals is forbidden, and raw meat is taboo. Navahos will never cut a melon with the point of a knife. They never comb their hair at night. No matter how crowded a hogan may be with sleeping figures, no Navaho may step over the recumbent body of another. Mother-in-law and son-in-law must never look into each other's eyes. Any kind of sexual contact (even walking down the street or dancing together) with members of the opposite sex of one's own or one's father's clan is prohibited. Most technical processes

are hedged about with restrictions: the tanner dare not leave the pole on which he scrapes hide standing upright; the potter and the basket-maker work in isolation, observing a bewildering variety of taboos; the weaver shares one of these, the dread of final completion, so that a 'spirit outlet' must always be left in the design. Let these few common examples stand as representative of the literally thousands of doings and saying which are *báhádzid,* or tabooed.

While the observance of avoidances is virtually universal, more positive religious activity is a good deal more variable from individual to individual. By far the most common of individual religious performances are songs, many of which conform to age-old formulas, while others may be 'owned' within individual families or clans, or even made up spontaneously. There are certain activities like traveling (especially on horseback), farming, weaving, gambling, and sweat-bathing which are nearly always accompanied by traditional songs. The songs are not performed in isolation, so to speak; they are interwoven with the different activities with which they are associated. People farm, or weave, or ride and sing at the same time. Some of the songs are so basic to certain activities that they might almost be considered as 'essential workplace skills.'

As with all other positive religious activity, there is a great deal of individual variability in the performance of songs. It is not entirely a matter of inclination; it may also be a matter of knowledge. Regardless of their intentions, some people are simply better equipped than others with the knowledge they need to deal with the world. 'I have always been a poor man,' one Navajo told W. W. Hill, 'I do not know a single song' (quoted in Kluckhohn and Leighton 1946: 220).

Pieces of white shell or of turquoise are very widely used both as votive offerings and for protection. Travelers place them on trailside cairns, or at hilltop holy places or springs; weavers attach them to their looms, and tanners to their poles. Farming involves a very wide variety of ritual practices, beginning with the special treatment of seeds before planting, and ending with a special way of storing the harvest.

Probably the most powerful of individual ritual acts is sweat-bathing. Along with purging, it is the supreme act not only of physical but of ritual purification. The sweat-house, a small conical structure of logs covered by earth, is always in a secluded spot some distance from the family hogans. In advance of actual 'bathing' it is necessary to build a fire and heat up the rocks that will then, with the aid of a shovel, be thrown inside. Before entering the sweat-house men (and formerly also women) shout an invitation to the *Dighinii* to come and join in the bath, and each bather throws fresh dirt on the roof. Sweat-bathing may be done by individuals, but is considered both more efficacious and more enjoyable when done by groups. While within the sweat-house, traditional songs are sung, and these like all songs acquire increased power when sung by multiple voices. The bathers should use only soap made from freshly dug yucca roots, not any commercial product, on their bodies. The ritual ends outside the sweat-house when the bather plunges into cold water, rolls in a snowbank, or (most commonly) douses himself with a bucket of cold water. Sweat-bathing however is not always and necessarily a ritual act. It may at times be undertaken just to get clean, in which case the songs and other observances are dispensed with.

Men vary in the frequency of their sweat-bathing, just as do Americans in the frequency of their bathing. It may depend partly on how often they need purification, either as participants in more extended ceremonies, or after polluting contacts or experiences. Notwithstanding those variable circumstances, a properly devout individual should probably take a sweat-bath at least once a month.

Attendance at ceremonies is of course the crowning act of religious participation, and it is one that just about everyone indulges in as often as circumstances will permit. Frequency of attendance depends to a considerable extent on the ability to travel. For just about every Navajo in every part of the reservation, there is likely to be a sing going on somewhere within a radius of fifty miles, every night of the year. Those who are free from conflicting obligations may attend a great many of them, but most people, most of the time, are not likely to attend a sing more then ten of fifteen miles away. They attend of course for a very wide variety of reasons, social and recreational as well as religious, and many are not involved in the ritual in any direct way, except perhaps in the group singing. But their mere presence helps in the collective effort to bring about the *hozhoni,* from which everyone benefits.

Religious instruction

Navajo singers—the only persons who really know the religion in any detail—acquire their knowledge and skills through a long process of formal instruction, at the hands of a previously established singer. Everyone else acquires his or her religion piecemeal, in the course of everyday living, and very largely within the compass of the family or 'outfit.' Children are, of necessity, taught the necessary avoidances at an early age: not just 'Don't touch that stove; you'll burn your finger' but 'Don't comb your hair after dark; a witch might get it' and 'Don't kill that bird; its spirit will come back and make you sick.'

More positive religious activities are learned in conjunction with the day to day activities with which they are associated. The boy learns the innumerable observances connected with farming as he works alongside his father in the field; the girl learns from her mother both the manual procedures of weaving and the songs associated with it. Additional knowledge is picked up through listening to and observing what goes on at sings. Many men aspire to be singers, for both the prestige and the income it may bring, and they make a conscious effort to memorize the songs and prayers they hear, and the manual activities they observe.

There are also certain occasions on which formal religious instruction may take place. It is common for grandparents or other elders to recite myths in the evening, for the entertainment of the whole family group but also for the instruction of the children. There is no formal tradition as to what should be taught at these times; it is entirely a matter of what the elders know, and feel like telling. In addition, there is a recognized time for speech-making, most commonly in the early evening hours, in the course of many ceremonies. On these occasions the lead singer, in charge of the ceremony, may admonish but at the same time instruct his hearers in regard to their religious duties.

*Change and
the future*

I think I probably knew, at Shonto, the last generation of Navajos who did not measure themselves by Bilagáana standards. Nobody had electricity; nobody had any kind of plumbing; nobody had any heat except firewood; very few had any amount of education in English. But people, except for the poor, had plenty of sheep, plenty of horses (the single chief measure of wealth) and plenty of 'hard goods' (silver jewelry). Many men also had some ceremonial knowledge, which was another important form of wealth. Navajos did not in the least think of themselves as poor, backward, or underprivileged; they thought of themselves simply as *Diné*, living as the *Dighinii* had ordained. They took every opportunity to obtain such benefits as they could from the proximity of the Bilagáana world, but with no desire to become Bilagáana.

That began to change with the advent of universal schooling—always in English—for the young, but it was also quite profoundly changed, in unintended ways, with the advent of Lyndon Johnson's War on Poverty. Poverty for everyone, regardless of ethnicity or culture, was defined by a single set of purely statistical measures, and according to them nearly all Navajos were counted among the poorest of the poor. The reservation thus became the target of many poverty programs, and saw the influx of 'poverty workers,' who saw it as their duty to rescue the people from what they regarded as unacceptable, substandard living conditions. Navajos were made aware that they were eligible for all kinds of special benefits, which they were generally eager to accept. At the same time they were almost obliged to think of themselves as poor, since poverty was the basis of their eligibility. A sense of deprivation was implanted in a people who had not previously thought in those terms.

The combination of extensive education in schools, run on strictly Bilagáana lines, and the ideology of poverty have instilled in nearly all younger Navajos a desire to leave behind at least the material circumstances of their traditional life. Everybody wants to live in a home with furniture and with electricity and running water, and now just about everybody can. Most people would rather have a wage job than undertake the onerous work of raising livestock, especially since the cash remuneration is much greater. Everybody wants as much education as possible, since that is the route to better jobs and more pay. The number of Navajo college students, and graduates, is staggering, considering that half a century ago there was only one. And there has been, all over the reservation, a wholesale acceptance of evangelistic Christianity. The so-called Native American Church, known also as the Peyote Religion, has also made very considerable headway, and some of its rituals have become blended with traditional Navajo rituals.

It is inevitable under these circumstances that much of traditional Navajo religion is disappearing. The state of public health has been vastly improved, reducing the formerly high disease rates, and the fear of using hospitals and Bilagáana doctors has wholly disappeared. Opportunities for the singers to earn a decent living are reduced in proportion. It is still true however that a great many people like to 'hedge their bets,' by having both hospital treatment and a sing, in time of illness. Nevertheless the number of top-flight singers is sadly reduced, as few young men are willing to invest the time necessary to become one. There are simply not enough rewards to be anticipated, either in the form of financial remuneration or prestige.

Probably the single most significant erosive force is not the rival religion of Christianity but the secular religion of capitalism. By making individuals economically self-sufficient, it has everywhere eroded the ties of kinship that were once basic to the structure and functioning of society. They were also, in the Navajo case, basic to the functioning of religion, for traditional religion and traditional society were intimately interwoven.

The future of Navajo religion is thus uncertain. It would almost certainly die out, or nearly so, without active efforts to reverse the current process of erosion. Those efforts are underway at the Navajo Community College (Diné College), where a formal program for the training of singers has been instituted. Fortunately for the program, there are hundreds of pages of myth and ritual, recorded in earlier days by anthropologists, that now serve as instructional materials for the Navajos themselves. Efforts are also being made to find elderly singers from whom additional, previously unrecorded myths and rituals can be learned.

There has also been, in the very recent past, an embryonic revitalization movement, comparable to many other such movements that have arisen among oppressed and colonized peoples whose cultures and religions were under threat. It was, as its votaries insist, instigated by a personal visit of the Hero Twins to a traditional Navajo woman, living in one of the most remote parts of the reservation. The Twins assured the woman that the current drought conditions (the worst in a hundred years, in 1996) were due to the people's neglect of their language, traditional culture, and above all ceremonial duties. The woman came to be seen as a true prophetess, and the area of the supposed holy visit became for a time a place of pilgrimage (for the details see Schwarz 1998). It is too early to tell, at this writing, whether the movement will persist, or will die out as the vast majority of such movements historically have done.

But there is also, among the educated young, a new sense of 'Navajo nationalism' which is quite different from the former, wholly tribal self-image. It is precisely those individuals who are becoming most assimilated into the general Anglo-American social and economic system, who are anxious to maintain a separate, Navajo identity within it. Their hopes are focused on two things specifically: the survival of the Navajo language, and the survival of at least some of the Navajo ceremonies. Consequently these individuals are often going out of their way to undergo, in adult life, ceremonies that are nearly as unfamiliar and exotic to them as they are to Bilagáana. How successful these efforts will be, only time will tell. If the history of other American Indian tribes is any guide, the ceremonies most likely to survive will be those with the greatest entertainment value. Fortunately their entertainment value, for Navajos, is enormous.

Navajo religion is a tribal religion, just as was early Judaism. As such its outlook is relativist rather than exclusivist. It is the religion of, and for, one people among many, and it is taken for granted that others have their own gods and their own ways of dealing with them. It is an open system, and has clearly borrowed many deities and many rituals from neighboring peoples. Its outlook is egalitarian, in that no Navajo is superior to any other by virtue of greater sanctity.

It is the religion of a people living in close, daily contact with nature, on which they have to depend for rainfall, for grass, for water, and for wood. The *Diné* have very limited control over those things, which are under the command of the *Dighinii,* and they must therefore make continuous efforts to influence the deities both to act in their behalf, and not to act to their detriment. There is at all times a sense of human weakness, in relation to the gods; the world at best is a dangerous place. The importance of nature in the Navajo world-view is reflected in the fact that many of the supernaturals are either animals, or natural forces like wind and rain.

Navajo religion is also the religion of a people for whom social relations are very largely embodied in a web of kinship, which extends beyond the immediate family to more distant lineages and clans. The supernaturals are conceived also to be related to one another through ties of kinship, which determine their relations to one another.

The foregoing observations could be made about almost any native religion in North America. It remains to add however that Navajo religion is the religion of an enormously creative and artistic people, who in myth and ritual have found rich expressive outlets for their verbal and pictorial artistry. Their achievements in this regard are matched by those of their Pueblo neighbors, but set them apart from most other tribal peoples in North America. The richness of religion, in the case of both Navajos and Pueblos, is a measure of their success in adapting to a world under Bilagáana rule.

3

ARAB VILLAGE RELIGION

The nature of peasantry

The religion that is mainly followed by Egyptian and Sudanese villagers is a variant of Islam, often called Sufism though that is not a very meaningful term. In somewhat variant forms, it has tens and perhaps hundreds of millions of votaries throughout the Islamic world, and among Iranians, Pakistanis, Afghans, and Turks as well as Arabs. It is not exclusively a village religion, for it has many adherents in the towns and cities also. It is however the primary religion of the villagers, for whom other and more orthodox forms of Islam are mostly inaccessible. My personal acquaintance with it is almost entirely at the village level, in Egypt and in the northern Sudan. I refer to it here as 'Arab village religion' simply because 'Egyptian and northern Sudanese village religion' would be too cumbersome a term.

The villagers are peasant farmers, as are at least two thirds of the inhabitants of the Islamic world, and at least half the population of the world at large. That means that they are the specialized food producers in a highly complex and differentiated society, in which they must produce enough not only to feed themselves, but also to feed all the different kinds of urban dwellers who are not food producers. Because the peasants can not be expected to do that voluntarily, society through the ages has found ways of extracting their surplus from them: by serfdom, by absentee landlordism, by enforced tithing, by debt peonage, or by taxation.

The villagers are generally left with just about enough to live on, which means that everywhere they are poor. They are also highly conscious of it, because many of the urban dwellers whom they feed are not poor. They are mostly uneducated and illiterate, because education—the only route of advancement in a stratified world—has rarely been available to them. Their living conditions are apt to be crowded and unsanitary, because they have been forced to crowd tightly together, partly for defense against marauders and partly so as not to take up valuable farmland, of which they never have enough. (These conditions are more conspicuous in Egypt than in the Sudan, where overpopulation and land shortage are not so severe.) The world-view of peasants, not surprisingly, tends to be pessimistic.

Not everyone of course is equally poor, here or anywhere else. And because the peasants live in a stratified and highly status-conscious world, they are status-conscious among themselves. Families may inherit status, through descent from the Prophet or from length of residence in a village, but they may also achieve it, through increasing their land holdings and hiring others to work for them. But there is an additional road to status through religion, and as such it has a role of its own in peasant life.

The peasants' world, in marked contrast to that of Navajos, is almost wholly a human world, from which nature has long been banished. They spend much of every day working the land, but it is a land that for millennia has been divided through human intervention into small plots, surrounded by irrigation ditches, and it is land covered by man-made crops. The desert in usually close within sight, but it is an evil and a dangerous place where peasants never go if they can avoid it. When not at work in the fields they live in crowded villages, surrounded not only by their kin but also by strangers who are potential rivals and enemies. There are dangers to be apprehended from nature (mostly when the annual Nile flood is too high or too low), but the main dangers that threaten daily life are from humans, or else from supernaturals. In a world so human-oriented and so far from nature, it is not surprising that the supernaturals are all conceived in human rather than in animal form.

Peasants and the larger world

In the characterization of A. L. Kroeber, peasants are 'part societies with part cultures.' They are part societies because their village community is part of a national whole that embraces also all the different kinds of urban dwellers. They have a part culture because in addition to their own rich body of folklore, folk medicine, folk law, and folk religion, which is perpetuated from generation to generation through oral tradition, they also try as best they can to participate in the larger culture of the cities.

Robert Redfield gave us the concepts of Great Tradition and Little Tradition. Great Tradition is the literate culture, embodied in scripture, law, and literature, that is generated by the urban elites. Because of its basis in literature, it is widely shared throughout the realm of any civilization. The Islamic Great Tradition is shared by all the literate classes from Morocco to Indonesia. The lower classes also participate in it to the extent that they understand it, but their understanding is limited by their illiteracy or very limited literacy. This problem is especially acute in the Arab world because so much of the literature is in Classical Arabic, a language that differs as much from the modern vernaculars as Chaucerian English does from the speech of today. Almost no villager understands it, though many can recite memorized passages from it.

Side by side with the Great Traditions there exist the innumerable Little Traditions that are indigenous to particular, often limited regions. These supply most of the culture of the peasants, most of the time, because they are fully accessible without the aid of literacy. In the Islamic world they will often be found to embody beliefs and practices that trace back to pre-Islamic, and even to Neolithic times. To a very large extent the villagers of Egypt and the Northern Sudan share parts of the Islamic Great Tradition, and at the same time a particular Little Tradition indigenous to the Nile Valley.

*The two
religious
traditions*

What has been said about peasant culture in general applies with special force to the domain of religion, for Arab villagers. To all intents and purposes they have two religions. They are both called Islam by their adherents, and yet they have only one meeting point, which is at the top. That is, they both proceed from the recognition of Allah as the pure and absolute embodiment of power, above considerations of abstract right and wrong because his actions define right and wrong. He is under no compulsion to act in predictable ways, although he often does so from force of habit. All supernatural power enjoyed by lesser beings flows originally from him.

Allah's gift to mankind has come in two quite distinct ways. To orthodox Muslims he has given an immensely complex and detailed body of laws, which are for most people the only path to salvation in the next world. Salvation comes neither from faith (which is taken for granted by everyone) nor from good works, but by strict obedience to the law. As a result ritual is very little emphasized; orthodox Islam is essentially a personal religion for each adherent. Even the Five Pillars of the Faith (see below)—the only performances that are absolutely prescribed—can all be performed by lone individuals.

God's gift to the poor and illiterate has come not in the form of laws that they can't read, but in the form of *baraka* (usually translated as 'blessedness,' though this does not fully capture the meaning). It is a complex and highly subtle concept, and will be further explored in later pages. Here it will be sufficient to suggest that *baraka* is a kind of spiritual capital that everybody requires to obtain the good things and to avoid the bad things in life. *Baraka* has been bestowed by God on specially chosen individuals, who call themselves 'clients' of God (*wali*, pl. *awliya*),[15] and by them it is transmitted in turn to followers, in a wide variety of ways. While obedience to the law is necessary for salvation in the next life, it is *baraka* that brings rewards in this life. And since peasants, at least until late in life, have to worry at lot more about this world than about the one to come, *baraka* is much more important to them than is law. However, the villagers' participation in both traditions is seen by them as important, and will be described in the paragraphs that follow.

Everyone recognizes that at least a minimal obedience to God's law is necessary for salvation, and the peasants comply within the limits of their knowledge and ability. The following are specific aspects of their adherence to the Great Tradition:

Participation in the Great Tradition

The name of Allah embodies enormous power in and of itself, and it crops up repeatedly in everyday discourse. Indeed it can hardly be avoided, for it is contained within just about every ritual of greeting and of parting, every exclamation of pleasure, pain, regret, surprise, and alarm. These utterances are not of course acts of worship; the name of Allah simply imparts intensity to the saying itself. But they serve continually to remind people that God is out there.

The name of God

Allah has ninety-nine other names, expressing his myriad attributes. They range all the way from 'the merciful' to 'the vengeful,' for God is all things to all men. Pious Muslims know the ninety-nine names, and recite them in a ritually prescribed sequence, aided by a rosary. Peasants probably also know most of the names, if for no other reason than that one or other of the names of God is always the second element in any personal name that begins with 'Abdel.' But very few peasants know the names in the prescribed ritual sequence, and can recite them.

This metaphor was coined by the Prophet Muhammad, to designate the five ritual performances that are absolutely required of all good Muslims.

The Five Pillars of the Faith

[15] In transliterating Arabic words I fellow the spellings that are usual in the Sudan, where my familiarity was acquired. Usage in Egypt is in some cases different.

They are recitation of the Profession of Faith ('There is no god but God, and Muhammad is his messenger'),[16] recitation of formal prayers (actually psalms) five times a day, fasting during daylight hours throughout the month of Ramadan, giving alms to the poor, and making the pilgrimage to Mecca once in a lifetime if you can afford it. Of these, only the recitation of the Profession of Faith (*shahada*) is consistently practiced by peasants (partly because it is a formula which recurs in many other Muslim prayers). Everyone knows also the Classical Arabic formulas that are to be recited in the five daily prayers (which are nearly the same each time), but each complete prayer takes from fifteen to twenty minutes to perform, and is therefore frequently an inconvenience for hard-working peasants. People vary enormously in their attention to the prayers, but few are absolutely strict about them. There is a tendency to postpone daily prayer recital until late in life, in the years of retirement, partly because more time is then available, and partly because of a belief, sometimes articulately expressed, that 'salvation can wait.'

There are however degrees of prosperity among the villagers, as I have already noted, and they correlate to a considerable extent with degrees of piety. Everyone's highest ambition is to acquire enough land so that other people can be hired to work it; to become in effect an idle landowner. Persons who achieve that exalted status are quite likely to begin saying regular prayers, for in Arab tradition religious virtuosity goes hand in hand with status. Recitation of prayers in public is a way of advertising your status, partly by making the point that you don't have to spend all your time working.

If recitation of the daily prayers is irksome, fasting all day during Ramadan (which includes a total abstention from water, and even medicines) is far more so for the village dwellers. The urban upper classes simply sleep all day and party all night; Ramadan for many of them is not a time of self-denial but a festival season. The farmers of course do not have that luxury. Many start the month each year with a pious resolution to fast all the way through, but few succeed. I suspect that one reason many find it impossible to keep Ramadan is that they are habitual smokers, and smoking too is forbidden during the daylight

---

[16]I prefer this translation to the more usual 'there is no god but Allah,' because the latter may suggest to Christians that their own god is regarded as a false god, since he is not named Allah. This is the belief of some uneducated Muslims, but it is not condoned in orthodox interpretation. The Christian god *in heaven* is one with Allah, the One True God, but Jesus is not. 'God is not begotten and does not beget,' as the Quran repeatedly asserts.

hours. As in the case of saying prayers, there is a tendency to postpone keeping Ramadan until the late years of life.

Almsgiving is not a practical possibility, most of the time, for people who have so little to give away. If they pay any kind of taxes they are apt to feel that that is alms enough. But before starting out on a hazardous undertaking people may seek out a beggar and give him something, as a kind of protective measure.

It goes without saying that few villagers have the resources to make the pilgrimage (*hajj*) to Mecca, even once. It is nevertheless everyone's lifelong dream, partly from a belief that making the *hajj* will insure salvation, even if the other Pillars have been neglected, and partly because the returned *hajji* enjoys enormous prestige in the village. He will very probably decorate the outside of his house with a painting of an airplane, boat, or bus, to show the means by which he made the trip. A few peasants each year do manage to make the pilgrimage, usually with the aid of donations and loans from a wide circle of relatives. Having a *hajji* in the family confers status on all of them.

Mosque attendance

Attendance at Friday prayers in a mosque is defined as meritorious rather than mandatory for orthodox Muslims. Still, all the peasants recognize that it is beneficial, and village men will usually attend if they have the chance. (According to folk tradition, women are generally excluded from the mosque.) But many smaller villages have no mosque, and some of the larger ones have a mosque but no preacher (*khattib*). Men will rarely travel any distance for the specific purpose of attending Friday prayers, but if they happen to be in a town or village where the prayers are in progress, they will often attend. Everyone knows the special formula for the Friday prayer.

The Friday noon prayer need not always be performed in a mosque, particularly if there are fewer that forty worshippers on hand. Sometimes a pious village elder will collect a group of like-minded men and lead the prayers in any convenient open space. However, the mosque service is considered to be more beneficial because it also includes a sermon.

Quran recitation

For villagers the Quran is a closed book, as J. S. Trimingham (1949: 117) puts it, for they don't understand the Classical Arabic words in it (nor do they sometimes understand the words in the prayers they recite). However, reciting the Quran, even without understanding, is defined as meritorious. As a consequence many boys are sent for one or two years to sit with a village *feki* (a kind of hedge-scholar, who possesses a Quran but who may himself be barely literate). He teaches the boys to chant, by rote, such verses as he himself knows, and also to write them on large wooden tablets. It is felt that this knowledge will provide the boys with a certain degree of divine protection in later life, to the extent that it can be recited in times of crisis or need. How much is actually retained of course varies enormously from individual to individual.

Festivals

Everyone in the villages celebrates and enjoys the two great *bairam* festivals, one at the end of Ramadan and one forty days later. The birthday of the Prophet Muhammad (*Mulid en-Nebi*) is also important in some Egyptian communities, though less so in the Sudan. However these, like Christmas for most Americans, have very little specifically religious content.

*Customary
law*

The Quran, containing 114 verbatim messages from God, makes up only a small part of orthodox Islamic scripture. There are also innumerable sayings attributed to Muhammad (*hadith*), and the whole body of customary law (*sharia*) to which the Prophet adhered throughout his life, even though he may have made no verbal reference to it. The peasants' knowledge of all three of these bodies of scripture is extremely limited, but they nevertheless acknowledge them as part of their Islamic heritage.

There is however one particular area of customary law with which they are familiar: the family law relating to marriage, divorce, property ownership and inheritance, and the care of widows, orphans, and elders. In regard to these matters the villagers generally follow established custom, and disputes may be referred to special *sharia* courts that are maintained both in Egypt and the Sudan. On the other hand they avoid the secular courts at all costs, for bringing the authority of the state to bear within the village is bad news for everyone.

Abstentions

Islamic law includes a very long list of forbidden foods, more or less comparable to the Abominations of Leviticus. Villagers generally know and observe some but not all of them. Everyone avoids pork, which is considered disgusting even on dietary grounds. On the other hand there is not much avoidance of alcohol, although everyone knows that they should do so. Egyptians have had a reputation as heavy drinkers since far back in antiquity, and it has not been extinguished under Islam. Sudanese tend to be somewhat more abstemious in this regard, and in fact are regarded as puritanical by their Egyptian neighbors. The prohibition against gambling is very widely ignored in both Egypt and the Sudan.

The foregoing paragraphs pretty much exhaust the list of peasant activities in conformity with the Islamic Great Tradition. There is however a great deal of knowledge, derived from the Great Tradition, that they preserve in oral form. Few if any can read the Quran, but people know many details of its content, just as many Christians who have never read the Bible know about Noah's ark, Lot's wife, David and Goliath, and other dramatic episodes. Details of the life of the Prophet and of his earlier followers are known in some detail, and there is often some knowledge of the later caliphates as well. It is that knowledge that allows the peasants to site themselves within a worldwide historical context of Islam, a factor vital in their self-image. It provides a feeling of solidarity with the upper classes from whom they are otherwise alienated. *Historical knowledge and self-image*

The principal religion of the villagers falls within that very broad domain of Islamic belief and practice that is called Sufism, though the term is not a very useful one. Just as the term Protestant embraces everything and everyone that is not Catholic, from Episcopalians to pentecostals, Sufism embraces every aspect of Islam except strict legalism. In theory, what all of the different Sufi beliefs and practices have in common is the belief that salvation can be attained through direct communion with God as well as through obedience to his laws. It was of course a very old and pervasive idea long before the coming of the Prophet. It was introduced into Islam by mystics in the early centuries after Muhammad, and was rather reluctantly accepted as legitimate by the orthodox leaders because of its broad popular appeal. They have always insisted however that communion with God must be direct, not through intermediaries, and it is on this point that the villagers depart from orthodoxy. Being humble and weak, they have to commune with almighty Allah almost entirely through intermediaries who are closer to their own level. *The folk religion of the villages*

The sufistic folk religion of the villages has two enormous advantages that scriptural Islam lacks: it is fully accessible to the illiterate, and it is accessible to the weak and humble. It is focused not in a remote and magisterial Allah but in a saint whose shrine is close by, who is not offended by colloquial Arabic speech, and who has a special feeling for 'his' villagers. For many there are other attractions not found in orthodox Islam: membership in an enrolled congregation, rich pageantry, and esoteric rituals. Finally, folk religion does not impose excessive behavioral demands, that can be very difficult for everyday folk to follow.

The super-naturals

Allah. As I have already suggested, village religion connects with scriptural Islam at the top, in the shared belief in all-powerful Allah. But his personality, as conceived by villagers, is somewhat different from that taught in the mosque schools. It has been magnificently delineated by the Egyptian novelist Naguib Mahfouz, especially in *Children of Gebelawi* (1981). Like the early Yahweh, Allah is a stern and unforgiving tribal patriarch, who has laid down for his children a strict and difficult path to righteousness, but who is forced continually to castigate them when they don't follow it. He seems to enjoy the role of disciplinarian. He never smiles, and whatever love he has for his children is the toughest of 'tough love.'

The invocation *Bismillah el-Rahman el-Rahim* (in the name of God, the merciful, the compassionate) is very frequently uttered, particularly at the outset of any hazardous or uncertain enterprise, like taking a taxi ride or setting out to cross the Nile. It is very clear from the context however that this is not meant as praise to God for being merciful and compassionate; it is a supplication to *please be* merciful and compassionate.

Allah is far too lofty and remote to listen to the poorest and weakest of his children, especially since he cannot be respectfully addressed except in Classical Arabic. All other languages are offense to his ears. Small wonder then that the attitude of the villagers is one involving equal parts of reverence and fear; indeed the two can hardly be separated. The general feeling is that he brings eternal salvation in the next world, but only trouble in this one. He must be continually propitiated, but in this life little or nothing can be expected in return.

The attitude of the villagers is nicely captured in a story told me by an educated Sudanese friend, who swears it is true. My friend was back in his home village, visiting with the old folks, and they were sitting outdoors one evening under a full moon. My friend pointed up at it and said, 'Isn't it amazing to think that the Americans were actually up there last month?' His uncle was totally incredulous, and said, 'Oh, that's just more American propaganda, isn't it?' (Thanks to Voice of America, most Third World peoples are subjected to a fair amount of self-congratulatory American propaganda, and they have developed a well-deserved skepticism.) In the course of half an hour my friend succeeded in convincing his uncle that the Americans had indeed landed on the moon, explaining in detail how it was done. The uncle's totally spontaneous reaction then was '*Ya salaam!*' (roughly, 'Oh, wow!'). 'I hope they don't bring God back with them!' (In Islamic folk belief, the moon is one of the dwelling places of Allah.)

Baraka. Despite God's stern and unforgiving attitude toward his unruly children, he relents from time to time by sending gifts to specially favored individuals, who are usually but not always men. His gift is in the form of *baraka,* a word derived from the verb 'to bless.' It is the spiritual capital that is needed to bring most of the good things in this world, and to prevent most of the bad ones. God is the only central bank that issues this precious currency, but it is disbursed by him to his 'clients,' the *awliya* (sing. *wali*) who are like branch banks, and who in turn disburse it to ordinary folk. *Baraka* has no very close equivalent in Christian thought; as nearly as I can tell its closest equivalent is found in the Polynesian concept of *mana.* It is not an innate quality but something you possess, and which is regularly acquired and regularly expended.

Since the *wali* is the primary local source of *baraka,* it is chiefly to him that one should apply. He may have died and gone to be reunited with God centuries ago, but he at the same time survives as a living and active presence within his tomb, on the village outskirts. All kinds of *baraka* can be obtained from visits to the tomb; especially if one can carry away pieces of it to serve as amulets. Because of this arcane practice, the tombs of the most venerated saints will often be seen in quite dilapidated condition, and must be recovered with whitewash annually. If the tomb has a guard, the next best thing is to carry away dust from the interior.

Baraka is inherited, and also transmitted by marriage. It is possessed in large measure by the wife of the *wali,* and above all by his descendants, who continue to disburse it after his death. It is contagious, through the air but especially by touch. People continually strain to approach and to touch the descendants of the *wali,* as well as his tomb and the things associated with him. Television watchers may recall how, after the death of the Ayatollah Khomeini, there was a near-riot as the faithful fought to approach and to touch the body. *Baraka* is obtained also by sitting at the feet of the *wali's* descendants and listening to their teaching.

Baraka is clearly connected with virtue, but it is not virtue in and of itself. It is possessed more by virtuous persons than by others, because it is much more readily given to them, and is less diminished by evil deeds or thoughts. Nevertheless, like all currency, it is expendable and must be replenished. It is diminished by bad acts and thoughts, but it is also expended in quite specific ways, as when a prayer addressed to the *wali* is granted. It can be replenished in any of the several ways I have indicated above. Fortunately the *wali* himself has an inexhaustible supply, because he can always travel to God and get more.

The saints. The *wali,* who is the clear focal point of all village religion, goes by a variety of names. In life he will usually call himself a *wali,* a word that means literally 'client' (i.e. a client of God). (He must be so designated because according to Islamic usage he may not be called a prophet, Muhammad having identified himself as the last of the prophets.) His followers will call him their *sheikh,* a word that in Arabic has much broader application than just to a tribal chieftain. After death he may still be called *sheikh,* but he is more likely to earn the honorific *sid* or *sayyed*—both words meaning 'lord.'[17] More familiarly he may be *sidi,* 'my lord,' or *sayyedna,* 'our lord.' In English, for want of a closer equivalent, we usually call him a saint, as do English-speaking Arabs themselves. He does indeed have many qualities in common with the saints of Catholic folk religion, but he has many other properties as well.

The saint may have been dead for a few generations or for centuries, but he remains a living and active presence within his nearby tomb. There are of course many other saints (thousands of them, in fact), and they all convey *baraka,* but the local saint is most of the time the most important, because he is very much a tutelary. He is always referred to by the villagers, with enormous pride of possession, as 'our saint.' However, people when traveling will endeavor to get such *baraka* as they can from any saint whose tomb they pass by. The miraculous achievements (*karamat*) of each saint are kept in collective memory through a rich tradition of storytelling, which has its counterpart in the myth recitations of Navajo elders.

Most saints are conceived to have purely local power, which does not extend far beyond the village or villages where they are worshipped. For that reason their tombs, though the subject of constant visit by locals, are not major pilgrimage centers. Since every village has its own saint

---

[17] In Egypt and some other areas, the title *sayyed* is reserved for blood descendants of the Prophet.

(or often several of them), there is no reason to seek out other peoples' saints. There are however a few 'super-saints,' like Sheikh Abdel Qadir and Sayyed Ahmad el-Bedawi, who are celebrated throughout the Arab world, and whose tombs are major centers of pilgrimage. Some of these 'super-saints' have 'tombs' in several places.

Unlike Allah, the saint is a mainly benevolent being. He loves his villagers and they love him, with an adoration that is unmixed with fear. He is always nearby and is never too busy to listen, and his ears are not offended by colloquial Arabic (or Nubian or Turkish or Farsi). He is a thoroughly tolerant, warm-hearted, and forgiving being—an island of comfort in a world ruled by stern religious as well as secular authority. I suppose he might be called a grandfather figure. He is nevertheless capable of bringing misfortune both to religious and to secular authorities who are vain or oppressive, or who cast doubt on his powers.

The Virgin. The Virgin Mary is honored in orthodox Islamic scripture, but she has a different and somewhat more exalted place in folk religion. As so often in the Christian world, she is a special patroness of women, and is supplicated above all to provide protection for their young children. She can however confer *baraka* on anyone. Some years ago in a poor Cairo suburb, an apparition of the Virgin was seen by a young Muslim man, above the roof of a local Coptic church. Thereafter for several weeks the square in front of the church was thronged by both Muslims and Christians seeking to derive *baraka* from the sight of the Virgin. Some female saints have a similar role among the villagers.

Evil spirits. There are rather vague conceptions about the Devil (*Shaytan* or *Iblis*), who does not play a very prominent role even in orthodox Islamic belief. He is an evil force that is always trying to lure people to damnation, as God is always trying to guide them to salvation, but like God he is remote, and not much involved in the everyday world. Most of the bad things that happen are attributed not to him but to *jinn*. They are the evil counterparts of the saints, and dwell in all kinds of nearby places. Above all they dwell in the desert, which is very much feared by the villagers.

Animistic spirits. *Jinn* have a place in orthodox belief, but there are also spirits that fall outside the realms of both orthodox and folk Islam, and are legacies of a much older past. Most important of these are spirits who dwell in the Nile, and who, among other things, are sometimes thought to be the 'real' parents of albino children. Villagers are aware that propitiation of these spirits is not countenanced within Islam, but they are also prone to say in self-defense that 'Islam isn't everything.'

Zar. These are a very special class of powerful spirits that take possession mainly of women in the Sudan, although in Egypt they may invade men as well. They are generally capricious and malevolent, and must be 'bought off' once they have moved in, by gifts and acts of propitiation. Nevertheless some women will go out of their way to attract them, because the woman while possessed has far more power than she will ever otherwise have, and the whole community will mobilize to try and rid her of the *zar.* Once exorcised, it stays near her for the rest of her life, and if properly propitiated can actually serve as a kind of guardian spirit, protecting her from other *zar.* It can repossess her at any time, and may be invited to do so when power is sought.

. The *zar* cult stands wholly outside of both Islam and Christianity. *Baraka* is not involved in it at any point, for possession by the *zar* can itself be a kind of substitute for *baraka.* The cult seems to have originated in Christian Ethiopia and crossed from there into Muslim North Africa, where it is chiefly found. It is not, like the belief in animistic spirits, a cult of high antiquity; it is believed to have originated no more than three of four centuries ago. Everywhere outside Egypt it is virtually a religion of and for women, compensating them for their exclusion both from the mosque and, often, from the religious brotherhoods (see below).

The evil eye. The evil eye is one of the most pervasive of beliefs, found not only throughout the world of Islam but through the whole of the Old World, except in the Far East. Of all the dangers that afflict people, it is the most feared because it is an evil without an identifiable source. It may cause harm to anyone or anything, but above all it causes harm to young children, and to animals. It is by far the most commonly invoked explanation for the illness or death of a young child, but also when a cow or goat fails to lactate, or goes dry. Psychofunctionalists have suggested that the value of the evil eye belief lies in the fact that it provides an explanation for intrusive evil without pointing the finger at anyone in particular. However, other theories have also been propounded; the pervasiveness of the belief as well as some of its specific features are still far from completely understood.

The evil eye is the eye of covetousness, which anyone is capable of casting, often quite unintentionally. There is a common supposition in the West that certain people 'possess' the evil eye, but this is not the way it is usually conceived by the villagers. Some people are of course more covetous by nature than others, but when a child or animal dies it is rarely clear who was responsible. My late colleague John M. Roberts was convinced that the tenth Mosaic commandment, against coveting, was actually an injunction against casting the evil eye (personal communication). It is the only Biblical commandment that has reference to feelings rather than to overt actions.

Among the villagers there are many rituals of exorcism once a person has been afflicted as a result of the evil eye, but rituals of protection against it are even more pervasive. Many kinds of amuletic objects confer protection: depictions of an eye, which will often be seen on boats or painted on truck bumpers; depictions of an open hand; representations of a chili pepper (often seen hanging from the rear-view mirror in taxis); and almost anything blue in color. It is very common, indeed nearly universal, for young children to wear one or more blue beads on a string.

*The human
condition*

Humans are corrupt and sinful, and more so now than in earlier times. God intended them to be righteous, and showed them the path to follow, but they are mostly too weak and too willful to obey as consistently as they should. Consequently they are always in danger of divine wrath, but fortunately Allah is usually too far away to be concerned with the doings or misdoings or lowly peasants. His rewards and punishments are reserved for the next world

The present world has its own much more immediate dangers, rewards, and punishments. Danger, which is never far away, comes from a host of evil beings, both human and supernatural, as well as from the disembodied evil eye. Suffering comes from the peasants' immemorial, downtrodden position within a stratified social system from which there is little hope of escape. Alleviation and rewards come from the saint and his living descendant, who are also never far away.

Kinship is as important to Arab villagers as it is to Navajos; it is the main economic safety net in both societies. It finds its divine sanction in the *Sunna*—the customary law of the Arabs by which Muhammad himself lived. Inheritance law spells out the degrees of kinship, and their rights and duties, with minute precision. But for villagers, kinship has an overt political dimension as well, for kin networks usually exist in a state of latent or overt hostility toward other groups, resulting most often from disputes over land.

Women are looked on in the same way as children. They are loved and protected, but are considered to have no capacity for moral judgment, and so must be under the guardianship of an adult male at all times. Left to their own devices they will become prostitutes, for they are insatiably sexual. It is that quality that makes them dangerous, and in need of restraint, for they upset men's judgment. Sexual transgressions stain the family honor, which is the proudest thing that many families possess.

The good life as envisioned by the villagers is almost the exact opposite of that sought by the Navajos. It is crowded, noisy, and busy. The highest available enjoyment is a trip to Cairo or Alexandria, there to be swallowed up in the swirling mass of humanity. It is the silent and empty desert that is threatening.

Mythology

Islamic scripture. In the broadest sense, the peasants may lay claim to the whole vast body of Islamic scripture as their mythology, for it 'comes with the territory' of being Muslim. But it is not a mythology of which they have any amount of knowledge, for it consists very largely of law, and has little bearing on the circumstances of their daily lives.

Saintly biographies. The mythology that matters is embodied in the biography of the local saint, preserved in oral tradition and often recited, sometimes in verse. There are strikingly recurrent features in these tales, which remind us irresistibly of the traditional life of Jesus. The saint is born under unusual circumstances, often accompanied by portents; he displays incredibly precocious religious erudition ('he could recite the entire Quran from memory by the time he was two'); when still very young he confounds the orthodox elders with his superior knowledge of scripture; he has a period of ascetic withdrawal ('time in the wilderness') during which he receives revelations; when he returns he is able to perform miracles, including curing the sick and raising the dead. Finally he dies and is instantly reunited with God, but at the same time he lives on within his tomb. Much of his biography is taken up with a recitation of the miracles he has performed, both before and after death. Some fundamentalist Christians may wish to believe that these tales are rip-offs from the recorded life of Jesus; in fact, they and the traditional life of Jesus draw on a common, older tradition of hagiography.

The episode of confounding the elders plays an important part in legitimizing the worship of saints, something that is regularly denounced as blasphemous by orthodox religious leaders. They are apt to suggest that saint-worship is the false religion of people who are too lazy and too ignorant to learn and follow the scriptures. Not so, says the myth; our leader was even more pious and more learned than you are, and could have followed your path had he wanted to. He chose another path because God commanded him to, and commanded us to follow him. Therefore, although we ourselves cannot recite scripture, we are justified in following his lead.

There are, according to Sudanese folk tradition, three 'levels' of sainthood, as reflected in the extent of their miraculous powers. All of them can walk on water, fly through the air, and read people's thoughts; those at a higher level can also cause things to come into being simply by saying, 'let it be.' The highest level is represented by those who become *qutb,* which in ordinary speech is the name of the North Star. There is debate as to just what this means in specific terms; some suggest that the *qutb* becomes the axis around which everything else revolves. There seems to be little doubt, however, that the *qutb,* when he wants to be, is virtually one with God.

The *Mahdi.* Orthodox Muslim belief shares with Christianity the belief that Jesus will return to earth at the end of time, and will establish a rule of righteousness. He will return however as a convert to Islam, and will kill all the swine, break the crosses, destroy the churches, and kill all the Christians who do not convert (Trimingham 1949: 149). In folk belief however the redeemer will not be Jesus but a descendant of the Prophet, called the Mahdi. His coming is widely expected in the Sudan, and to a much lesser extent in Egypt.

Although the Mahdi tradition as such has no sanction in scripture, there have been many self-proclaimed Mahdis, especially in North Africa. No one can claim to be a second coming of Jesus, but anyone can claim to be a descendant of the Prophet. The aim of the would-be Mahdis has always been to gather an armed following and to banish evil with the force of the sword, as tradition stipulates. In the Sudan the Mahdi Muhammad Ahmed achieved very great success in the late nineteenth century, defeating a British army and freeing the country from Egyptian control, as all students of history know. Yet the peasantry did not rally in large numbers to his support, which came chiefly from among nomad groups. Among the villagers the Mahdi remains an expectation, but a very distant one. Nobody is holding his breath.

Apart from mythology, there is a great deal of specific knowledge about all kinds of lesser supernatural forces, and about magic and witchcraft. Much of this is very practical knowledge having to do with the causes

Folk wisdom

and the cures for disease. The evil eye belief, already mentioned, falls into this category.

Ritual   **Festivals.** The one great folk ritual shared in by all villagers of both sexes is the birthday festival (*mulid*) of the local saint. It is a great outdoor celebration, with all of the usual components of feasting, singing, and dancing. Many of the songs and dances are specific to the saint in question, and it is noteworthy that they are performed much of the time by women. The *mulid,* along with weddings, is their one great opportunity for ritual participation. The *mulid* is the time when everyone should visit the saint's tomb, and it is an especially propitious time to make requests of him. Weddings and funerals are the other great folk festivals for the villagers, but they have very little specifically religious content, although a Quran reader is sometimes hired to recite to the assembled crowd at major funerals.

Brotherhoods and *hadra*. We now come to the esoteric dimension of village religion, which is one of its most striking features. God gave to many of his *awliya* not merely *baraka,* but a very specific set of esoteric rituals through which it can be obtained. These rituals are taught by the *wali* to followers, who after mastering them are admitted into an enrolled society called a *tariqa* (pl. *turuq*). In English they are usually called brotherhoods, although most have female as well as male members. It is important to notice that not everyone who is a worshipper of the saint is also a member of the brotherhood he founded. There are always some villagers who don't want to take the trouble, for the *tariqa* rituals are time-consuming, and in some of the groups women are excluded. There are also many venerated saints who never founded a *tariqa*.

Turuq are revealed religions, but not for everyone; they are esoteric by intention.[18] The *wali* is not a messiah, bearing an urgent message of reform and salvation for the whole of mankind. His message is only for the chosen few, and it is not conceived to be the only way to *baraka* and salvation. It is just God's latest brainstorm, if I can put it that way.

Like all the other aspects of folk Islam, the brotherhoods are not by any means confined to the villages, and not by any means confined to the poor and illiterate. There are some famous brotherhoods that count members throughout the Islamic world, and that maintain hostels for their followers at Mecca. The great majority of brotherhoods however are highly

---

[18]In this respect they differ from minority Islamic sects like the Druze and the Alawi, which were meant to bring salvation to everyone.

localized, because they center around the persona of a local saint. It is very largely to these that villagers belong. Estimates vary widely as to what percentage of them belong; my own hunch is that it's at least sixty percent in the case of males.

The *tariqa* is virtually a complete religion within a religion. In the persona of the founding *wali,* his biography, and his tomb, it has its deity, its mythology, and its holy shrine. This much is shared with all the villagers, whether or not they are enrolled in the brotherhood. But the *tariqa* has in addition a strongly esoteric aspect: a set of complex rituals, involving prayers, songs, and dances that are known only to the members. These were God's special gift to the founding *wali.*

The priesthood of the *tariqa* consists in the first instance of a descendant or descendants of the founding *wali.* He has inherited much of the founder's *baraka,* and is a continuing source of it to others. He regularly receives gifts from the brotherhood members, which he uses to maintain a lifestyle appropriate to one of God's chosen, but also to pay for major celebrations like the *mulid,* and for occasional disbursements to the needy. He is referred to as the living *sheikh,* although his ancestor in the local tomb may also be called the *sheikh.* Below him are those who have become fully adept in the rituals and lore of the *tariqa,* who are usually referred to as adepts (*munshid*). It is to these individuals that one applies for membership, and, if accepted, is given a formal status of a learner. In time and with sufficient mastery, the learner graduates to the status of an adept himself.

Each *tariqa* has many distinctive features, conspicuously including costumes and banners. On festival occasions parading in costume and under the banner, to the accompaniment of singing and drumming, is one of the signal joys of *tariqa* membership. The various local brotherhoods generally exist in a state of friendly rivalry, for only a few of them deny the legitimacy of the others. One can even, in theory, belong to more than one, but very few people do so because of the commitments of time involved.

Hadra. The central ritual of each brotherhood is a weekly gathering called a *hadra.* It is held in a place called a *zawiya,* which may or may not be a mosque; often it is just a cleared area in the open. The hour and day chosen is a matter of convenience, and varies from village to village. The *hadra* itself has many components, and usually lasts at least three or four hours. It high point however is an ecstatic group performance (*dhikr*) in which the participants are 'intoxicated' by dizziness, hyperventilation, or some other form of self-induced trance. In that state they are possessed by God, and receive *baraka* directly from him. Participants in such rituals are often called dervishes (*darawish*), although the word also has wider applications.

The extent of individual participation in the *hadra,* as in orthodox Islamic practice, varies from person to person. Some attend religiously every week, some much less frequently. Some never get beyond the learner stage, while others become *murshid,* who are instructors in the ritual, and *munshid,* who help direct the performances. A good many people attend the *hadra* who don't actually join the brotherhood, and this is especially common among women, who may not be permitted full membership.

Obviously, the brotherhoods offer many attractions that are lacking in orthodox Islam: membership in enrolled congregations, colorful pageantry, complex ritual, and ecstatic experience.

Zar rituals. There are a great many rituals, some of them quite elaborate, both for appeasing the *zar* spirits and for exorcising them. They are appeased by ecstatic dance, songs, gifts, and sacrifices. In the ritual of exorcism, they are first called on to identify themselves by name (since a woman can be possessed by any of a number of individual *zar*), and then are asked in effect what it will take to get them to come out. The ritual that follows depends on what the spirit has asked for. As Trimingham (1949: 174–5) has remarked, the whole system involves a kind of spiritual extortion.

Rites of passage. Apart from the *mulid* of the saint and the two orthodox *bairam* festivals, the great festival occasions in the village are weddings, circumcisions, and funerals. Weddings are especially festive, and are a high point in the religious life not only of the bride but of women in general; they have a chance to sing and dance as they do on few other occasions. Wedding celebrations often last for several days. Funeral celebrations, which may also last for several days, are for obvious reasons more solemn and less festive, and they involve men to a larger extent than women. In place of singing and dancing there is a great deal of collective prayer for the soul of the departed, an sometimes a public Quran reading by a hired expert. Circumcision ceremonies involve communal feasting of all the boy's relatives, and an elaborate ritual surrounding the actual act of circumcision.

The *feki*. Orthodox religion is represented in the village, to the extent that it is, in the person of the *feki*. He is the possessor of a Quran—often a rather battered one—and has learned to recite and to write some or all of the verses. His main job is to teach the village boys to do the same, which he does at an informal school (*khalwa*), usually held outdoors under a tree. For this service he is paid mainly with food, and he will take many of his meals with one or another of the village families. He will also, for a fee, write protective verses on scraps of paper, which are then folded and sewn up in leather amulets (*higab*).

The *feki* may also be called on to recite the appropriate verses at a funeral, and to draw up marriage contracts. It will sometimes be found however that the extent of his literacy is not up to this latter task, and a more learned *feki* must be hired from another village. The *feki* often does not enjoy high prestige in the village, in part because he is usually landless and poor, in part because the extent of his religious knowledge is obviously limited.

Officers of the brotherhoods. The living *sheikh el-tariqa* of any brotherhood is a religious practitioner simply by virtue of his descent from the founder, for it is he who carries on the founder's *baraka,* for which he is approached by others. He is the main repository of myth, in the form of his ancestor's biography, and he can also instruct in the esoteric details of the *tariqa.* That job however is more often left to the *murshid* (literally, 'guides') who are formally appointed teachers. Within the *dhikr* performance, and also in parades, there are *munshidin* who lead the congregation in the chanting of litanies. Since the brotherhoods are usually quite formally structured, they may have other officers as well, bearing a variety of titles.

***Zar* practitioners.** The *zar* cult, described earlier, has its own practitioners, who are nearly always women and are called *sheikha*. They are skilled in the complex rituals necessary to exorcise the *zar* spirits.

The *gubba*. The habitual abode of a saint, when he is not traveling abroad, is in his tomb. As a shrine, it should properly be called a *maqam*, but it is much more commonly called a *gubba*. The word simply means 'dome,' and refers to the fact that the tombs of saints are nearly always covered by some kind of domed structure. *Gubbas* vary widely in size and elaborateness, depending largely on the number and the wealth of the saint's followers. They are usually whitewashed annually, but may nevertheless appear dilapidated because pious visitors have chipped away pieces of them, for the sake of the *baraka* they confer. Within the *gubba,* the tomb proper (*tabut*) is a rectangular structure of brick or stone, about the size of a sarcophagus, which will often be found covered with offering cloths. In large *gubbas* it may be within a sacred enclosure, called a *maqsura.*

The rural *gubba* is usually on the outskirts of a village, though occasionally somewhere within it. This is particularly true in the case of saints who are founders of a *tariqa,* and who are needed close at hand. There are a great many other saint's tombs on hill and mountaintops, but they are usually not centers of regular or organized worship. They may nevertheless be foci of pilgrimage, in the case of saints who are identified in local tradition as having special power. There are also crumbling tombs at which the name of the resident saint has been forgotten, but which retain a certain amount of *baraka* nevertheless.

The shrine of an active saint is a place of continual comings and goings. On an average day the visitors will number more women than men. Excluded as they are from the mosque, and almost wholly ignorant of scripture, the saint is very nearly all the religion they have. He is a constant source of comfort in a world where they are endlessly reminded of their inferior status, and where fertility and the health of children are continual worries. Also, the saint's shrine is one of the very few public places where they can legitimately spend time away from home.

The *gubba* is infinitely the most sacred place in folk belief; as much so, in the eyes of many, as the *Kaaba* at Mecca itself. Indeed it is sometimes said that a pilgrimage to the shrine of an especially powerful saint is as good as a pilgrimage to Mecca; it satisfies the Quranic requirement of the *hajj.*

Gubbas, since there are thousands of them, provided the villagers with all the holy places they need. Neither the Friday mosque nor the *zawiya* is holy, except when services are actually or progress. At other times people may sleep, eat, transact business, or do just about anything else except gamble.

Holy things

Since the religion of the villagers is above all a practical religion, holy things are those things that provide success or protection. They are of three sorts:

Higab are prayers, often though not always involving Quranic scripture, that are written on small pieces of paper, then folded and sewn up within leather amulets. These fall within the realm of orthodox religion to the extent that they are always addressed to Allah, not to a saint. They are generally requests for success or luck in some kind of enterprise, rather than for protection. They may be written to order by a *feki,* in which case they will invoke blessing specifically in the name of the wearer, but they can also be purchased from merchant dealers, in which case they will invoke blessing on behalf of the unnamed bearer. We have unearthed and opened a number of these in archaeological excavations, and found that some of them are beautifully written in Classical Arabic, and some are mere meaningless marks, evidently executed by an illiterate *feki. Higab* are most commonly worn by men, and some men may carry several, to bring success or protection in different kinds of enterprises.

Relics. Other kinds of amulets, which have no specific name, are those that partake of the *baraka* of the saint. Anything he has touched may serve, but the most common amulets are those made from pieces of the saint's tomb, or from dust within it, usually sewn up in a piece of cloth. These amulets serve much more specifically for protection than do the *higab.* They may be worn by persons, but can also be seen attached to animal harnesses, and even to plows and waterwheels that are left unattended.

Tamima are beads, nearly always blue in color, that are worn specifically for protection against the evil eye. They may be individual beads, worn on a string around the neck or wrist, or they may be in strings, which are often woven into the hair. Every young child should have *tamima.*

Iconography and symbolism. The poverty of iconography and symbolism, both in orthodox and in village Islam, provides perhaps the single most striking contrast with Navajo religion. The injunction against graven images (the second Mosaic commandment), ignored by nearly all Christians, is taken very seriously by both Muslims and Jews. The traditional culture of the Near East has always been a highly verbalizing culture, and perhaps this is why the supernaturals expect to be addressed almost entirely with words, rather than through art, architecture, and icons. The great architectural monuments of Islam are meant to celebrate not the glory of God, but the majesty of the ruler who commissioned them.

World-view

The world-view of the peasants is decidedly degenerationist (as it is also for many orthodox Muslims). In the days before Muhammad everyone was sunk in ignorance and idolatry, but for six hundred years afterward (the so-called 'Islamic Era'), people were just and righteous. Since the fall of the Abbasid Caliphate (A.D. 1258) however it has been all downhill, and today the world is rife with evil. The end of time and the coming of the Mahdi is therefore an appealing prospect, though for most people a remote one.

Many peasants also exhibit the low self-esteem that comes with poverty, ignorance, and the unconcealed contempt of the more fortunate classes. 'We're sorry folks' is an expression I've heard more than once, both from Egyptian peasants and from people in Appalachia. Those feelings however are not products of religion; on the contrary it is religion that provides the main escape from them. Islamic identity is the one thing that makes the peasants the equal of the rich and powerful, in the eyes of God, and it is something of which they remind themselves and one another, even if they don't dare breathe it to the rich and powerful.

Religion in everyday life

In the cities, educated Arabs have the same options as do educated Christians; that is, they can make their own choices between religion and science, in their attempt to understand and to deal with the world around them. That option does not exist for the villagers, any more than it does for traditional Navajos. At the level of cognition they are all 'true believers,' to the extent that they believe unquestioningly in Allah and in the saints, for they have no other way of understanding the world around them. People may however question the power or even the existence of particular saints.

At the level of religious activity there is, as always, a great deal more variability from individual to individual. A clear division exists between those who follow the strictures of orthodox Islam and those who don't. The minority who follow the way of the Prophet necessarily spend an hour or more each day in the recitation of the five daily prayers (that is, fifteen minutes or more each time), and they may invest additional time in Friday mosque attendance, and even in Quran reading, though very few peasants have the necessary knowledge for the latter. Observance of the Ramadan fast involves its own set of special behaviors, if nothing else because meals must be taken at special times, after dusk and before dawn. But no matter how diligent they are in the observance of the 'Five Pillars,' peasants will nearly always follow also some of the immemorial practices of folk religion, including visits to saints' tombs, the wearing of protective amulets, and the recitation of the innumerable formulas for protection from the evil eye and from *jinn*.

For the great majority of peasants who do not rigorously follow the Five Pillars, there is very much less overt religious activity. On an ordinary day it consists mainly of the recitation of verbal formulas, some to avert misfortune and some to achieve success in this or that enterprise. There is no set time for these; like Navajo songs or observances they are appropriate to particular activities rather than to particular times. There are prayers to be said, or formulas to be recited, at the beginning of the day's irrigation, when setting out on a trip, when approaching a powerful official or landlord, before undertaking a major purchase, and a host of other occasions. The prayers may be addressed either to Allah or to a saint; in some cases it is not entirely clear who is the intended hearer. The most common of prayers, those that ask for a specific boon, are addressed to the saint. The frequency of recitation varies of course from person to person, but also from day to day, as circumstances do or do not require. In times of misfortune, such as illness or heavy debt, there is likely to be a regular litany of prayers, offered especially by women.

Visits to the nearby saint's tomb are for most people the most common of non-verbal religious activities. People, especially women, are likely to go very often to ask the saint for specific favors, but everyone will go from time to time just to increase his or her stock of *baraka*. Visits to the *sheikh* himself are also common, though unlike the saint in the tomb he is not always readily accessible.

For active participants in the *turuq,* attendance at the weekly *hadra* is of course another major activity, consuming four hours or more on each occasion. Only a minority of peasants however will be that diligent. Although as many as sixty percent of men may belong to one or other of the brotherhoods, most do not attend the *hadra* every week. Most however will try to take part in the parades, with their costumes and banners, on festive occasions.

There is an enormous body of everyday practices connected with averting the evil eye and other evil influences. They include the wearing of many kinds of amulets, attaching certain objects over the house door, painting an eye design on houses or boats, dressing children in ragged clothing (so as not to attract envy), and the inevitable plethora of verbal formulas. Illness, supposedly caused by the evil eye, brings into play a host of additional, exorcistic rituals, some involving the mumbling of Quranic passages in a special way and others wholly non-Islamic. As with Navajos, a considerable amount of religious activity consists in avoidances: of the many forbidden foods, of certain substances and places, and especially of impious or dangerous utterances.

Perhaps the single most important point to make about nearly all Islamic religious practice, orthodox as well as folk, is that it is compartmentalized. That is, there are clearly specified occasions for religious utterance or activity that are different from the times for secular activity, for both Allah and the saints demand the full attention of the votary. It is an offense to them to say a prayer while at the same time engaged in some other activity. In this respect the practice of Muslims is clearly comparable to that of Christians and Jews, while differing altogether from that of Navajos, for whom religion and secular activities are continually intertwined.

*Religious
instruction*

Village children, like Navajo children, learn within the family, and at an early age, the many avoidances that are necessary for their basic protection. More positively they learn, at an early age, to recite the Profession of Faith, for it is this that entitles them to God's protection. Eventually they are likely to learn also the formulas for the five daily prayers, for everyone knows these, even if they don't perform them.

Any further instruction in orthodox Islamic belief and practice will be confined to boys, and will be received at the hands of the village *feki,* at the informal school (*khalwa*) that he conducts under a tree. The curriculum consists almost entirely of learning to recite, and to write, passages of the Quran. These performances are learned entirely by rote, for the boys are not taught the meaning of the words, which the *feki* himself may not know. The *khalwa* are not found in every village, but where they are present, most boys will attend for one or two years. The amount of retention from these experiences is highly variable, depending on the effectiveness of the teacher and the inclination of the learner. Many boys remember almost nothing a few years later.

For those who adhere to orthodox practice, additional instruction comes in the form of the sermons, which are part of the Friday service at most mosques. Through these a man may in time acquire a very substantial knowledge not only of scripture but of the many non-scriptural traditions that are part of the Islamic Great Tradition. However, the preachers (*khattib*) at village mosques, where they exist, are usually not very well educated. At one village mosque in Jordan, it was reported that the preacher had delivered the same sermon every Friday for thirty years.

Those who follow the *turuq* rather than the orthodox road receive very lengthy and specific instruction from the specially designated individuals who are chosen as *murshid* (guides). The mass of peasants, however, acquire such religious knowledge and practices as they need informally and by word of mouth, in the course of everyday living—just as do Navajos.

To convey something of the flavor of Islamic folk religion, I will conclude by recounting briefly an experience of mine, in Egypt. It took place not in a village but in the great funerary mosque of Sayyed Ahmad el-Bedawi, in the city of Tanta. At the time of my visit a *dhikr* was in progress within the mosque interior, occupying nearly all of its extensive floor space. At the very center of it, a youngish woman was holding a rose aloft, and slowly turning around and around while looking up at it. I guessed that she was seeking for a self-induced hypnosis; she was not turning fast enough to bring on a whirling trance. She was not wearing the plain outer garment (*tob*) demanded by Islamic modesty, but a quite attractive flowered house-dress of Western style. As far as I can remember, it did not extend below the knee. I assumed that she was a descendant of the saint, because no other women were allowed within the performance area. However, she may simply have been *maqzuba* (smitten by the saint), for women in that condition are exempted from the rules that normally exclude them from the *dhikr.*

A personal experience

Around this central figure, several men were standing in an orderly circle, rhythmically bowing and straightening up, in unison. Elsewhere the whole remainder of the floor was occupied by other men doing the same thing. They were probably standing in some kind of prescribed ranks, as is required in most *dhikr,* but this was not evident from where I stood. Their movements were not in unison. While bowing they were at the same time uttering a word or words that I'm sure involved the name of Allah, although I could not catch them. They must have been hyperventilating, because from time to time a man would fall down, and then would be gently lifted and led away by the *munshidin.* Nearly all the men were in Western-style street clothes rather than in the traditional Islamic gown (*galabiya*) and turban; they had probably interrupted their ordinary day's labor long enough to take part in the *dhikr.* (Villagers will much more often dress in traditional fashion when attending a *hadra,* because the *galabiya* and turban are the only 'good clothes' they possess.)

All around the perimeter of the performance area, young men were stationed as guards to prevent the entrance of women, and probably also of children, Christians, and other undesirables. As I watched, several women tried to break through or to sneak past the guards, in order to obtain some of the *baraka* that could be had within. However they were seized and quite rudely thrust back by the guards. I'm sure they knew that they couldn't get away with it for any length of time; they must have felt that even a moment's entry would bring its share of blessing.

The actual tomb of the venerated saint Ahmad el-Bedawi is in a room adjoining the mosque proper, and entered from it. Women as well as men were allowed to pass along the outer edge of the performance area in order to have access to it, and they were continually coming and going. Inside the chamber, the tomb (*tabut*) itself is enclosed within a very ornate *maqsura* of cast brass, having the appearance of a gilded cage. Visitors were continually circumambulating this, and others crowding to touch it with their hands or lips. Women who had brought young children, as many had, made especially sure that the children touched the holy structure. Prayers, written on small scraps of paper, were tucked into the crevices of the *maqsura* structure. Outside the mosque there were seated *fekis,* ready to write these blessings for a fee.

I have described this occasion because it so beautifully illustrates the two complementary and intertwined aspects of folk religion, which Reeves (1990) has called the *tariqa* complex and the *wali* complex. The one, mainly a religion of and for men, involves *tariqa* membership and the performance of the *hadra* rituals; the other, for both sexes but of more central importance to women, involves simply the worship of the saint.

An overview   In contrast to Navajo religion, Islam, in both its orthodox and its folk variants, is a religion for a man-centered world; a world from which nature has long since been 'banished to the sidelines.' In the beginning God gave man dominion over all the beasts in the field, and since that time a sense of mastery over nature remains strong in all the Abrahamic religions. The world is full of dangers, but they are nearly all of human origin. Thus, virtually all of the supernaturals, good and evil, are conceived in human form. For that reason, they are addressed very largely with verbal formulas, rather than through artistic or magical forms of invocation.

The Allah of the peasants is not quite the same deity who spoke to Muhammad. The Prophet lived his life in a world of contending sheikhdoms, beyond the orbit of the great totalitarian empires of antiquity. His god was the quintessential tribal sheikh, stern and demanding of total loyalty but at the same time devoted to the welfare of his tribe. The peasants on the other hand have lived under totalitarian regimes for millennia; regimes that all too often have taken everything and given nothing in return. Their world has been ruled not by law or by right or by virtue, but by pure, naked authority. Allah is the divine embodiment of that principle; the celestial equivalent not of the sheikh but of the Pharaoh.

For villagers, it may be said that scriptural Islam is a religion for the next world, and folk religion is a religion for this one. Both are important, but it is this world that almost always needs urgent attention. It may also be said in a general way, and not without exceptions, that scriptural Islam is a religion for the upper classes, and folk religion for the lower classes. The rich, relatively secure in their worldly circumstances, can afford to devote their time and thoughts to the life to come. The peasants, continually faced with the threat of floods, drought, plagues, landlords, thugs, and taxes, can hardly afford to look beyond next month.

But folk Islam is a religion for the poor in another and more fundamental respect, it which it holds a kind of mirror up to Islamic society. That society has traditionally been, and is still to a very large extent, a society ruled through patronage. Governments, under the Caliphs and under the Sultans, were simply vast patronage networks, in which power flowed from patrons to their personally recruited clients, and from them in turn to their own clients lower in the system. Unquestioned personal loyalty to the patron was the one principle on which the whole system depended. The client's abilities to perform competently, in specific contexts, were much less important than his loyalty.

Within the rigidly stratified society of the traditional Middle East, opportunities to advance through personal achievement or personal merit were few and far between. The need of the poor man was and largely is not for advancement, which is beyond reach, but for favors and protection, and they come from patrons who are placed higher in the system. The strategy for survival is to attach yourself to a patron, make him such small gifts as you can, and perform such services as you can, for which at the time you may receive no more than the most perfunctory acknowledgment. The patron's turn comes when your wife needs an operation or your son needs to get into technical school or your cousin needs his bail paid. If the patron has accepted your gifts and services, he is honor-bound to do his part. The system works because it confers benefits on both client and patron. The client, with his little gifts and services, has bought insurance against big risks. The patron, in accepting the clients, has bought power. The more clients, the more power.

It is hardly necessary to point out, then, that the religion conceived and practiced by the village folk is a vast divine patronage system. Patronage is dispensed from God to his *awliya,* from them to their descendants, and from the descendants to their followers. This is overtly recognized in Egypt, where the congregation of saints is sometimes referred to as 'the hidden government' (Reeves 1990).

Two final points are worth making. First, the folk religion of the villagers is a source not only of protection but of enjoyment, which the practices of orthodoxy usually are not. The pageantry of the *tariqa,* the pleasure of belonging to a brotherhood, not unlike a Masonic lodge, and the comforting presence of a nearby and benevolent saint, are all features not found in scriptural religion, and frequently condemned by its spokesmen. Second, the village religion is quintessentially a practical religion, an aspect that I will discuss further in a later chapter.

In and of itself, each *tariqa* is very much 'a unified system of beliefs and practices,' thus satisfying Durkheim's (1915: 47) definition of religion. But when the *turuq* are taken together with the *wali* complex, with belief in the evil eye and *zar,* and with elements of orthodox Islam, it will be evident that the religion of Arab villagers is anything but a unified system of beliefs and practices. Adherents of Durkheim might perhaps argue that the villagers have not one religion but several, but I will suggest in later pages that if this is true of them, it is true also of many other peoples, including Christians.

*Change and
the future*

The world I have just described is gradually changing, thanks to various rural improvement programs. In Egypt, electricity and clean water bring increased comforts and a reduction of the very high disease rate in the villages, especially among small children. They do not however alleviate the grinding poverty that results from acute land shortage. A great many families are struggling to support as many as eight or ten persons from the produce of a single acre. Village schools also do nothing to improve the conditions of peasantry as such. What they do instead is offer an escape from peasantry, and it is an escape that thousands have taken.

Conditions are also improving for Sudanese peasants, but in a sense it is at the expense of others. The hideous, endless civil war in the southern Sudan has driven tens of thousands of destitute refugees northward. Penniless and without education, they are forced to live in any way that they can, and many have become peons in the fields of the northern peasants, working for nothing but food.

What is not happening, among Egyptian and Sudanese peasants, is secularization. The saints and their cults flourish as strongly as ever, simply because clientage remains the basic feature of society. Readers should be clear however that the peasants have little or no part in the fanatical Muslim movements that have sprung up in the towns and cities. Those movements are always rooted in the cities, and their 'armies' are gangs of rootless and jobless urban youth. So have most volunteer armies been, at most times in history. Peasants are almost never fanatics, unless and until they are dispossessed of their land. As long as they have an acre to call their own, it remains the whole focus of their existence, and their circumstances force them to be quintessentially pragmatic.

COMMONALITIES AND CONTRASTS

Navajo religion is in all its essentials a tribal religion, and Arab village religion is a typical peasant religion. The contrasts between them are enormous, for they developed out of and are adaptive to vastly different worlds. I propose in this chapter to see how much enlightenment can be drawn from a comparison between the two, with occasional side glances at Christianity and at scriptural Islam. I have to reiterate that my characterizations apply to the two religions as I knew them half a century ago, and they may not hold completely true today. I continue to use the present tense, however, to stress the fact that these were, at the time I knew them, living and vital religions and not relics.

Environments   One thing common to the Navajo and the Arab village religions is that both are religions of the weak. Weakness, however, stems from very different sources. Navajos have to deal with a natural environment over which they have little control; villagers are caught up in a human environment over which they have little control. The differences between their two religions are very much a reflection of those circumstances.

The physical environment   Navajos and Arab villagers are both agrarian peoples, and the land is equally important to both. But the Navajo world is an untamed natural world, where only a few thousand acres out of twenty million are under cultivation, and where until a generation ago there was not a fence from end to end of the reservation. Signs of human intervention are insignificant; the world beyond the hogan door is a world of wide open space and sky. The environment has great physical beauty, which is very much appreciated, but it also contains dangers, especially from the unpredictable weather. Animals, the main source of livelihood, are dependent on grass, and grass is dependent on summer rains and winter snows, neither of which is dependable.

72

By contrast, the first things that meet the peasant's eye, as he or she steps out the door, are other houses, crowded all around. Beyond the limits of the village lies a world of man-made fields and ditches, and beyond that, the ever-flowing Nile. It is a world in which nature was tamed long ago, under a succession of state-imposed irrigation regimes. Even without human intervention nature is fairly dependable, for the Nile rises and falls at nearly the same time every year, and as long as it is there, rainfall is unnecessary. Occasional floods are a problem, but disastrous storms are too rare to present much of a danger.

*The social
environment*

The social environment of Arab villagers is much more complex, and much more important, than in the Navajo case, because the peasants live in a man-made and man-dominated world. At the most basic level, however, the Navajo and Arab social worlds are alike in that both are founded on kinship. Both peoples have wide-reaching kinship networks in which the extended family is the basic residential and corporate unit, but is embedded in turn in more ramified lineages and clans. Those groupings are, for both peoples, the basic safety net in time of need. There are plenty of non-kin around as well, but they are undependable and a potential source of danger.

For Navajos however the danger from non-kin is much less than it is for Arabs, because they are not living anywhere within sight, and they can be avoided to a very large extent. For Arab villagers the non-kin are right outside the door, so to speak, and they can never be avoided. And because the crowded conditions and limited land give rise inevitably to quarrels, the Arab lineages are generally more important as a political support network than they are for economic support. Kinship has a weak political dimension among the Navajos, but a very strong one among the villagers. 'Me against my brother; me and my brother against my cousin; me, my brother and my cousin against the world' is a common saying among them.

Like many tribal societies, that of the Navajos is egalitarian within limits. Everyone, even the singers, makes his or her basic living raising livestock and farming, and there are no inherited differences of rank. Every man and woman belongs by birth to one of sixty-three clans, but no clan is consistently recognized as superior to any other. There are recognized differences in personal wealth, and in the prestige that comes with the possession of wealth (including ceremonial knowledge), but all such prestige is acquired rather than inherited.

Wide-ranging kinship ties, although unimportant politically, provided the only formal structure within traditional Navajo society. And beyond the web of kinship, there were only other Navajos; non-Navajo peoples were outside the system altogether. It was not a highly competitive world, because until recently there was felt to be enough grazing available for everyone.

By contrast, peasant village society has been embedded within a rigid, formally stratified and economically differentiated society since the rise of the first empire five thousand years ago. To the peasants has fallen the task of raising enough food not only to feed themselves, but to feed all the city-dwelling artisans, merchants, and elites. To make that possible, they have been consigned to a very low level in the social order, which allows the city-dwellers to extract the food they need through coercive measures. Within that underprivileged context, kinship ties alone were never enough to ensure safety. Ties of clientage had to be developed with persons higher up the social scale.

The political environment

Among the Navajos there was no political organization as such; authority was conferred when needed, and to the extent needed, on situational leaders who had only persuasive, not coercive powers. There was almost no law except the law of tort; that is, all crimes except witchcraft were private rather than public wrongs, for which the victims had to exact restitution as best they could. But peasants have for millennia been subject to highly authoritarian political regimes over which they have no control whatever. Even the village headman (*omda*) has usually been appointed by the state. The villagers are subject to taxation, corvée, military conscription, and may be punished by the state for all kinds of infractions. It is small wonder that politics is a subject of passionate interest to the villagers; they cannot afford to be ignorant of who has what power. Their attitude toward the political regime is similar in that respect to the Navajos' attitude toward their gods.

The historical environment

Like most tribal peoples, the Navajos live at the center of the world, as they conceive it. They have arrived there after a long and adventurous search which the *Dighinii* directed them to make. Around them are other peoples who may be important as trading or raiding objectives, or both, but who until recently were not essential to Navajo survival and had almost no influence on the Navajo world-view. One could always take them or leave them.

The peasants have a very strong sense of historical identity, as the successors to pharaonic peasantry but more importantly as members of the Islamic community. They have considerable knowledge of Islamic history, as Navajos have of their Emergence Myth, and it is a history that provides them with their main source of pride. But the Islamic world is a very large one, extending far beyond the limits of their ken, and it is one in which they are more nearly at the edge than at the center. It is not a world in which peasants have ever played a very large historical role. In terms of self-identification it might be suggested that Navajos look outward but peasants look upward. Navajos live at the center of their world; Arab peasants live at the bottom of the social ladder.

The deities

At first glance it might appear that both Navajos and Arab peasants have very large pantheons. Such a statement is misleading however because most of the peasants' pantheon is made up of saints, who are more or less clones of one another. It is not quite true that 'when you know one you know them all,' for there are a few super-saints like Sayyed Ahmad el-Bedawy, but all of the saints except the local one can be safely ignored. The number of supernaturals with whom the villagers absolutely must deal is very small, while for Navajos it is very large. Only a few of the Navajo supernaturals can be safely ignored.

The Navajo pantheon is obviously much more diversified than that of the villagers, reflecting their much greater involvement with undependable nature. In addition to anthropomorphic deities there are animal spirits, gods of weather and natural phenomena, and monsters. The deities of the villagers are all anthropomorphic, a reflection of the man-dominated world in which they live.

The following are specific and instructive points of comparison:

Father figure. Both the Navajo and Arab pantheons include a father-figure of sorts: the Sun in the Navajo case and Allah in the Arab case. Both are very remote and supremely powerful male beings, but because of their remoteness they have little part in daily, practical religion. It is an interesting paradox that the Sun of the Navajos, though not human in form, is a progenitor, while Allah emphatically is not. 'God is not begotten and does not beget,' as the Quran has it.

Mother figure. The parallel between Navajos and Arabs is much closer in the case of the mother-figures: Changing Woman for the Navajos and the Virgin Mary for Arabs. Both are kindly and nurturing beings, incapable of harm. Changing Woman however has an explicitly sexual nature, while the myth of the immaculate conception (accepted in Quranic as well as Biblical tradition) removes the 'taint' of sexuality from the Virgin.

Saviors. Neither Navajos nor Arabs have any concept of a savior comparable in any way to the Christ. Muhammad is self-described as a messenger, not a savior, and always denied any personal divinity. He enjoined his followers to pray *for* him rather than *to* him, as in fact they still do. In a broader sense, however, the Hero Twins of the Navajos and the *awlia* of the Arabs occupy savior roles, because they performed heroic and miraculous deeds for the benefit of the people. The Hero Twins slew most of the Monsters, and the *awlia* brought special ways of achieving salvation, without having to know scripture.

Relationships. One of the most telling contrasts between the Navajo and Arab pantheons can be seen in the different relationships that are believed to obtain among the gods. The major Navajo deities are related by kinship, while for villagers they are connected through clientage. It is also observable that, although the Navajo deities vary considerably in the extent of their power, there is no well-defined hierarchy among them. For villagers, the hierarchy from Allah to the client saints, and from them to their own client followers, is very clearcut. Among the saints themselves there are different recognized levels of miraculous power. For both peoples, the pantheon models the existing social order.

Personality of the deities. For Navajos, most of the supernaturals have capacities for both good and evil. Some are usually benevolently disposed to man, and others not, but this is not in most cases an absolute quality of their personalities. They are judged simply by how helpful they are when summoned. Village Islam however exhibits the dualism that is characteristic of all the Abrahamic religions. All of the deities are either all good or all bad. *Zar* spirits are an exception; like Navajo deities they can be either helpful or harmful. However, they are part of a religious system that lies outside the boundaries of Islam.

The Abrahamic supreme deity, like any human autocrat, is highly susceptible to flattery; in fact he demands it, in the form of constant praise. Village saints are much less demanding in this respect, but they too receive their share of spoken adulation. Navajo deities lack altogether this self-absorbed quality; they must be compelled rather than cajoled, through ritual activity.

Immanence. The local saint, the most important deity of the villagers, dwells close by and is always 'on call.' For Navajos there is no one comparable; all of the *Dighinii* live far away, on the mountaintops or in another realm. However, some of them (the *Yei*) can be summoned to come to the human realm in the course of ceremonies.

Tutelaries. In complex, polytheistic religions, some form of tutelary relationship between human individuals and individual gods is expectable. There are just too many supernaturals to try and worship them all; the important thing is to find one who is helpful to you. The tutelary feature is very conspicuous in Arab village religion, where the local saint is very much the tutelary of 'his' village and 'his' people. It is rather surprising to find that nothing comparable has been reported among the Navajos, considering the size and diversity of their pantheon, and the fact that guardian spirits have an honored place in many American Indian religions.

Evil beings. There has to be someone, besides oneself, on whom bad luck can be blamed, and for both Navajos and Arabs this role is filled by various evil beings. For Navajos there are the Monsters, and for villagers the *jinn*. Both peoples also believe in and fear witches, and practice many rituals of avoidance and of exorcism. The villagers also have a supreme evil being, *Shaytan,* another evidence of their hierarchical world-view. There is no one supremely evil being for Navajos.

The central focus of Navajo religion is the attainment of *hozhoni*; for Arabs it is the obtaining of *baraka.* The contrast between these two highly abstract concepts is partly implied in the two verbs I have used: attaining and obtaining. *Hozhoni* is not property; it is a prevailing condition of harmony throughout the community, from which everyone benefits, and it is attained through the collective ritual efforts of a large group of people. It is not something that can be quantified; it either prevails or it doesn't. It does not bring special advantages, but merely restores the world to its proper harmonic balance.

*The central
concept*

Baraka on the other hand is strictly individual property, benefiting only the possessor and such others as he or she may choose to bestow it on. It is mostly obtained through individual rather than communal efforts, and it is possessed much more by some individuals than by others. It is a concept for a competitive world, and is one of the important ways of 'getting ahead of the game' in relation to other people.

Mythology   It would not be exactly true to say that the Navajos have a lot more mythology than have Arab peasants, for in the broadest sense the whole vast corpus of Islamic scripture is the mythology of the peasants. They don't know very much of it, but there are also a great many Navajos who don't know much of their mythology. Peasants and Navajos alike can access mythology through those learned persons who know it, although this is much easier within the egalitarian context of Navajo society than it is for the villagers, whose learned religious scholars (*alim*; sing. *ulema*) hold them in contempt, and who in any case live far away in the cities.

The boundaries of the domain   The mythology of the Navajos is almost their entire system of codified knowledge, and as such it has to explain everything in the universe, as well as giving the people the whole of their law. It is a system of knowledge alike of the natural and of the social worlds. There is really no such thing as a secular domain. Islam also is intended to give people the whole of their law, but it provides relatively little knowledge of the natural world. It has always co-existed with a large domain of purely secular knowledge, and for a time, during the 'Islamic Era,' the great Muslim cities of the Near East and Spain were centers of secular inquiry and learning. Islamic law has also, in the modern world, had to co-exist with a large body of secular law. The mythology of Islam, although extensive, is therefore much more limited in scope than is the mythology of the Navajos.

It is important to recall in this connection that the world was in existence long before the coming of Islam, a fact readily acknowledged by all Muslims. Although the pre-Islamic era is traditionally called the 'age of ignorance,' everyone recognizes that a great deal of useful and valuable knowledge of the world has been handed down from the days before the Prophet. It is therefore not part of the specific gift of Islam, for the sciences and the arts were imparted by Allah to the Greeks and Persians in much earlier times. There is, thus, a large specifically non-Islamic component in the knowledge of all Muslims.

Until a few generations ago there was nothing similar in the case of Navajos; their entire knowledge of the world was encompassed within their religion. There was also a pre-Navajo time in Navajo mythology—the various earlier worlds that were destroyed by disaster, before the creation of the *Diné.*—but whatever knowledge survived from those times was passed on by the *Dighinii* themselves. Since the coming of Bilagáana education, however, this is no longer true. Secular knowledge of Bilagáana origin is taking its place alongside religious knowledge, much as scientific knowledge of Greek origin long ago took its place alongside Islamic knowledge.

It is interesting to notice the different roles of Allah and of the Navajo deities as culture-givers. Allah has been all-wise since the beginning, but he has passed on his wisdom to mankind only piecemeal, in a series of revelations. In contrast, the Navajo deities were by no means all-wise, and in fact were very foolish at times. The various earlier worlds were a learning time for them, at the end of which they passed on such wisdom as they had acquired, before departing to live in other realms. The Navajo religion of today embodies the sum of that wisdom, but it is by no means conceived as a perfect system.

It is not the quantity but the content of mythology that differs profoundly in the Navajo and Arab cases. Throughout the whole body of orthodox Islamic scripture there are really only four explanatory principles: almighty God, his Prophet Muhammad, Shaytan, and the *jinn*. The ninety-nine sacred names are evidence of how much of the burden of explanation is placed on the shoulders of Allah alone; he is really ninety-nine beings rolled into one. He alone is responsible for all weather phenomena, for example. At the same time, a great deal of the peasants' world is understandable without reference to supernatural activity, since they have for millennia lived under authoritarian regimes and man-made laws that have pretty much decreed what's what. For them, law very largely takes the place of mythology in the more usual sense. Allah is a culture-bringer mainly to the extent that he is a law-giver.

The explanatory dimension

The small number of explanatory beings, and their remoteness from the everyday sphere, has clearly been inadequate to meet either the cognitive or the emotional needs of the villagers. They need somebody close at hand, and have accordingly peopled their world with all kinds of saints, witches, *Zar* spirits, and Nile spirits that lie outside the domain of orthodox belief (and are regularly denounced by the *alim*). Those beings are nevertheless the subjects of their own folk mythology.

For Navajos, who have never acknowledged human autocrats or man-made law, almost nothing in the world is understandable without reference to supernaturals. Their mythology therefore has a great deal more to explain than has that of the villagers. Within the diverse Navajo pantheon, the burden of creation and of explanation is widely shared. The Sun was perhaps the original creator, but a great many of his creatures became creators and culture-bringers in their own right. No fewer than twenty-four beings have some responsibility for weather phenomena, and the number who may be responsible for disease is at least equal.

This latter feature is in some respects a point of resemblance between Navajo and Arab folk religion. For both peoples, there are many beings who can be blamed when things go wrong, and many who can be thanked when things go right. The difference lies at the level of explanation, which is much more explicit in the Navajo than in the Arab case. Navajo mythology, aided by diagnosticians, is often able to determine quite specifically what deity has been offended, in what way. Arab peasants are more likely to blame misfortune on *jinn,* without identifying any one in particular. It is especially noteworthy that the peasants attribute a great deal of misfortune to the evil eye, a malevolent influence that has no identifiable source. I think it is fair to say that the Arabs are much less interested in explanation for its own sake than are Navajos, perhaps because they have for so long lived under authoritarian regimes that stifled and at times even punished curiosity.

The regulatory dimension

For Arabs and Navajos, as for the vast majority of other peoples, God or the gods are the source of all law. But although Islam is much less explicit than Navajo religion in defining the natural world, it is much more so in defining the social world. Orthodox Islam, like other Near Eastern religions back to Sumerian times, is quintessentially a system of laws, which spell out in minute detail the obligations of the individual. It is in that sense a statist religion, in which virtue is defined as obedience.

In the Navajo case the rules of behavior are very far from explicit; they must be teased out from a mass of mythology. There were many culture-bringers, but there was no law-giver. The only two 'public laws' that are clearly discernible are the prohibitions on witchcraft and on incest. (They are really pretty much the same thing, since witches are always accused of practicing incest.) The main thrust of law is not to suggest that people should live in obedience to the decrees of a single divine autocrat, but that they should live in harmony with all the powers and with one another. To a large extent, however, they are left to figure out how to do so on their own. It is in this connection that singers—the main authorities on mythology—are very often consulted for advice in uncertain social situations.

The institutions of kinship are very important to both Navajos and Arabs, but they are not equally reinforced by mythology. Kinship obli-

gations are explicitly sanctioned in Islamic law, which specifies how estates are to be divided among heirs, and who is responsible for the care
of widows and orphans. There are many exhortations in the Quran to
honor the obligations of kinship. On the other hand Muhammad specifically disavowed the importance of genealogies, stating that all persons
are equal under Islam. Of all his decrees, this is perhaps the one that has
been most consistently disregarded, for all self-respecting Arabs can recite a lengthy pedigree which leads back, if not to the Prophet himself, at
least to a noble and exalted ancestor. Among peasants it is the one thing
most necessary to establish their entitlement to respect, in a world where
respect is not easy to come by. The pedigrees are in a real sense an important part of folk mythology. In addition to personal or familial pedigrees,
there are also pedigrees of saints, establishing their relationship to the
Prophet, and sometimes to one another.

In the case of Navajo mythology the sanction for kinship is much more
implicit; the gods are related through kin ties because no other principle
of organization is imaginable. There are specific origin myths for many
of the clans, but they do not serve to establish the greater importance of
one or another.

A point of marked difference between the two mythologies is seen in
their respective attitudes toward sexuality. Both regard it as potentially
dangerous, and in need of regulation. But Navajos do not think of it as
inherently sinful or corrupting for that reason. It is one of the interesting
and enjoyable gifts of the gods, and it crops up again and again in mythology. Muslims are heirs to an age-old Near Eastern tradition that holds sex
to be corrupting, and that blames it entirely on women. It plays no significant part in mythology, although one of the 'miracles' attributed to
Sayyed Ahmed al-Bedawi was that of resisting the advances of a ravish-
ingly beautiful she-demon. Allah, although male, is not a sexual being,
as is made clear in the saying that he 'does not beget.' The Virgin Mary
is also as sexless as myth can make her.

All of the Navajos' history, at least up to the coming of the Bilagáana,
was embodied in their mythology. Most of Arab history, which has been
recorded for centuries both by themselves and by outsiders, stands outside the realm of mythology. There were and are many learned and celebrated historians, who are not necessarily possessed of religious learning.
However, there are also mythical or semi-mythical folk traditions about
the life and doings of Muhammad and his early followers, that may be

*The
historical
dimension*

counted as religious mythology although they are not part of orthodox tradition.

Among Arabs, the history that is embodied in mythology is mainly personal rather than collective. It comprises, first of all, the hundreds of personal pedigrees that were mentioned previously. However, the most important and detailed history is that contained in the folk biographies of the saints. These are important for the same reason as is Navajo mythology: they provide the justification for the existence of religion itself. In terms of specific content, they share with nearly all mythologies the fact that they are full of marvels and miracles and superhuman heroes.

The ritual connection

The Navajo and Arab village mythologies have in common the fact that they are both directly connected with ritual, something that is not always true of mythology. All the major Navajo ceremonies are connected with specific myths, which tell how they came into being and how they should be performed. For Arab villagers, the rituals of the brotherhoods (*turuq*) are explained as part of God's initial revelation to the founding *wali*. On the other hand there is very little connection between orthodox Islamic mythology and ritual, except in the specification of the five daily prayers, and the sacrifice of a sheep or goat at the *bairam* festival. There is an enormous number of additional, very specific rituals required of pilgrims to Mecca, but these are far removed from the sphere of day-to-day living.

Ritual

Some form of collective ritual is found in virtually every religion; it is the chief way in which religion fulfills its social function of unifying the community. In comparison with other religions, however, ritual is relatively little emphasized in the Abrahamic faiths. All that is required of votaries is that they get together regularly to do homage to God, and even this is not considered essential to salvation by many persons. The Catholic and Eastern Christian sects have of course carried collective ritual to much greater heights of elaboration, while Protestants as well as Muslims and most Jews stick to simple, communal homage.

But a great many Arabs, in villages and elsewhere, have found the simple Friday mosque service insufficient to their ritual needs. For them, the brotherhoods and their weekly *hadra* provide a much richer ritual life than orthodox Islam is able to do. The *hadra* has both a collective and a personal dimension. The members chant prayers and sing songs of praise collectively, imitating the practice of orthodox Islam, but in the *dhikr* each participant seeks individually to be possessed by the holy spirit.

In the worship of the village saint, however, individual acts of worship, including visits to his shrine, are more important than collective acts, because *baraka* is a personal acquisition.

Acts of individual worship exhibit a good many commonalities. For both Navajos and Arab villagers there is a heavy, indeed preeminent, emphasis on avoiding or placating evil forces, including witches. There are all kinds of verbal formulas for averting their influence, and some substances are believed to have special protective powers. There are also a great many outright avoidances, above all of forbidden foods. On the more positive side, the Arabs' visits to the saint's shrine have their counterpart in the Navajos' practice of leaving small offerings at trailside shrines, springs, and other holy places.

In contrast to the Arab villagers, and also to many North American Indians, there is no ecstatic component in Navajo religion. The emphasis throughout their culture is on moderation in all things, including ritual behavior.

Means of appeal

Collective ritual is much more essential in Navajo religion than it is for Arab villagers. The conjoined voices of many are needed to influence the Navajo supernaturals, but not Allah or the village saint. Allah is mostly beyond the reach of the peasants' voices, no matter how unified, while the saint responds readily to individual appeals.

The means that Navajos and Arab villagers employ to influence the supernaturals are also markedly different. The Near Eastern world is a highly verbalizing one, and the Arabs' approach to nearly all the supernaturals is verbal, through flattery and supplication. The prohibition against graven images, taken very seriously by both Muslims and Jews, has tended to channel religious expression into the verbal domain. Even within this domain, however, the absence of song (except in some *hadra* rituals) is striking. For Navajos, verbal appeals always gain power when set to music, while for Arabs they clearly do not.

Navajos appeal to their deities in a much wider variety of ways than do Arabs, through verbal formulas and songs but also by prayer sticks, ritual food offerings, masked dances, and sand paintings. While praise of God is the single most important component of ritual in all the Abrahamic religions, it has only a very minor part in Navajo religion. The deities are compelled rather than cajoled, through elaborate and carefully followed ritual formulas.

A preoccupation with disease is characteristic of both Navajos and villagers, for good reason in view of their living conditions. For Navajos it provides the chief focus of ritual activity, and it plays an important part in the villagers' ritual as well. The peasants' approach is mainly preventive: *baraka* is the best available insurance against illness or any other bad luck. Visits by women to the saint's tomb are most often for the sake of insuring either their children or themselves against sickness. For Navajos the Blessingway ceremony has the same preventive virtue; in this context, *hozhoni* has the same value as *baraka.* However, all other major Navajo ceremonies are conducted for the treatment rather than for the prevention of disease. The *Zar* rituals of the villagers are more nearly like Navajo ceremonies in this respect; their emphasis also is on exorcism rather than prevention.

Rites of passage, marking basic changes in the social status of each individual, are important to Navajos and Arabs as they are to most other human groups. There are interesting parallels as well as differences in the two cases. For both Navajos and villagers, the survival of newborns is always uncertain, and there are many very specific pre-partum and post-partum observances for mother and child, and for the father too in the Navajo case. In both societies there is a formal naming ceremony, after there is a reasonable assurance that the child will survive, and the name is conferred by a ritual practitioner.

Arab boys undergo circumcision between the ages of three and six, following an age-old Near Eastern custom that has no parallel anywhere among Indians. Navajo boys and girls are introduced to full ritual life in a formal initiation ceremony at about the age of seven. There is nothing exactly comparable among the Arabs, but boys begin to take their place in the men's world about the age of twelve, after which they may attend mosque, take their part in collective prayers, and be accepted as learners in a brotherhood.

It is characteristic of the very different attitudes toward sex that Navajos celebrate a girl's puberty with a major public ceremony, while Arabs celebrate her marriage. In the Navajo case the girl's new sexual identity is an occasion for rejoicing, while for Arabs it is kept hidden until her sexuality can be safely channeled through marriage. Only then is she formally acknowledged as a sexual being. Marriage for Navajos is a relatively minor and private ceremony, for it does not establish a bond between kin groups as it does in the Arab case. Each partner retains a primary loyalty to his or her natal family and clan throughout life.

The most striking contrast between Navajo and Arab practice is seen in the case of funerals. It is true in both groups that the dead must be buried as soon as possible, after preparation of the body, but for Navajos the only ceremony is the extensive purification that must be undergone by everyone who has touched the body, or been near it. For Arabs there is nothing polluting about the corpse, and the funeral is an occasion for the whole kin group to mourn the passing of one of its members, and at the same time to recall his or her accomplishments in life. There are also post-mortem observances, involving visits to the grave by relatives forty days after death, and a year after death. In the villages I have often observed offerings of food left on the graves, although the men assure me that 'this is something foolish that women do.'[19]

Practitioners

Although there are two kinds of local religious practitioners for both Navajos and Arabs, there are few parallels among them. The Navajo singer and the Arab *feki* are both supposed to be possessed of formal religious learning, but it is far greater in the Navajo case. The singer at his best is much more learned than any village *feki,* and bears comparison to the learned *alim* of the great city mosques, who are the official repositories of Islamic wisdom. The apprentice singers and the dropout singers might perhaps be compared to the *feki,* in that both possess and administer fragments from a much larger system of knowledge. The *feki* however is only a private purveyor, not a ritual director as is the singer.

The singer and the *sheikh el-tariqa,* or his deputy, have in common the fact that both are ritual directors, and in this capacity each may command various subordinates. The *sheikh' s* position however has been inherited, and depends as much on his inheritance of the founder's *baraka* as it does on his knowledge of the *tariqa* ritual. He must nevertheless have that knowledge, and also be able to recite his noble ancestor's biography. The singer's position is wholly acquired through learning, although it is very often the case that he has learned from his father or maternal uncle. The large amount of time that must be spent together by teacher and learner makes it difficult to establish an apprentice relationship with anyone not living nearby.

The Navajo diagnostician's practice is purely medical, and involves no collective ritual. Its closest parallel among Arabs is found in the person

---

[19]Mortuary religion, including regular post-mortem feasts, is far more developed in Egypt than in any other Arab country, and must surely represent a survival of pharaonic tradition.

of the *zar sheikha,* and it is significant that both these individuals may be females. The *sheikha* is however a director of collective ritual as well.

The practical functions of religion

All religious systems include within them a certain number of practices, and their associated beliefs, that have been called practical religion (cf. Leach 1968). They are practices undertaken by individuals or groups not for the sake of veneration or social respectability or spiritual uplift, but to achieve immediate, practical ends. The importance of practical religion, as a subset of religion in general, varies greatly from individual to individual, and perhaps even more from society to society. To some extent, it varies inversely to the development of science. That is, the less that can be achieved through the control of scientific forces, the more must be attained through appeal to the deities.

It will be apparent that the practical component in both Navajo religion and Arab village religion is very large, as is expectable in the case of relatively powerless peoples. Most though not quite all of the major Navajo collective ceremonies are undertaken specifically for the treatment of illness or the exorcism of evil, although in earlier days some were undertaken also for success in hunting and in war. Some Arab villagers' practices are also undertaken for therapeutic purposes, although the emphasis in their case tends to be more on prevention than on cure. But *baraka,* in any case, is conceived as a very practical form of insurance.

For both peoples, the number of ways in which the supernaturals can be influenced is very large. In orthodox Islam and in Christianity, by contrast, the practical aspect is relatively unimportant, and the deity can really be influenced only by verbal supplication and by obedience to laws.

The human condition

Navajo religion and Arab village religion are, as I have said, religions of the weak, but that is not a very meaningful statement; so also are nearly all other tribal and peasant religions. It is only we, the educated upper classes in the literate civilizations, who have any strong sense of mastery over our fates, and who can approach the supernaturals with a degree of confidence.

In Navajo and Arab village societies, the sense of weakness finds expression in very different ways. The Navajos' weakness is felt only toward the *Dighinii,* not toward any living people, and it is nobody's fault. It is a fact of nature. Arab villagers feel their weakness both in relation to humans higher up the social scale, and to Allah. In the former case it is not their fault; they are victims of a system that has been in place for thousands of years. With regard to Allah however their weakness is their fault; it is due to their failure to follow his commands. But the Arabs have, to compensate, 'someone to watch over them' in the person of the saint, a comfort not enjoyed by Navajos. Disregarding the deities altogether, however, both peoples are very prone to blame their troubles on witches—a convenient target that removes any suggestion of fault on their part.

The afterlife

In common with most peoples, the majority of Navajos and nearly all Arabs believe in an afterlife. However, ideas on the subject are very different in the two cases. In Islam, as in all the Abrahamic religions, salvation is at least theoretically the central concern, and the afterlife is quite explicitly a place of rewards and punishments. For Navajos it is 'just something that will happen,' and there is no way to prepare for it. It is therefore hardly more than an afterthought, and people don't spend any time worrying about it.

Arab eschatology and Navajo eschatology have nevertheless one feature in common. Among both peoples, ideas about just what to expect in the next world are not clearly focused, and are quite variable from person to person. Indeed this seems to be true in nearly all religions—even those that, like evangelical Christianity, place overwhelming emphasis on salvation. Christians are promised a 'paradise of delights,' but scripture gives very few hints as to just what the delights will be. And for the most pentecostal of Christians, salvation seems to be much less a case of attaining delights than of avoiding damnation.

Analysis

In this discussion I have sought to identify as many parallels as possible between Navajo and Arab village religion, but it must be apparent that there are not many. Insofar as the two have common features, they are mostly features common to many religions. It is the differences much more than the commonalities that contribute to our understanding of the complex phenomenon of religion. Those differences, I think, must be understood from five perspectives: ecological, economic, political, historical, and evolutionary.

*The
ecological
factor*

Navajos and Arab peasants are both agrarian peoples, dependent on soil and water for their livelihood. But Navajos must make use of very large areas of soil that are not theirs—grazing land belongs to everyone—and they must rely on water from undependable rainfall and snowfall. Peasants own outright the small plot of land on which they depend, and they draw water from the ever-flowing Nile, through irrigation schemes in which they have specified rights. For Navajos the natural environment is much more problematical than is the human environment, while for Arabs the reverse is true. I have already suggested how this difference of perception plays out in the mythologies of the two peoples.

The ecological factor plays a part in another way as well. Because of the reservation system and population pressure, Navajos have not been fully nomadic for a long time. Nevertheless, dependent as they are on grazing, they must be prepared to change their residences whenever their animals require it, and most families did so at least a couple of times a year. Navajos never had a strong sense of attachment to any one place, and therefore neither did their deities. When they migrated, the gods had to go with them. But earthbound peasants, rooted in perpetuity to the plot of land on which their survival depends, live within a world of very narrow horizons, and they need a deity as localized as they are. This surely explains the importance of local tutelaries not only in the Arab world, but equally among the peasants of southern Europe, India, and China.

The economic factor

The religion of Arab villagers is a religion of the weak primarily because it is a religion of the poor and struggling. It is also, it must be stressed, a religion of the busy. The peasants' life is one of constant toil to wrest a living from a tiny plot of land, through a ceaseless round of field preparation, planting, weeding, irrigation, harvesting, and post-harvest storage and marketing. There are also a few animals that must be tended throughout the year, and fodder must be raised for them. With the best of intentions, few people can afford to devote either much time or much thought to religion. Weddings and funerals largely consume such extra resources as they can spare, and these occasions usually require a great deal of borrowing that must later be repaid. The worship of the local saint, which can be undertaken when and as convenient for each individual, and which costs nothing, is most adaptable to their needs. *Hadra* performances too can be scheduled according to the convenience of the group, and in any case there is no absolute necessity to attend except for the officers.

It is conspicuously evident among the Arab villagers that, the more wealth the more religion. Those with many sons can delegate most of the tasks of cultivation, and those few with large land holdings can hire cultivators. Such individuals have at least more time than others, and also more money in some cases; they can and often do invest both in religion. They may show their greater religiosity either by contributing to the *tariqa,* its *sheikh* and its rituals, or by regularly reciting the daily prayers and keeping the Ramadan fast. The most successful of them will crown their religious lives by making the *hajj* to Mecca.

Navajos like Arabs vary in the extent of their personal wealth, which in their case is measured by livestock holdings rather than by land. However, even the poorest of them are not dispossessed, since the open range belongs to everyone. No one is trapped in poverty in the same way as are peasant farmers. It was conspicuous when I was trading at Shonto that virtually every family had more horses than were needed for any practical purpose, with the result that many were never ridden. Navajo religion, in other words, is a religion of the weak but decidedly not a religion of the poor.

It is also not, most of the time, a religion of the busy. Navajo subsistence activities are far less time-consuming than are those of the Arab farmers—something that is true of all pastoral peoples. There are times of intensive, almost around-the-clock activity, at lambing and shearing seasons, but there are also long periods when most of the livestock tending is turned over to children, leaving the adults with time to spare. The most intensely busy season for everyone is the short summer farming season, for every self-respecting family needs a cornfield. The growing season however is only about 120 days, and during that time there is relatively little ritual activity. The mid-winter months are pre-eminently the ceremonial season, and it is a season when nearly everyone has time to attend sings. In the process, many men will invest time in learning some of the ritual songs, and perhaps in learning how to help with sand-paintings.

Sponsorship of sings is a more serious matter, and here, as in the Arab case, wealth has a role. Sponsoring one of the great nine-day Holy Ways is an expensive proposition; not only must the head singer and his assistants be paid, but all of the numerous attendees must be fed, and many must be given gifts. In this respect a Navajo nine-day sing is like an Arab wedding; on both occasions a whole kin group must usually mobilize. It is noteworthy however that the Navajo world is not competitive in the same way as is the Arab world, and sponsorship of a large sing is seen not as a sign of greater religiosity but only as a sign of greater generosity— something expected of the wealthy. Religiosity is measured not by ritual sponsorship of sings but by possession of religious knowledge, which may be brought into play at any sing, regardless of the sponsor.

In sum, the whole elaborate edifice of Navajo ceremonial life is made possible by leisure time; something of which the peasants have precious little.

The political factor

Arab peasants, like most other peasants, had lived for millennia under totalitarian regimes that, from their perception, were ruled by absolute, naked authority. That authority was conveyed through enactments of law—laws based not on principles of right or justice, but simply on the authority of the giver. It is no wonder then that the peasants' conception of the highest deity embodies the same principle. If the authority of the state was something foreign and threatening, but fortunately remote, so also was the authority of Allah. Navajos on the other hand never lived under any authority more formal than that of immediate kinsmen, and never under a regime of laws. It is conspicuous in this connection that none of their deities is an authority figure, and none is a lawgiver. The Sun, though powerful and remote like Allah, is not an autocrat; he does not give orders to his people.

The historical factor

No domain of culture seems more susceptible to diffusion and borrowing than is religion. Nearly every people's religion has similarities to that of the nearest neighbors, regardless of ethnic or linguistic or national differences. For reasons that are not well understood, this is particularly true of Athabascan-speaking Indians everywhere. Whether in the far Northwest, on the Pacific Coast, in the Southwest, or in Oklahoma, their religion is closely similar to that practiced by their nearest neighbors.

The Navajos, after arrival in the Southwest, became participants in a religious tradition that is common to most western American Indians. Its emphasis is on communal rather than on individual acts of worship, and on moderation rather than excess in ritual behavior—both points of contrast with tribes farther to the east. The most specific resemblances, as might be expected, are between Navajo religion and that of the immediately neighboring Pueblo tribes, who were already on the ground when the Navajos arrived in the Southwest. The Emergence Myth, although much embroidered in distinctly Navajo ways, is clearly of Pueblo origin, as are many individual gods and ritual elements. The heavy emphasis on moderation and harmony is also a distinctively Pueblo trait. For the Pueblos it is a matter of great practical importance, since they live as closely crowded together as do Arab villagers. For Navajos however it must be accounted for on historical rather than on functional grounds, since it is not essential to the maintenance of peace among the widely scattered families. It is just something picked up from the Pueblos, along with many other aspects of religion.

Arab village religion is heir to many age-old and distinctly Near Eastern religious traditions, including nominal monotheism, dualism, legalism, salvationism, and the messianic tradition. It has combined these with other features having a regional distribution, such as the evil eye belief and the *Zar* cult. Certain elements, such as the belief in Nile spirits and in the *jinn,* as well as mortuary practices, are quite probably legacies from pharaonic or even from Neolithic times.

The evolutionary factor

Simplistic evolutionary theories of religion were so overworked a hundred years ago[20] that they have come in for considerable and justified criticism by modern anthropologists. Still, the baby is far too large to go out with the bathwater. Making every allowance for environmental and historical factors, cognitive and social evolutionary factors still provide a more coherent framework for the understanding of religious similarities and differences than do most other factors.

The evolutionary factor seems especially apparent in the contrast between Navajo religion and Arab village religion. When all is said and done, Navajo religion is a tribal religion, albeit an unusually complex one, and Arab village religion is a peasant religion. They are adapted to the vastly different worlds in which tribesman and peasants live.

The traditional Navajo world was to all intents and purposes a Neolithic world. It was a world in which human mastery over nature was decidedly limited, but so also was human mastery over other humans. It was a roughly egalitarian world in which everyone made his living in pretty much the same way, and in which powerful chiefs and monarchs had not yet emerged, nor had social stratification or man-made law. The greatest dangers to be apprehended were from nature rather than from humans, and the supernaturals were conceived accordingly. Many were animals or natural phenomena, and none had the characteristics of a human autocrat. Since the gods were so much more powerful than humans, no living human could be taken as a model for them. And as human society was relatively egalitarian, so also was the society of the deities; as human society was organized primarily on the basis of kinship, so also was the society of the *Dighinii.*

---

[20]They still are, within the discipline of *Religionswissenschaft.*

Peoples who evolved beyond the Neolithic stage, as many did in both the Old and the New Worlds, gradually developed all those characteristics that we associate with literate civilization and complex society. First came powerful, hereditary chiefs, claiming either personal divinity or divine ordination; later came cities and economic differentiation, and the social stratification that inevitably goes with economic differentiation. As the society and economy became too complex for purely personal rule, the chief became a formally designated king or emperor, aided by a ruling elite of priests and officials. Literacy, at first confined within the ruling elite, led to the codification of mythology and law codes, which became the Great Traditions of the early civilizations. Such were the institutions of the state, as it first emerged in Egypt, in Mesopotamia, in India, in China, and in the New World

But the early civilizations did not stand still. In the areas where they had first emerged, there was over time a gradual process of secularization. Literacy became diffused from the priests to a merchant class who were not part of the official state hierarchy, and these folk developed a secular power hierarchy of their own, and increasing bodies of purely secular knowledge. As commerce provided avenues for advancement through wealth, the hierarchical social system became somewhat more fluid than it was in the beginning. The peasants however were excluded; they were tied to their land either by formal legal enactments, or by the ignorance and the lack of resources that would have allowed them any escape from their immemorial role. And as in all early civilizations, the status of women was more depressed than was that of men; they no longer had a significant role in food production activities.

Such was the world, or at least a large part of it, into which Islam was born, in the seventh century A.D. But is was not born within the confines of one of the ancient civilizations or state societies, but into what was still in many ways a tribal world, lying just beyond the borders of the civilized states. The Arabs were, in Toynbee's phrase, an 'external proletariat.' The city of Mecca, dominant at that time as a trade center, was ruled by a merchant oligarchy, of which Muhammad was a member. He lived throughout his life within the framework of Arab tribal law and political tradition, and yet he was thoroughly familiar, through close personal contact, with both Jewish and Christian religious traditions.

The utopian religion which the Prophet sought to create was a blend of Arab customary traditions, and traditions adopted from the neighboring, literate civilizations of the Byzantine, Jewish, and Persian worlds.

Within a century, however, something happened which the Prophet had never really anticipated. Through conquest the Arabs became masters of a very large part of the civilized world that had for so long excluded them, including Egypt, the Levant, and the whole of the Persian domains. Suddenly, almost all the greatest centers of urban learning, and most of the major centers of commerce, were within the Islamic domains. The development of Islamic thought and law passed very rapidly from Arab tribal leaders and merchants to the long-established urban elites in Alexandria, Antioch, Damascus, and Baghdad. Islam in the process was transformed into something more than just a salvationist religion; it became an urban-dominated civilization with all the same features of economic differentiation, social stratification, law, and literature that its predecessor civilizations had possessed.

Peasants within the Arab domains adapted as they have always adapted. In the sphere of religion, they grasped as much of the new Great Tradition as they could understand without the benefit of literacy, but it was reconfigured to fit their particular, limited world and their particular needs. Allah came to embody all the characteristics of the Pharaoh and the Byzantine Emperor, but like them he was too remote to be of practical concern. He could not hear their feeble voices, and therefore would never grant requests, but at the same time the villagers didn't have to spend a lot of time praising him as the urban dwellers did. As a simple matter of practicality, the peasants retained the myriad folk traditions on which they had always relied. This was especially true of women, for even more than men they were cut off from access to the Great Tradition. There were certainly local saints among them long before the coming of Islam,[21] and these were partially reinterpreted and renamed, to fit a new, distinctly Islamic folk tradition in regard to revelation. Since Egyptian and Sudanese peasants had been Christian before the coming of Islam, the worship of the Virgin was well established and was continued as a matter of course. Beliefs and practices in regard to *jinn,* the evil eye, and Nile spirits were retained from a still more remote antiquity. Long before Islam those beliefs had undoubtedly been condemned by Byzantine and Coptic priests, as they were later to be by Islamic clerics, but the villagers stubbornly clung to practices that had always served their needs.

In almost every respect, then, the religion of Egyptian and Sudanese

---

[21] During archaeological survey in Nubia, we found that some of the local saints' shrines had been foci of pilgrimage since long before the coming of Islam.

villagers is a typical peasant religion, adapted to the special circumstances of an underprivileged people within a complex and differentiated society. It exists under the umbrella of a Great Tradition, but perpetuates local beliefs and practices that have been found effective since time out of mind.

The issue of religious evolution will be discussed from a much broader perspective in Chapters 14 and 15.

PART 2

THE THEORY OF RELIGION

5

INTRODUCTION TO PARTS 2 AND 3

In the Introduction to Part 1 I explained, albeit briefly, how I came to know what I know about religion. Here I want to explain, in somewhat more detail, how I came to think what I think, for it is chiefly ideas rather than data that will occupy the remainder of my book.

Anthropologists have always listed religion among the universal features of human culture, and I've never had any difficulty in accepting that proposition. But like all such generalizations it is not very enlightening, partly because, like all such propositions, it is a normative statement. That is, it conveys the impression that all peoples are equally religious, and might even suggest that all individuals within any society are equally religious. If one is truly to understand religion as a cultural phenomenon, one must be prepared to recognize not only its variability in quality (i.e. the differences between one religion and another), but also its variation is quantity, from person to person and from society to society. Religion is not lacking in any society, but some people are more religious than others, and some societies are more religious than others.

Although I have never been religious, my personal experiences have nevertheless convinced me that no anthropologist worthy of the name can afford to dismiss or to disparage something that has played so pervasive a role in human affairs. That perception, of course, is hardly original with me. Many of our most eminent social scientists—Durkheim, Weber, William James, and Malinowski come readily to mind—have made it the central feature of their study, and I have read their works with a great deal of profit. And yet they leave me ultimately dissatisfied, for a variety of reasons that I'll explore more fully in the chapters that follow. Suffice it to suggest here that they offer incomplete answers to the two most basic questions: *what* is religion? and *why* is religion? These chapters represents my personal attempt to answer those two questions, and a few others, in a way satisfactory both to logic and to my ethnographic understanding.

Three-quarters of a century ago, Henri Bergson gave voice to the problem that has confronted every student of religion since time out of mind: 'How is it that beliefs and practices which are anything but reasonable could have been, and still are, accepted by reasonable beings?' (originally in Bergson 1935: 93; paraphrased in Evans-Pritchard 1965: 15.) Philosophers have offered a wide variety of answers, but social scientists have usually taken refuge in a functionalist explanation, showing how religion satisfies universal human needs. More than two centuries ago, Montesquieu (1762, vol. 2: 131) opined that 'religion, though false, is necessary.' It is an important insight, and one I will pursue in later pages, but it is not the whole answer. It explains why people need to have beliefs and practices, but not why they have the ones they have. And it ignores altogether the question of what religion is.

By way of 'deconstructing' Bergson's problem I suggest that for 'reasonable' we substitute 'intelligent,' by which we mean 'possessed of intelligence.' The latter word has two meanings. Its most common usage designates a quality and capacity of the mind, otherwise sometimes called sagacity. But it can also mean simply information, as in the case for example of military intelligence. I want to suggest in this book that most people most of the time act intelligently on the basis of the reasoning power that they possess *and the information they possess.* This latter point, I will argue, is critical to the understanding of religion, because it is, before all, a system of intelligence. Most religious beliefs and behaviors are reasonable, or logical, within the context of the information available to their practitioners.

That is, religions are ethno-logical. I use this word as cognate to ethnoscience, ethnobotany, and so on, to designate the *emic* domains of culture. They are systems of knowledge and action that prevail among peoples, based on their apprehension of the universe around them.

To suggest that other peoples' religions appear illogical to us, but not to them, is hardly a new insight. The statement on its face is tautological: for most peoples religion is not only logical, it *is* logic. What I seek to do in this book is to go beyond the obvious, to suggest that there are commonalities among all religions not only because they satisfy the same basic human needs, but because there is a certain logic common to them all, based on perceptions that are common to all.

I am going to suggest in later pages that all religions involve the three basic components of believing, belonging, and behaving. Most also involve a great deal of affective feeling. Virtually all scholars have agreed on this point, but they have disagreed as to the relative importance of the different components. Sociofunctionalists place the heaviest emphasis on belonging and behaving (i.e. ritual), while psychofunctionalists place emphasis on the feelings that religion engenders. The important thing about religion, for both kinds of functionalists, is what it does rather than what it is. The beliefs that rationalize behavior and that underlie feelings are not considered important in and of themselves.

As an example of the functionalist perspective, let us consider the definition of religion offered by Anthony Wallace, one of the most thoughtful anthropological students of the subject. Religion is, for him, 'a set of rituals, rationalized by myth, which mobilizes supernatural powers for the purpose of achieving transformations of state in man and nature' (Wallace 1966: 107). To say that religion *is* a set of rituals (behaviors), rationalized by myth, is in effect to make myth (beliefs) a secondary feature; a dependent variable. Seemingly, religious beliefs exist only because they provide legitimation for ritual behavior. (There are other problems with Wallace's definition that I will consider in a later chapter.)

From the standpoint of a logician, this is unsatisfactory. The student of religion must explain its forms as well as its functions, and forms are never wholly defined by functions. More to the point, though, it is unsatisfactory from the perspective of cognitive psychology itself. Except in the case of instinctual behavior, human actions are always preceded by and based on perceptions; we react to what we see or hear or feel or smell. To try and explain any behavior without reference to the perception that gave rise to it is not merely putting the cart before the horse, it is making the cart move without any horse.

In the case of religion, then, I suggest that behavior (ritual, for short) cannot be understood except in terms of the belief (myth, for short) that has prompted it. Myth, understood in the broadest sense, does not simply rationalize ritual; it *causes* ritual. In this study therefore I see no possibility except to begin at the beginning: to consider the cognitive aspect of religion first and its behavioral or affective aspects afterward, simply because perception must precede reaction. It is the action, not the thought, that is the dependent variable.

In short and in sum, my thesis is that the religion of every people begins as an attempt to *comprehend* the experienced world, rather than as an attempt to deal with it. Above all it seeks to answer the most fundamental and the most difficult of human questions: *why?* Why does the sun rise and set? Why do the seasons change? Why do people become ill, and die? For most peoples it is religion that provides the answers, and it is on the basis of those answers that methods of dealing with, and to a degree controlling, the experienced world are developed.

Pure and applied religion

Scientists have long made a distinction between pure and applied science. The former is a system of knowledge for its own sake, including a great deal of knowledge that has no apparent practical value. The latter involves the application of scientific knowledge to the achievement of practical human ends.

I think it is useful to make a similar distinction in the case of religion, for it too is both a system of knowledge and a system of action based on that knowledge. Mythology is pure religion, and like pure science it includes a great deal of information that is of no practical value to the believers. That is, it does not provide a basis for any kind of ritual action; it is merely a way of knowing how and why things are. It satisfies the mind's eternal quest to know more and to explain more. Navajo mythology, for example, names a great many Powers that are not subjects of propitiation or veneration, but that provide the explanation for natural phenomena. Ritual on the other hand is applied religion, addressed to those Powers that people have learned how to deal with.

In my view, the basic deficiency of all functional theories is their failure to recognize that not all religion is applied religion. They thus dismiss as irrelevant all those large bodies of belief about the supernaturals that don't find expression in ritual, and for which there is no obvious practical explanation. But just as there can be no understanding of applied science without a prior understanding of pure science, so also there can be no understanding of applied religion without a prior understanding of pure religion.

The ethnographic perspective

My discourse, from here onward, is not ethnographic, in the traditional sense of focusing on the description and understanding of a single people. Its target population is nothing less than the whole of humankind, past and present. It is also not ethnographic in its methodology. Some of my data have come through direct observation, but much more of it has come from reading. None of it has come by participation, in any meaningful way. The study is ethnographic simply in the approach that it brings to its subject matter: that of a keenly interested and appreciative Other, trying to understand but without a desire to convert.

The term 'ethnography' has a considerably wider meaning today than it once had. It seems to encompass just about any study of any human behavior, including one's own. It even includes the study of idiosyncratic behavior that cannot be traced to a cultural origin. Thus undertaken, it becomes a study of behavior as an ultimate datum, rather than of behavior as expressive of culture.

In my generation (roughly, the middle years of the twentieth century) ethnography was much more explicitly a cultural enterprise, and usually a cross-cultural one: the study of an alien people, usually speaking an alien language. Ideally, we went among them for a protracted period, tried within reason to live as they did, tried to learn their language, and hoped in the end to be able to see the world—*their* world—through their eyes. It was quintessentially a humanistic enterprise, whose aim was understanding rather than prediction or explanation in any narrowly scientific sense.

It was not a search for self-understanding. Anthropologists, like other Americans, were much less self-absorbed then they are today. For better and worse we took ourselves for granted, and had confidence in our ability to function in the field as disinterested observers, recording what we saw and heard without imposing ourselves upon it. We adhered as best we could to one of the axioms of good newspaper reporting: that you never want to become part of the story you're writing. Lately the revisionists have suggested that this was never completely possible; you can't intrude upon a field of inquiry without affecting it. They have a point, although they consistently overstate it. The great majority of quotidian culture that we see and record is really non-problematical; observer and observed can agree on what it is and what it means without much argument.

In our guise as objective recorders, our aim was to see rather than to feel. We wanted to understand how the world looked to a Navajo or to a Nubian, but we didn't necessarily want to share their feelings toward it. We didn't for example want to go through life in fear of witches or of the evil eye. We wanted to understand the feelings and values that led some people to have those fears, and that led others to abuse their environments, to neglect their children, and sometimes to treat animals inhumanely, but we had no desire to share the same feelings or values. As cultural relativists we sought maximally to empathize with our subjects, but not to identify with them. In short the ideal ethnographer, as we conceived him or her, was an innocent, without preconceptions and without biases for or against anyone or anything.

Ideally, our ethnographic studies were comprehensive. That is, we sought to describe and to understand each culture as the sum of all its parts, not just some of them, and we did not presuppose that any of them were unimportant to the people involved. This is the approach that I have taken to the study not only of individual religions but to religion as a whole. Readers of the preceding chapters will have noticed already that I devote a great deal of space to the discussion of what are usually considered minor features or even mere superstitions, because I've noticed that they really constitute a very large part of the day to day religious life of many peoples. In sum, it is the ethnographic perspective that I have brought toward the study of religion, rather then the theoretical perspective brought by most other commentators.

In the beginning, religion was for me a domain as alien and exotic as were the cultures of the Navajos and the Nubians among whom I resided for protracted periods. I was simply brought up without it, as I was brought up also without Navajo or Nubian culture. But it is important to make the point that I was not brought up anti-religious, any more than I was anti-Navajo or anti-Nubian. It was just something that lay beyond my personal horizon.

While I had no negative feelings toward religion, for a long time I considered it unimportant, and therefore uninteresting. It was not only unimportant in our family; it seemed so to just about everyone else we knew. Most professed a belief in God, and many went to church, but religion seemed to play very little part in their daily lives, and almost none in their thinking. I was, and remain, convinced that a majority of Americans may be religious, but they are not very religious, as I have since come to understand religion. I suppose this reflects my lifelong feeling that what's important about people is what they think, not what they do.

My rather cavalier attitude about religion began to change when I lived and worked among the Navajo, for whom religion is vitally important. It changed much more when I went to live and work among Nubians and other Arabs. I came to appreciate that religion was not only a pervasive force in their daily lives, but had played a large role in shaping their history over several millennia. Subsequent travels, reading, and teaching have all served to reinforce the conviction that religion has been very important indeed to most peoples, at most times in history. They were and are simply much more religious than are most Americans.

In making that statement I have to stress again that I'm thinking of religion, and religiosity, first and foremost in terms of cognition, not of behavior. Sudanese and Egyptians of my acquaintance vary enormously in the rigor with which they perform their religious duties, but very little in their ultimate belief in Allah and his saints. Many neglect their daily prayers, and few succeed in keeping the Ramadan fast all the way through, but they all recite the Profession of Faith. To the extent that they neglect religious duties, they do so in the same spirit in which we often disobey secular laws: not because we don't believe in them but because we hope we can get away with it. In my early days in the Sudan I incautiously told one or two people (whom I thought were equally 'enlightened') that I did not believe in God. It was clear from their reaction that this was beyond their comprehension, coming from an otherwise intelligent being. In a sense they were turning Bergson's problem on its head, and thinking, 'How can anyone who otherwise seems intelligent be so stupid as not to believe in God, when every day brings fresh confirmation of his existence?' (M. N. Srinivas [1976: 98] reported an identical reaction among the villagers whom he studied in south India.) More than a performer of actions and a subject of worship, the god of my Sudanese and Egyptian friends is a basic explanatory principle, without which the endless, unpredictable events of daily existence are unintelligible.

As I have already suggested, no anthropologist worthy of the name can afford to ignore or to disparage something that is not only present among all peoples, but is vitally important to so many of them. I have therefore been engaged for over half a century in an effort to comprehend it, just as I've striven to comprehend the cultures of the Navajos and the Nubians. At the same time I am not and have no desire to be religious, just as I have no desire to be a Navajo or a Nubian. For better and worse, it is this detached ethnographer's perspective that I bring to the present study. I remain, in the tradition of twentieth-century anthropology, a relativist, according neither more nor less respect to one religion than to another.

My perspective, like that of most ethnologists of my generation, is culturological rather than behavioral. That is, I approach religion as a set of codes for belief and behavior, that exists above and apart from the behavior of individuals in specific contexts, in the same way that language stands above and apart from individual acts of speech. It has discoverable rules, even though people don't always obey them in everyday life. This is something readily apparent in the case of the scriptural religions, which have a canonical or ideal form that is overtly proclaimed by the clergy. In the case of the non-scriptural religions of tribal peoples the basic rules may be much more difficult to elicit; they are discovered only through a great deal of observation and inquiry. I am convinced nevertheless that the rules are always there, underlying and informing specific behaviors, in the same way that rules for language usage are always there, even among peoples who have no grammarians.

My book is thus about what religions are like, not about what religious people are like. The latter is indeed a vitally important field of inquiry, and the subject of a great deal of insightful literature, but it is not one on which I'm well qualified to comment, since I've never been a participant observer.

It is hardly necessary to add that, from the relativist and comparative perspective, all religions are of equal importance, regardless of the number of their votaries. We have to remember that the three Abrahamic faiths, despite their millions of adherents, are only a tiny minority among the world's hundreds of religions, and a rather atypical minority at that. Viewed in that light, an understanding that applies to most religions, but not to the Abrahamic faiths, is of more value than an understanding that applies to the Abrahamic faiths but not to most of the others. My concern has always been to develop an understanding that is applicable to as many religions as possible.

*Teaching
experience*

I spoke in the Introduction to Part 1 about the part that direct ethnographic experience, as well as ethnographic reading, has played in developing my ideas about religion. Here I want to say a word further about the very important role that teaching has played, for throughout most of my adult life I've been first and foremost a teacher.

For me the most exciting of all experiences is learning, and the way to learn is to teach. Not only does it involve an enormous amount of library research, but I have found again and again that inspiration comes, unbidden, in the act of communication. So, for enjoyment as well as for intellectual profit, I taught over thirty different courses in the Department of Anthropology, and two in the Religious Studies Program, at the University of Kentucky. A few of those courses have added very substantially to my understanding of religion. Indeed, many of the ideas and much of the material presented in this book was developed originally for delivery in the classroom. The most important courses relative to religion, were:

RS 301: Understanding Religion. In this course, taught in the Religious Studies Program, I reviewed briefly and then compared each of the major approaches to the study of religion: Theology, History of Re-ligions (*Religionswissenschaft*), the Sociology of Religion, the Psychol-ogy of Religion, the Anthropology of Religion, and the Philosophy of Religion. Much of the understanding I developed has found its way into the chapters that follow.

ANT 430: Comparative religious systems. This course opened with a discussion of the problems in defining and in explaining religion. It was followed by detailed ethnographic descriptions of four specific religions: the shamanic religion of the Yupik, the communal religion of the Nava-jos, the Olympian religion of the ancient Sumerians, and the 'monothe-istic' religion of Arab peasants. The material developed on Navajos and on Arab peasants has contributed extensively to Chapters 2 and 3.

Other courses that contributed substantially to my understanding of religion were Indians of the Southwest, Peoples of the Near East and North Africa, Peoples of Inner Asia, Egyptian Civilization, and Compar-ative Civilizations, as well as three graduate seminars devoted specifi-cally to the topic of religion.

Teaching abroad. Apart from those courses in the United States, I have also taught courses on religion both in China and in Kazakhstan. In both countries I had some command of the native language, but not enough to deliver lectures on so abstruse a subject as religion; my lectures were all given in English. In both countries I had to approach the subject very nearly from 'square one,' because much of the common knowledge about religion that we take for granted in Europe and America had been either erased or distorted by generations of Communist indoctrination. In Kaza-khstan, one of the senior professors at Almati State University told me, in all seriousness, how delighted she was to learn that Muhammad had been a real person, and not a mythical figure!

In China the problem was less of total ignorance than of misinforma-tion. Many of my Chinese hearers (a lot of whom were faculty mem-bers) were Communist Party members, and they had read and discussed Lewis Henry Morgan's *Ancient Society* (1877), as all dutiful Commu-nists should. They were thus full of nineteenth-century evolutionist no-tions about religion, which had been taught to them as dogma. I found however that they were just as eager as were Kazakhs to hear new and different ideas.

The problems of pedagogy were a bit different in the two countries, but were interesting and instructive in both cases. In China my lectures were translated on the spot—more or less paragraph by paragraph—to listeners some of whom had little or no English. The problem was therefore one of translation, into a language that has no exact equivalents for many of our most basic analytical concepts. Calculated ambiguity is one of the most salient and delightful features of Chinese discourse, but it was of course something I hoped to avoid. I spent hours, in advance of each lecture, going over it with the translator, and trying to decide on the appropriate Chinese terms for important concepts. In Kazakhstan I lectured to advanced students of English, many of whom took the courses chiefly to improve their English, and my lectures were not translated. Consequently, I had the problem of confining myself to a vocabulary of basic, everyday terms that they might be supposed to know. In the case of a subject like religion, it is not an easy challenge!

Advantages and disadvantages of the ethnographic perspective

By this time, devout believers may have decided that they don't need to read any further. How, they may ask, can anyone who has never known religion from the inside possibly speak about it with any degree of insight? I can only respond with the traditional ethnographer's view: that the outsider's perspective has its own advantages, as well as disadvantages. As evidence of the advantages, I can point to six outstanding field studies that I've had the pleasure of reading: Alfonso Ortiz' *The Tewa World* (1969), Hamed Ammar's *Growing Up in an Egyptian Village* (1966), Abdulla Lutfiyya's *Baytin—a Jordanian Village* (1966), Jomo Kenyatta's *Facing Mount Kenya* (1938), M. N. Srinivas' *The Remembered Village* (1976), and Mao-ch'un Yang's *Chinese Village* (1945). To my mind, those works represent ethnography at its absolute best, combining insights that are possible only to an insider with others that are possible only to an anthropologist. Each author returned to his native community after having studied anthropology or sociology abroad, and each then saw it through entirely new eyes, achieving understandings of things that were long familiar, year never really seen in a clear light.

My relativistic outsider's view of religion is, needless to say, hardly unique to me. It was very succinctly expressed by Émile Durkheim nearly a century ago: 'In reality ... there are no religions which are false. All are true in their own fashion; all answer, though in different ways, to the given conditions of human existence' (Durkheim 1915: 3). Where Durkheim and many like-minded scholars have gone astray, I think, is not in the attitude that they bring to the study of religion but in the specific knowledge that they bring, based on their prior experiences in the

Judaeo-Christian tradition. I will deal with some of their more common ethnocentric misperceptions in Chapter 7. My advantage, in contrast to Durkheim and other predecessors, is simply that of ignorance. I have no ethnocentric preconceptions simply because I was not brought up in any religious tradition.

But it is, of course, a weakness as well as a strength. Like any ethnographer, I may be able to see things that insiders can't see, but I cannot feel things that they feel. As a result I'm better equipped to understand some aspects of religion than others. I'm best equipped to understand its cognitive domain, and worst equipped to understand its affective domain. However, since the life of the mind has been my chief concern throughout my career, it is the cognitive domain of religion that interests me most. I have the conviction that this aspect has been unduly neglected by other modern students, perhaps because the intellectual content of religion is so difficult to account for. But religion is nothing if not a system of knowledge and explanation about the nature of the universe, and for most peoples at most times it has occupied the entire ground now pre-empted by science. And because knowledge must precede action, that is my point of departure in the analysis of all religions, as I've already suggested.

Non-credo

Readers who proceed beyond this page must, then, be fully aware that they have in their hands the work of a freethinker, but not of a critic or disparager. But this does not really make me so very different from most of my fellows. Within the tradition of Abrahamic exclusivity, every devout Jew, Christian, and Muslim is an unbeliever in hundreds of religions—in every one but his or her own. I am merely an unbeliever in one more religion than are they. I share with Jews an unbelief in Christianity and Islam, with Christians an unbelief in Judaism and in Islam, and with Muslims an unbelief in Judaism and Christianity. But because I have no faith of my own to defend, I may be more accepting of the others than are they.

As regards religion I am, nevertheless, a scientist and not an atheist. Science operates (ideally) on the provisional assumption that there are no gods, and attempts to build systems of knowledge and action that leave them out of account. Atheism asserts that they don't exist as a first premise, requiring no confirmation. The scientist says only that up to now he has found no empirical evidence to confirm the existence of gods; the atheist says that is proof enough that they don't exist. But mankind all through history has had a tendency to deny the existence of things, that were afterward discovered. Of course, many scientists are atheists, but insofar as that is a dogma independent of confirming evidence, it is itself really a religious belief and not a scientific one.

Scientific theories, no less than religious tenets, are at times dogmas for the unthinking. Thinking is hard work at the best of times, and often stressful when it involves decision-making. Most people (not excluding myself) would like to avoid it some of the time, and some people would like to avoid it all of the time. Dogmas, scientific as well as religious, offer an easy way out.

As a result, I am nearly as much a freethinker in regard to science as I am in regard to religion. The most doctrinaire of scientists make absurdly exaggerated claims as to how much of nature we can really explain, on the basis of the laws we have so far discovered. All of the natural selection and genetic drift and sociobiology and other principles that have so far been adduced don't begin to explain all of the marvelous regularity, the 'grand design' of nature, that is patent to any observer. Consequently readers will (I hope) find a conspicuous lack of theoretical orientation in these pages. I will suggest in later pages that all the great theories about religion are true in some contexts and untrue in others. I have tried to keep the book free of dogma, either religious or scientific, so that readers as well as myself are free to think.

I don't despair of the possibility that we may one day be able to explain all of nature without reference to deities—the ultimate goal of all science—but I also don't shut the door to the possibility that deities may turn out to be involved. In the meantime I'm content to live in ignorance, acknowledging that neither religion nor science explains nearly as much as it pretends to. On the other hand I'm decidedly not a mystic; I don't believe that anything is ultimately beyond discovery.

If there are any deities, however, I suspect that there will turn out to be a lot of them, just as there are a lot of different and unrelated scientific laws. I can see no logical reason for attributing all the happenings in nature to the action of one single will, except as a concession to the so-called 'law of parsimony.' It is not a principle that has any appeal for me, unsupported as it is by empirical evidence. The simplest explanation for any phenomenon is almost invariably the wrong one; the universe is not a simple place. Einstein spent the last twenty years of his life trying to develop a 'unified field theory' that would collapse a lot of the disparate theories of physics and astronomy into one grand overarching scheme, but he was not successful. There are just too many different things that need explaining.

I thus share with the Deists of the Enlightenment the acceptance that there may be sentient powers out there, but that none of the religions to date have satisfactorily captured them. I differ from the Deists in the assumption that if there is one, there must be only one. I suppose therefore that I might be called a poly-deist.

*Religion and
religions*

It should be clear at this point that, as a sympathetic outsider, my effort is not to try and understand any one religion, but to achieve a level of understanding that will apply equally to all of them. At the outset I found them all equally incomprehensible. What I hope to achieve, for my own benefit if not that of others, is to render them all equally comprehensible. That will be my frame of reference throughout the remaining chapters of this book, in which I will be talking mostly at a high level of abstraction. I will be talking about religion in the generic and singular sense, rather than about religions in the partitive and plural sense, because that is the level at which I strive for understanding.

And yet, as all social scientists know, our abstract theories and concepts will carry us only so far in understanding, much less predicting, the daily thought and actions of actual people. Abstractions are necessarily and inherently oversimplifications. Quite simply, in the case of nearly all social science theories, they profess to explain much more than they can actually predict. At the same time we cannot achieve any kind of real understanding without them: they are our basic vocabulary of cognition.

At any rate I will, until the last chapters, be concerned with religion rather than with religions. In Chapter 17 I will belatedly consider how my generalized understandings play out 'on the ground,' in actual, observable human thought and behavior.

6

CLEARING THE GROUND

The three major problems that confront every student of religion are those of defining it, explaining it, and understanding it. What is religion, why does it exist, and how are we to relate to it? The three questions have often been confounded; particularly by functionalists who assume that religion is sufficiently defined and understood by explaining what purposes it serves. In fact however they are separate issues that must be separately addressed. The definition of religion does not really specify anything about its content, and the content does not determine the functions of religion. But before tackling those issues it is necessary to clear away some of the encumbrances of terminology that entangle them, and some of the encumbrances of ethnocentrism that often confound them. I will address problems of the first type in the present chapter, and problems of the second type in the next chapter.

The termino-
logical
thicket

Robert Lowie long ago observed that 'The clarification of concepts ... directly gauges scientific progress' (Lowie 1937: 281). More so, I would add, than does the development of new theories, which often turn out to be very old wine in new bottles.

The matter can be well illustrated in the case of human social organization. Forms of kinship organization had been of interest to social philosophers from Greek times to the Enlightenment, but in the vernacular languages there was really only one term, 'the family,' to designate all kin-based groupings. This led to an implicit and thoroughly erroneous assumption that the patrilineal nuclear family as we know it in the West was the basic residential and economic unit in all societies. Then, in the last half of the nineteenth century, came Johan Bachofen, Henry Sumner Maine, John McLennan, and Lewis Henry Morgan to provide us with a whole new conceptual vocabulary, encompassing such terms as matriliny, exogamy, cross-cousin marriage, sororate, lineage, and a host of others. Basically, the whole field of social anthropology was born out of that terminological breakthrough, as we were enabled for the first time to appreciate and to analyze the enormous diversity of functioning kin groups that may be encompassed under the term 'the family.'

In the study of religion, anthropologists have devised some useful analytical concepts, like 'animism' and 'shamanism,' but there has been no conceptual revolution similar to that in the study of kinship. We are still constrained by a vocabulary of age-old terms like 'gods,' 'myth,' 'ritual,' 'prayer,' 'sacrifice,' and others, whose meanings are no more precise than is 'the family.' To make matters worse, many of them have positive or negative affective associations in popular usage. 'Holy,' 'sacred,' and 'divine' generally have positive connotations, while 'myth,' 'ritual,' and 'idol' often have negative ones; they designate things that other peoples believe in or do, but we don't. Thus an image of the Buddha is an 'idol' but an image of Christ on the cross is not; a Navajo prayer-stick is a 'fetish' but a rosary is not.

Let us consider now some of the most common terms that are employed in the discussion of religion, and that are really problematical for analytical purposes. The list should properly begin with 'religion' itself, but I will bypass that one for now, since it is the subject of extended discussion in later pages.

Vernacular terms

Supernatural. This is probably the single most commonly employed term in the discourse on religion, and the most unavoidable. As a noun it may designate any or all of the myriad powers that peoples believe in, and that in various contexts we have labeled as gods, spirits, ghosts, demons, and by a host of other names. As an adjective it may designate any or all of the special qualities possessed by those powers, and not possessed by the rest of us.

The term is only objectionable when it is used in a dualistic context; that is, in contrast with the word 'natural,' in such a way as to suggest that there is a clear dividing line, or that the supernaturals are somehow *un*natural. That kind of dualistic division, between the 'sacred' and 'profane' realms (read: supernatural and natural), is a recurring feature of Western religious thought, but it is not shared by many other peoples, for whom the two are parts of an unbroken continuum of nature. The deities and other powers are not merely a part of nature; they *are* nature. The Navajos make a distinction between 'Earth Surface People' and 'Holy People,' but the two dwell together in the same cosmos, and they interact at many points and in many places. The Visitor Gods (*Yei* to Navajos; *Katcina* to Pueblos) spend part of the year among humans and part of the year apart from them.

The learned churchmen who met at Chalcedon in 453 A.D. formally established the dualistic principle for most Christians, when they decided that Jesus had separate human and divine natures, because the two could never be blended. But the Monophysites (today's Armenians, Syrians, and Copts) refused to accept the decree, and continue to believe that, at least in the case of Jesus, there is no sharp dividing line between the divine and the human, or in other words between the supernatural and the natural.

In writing this book I had hoped initially to avoid the term 'supernatural,' because of its all too frequent dualistic connotation. However, I have found it impossible to do so. Be it understood, therefore, that in my usage the prefix 'super' means 'more than ordinarily' natural rather than 'apart from' the natural.

Gods and goddesses. All peoples, including Christians, Jews, and Muslims, recognize a wide variety of unseen powers, but the terms 'god' and 'goddess' are applied only to some of them. Others, in the Abrahamic religions, are variously called archangels, angels, spirits, saints, *awlia,* and demons. Western theologians, in an exercise of word-play, have worked out the fine distinctions between these various types of beings—but what about the case of the non-Abrahamic religions? Most of them also recognize a horde of powers, great and small, which go by a prodigious variety of individual and collective names. We have, often quite arbitrarily, applied the terms 'god' and 'goddess' to some of them, while calling others 'spirits,' 'ghosts,' etc. But there is often no real dividing line separating the various categories of beings. Indeed, some of them can 'morph' very readily into a wide variety of forms, as the Greek Zeus was able to do.

Gladys Reichard faced the problem of nomenclature when she attempted to sort out the Navajo pantheon, through an analysis of recorded and unrecorded mythology. Avoiding the terms 'god' and 'goddess,' she ended up classifying the various personae as deities, helpers, intermediaries, dangers conceived as deities, and monsters, while at the same time acknowledging that the scheme and the nomenclature were her own, and that the categorical boundaries were very imprecise (Reichard 1963: 63–79). It was no use asking a Navajo singer (religious practitioner) for guidance, for any singer would say: 'All we know is what the myths tell us, and you can interpret them in your own way.'

The anthropologist clearly needs a single term to encompass all the different kinds of powers that be, rather than trying to place them in a hierarchy or in distinct theonomic categories. In the case of Protestant Christianity it would have to embrace, at a minimum, the Trinity, the Virgin, the archangels, the angels, and the Devil. To Catholics the list would be considerably longer. Throughout this book I will refer to them sometimes as supernaturals, and sometimes simply as Powers, Sentient Powers, or Beings. I will capitalize these latter terms whenever necessary to make it clear that I am using them in a special sense. (I will also capitalize God when it is used as a proper rather than a common noun; that is, when it serves as the name of a single deity, in the Abrahamic religions. This usage is necessary for clarity; it should not be interpreted as an indication of a greater respect for this deity than for others.)

Pantheon. The same problem applies here as in the case of gods and goddesses. That is, the term is usually applied to some but not all of the powers, as was the case in Greece, where the term originated. There is usually an assumption of hierarchy, with the 'higher' powers being included within the pantheon and the 'lower' ones excluded. But, as I have already suggested, the powers that many peoples believe in cannot be arranged in a hierarchy; there is simply a continuum of diminishing power from top to bottom of the group. To the extent that I am forced to use the term pantheon in this book, it will refer to all of the powers from the Sun God to the lowliest demon.

Monotheism. This term is misleading if it is taken to mean that all supernatural power is embodied in one single being. So far as I know, there is no religion in the world that fits that category. All three of the Abrahamic religions have a place for the Devil and for the angels; in Roman Catholic usage the Virgin is quite clearly a separate deity, as is the Archangel Michael in Eastern Orthodox belief. Monotheism becomes a meaningful term only if we apply it to belief systems in which there is a single supreme, creator deity, who is the original source of all the powers enjoyed by the other beings. When I use the term in this book, it will simply apply to religions that call themselves monotheistic.

Ghosts and spirits. A great many peoples recognize the existence of beings who were once ordinary mortals, but who after death became supernaturals, while continuing to act within the human realm. Often they are malevolent, in which case we call them ghosts, but they can also be benevolent, in which case we call them ancestral spirits. There are also beings who have an equal capacity for both, whom we usually call simply spirits.

Holy, sacred, divine. These are among the most affectively loaded words in our religious lexicon. Within the dualistic tradition of Abrahamic thought, they refer only to an indwelling charisma possessed by good Powers, and to persons, things, and acts associated with them. The charismatic quality of evil Powers we call unholy, meaning not merely non-holy but anti-holy. But, as I will suggest later, most peoples outside the Abrahamic realm do not have a dualistic tradition, and many of their Powers are equally capable of good and bad deeds. As a consequence, we as outsiders do not usually apply to them the terms 'holy,' 'sacred,' or 'divine.' Many of the Navajo Powers have indeed been designated by anthropologists as Holy People, but this is simply the best translation we could come up with for the Navajo term, *Dighinii,* which really has no English equivalent. It simply refers to the special power possessed by these beings, which may be used equally for good or for harm.

Myths and mythology. When anthropologists say that religion consists basically of myth and ritual, they mean only that it has always a cognitive and a behavioral dimension. Used in that sense, 'myth' and 'mythology' refer to all the different forms of religious knowledge and beliefs. But 'myth,' even when stripped of its all too common negative connotation, usually refers only to those areas of religious cognition that are formally codified, in scripture or in recitation or in song. There are at the same time large areas of religious cognition that are simply shared folk wisdom, never formally codified, and sometimes spoken of only in whispers. Most Navajo beliefs about ghosts and witches fall into this category, as do the ideas that many European peasants have about the differing powers of different saints, or of different manifestations of the Virgin (cf. Christian 1972). These beliefs are sufficiently powerful so that they give rise to a great deal of overt behavior—avoidance of certain places or things, pilgrimages to specific shrines, and the like—yet they don't rise to the level of formal mythology.

A further difficulty arises from the fact that not all myths are religious, or wholly so. The versions of our national history that are taught in the early school grades, and hero tales about great explorers or sports figures, are examples of purely secular myths. Even those myths that we identify as specifically religious, like many of the books of the Bible, often have a good deal of verifiable history interwoven with their accounts of marvels and miracles. Again we lack, and need, a generalized term to encompass all the different kinds of religious knowledge and belief, including those that are vulgarly called superstition. In this book I will have to speak, when necessary, simply of religious cognition.

Faith. Used in its partitive sense, *a* faith is usually a synonym for a religion, irrespective of the kinds or degrees of belief required of the votaries. In its generic sense, faith refers to a particular kind, or I should say a particular intensity of belief: an unshakable belief that does not rest on empirical evidence, and cannot be undermined by empirical evidence. The term undoubtedly has some utility in the psychological and perhaps in the philosophical study of religion, but it is not very useful to the anthropologist, because it is really pretty much an individual matter. Within every society, people vary not only in the degree of their religious faith, but in what they have faith in. Most American Christians have strong faith in the existence of an afterlife, but much less faith in the necessity of going to church in order to get there.

Ritual. What was said about myths applies equally to the term 'ritual,' which anthropologists sometimes use to designate any kind of religion-inspired behavior. In lay parlance however it usually refers to a formally specified and a repeatable performance. But a great deal of religiously inspired behavior consists of impromptu actions, and much of it also consists not of acts but of avoidances. The Navajos' refusal to touch anything that has been struck by lightning is certainly based on religious belief, but most people would not think of such avoidance as a ritual.

As in the case of mythology, so also there are many purely lay rituals. Even great religious rituals, like the Navajo 'sing' and the Arab villagers' *mulid* (birthday of the saint) are often at the same time great lay festivals. Once again, we need a more general term for all forms of religion-inspired behavior. I will refer to them when necessary simply as religious activity.

Worship. This term has both affective and behavioral connotations. It may refer to feelings of veneration, whether or not accompanied by any overt acts, but it may also refer to acts of propitiation, whether or not accompanied by any special feelings. As examples of the latter sort, I have witnessed French villagers mechanically repeating 'Hail Marys' while their minds were a thousand miles away, and I have seen Tibetan monks absent-mindedly spinning prayer wheels as they walked by , without bothering to look at them. These are, in the broadest sense, acts of worship but hardly of veneration. We really need different terms to refer on the one hand to veneration, and on the other hand to actions, of the kind that were once called 'devotions.'

Prayer. We tend to use this term to designate any words that are addressed to the Powers. From that broad perspective it is safe to say that prayer is a human universal. There are many ways of communicating with the deities, but the use of language is surely the most common of them. But the term 'prayer' covers such an enormous variety of verbal performances as to have little analytical utility. Christians nearly always think of it as involving an element of supplication, but the so-called prayers that are performed five times a day by devout Muslims have no such component. They are paeans of praise; essentially a kind of psalm. The formulaic prayers recited by many Southwestern Indians are, like Christian prayers, meant to elicit divine action, but it is not so much by supplication as by compulsion. If the verbal formulas are correctly recited, the Powers have no alternative but to act in expectable ways (cf. Reichard 1944).

Sacrifice. This term in popular parlance always carries a notion of self-denial, as when we give something costly away, or abstain from some form of pleasure. Yet we find the term applied also to offerings to the Powers which really involve no self-denial on our part. The term is regularly used when animal food is offered to the Powers ('blood sacrifice'), but not when plant food is offered. Used in that sense, 'sacrifice' simply means ritual killing. Bio-medical researchers routinely use the term when an animal is killed in the course of experimentation, an action that obviously involves no self-denial. In the case of religion, we should really distinguish between what are basically acts of generosity, and what are basically acts of self-denial.

Shrine. Some places are special because Powers actually dwell in them, while others are special simply because they are advantageous places from which to address the Powers; we use the term 'shrine' to designate both. The common denominator is that they are places that are beneficial to visit, i.e., usually, places of pilgrimage. In either case, the term carries very much a connotation of individual benefit. Churches, mosques, and temples, the sites of regular communal worship, are usually not designated as shrines, though there may be shrines within them. One goes to the church, mosque, or temple as a member of a community or congregation, to participate in collective acts of devotion; one goes to a shrine as an individual, to seek individual benefit. We usually think of a shrine as a place where something has been erected, but this is not a universal or necessary feature. 'Holy places' visited by members of tribal societies are often referred to in our literature as shrines, even through they may be no more than natural outcrops or caves.

Idol, icon, fetish. These terms are used to describe material things that become foci of supernatural power. They are often thought by outsiders to possess an indwelling power, but that is usually incorrect. They serve to attract and focus power from some external source, in the same way that a magnifying glass attracts and focuses the light and heat from the sun. But the trouble with all these terms, as in the case also of 'myth' and 'ritual,' is that they too often suggest something that other peoples believe in but we don't. An image of the Buddha is an idol, but an image of Christ is not; a Navaho prayer-stick is a fetish, but a hand-held crucifix is not. To avoid such pejorative connotations, I will generally have to refer to such paraphernalia simply as religious objects.

Magic, sorcery, witchcraft. There has been continuing debate as to whether these beliefs and practices should be placed in the category of religion, in the category of science, in both, or in neither. But the terms tend to be used so loosely that there is no simple answer to the question. I will here use 'magic' to designate a body of specific practices which are, if you like, the technology of sorcery and witchcraft. That is, they stand in relation to sorcery and witchcraft as ritual does to religion. But the question of whether or not sorcery and witchcraft should be classed as religious phenomena I will defer until a later chapter.

Judaeo-Christian. This term is satisfactory and unambiguous as far as it goes, but it fails to include the third major religion that proceeds from the same source: that of Islam. Almost all generalizations that can be made about Judaism and Christianity apply also to Islam, and for that reason I need a term to encompass all three. I will use the term 'Abrahamic' religions, which I have borrowed from the *Encyclopedia of Religion.*

The analytical terms devised by anthropologists have helped to bring a degree of clarity to the discourse on religion, but they are not without ambiguities and misconceptions of their own. Two, in particular, have come to be used so widely and uncritically, by both anthropologists and non-anthropologists, that they have lost much of their value.

*Anthropo-
logical
terms*

Animism. This term was originally coined by E. B. Tylor in the 1870s, to describe the belief that there is an indwelling spirit, endowed with supernatural power, in all living things. Tylor believed that this represented the primordial form of religion, because the earliest humans could not conceive of powers beyond the immediately experienced world. Such a belief is indeed widespread among tribal peoples, and to that extent the term is a useful one. The problem lies in the fact that it has become in the minds of evolutionists a rigid evolutionary stage—a type concept applied to all primitive religions. For example, we often hear the tribal religions of the southern Sudan described in the press as 'animistic,' simply because they are neither Christian nor Muslim, whereas animism actually plays only a small part in these religions. In reality, animism is present to varying degrees in a great many religions; it is not the sole component of any.

Totemism. This term, of Algonquian Indian origin, refers to the mystical association between an extended kin group (lineage, clan, or tribe) and particular species of animals or plants, or sometimes other natural phenomena such as geological forms, which are worshipped and propitiated as the ancestors and guardian deities of the group. Although the term is found in ethnographic literature dating back to the early nineteenth century, it did not become an important organizing concept for anthropologists until nearly the end of the century, when the first ethnographic studies of the native Australians were published. It then appeared that totemism was the central focus of Australian religion, and, because anthropologists had (mistakenly) jumped to the conclusion that Australians were the most primitive of living peoples, they jumped also to the conclusion that totemism was one of the defining features of the earliest religions. It was a logically convenient assumption because it provided a link, hitherto missing, between religion and kinship institutions—the other major preoccupation of the early anthropologists. On the basis of that assumption Frazer, Freud, and Durkheim all published books on religious evolution taking totemism as the starting point, and their error can still be found today in much semi-popular writing about religion.

The early anthropologists were wrong on two counts. First, the Australian aborigines are not by any means the most primitive of peoples; their social institutions are far more advanced and complex than are those of many peoples dwelling in high latitudes or in dense tropical forests. Second, totemism is not at all a prevalent feature in the religions of those simplest societies, which are mostly lacking in widely ramified kin groups. It is found primarily among peoples who have arrived at the tribal or chiefdom level of social organization, not those who remain at the band level. This issue that will be further pursued in Chapter 14.

While I have sought to identify the serious problem of terminology that confronts all students of religion, it is not my desire to propose a new and more precise lexicon, for general use. Neologisms and unfamiliar conceptual terms are apt to wave a red flag for many readers, as they do often enough for me. At the same time I don't want to use terms that have unintended popular connotations. The following is a glossary of the terms (all those either in boldface or in italics) that I will mostly employ, in the attempt to avoid both neologisms and terms with extraneous connotations.

Supernaturals (n). All the different kinds of sentient powers that are at work in the universe, and that can do things that ordinary mortals can't. I will also refer to them at times as *Powers*, *Sentient Powers*, and *Beings*; the three terms should be read as synonymous. I will develop later the distinction between sentient powers and non-sentient powers, which are not supernaturals. I will call them *Forces*.

Supernatural (adj). The special quality possessed by supernaturals that sets them apart from ourselves. It consists chiefly though not exclusively of *Power.* It may be transmitted by supernatural beings to persons, places, and things that are not in themselves supernatural, and they may possess it in varying degrees.

Religious cognition. The whole body of shared knowledge and belief about supernaturals, including both formally codified knowledge (*Myth*) and uncodified common wisdom.

Religious action. The whole body of acts prompted by religions belief, including formally specified acts (*Ritual*) as well as impromptu acts and avoidances.

Religious sentiment. The whole body of feelings evoked by religion, including but not limited to feelings of exaltation, of veneration, of fear, and of revulsion.

Religious places. All places that have a special, religious significance, either because power is focused in them or because they are advantageous for addressing the Powers. They may be either places to visit or places to avoid, depending on the kind of power associated with them.

Religious objects. Material things in which power may be focused, or through which it may be addressed.

Abrahamic religion. A blanket term for Judaism, Christianity, and Islam.

Practical religion. Those religious practices, and the associated beliefs, that are devoted to the attainment of immediate, practical ends.

7

CLEARING THE AIR

Just about everyone was reared within the context of one religion or another, which has shaped his or her conception of what religion is and isn't. Usually also it has imbued the person with strong feelings, both positive and negative, for the ability to generate passions is one of the conspicuous features of religion. In this chapter I hope to dispel some misconceptions that are common among followers of the Abrahamic religions (i.e. most Americans, Europeans, and Near Easterners), but also some misconceptions that are found among scientists.

I have suggested in foregoing pages that much popular thinking about religion is colored, and sometimes discolored, by the Abrahamic and Mosaic traditions in which most of us were reared. The three Abrahamic religions of Judaism, Christianity, and Islam share in common a number of very powerful and very distinctive features, which their votaries are apt to assume are common to other religions as well. I will consider a number of those features here, and will suggest that none of them are by any means universal.

The legacy of Abraham and Moses

Early Judaism, the forerunner of all the Abrahamic religions, was not really monotheistic, nor was any other religion of the same era, as far as I know. When Yahweh said to Moses, 'Thou shalt have no other gods before me,' he did not say, or mean to imply, that he was the only god extant. If he had meant that he would have said so, for in those days he was nothing if not plain-spoken. But his meaning is made perfectly clear by his next words: 'for I the Lord thy God am *a* jealous god ...' Obviously, he could not be jealous if there were no one to be jealous of. He was merely reminding the Jews that they had signed an exclusive contract with him, and henceforth must take their business nowhere else. He was not condemning all the rest of mankind to a state of perpetual

Exclusivity

godlessness. It was probably not until the Babylonian captivity, centuries later, that Judaism became genuinely monotheistic, and the gods of all other peoples were declared to be false.

Notwithstanding, the exclusivity enjoined by Yahweh has been a feature of all the Abrahamic religions from the time of Moses to the present. Whether or not the existence of other religions is acknowledged, or tolerated, the injunction is: '*You* shall have one and only one religion, and *you* shall worship one and only one god.' Clearly implied also is the feature of renunciation: you shall renounce whatever other gods you may have been worshipping, and any beliefs and practices associated with that worship. In short, the Abrahamic religions are *closed systems.* This very salient feature of all three of them has led many persons to assume that exclusivity is an essential feature of religions in general.

Nothing could be farther from the truth. Nearly all polytheistic religions (which is to say the great majority of the world's religions) have grown by accretion, with the continual addition of new gods and goddesses, and there has never been a suggestion that when you begin to believe in one you may no longer believe in another. Most religions in other words are *open systems,* ready to accept anything that seems believable, or efficacious, and demanding nothing in the way of renunciation. It is up to each individual to decide how many different things he or she can believe in at the same time.

Some years ago, in developing this point for a non-scholarly audience, I devised the following imaginary dialogue with a traditional Navajo:

Outsider: 'What is your religion?'

Navajo (after a long, puzzled pause): 'I guess I'm a Navajo.'

Outsider: 'But what do you believe in?'

Navajo: 'Why, everything that exists, of course—the rocks, the trees, the animals, the earth surface people, and the Holy People.'

Outsider: 'What gods do you specifically believe in?'

Navajo: 'All of them.'

Outsider: 'Including the gods of the Hopis and Utes?'

Navajo: 'Sure. I don't know anything about them, because they don't do anything for Navajos, but why would anybody talk about them if they didn't exist?'

Outsider: 'What about the Christian god?'

Navajo: 'Same thing. Your people are always talking about him, so of course he must exist. I don't know whether he does anything for Navajos or not; different people have different ideas about that. Maybe he helps some people and not others, like some of the Navajo gods do. So far, I'm getting along OK without his help.'

The idea that the sacred and the profane (read: supernatural and natural) are separate and distinct realms is clearly expressed in Judaeo-Christian and Islamic theology, and it continues to resonate even in the work of many anthropologists. It was strongly emphasized by the great Emile Durkheim (cf. 1915: 37), who made it one of the bases of his definition of religion. But, as I have already suggested, many peoples do not differentiate between the supernatural and natural realms; on the contrary the supernaturals *are* nature. Moreover, insofar as the supernatural is defined by the possession of special power, that power is possessed in highly varying degrees by different beings and persons. There are, in that sense, many different degrees of 'supernaturalness.'

The dualism of sacred and profane

There are two recurrent, but fundamentally opposed, currents that run through all Western thinking about the nature of man. One view holds that he is naturally evil, or at least brutish, and is saved from his own bestiality by the social and cultural institutions of his own making. It is a subtext that is evident in nearly all of sociology (except rural sociology), in which society is venerated as the institution that has brought us up from savagery, and the city is seen as its highest expression. The opposite notion, dear to the hearts of New Agers but also of many primitivist anthropologists, is that man in the pristine state was fundamentally good, but has been corrupted by the institutions of his own civilization. I say 'civilization' rather than 'culture' because the city, above all, is abominated as man's most ignoble creation. Both conceptions can be traced back to remote antiquity: the progressivist view to the Platonians, and the primitivist view to the Stoics.

The dualism of good and evil

Both perceptions are contained also in the Book of Genesis, although grace and damnation are of course attributed to supernatural forces rather than to man's own efforts. Man before the Fall was pure and good, as conceived by the primitivists; since then he has been fundamentally sinful.

At least within the Abrahamic tradition there seems to be no middle ground; no room for a conception of both men and gods as exhibiting equal capacities for good and bad deeds. Thus, all of the Abrahamic religions make a clear distinction between Good and Evil, and attribute the two to the activity of different deities, or powers: a good god and a bad devil or devils. Yet this was not an original feature of Judaism: the original Yahweh was an absolute power above considerations of right and wrong, and capable of considerable cruelty and vengefulness. Judaeo-Christian and Islamic dualism probably reflects a latter-day influence from Zoroastrianism, though that in turn may derive from a still older Indo-Iranian tradition.

Again, most religions do not have a dualistic tradition. The gods and goddesses of non-Western peoples are much more nearly human in their characteristics; like the rest of us they are capable both of good and of bad deeds. They are simply powers-that-be, and as such are both potentially helpful and potentially dangerous. Even within the Abrahamic tradition, the common folk conception of Allah is of this nature, as I have already suggested in Chapter 3.

Sin, guilt,
and
atonement

The emphasis on guilt and atonement is the single most outstanding feature of Judaic religion. If religions are meant to evoke the feelings that we enjoy most, as many interpreters have suggested, it is hard to escape the conviction that the Jews enjoy suffering. The emphasis on guilt and atonement has come through into both Christianity and Islam, though not in quite so extreme a form, except in the case of certain Protestant sects. It has nevertheless led many scholars of religion, and especially those from a Judaic background, to assume that this is an important feature of other religions as well.

Certainly, all religions have very clearcut ideas about transgression, and what to do about it. Someone has knowingly or unknowingly upset the supernatural order, in a recognizable way, and something must be done to set things right. However, this can rarely be equated with the Abrahamic conception of sin, which always involves evil intentions for which the actor must feel guilty, and must atone. The Jewish or Christian sinner must punish himself or herself, to forestall punishment by God in the next world. But the Navajo transgressor has very often done so unknowingly, and does not realize he has transgressed until he is visited by punishment, in the form of illness or bad luck. The punishment itself must be alleviated, by appropriate mollification of the offended Powers, but no atonement on the part of the transgressor is required, or expected. The offender, having suffered the consequences of his acts, feels regretful rather than guilty. The Navajo deities are not offended by the mere presence of evil capacities in humans, because they have all the same capacities themselves.

Salvationism, with its emphasis on preparing for a life to come, has been *Salvationism*
a very powerful current in Western religious thought, and it is at least
nominally the central concern in all of the Abrahamic religions. It is not
however a very ancient idea. It seems to have originated in India, and
from there to have spread westward through Iran and into the Mediterranean world, mostly in the last centuries BC and the first centuries AD.
It diffused through the Graeco-Roman world with almost revolutionary
force, giving rise to Mithraism, Isis-worship, the Eleusinian mysteries,
and a host of other salvationist cults, including Christianity. Meanwhile
Buddhism, a different form of salvationism, spread eastward from India
through the whole eastern part of the Asian continent. The essential consequence of all these cults was the personalization of religion, which had
formerly been much more a communal affair. But salvation is achieved
only by one and by one; you can't take another person with you into the
hereafter.

Probably the single most persistent ethnocentric misconception among
Westerners is the notion that all religions are similarly concerned with
the afterlife. It is true that all peoples (though not necessarily all individuals) seem to have some kind of belief in a life after death. Often enough
however it is a rather vague one; a kind of pervasive folk belief that is
not supported by any explicit mythology. This was pretty much the case
for the early Greeks, as it is also for Navajos. The afterlife, being a realm
of uncertainty, is something they would rather not think or talk about.

In any case, for most peoples the afterlife is not something that you
can prepare for, except perhaps by having various goods buried alongside
you that you'll need in the next world. But it is not a place of rewards
and punishments. The Powers are much too impatient, and too immediately involved in the human sphere, to wait until you die before meting
out their rewards and punishments. You propitiate them for the sake of
what they will or won't do this week, next week, or next year; not in
another life that is too distant to worry about. Indeed I will suggest, in
later pages, that the ideas many peoples have about the afterlife should
not really be considered as religious beliefs, because the supernaturals
are not involved.

The missionary spirit is a quintessential feature of American Protes- *Evangelism*
tantism. The various sects not only send forth missionaries to convert the
heathen; they also seek actively to recall their own strayed parishioners
to the fold, and even to entice converts away from rival denominations.
In one sense or another, they are always in search of converts.

The evangelical zeal of American churches is not unconnected with the well-known American penchant for aggressive marketing—a feature of our national character. European visitors often find it surprising, and a trifle offensive. By contrast, Americans traveling abroad may be surprised to find that the European churches—especially the established churches—are much less fired with evangelical zeal. Like physicians, the European pastors or priests are apt to feel that those who want or need their services will come to them.

The practice of evangelism requires both self-confidence and self-righteousness—two other common American traits. The evangelist must have an unshakable belief in the rightness of his own beliefs and practices, and also a belief that converting other people to the same beliefs and practices will be beneficial either to him or to them. Persons of many faiths have held those convictions, and they are characteristic of all messiahs. They are nevertheless less common in other countries than in America, and they are uncommon outside the Abrahamic realm. Most people in most religions are relatively humble in their religiosity. Even their most learned religious practitioners are all too aware of the limitations of their religious knowledge, and of their capacity to influence the gods. There is so much out there that they can't really understand, so much that they can't predict, so much that they can't control. There is in other words a degree of uncertainty in their religiosity, and the last thing they feel inclined to do is try to impose their views upon others.

The salience of the church

Christians, and in particular Americans, often think of religion in terms of church membership. Thus conceived, religiosity becomes a matter not so much of believing, or even of behaving, as it is of belonging. Obviously, however, such a conception is relevant only in societies where there are rival sects at work. In most tribal societies, and for that matter even in orthodox Islam, there are no organized bodies of worshippers—no institution comparable to a church. Religiosity is measured by acts of personal devotion rather than by membership in a sectarian group.

Secular and scientific ethnocentrisms

Understanding of religion may be clouded by secular as well as by religious enthnocentrisms. There is to begin with a generalized Western ethnocentrism, resulting from the conviction that our own particular logic corresponds to immutable truth. There are also more specific ethnocentrisms, when we assume that everybody else is just like us—ignoring the fact that we ourselves don't remain the same from generation to generation.

All Western scientific thought is rationalistic; it is probably the single unifying feature common to all the sciences. There is an assumption of uniformity of cause and effect, at all times and places, and an assumption that every effect is explainable in terms of some cause or causes. This is established scientific truth, within the canons of science, and has been subjected to repeated empirical verification. But there is also a common assumption of linearity and directionality: if something has been going in the same direction for an observable length of time, it is our automatic assumption that it will continue to do so, because there must be a reason for it. Almost all our evolutionary theories involve such an assumption. It is not established scientific truth; it rests on specifically Western logic, which not all peoples share. Traditional (East) Indians, for example, take circularity as much for granted as we take linearity. Both are viewed as laws of nature, respectively in India and in the West.

Generalized Western eth- nocentrism

Progressivism. Both scientific agnostics and many true believers share the belief that today's monotheistic religions are the outcome of a linear developmental process, which the agnostics call evolution and the believers call enlightenment. There is disagreement as to where we'll go from here, but both scientists and believers take it for granted that we won't go 'backward;' that is, we won't revert to polytheism, animal worship, or whatever. I'm not sure in my own mind that this is an entirely safe assumption. But progressivism in any case may distort our understanding of other people's religions, insofar as it causes us to think of them as more or less 'advanced,' relative either to modern monotheism or to atheism.

The legacy of atheism. Atheism is a logical outgrowth of Western progressivism. If we can recognize, over time, a continual reduction of the pantheon until it is all collapsed into a single deity, and also a continual reduction of the religious 'sphere of influence,' it becomes possible to envision an ultimate vanishing point for both. It was something that many of the rationalist philosophers of the Enlightenment devoutly hoped for.

It is no wonder then that atheism as an organized body of thought, rather than an expression of personal dissent, is almost wholly a Western phenomenon. It springs fairly easily and logically from Abrahamic monotheism because there is only one god to deny, instead of a host of them. It has been spread over much of the world as an official doctrine of Communism, but Communism itself is quintessentially Western in its origins, and thoroughly ethnocentric.

As Evans-Pritchard has reminded us, the comparative study of religions was actually born out of atheism. That is, it was a deliberate effort on the part of Enlightenment rationalists to make the Abrahamic religions look ridiculous, by showing how much they shared with the religions of painted savages. 'They sought, and found, in primitive religions a weapon which could, they thought, be used with deadly effect against Christianity. If primitive religion could be explained away as an intellectual aberration, as a mirage induced by emotional stress, or by its social function, it was implied that the higher religions could be discredited and disposed of in the same way.' (Evans-Pritchard 1965: 15). This outlook is still clearly detectable in the work of some of the early, armchair ethnologists, like Frazer.

Present-day anthropologists, who have left their armchairs to experience the non-western world and its religions at first hand, are generally much less negative in their feelings. In the best tradition of relativism, they hope as I do to bring an equal appreciation to all religions. Nevertheless, aspects of the older tradition of invidious comparison can still often be found in their work, as a kind of unintended subtext. That is, they are inclined to make gratuitous comparisons between the religion they study and Christianity or Judaism, with an implied preference for the former. Their intention is no longer to discredit all religion, but there is still at least an implied discrediting of the Abrahamic religions, from which the anthropologists are often dropouts.

Scientific ethnocentrisms

There are, I have observed, two kinds, or levels, of ethnocentrism. There is the intolerant ethnocentrism of the first- (and probably last-) time tourist who says, 'Ugh—these dirty foreigners. The go around half-naked, they eat nasty foods, and they have no manners at all.' That was the attitude succinctly expressed by the missionary who, when asked to fill out a questionnaire about native customs, wrote 'Manners: none; Customs: beastly.' But then there is the more subtle and self-delusive 'tolerant ethnocentrism' that comes from a fuller but still incomplete acquaintance, and that says: 'Gee—when you get to know them, they're really just like us.'

As someone with extensive cross-cultural experience, and a command of several languages, I'm here to testify that when you *really* get to know them they're not at all just like us; at least not in the way they think. Navajos, who are quintessentially literal-minded, insist that the thought, the word, and the deed must exactly coincide; otherwise one or other of them must be wrong. For traditional Arabs the thought, the word, and the deed exist on separate planes of reality, each obedient to its own rules of understood usage. There are many situations in which the word and the deed cannot and should not coincide. The thought is your own; the word is what you want other people to hear, or what they want to hear; the deed is what circumstances compel you to do. For traditional Chinese word and deed can never totally coincide, because all words and all deeds are subject to multiple interpretations. If a Navajo says he is coming at 12:00, and comes at 12:15, he has broken his promise, regardless of extenuating circumstances. If an Arab villager says he is coming at 12:00 and shows up at 2:00, he has kept his promise, because he honestly meant to come at noon. A traditional Chinese has kept his promise in some respects and broken it in others.

In spite of our best efforts at objectivity, a great deal of 'tolerant ethnocentrism' finds its way into modern social science, which consciously or unconsciously takes our own cultural interests and values as the measure of human nature. If in religion we often find that man makes god in his own image, modeling the celestial order on the social order of the time, something similar occurs in history and in the social sciences. Each age assumes that people in other times and places have been 'really' just like themselves. This propensity is illustrated by three recent movements in anthropology.

Materialism. Ours is a highly materialistic, self-indulgent, and this-worldly age, so the materialist assumes that under the surface everyone else is really like that too, and always has been. Just like many Americans, they suppose, other peoples aren't *really* religious; at least not to the extent that it might be detrimental to their material welfare or survival, as we perceive them. But those other peoples might have very different conceptions of welfare and survival than we do; they may be thinking about welfare in a future life rather than in this one.

An evident deficiency of all materialist theory is its emphasis on practical religion—those practices and beliefs intended to obtain specific ends—as the most salient feature of all religions. As I have suggested before, this is really something variable from one religion to another. It is more true in Navajo than in Arab village religion, and it is much more true in both of them than it is in scriptural Islam or Christianity.

Most forms of materialist theory involve harshly inflexible ideas about survival and extinction, which remind me of Judaeo-Christian ideas about salvation and damnation. Extinction, according to materialists, hangs like a sword of Damocles over the head of any species and any society that does not adapt itself to *our* environment according to *our* rules of logic, as they prevail at the moment. I think the materialists vastly underestimate the human capacity for survival under all kinds of circumstances which, according to materialist theory, should lead to extinction.

Deconstructionism. If we believe that other people are just like us, this necessarily means that when we change, as we do every generation or two, our ideas about other peoples change also. In this connection, today's deconstructionists exhibit the same basic ethnocentrism as do the materialists whom they oppose. It is however ethnocentrism in a new and more purely egocentric guise, reflective of today's chaotic and self-preoccupied age. Deconstructionism is, as its name implies, an anarchic doctrine for an anarchic age. We are living in a time of kaleidoscopic change, when nations and societies and cultures are visibly disintegrating. Old social and cultural traditions, unless enforced by legislation, have diminished compulsive value, since they no longer seem adaptive to the world as we now know it. Individuals in a great many circumstance have to make their own, existential decisions without relying on tradition.

Therefore, suggest the deconstructionists, it has really always been like that; we just couldn't see it through our rose-colored glasses. Culture per se never had any real compelling force; it was something that individuals followed, manipulated, or disregarded as self-interest dictated. Many of today's anthropologists seem unable to conceive that anyone could act other than in self-interest, unless forcibly compelled.

One difficulty with that perspective lies in its assumption that everybody is thinking, and calculating the odds, all the time. It may be unavoidable in our own turbulent world, but it certainly hasn't always been like that, nor is it for many peoples today. Most people most of the time would rather not make existential decisions if they can avoid it; they would rather follow fixed rules that most of their fellows agree on, and in which there is safety. Therein lies the compelling strength of culture, including religion. For traditional Navajos whom I knew, culture and especially religion provided their only map of the very dangerous world in which they lived, and as such it had a very compelling force indeed. A traditional Navajo was always navigating a minefield of supernatural dangers, and no sane person navigates a minefield without a map, as long as one is available.

Psychofunctionalism. This approach to the explanation of religion, popular among psychologists as well as many anthropologists, involves a special, reductionist kind of ethnocentrism. For modern Europeans and Americans, most of the formerly large cognitive domain of religion has been pre-empted by science, to which people now turn for the explanation of natural phenomena. Similarly, most of the formerly large social domain has been pre-empted by the purely secular institutions of the modern state. The affective domain—the realm of feelings—remains as the main aspect of religion that has not been heavily undermined by secularization, and that is still fairly robust. This has led a great many even of our most advanced thinkers to assume, incorrectly, that the affective is the most important functional domain in all religions. The various psychofunctional approaches to religion, to the extent that they are reductionist, all rest on that assumption. In fact, the importance of the psychological domain, which is essentially the personal domain of religion, varies enormously in importance from one person to another, and from one society to another. This issue will be pursued further in Chapter 11.

From the open-systems perspective of the polytheist, there are not necessarily any false religions or false gods. There is no need for a category of 'superstition.' In that respect, adherence to one of the polytheistic religions should generate an appreciation and understanding of religion in general. Within the closed-system context of Abrahamic monotheism, the opposite may be true. The fundamentalist Jew or Christian or Muslim is apt to believe that he understands religion because he is religious himself, when in fact his conception of what is and isn't religion is wholly defined by the boundaries of his own faith, with everything outside being consigned to the realm of 'superstition.' Conceptually, it is only a short step from that kind of monotheism to atheism. The atheist is convinced that all of the world's myriad religions are false; the rigid monotheist in convinced that all but one of them are false.

Clearly the seeker after a genuine, cross-cultural understanding of religion cannot begin with apriori assumptions about truth and falsity. He can only adopt a relativistic, utilitarian perspective, in respect to which questions of truth and falsity are irrelevant. Religion, as all its students agree, exists because it serves human needs, and it can therefore be judged only by its utility to those needs.

This does not mean however that there is no basis for judgment. The egalitarian notion that all societies are equally well served by their cultures was dear to the hearts of an earlier generation of anthropologists, but it was a doctrine for a stable world. We live today in a notoriously unstable one, and, because there is a considerable inertia in all religions, they may and often do become maladaptive—not only as seen by us but as seen by their own adherents. We are therefore legitimately entitled to ask how effectively any religion is serving the needs of their adherents, just as the adherents themselves do.

8

THE PROBLEM OF DEFINITION

The enormous differences between the Navajo and Arab village religions should make sufficiently clear the problem of defining religion in the abstract. It is certainly not, among most peoples, a self-defining category. Ethnographers have noted repeatedly that there is no word, among the peoples they study, that can be translated as 'religion.' They could observe with equal legitimacy, however, that there is also no word for 'art,' no word for 'economy,' or for most of the other analytical categories into which we subdivide culture. Most peoples think of their cultures, consciously or unconsciously, as seamless wholes, and do not analyze them into discrete 'systems.' Yet our logical and analytical minds demand that we do so, for most of us cannot achieve understanding in any other way.

The anthropologist's dilemma

Here we encounter a fundamental paradox. We, or at least many of us, strive to *understand* each religion in an emic sense; that is, we try to see the world of the gods and the other powers through the eyes of those we study. Yet we can only *define* it in an etic sense, in terms of our own, peculiarly Western, analytical categories. We have to do this to make it intelligible to ourselves, by finding analogs in our own experience. Someone has correctly remarked that the fundamental process involved in ethnology is that of reasoning by analogy, or in other words translation. But the problem, in the case of religion, has proved extraordinarily difficult, partly because we have never finally decided what is and is not religion even among ourselves.

The problem faced by the anthropologist is unique in this respect, at least among social scientists. We are alone in our attempt to understand religion as a human universal, and therefore to fit all of the world's myriad religions within one single frame of understanding based not on logic or theory, but on actual field observation and participation. Our approach, if not wholly empirical, is at least more so than is that of sociologists, psychologists, political scientists, and historians of religion. It has required us, at the outset, to decide what was and wasn't religion among the peoples we studied—an enterprise in which we usually got no help from the peoples themselves. The problem of defining religion has been addressed in many disciplines, but for anthropologists alone it has been of practical as well as theoretical concern. It has therefore received proportionately more attention from anthropologists than from others.

And yet—we find in the end that religion really cannot be defined empirically; that is, by any specifiable content. There is nothing within religion—neither myth nor ritual nor affective feelings—that does not exist outside it as well. Not only are there purely secular myths and rituals, but a great deal that we identify as religious mythology and ritual has plenty of secular content as well. The reverse is also true: there is little if anything outside religion that cannot also be found within it, in one society or another. In short, religion in practice has no clearly defined boundaries. This problem will be further pursued in the next chapter, and again in Chapter 13.

A misconception found in much anthropological literature is the tendency to separate out religion as one of the several discrete categories of culture, coordinate for example with technology and social organization. This can be seen very readily in the table of contents in many standard ethnographies, and even more conspicuously in elementary anthropology textbooks. There are successive chapters dealing with subsistence, technology, housing, social organization, political organization, and so on, with religion usually coming at or near the end. But such an analytical model is really relevant only as it applies to behavior. It really is possible, much of the time, to identify and to label discrete behaviors as religious.

Within the cognitive domain however no such partitioning is possible. Religion is not a bounded category like technology or social organization; it is a way of thought which overarches many and sometimes all of the different aspects of culture, giving meaning to the institutions and practices of farming, of cooking, of pottery making, of house building, of kinship and of art. Viewed from that perspective, *religion cannot be defined either by its boundaries or by its content, but only by its mode of thinking.* Insofar as it is a cultural category, its only counterpart is Science. This issue will form the theme of the next chapter.

The problem as seen by Melford Spiro

Many authors have acknowledged the difficulty of defining religion, but have attempted to do so nevertheless. Very few however have considered

in any detail why it is so difficult to define. One who has done so is
Melford Spiro (1966), and his ideas are worth considering here.

To begin with, Spiro points out that logicians recognize two kinds
of definitions, which they call nominal and 'real' (cf. Hempel 1952: 2–
14). Nominal definitions are those in which we define an unfamiliar term
purely in words; that is, by relating it to other words having familiar and
generally accepted meanings. But this kind of definition, if not impossible, is extremely difficult in the case of religion, because all of the words
to which we might relate it, like gods, myth, ritual, and the like are themselves ambiguous. Instead of arguing over the definition of religion itself,
we end up arguing over the definition of the words that we chose to define
it. Tylor's 'minimal definition' of 1874, 'belief in spiritual beings' (Tylor
1874: 424) provides a case in point. The statement, although incomplete,
is unarguable as far as it goes—but what are spiritual beings?

'Real definitions' are those that go beyond mere verbal labeling, and
attempt to make a statement about the thing defined that is verifiably
true, usually on the basis of empirical evidence. The trouble in the case
of religion, of course, is that you can't point to something and say 'this
is religion' unless you have already decided what religion is. As Spiro
observes, controversies over the definition of abstract concepts admit of
no empirical resolution (Spiro 1966: 86).

Spiro goes on to observe that some anthropologists have attempted to
sidestep the problem of rigorousness or inclusiveness by identifying the
'essential nature' (i.e. universal core) of religion, while leaving open the
question of where its boundaries lie. But all such attempts at definition
bring us into an area of variable human perception and judgment, because
there is clearly no general consensus on what is the 'essential nature' of
religion, or of most other things.

Spiro points out also that many attempted definitions of religion are
functional in nature, defining it by what it does. But these statements,
though often verifiably true, are characterizations and not definitions. It
is verifiably true that religion often serves as a foundation for social solidarity, and also that it may provide psychological comfort for individuals
in an uncertain world, but those things are not defining features of religion, for many other things besides religion perform the same functions.

Finally, and more problematically, Spiro contends that the anthropologist's insistence on universality is the bugaboo that makes definition
ultimately impossible. 'The insistence on universality in the interests of
a comparative social science is, in my opinion, an obstacle to the com-

parative method, for it leads to continuous changes in definition and, ultimately, to definitions which, because of their vagueness or abstractness, are all but useless. (And of course they commit the fallacy of assuming that certain institutions must, in fact, be universal, rather than recognizing that universality is a creation of definition)' (Spiro, 1966: 86–7). There is much food for thought in that statement, but I would point out nevertheless that usefulness is not the same thing as truth. I will try in the next chapter to develop a definition of religion that, however little practical utility it may have, really does satisfy the criterion of universality.

My view, in the meantime, is that Spiro has slightly missed the mark here. The problem is not to frame a definition of religion that will fit all cultures (something we can and should do) but to frame a definition that will embrace all the different kinds of 'non-rational' belief and behavior that have been identified as religious. Henri Bergson (quoted in Chapter 1) did not ask 'why do people believe,' he asked 'how can people believe *this stuff?*' It has been a standing joke among archaeologists for decades that any unidentifiable artifact becomes, in the catalogue, a 'ceremonial object,' but it is almost equally true among ethnologists that 'religion' is the residual category of the non-rational. Beliefs and behaviors are consigned to this category when we can find no practical explanation for them, according to our conceptions of practicality. Thus conceived, the defining characteristics of religious thought and action are purely negative. Our problem is to find a positive defining characteristic, or characteristics.

A review of definitions

While a great many students of religion have recognized the critical necessity of beginning with a definition, Spiro seems to be one of the few who has given any extended thought to the problem involved in definition. The definitions offered by most other scholars tend to be cursory, and often they do not provide an adequate foundation for the scholar's own discussion in the pages that follow. Most of them are more nearly descriptive than definitive; none of them achieve anything like rigor. Nearly all of them also are reductionist. The following is a review of definitions offered by some of the most outstanding students of religion.

E. B. Tylor, *Primitive Culture* (1874: 424): 'Belief in Spiritual Beings.' This is unarguable so far as it goes, but it is a very incomplete definition. Like so much of Tylor's writing, it focuses purely on belief (the cognitive domain of religion), leaving out altogether the domains of action and of affect. In other words it is a purely formal definition, without reference to the functions of religion. There is of course the further problem of defining 'spiritual beings,' mentioned earlier.

Emile Durkheim, *Elementary Forms of the Religious Life* (1915: 47): 'A unified system of beliefs and practices relative to sacred things, that is to say, things set apart and forbidden—beliefs and practices which unite, into one single moral community called a church, all those who adhere to them.' This statement shifts attention from the cognitive to the social aspect of religion. The second half in fact is a functional characterization rather than a definition, and it succinctly captures the whole Durkheimian theory of the sociology of religion. It is a powerful insight, and one that continues to resonate in social science today, but it does not answer the problem of definition. At the same time there are all kinds problems with the first half of the statement—the attempted definition—that reflect the author's specifically Judaic background.

The words 'unified system' are problematical to start with. If we examine the total body of religious beliefs, practices, and feelings found among any one people, including those relating not only to deities but to spirits, demons, and ghosts, we are likely to find that they add up to a very disparate collection, which can hardly be called a system. This is conspicuously true in the case of Arab village religion. Then there is the problem of what is meant by 'sacred things;' is the author referring to Powers, or to actions, or to material objects? In any case, 'the sacred' is identified as 'things set apart and forbidden,' which is again highly problematical. I assume that this phrase in the broadest sense is equivalent to Tylor's 'spiritual beings,' but the choice of words is unfortunate. Not all things that are 'set apart and forbidden' are necessarily sacred; electric transformers and many kinds of military installations are just as set apart and forbidden—usually with the aid of cyclone fences and barbed wire. And it is intuitively obvious that not all things endued with power are forbidden; 'dangerous' would be a much better word.

Finally, the use of the word 'church' expresses Durkheim's lifelong conviction not only that all religions exist within a social context, but that the social context is their reason for being. This is a valuable insight, as far as it goes, but it leaves aside the whole domain of personal religion. It may be true that there is no religion that has no organized body of votaries anywhere, but it is also true that many religions have thousands of votaries who belong to no such congregation or community. Thus, Durkheim's definition runs counter to his own stipulation, that 'we have neither the right nor the logical means of excluding some and retaining others' (Durkheim 1915: 24).

Max Weber, *Wirtschaft und Gesellschaft* (paraphrased in Parsons, 1937: 564): 'Religious as distinct from secular actions involves qualities, forces, etc. which are exceptional, removed from the ordinary, to which a special attitude is taken and a special virtue attached.' The things which are 'exceptional, removed from the ordinary' are of course the same as Durkheim's 'things set apart,' but here the emphasis shifts from the social domain to the domain of individual or collective feelings. The definition in that respect is less functional, and more affective. But of course it leaves unanswered the question of just what is 'special' about the attitudes and the virtues that are mentioned. Many actions besides religious ones evoke a special attitude, and many things besides religious ones have a special value.

William James, *The Varieties of Religious Experience* (1902: 31–2): 'The feelings, acts, and experiences of individual men in their solitude, so far as they apprehend themselves to stand in relation to whatever they may consider divine.' It is at once clear, from the mention of 'individual men in their solitude' that the author was a psychologist and not an anthropologist or sociologist. No anthropologist or sociologist would dream of defining religion while deliberately excluding its collective dimension.

James was clearly guilty of ethnocentric fallacy on this point. Because Christianity and other salvationist religions are so essentially personal, he evidently assumed that all other religions are the same. In fact, the idea that religion is basically a personal matter would strike most peoples as bizarre. Apart from that peculiarity, the definition of James shares with that of Weber the emphasis on feelings rather than either belief or behavior as the most important feature of religion.

Robert H. Lowie, *Primitive Religion* (1924: xvi-xvii): 'Religion is ... a universal feature of human culture ... because all recognize in some form or other awe-inspiring, extraordinary manifestations of reality .... Those cultural phenomena ... center about or are somehow connected with the sense of mystery or weirdness.' Lowie's definition is important in recognizing that religious phenomena are manifestations of reality, not something apart from it. Apart from that he, like James and Weber, placed primary emphasis on feelings rather than on either beliefs or actions. But his use of 'weirdness' to characterize the supernatural was ill-chosen, given the frequently pejorative connotations of that word. I think what he really meant was things that it are inexplicable in ordinary terms.

Paul Radin, *Primitive Religion* (1937: 1): 'It consists of two parts: the first an easily definable if not very specific feeling; and the second certain specific acts, customs, beliefs, and conceptions associated with this feeling.' Radin follows Lowie, James, and Weber in giving primacy to feelings, while mentioning beliefs and actions in such a way as to suggest that they are secondary features. While I can't speak from personal experience, I think that the notion of a single 'easily definable if not very specific feeling' is highly debatable. It seems to me that religion engenders a very wide range of feelings, from exaltation to execration. I suspect that Radin was generalizing from his own personal experience.

Guy Swanson, *The Birth of the Gods* (1964: 27): 'Religion consists of behaviors directed toward influencing the purposes of ... spirits.' This is the first definition of religion in purely behavioral terms, ignoring both its cognitive and its affective dimensions. It thus places Swanson at the opposite extreme from Tylor. The definition seems somewhat out of character, however, since the bulk of Swanson's book is actually about the cognitive content of religion, not the behavioral content.

Robert Bellah, *Religious Evolution* (1964: 359): '... a set of symbolic forms and acts which relate man to the ultimate conditions of his existence.' For me at least, 'the ultimate conditions of his existence' is so vague as to be nearly unintelligible, though I have to assume that the reference is primarily to deities. What is of positive interest about this definition, in contrast to those discussed above, is its identification of religion as a system of symbolic interaction with something or other.

Melford Spiro, *Religion: Problems of Definition and Explanation* (1966: 96): 'An institution consisting of culturally patterned interaction with culturally postulated superhuman beings.' Here we encounter again the concept of interaction, though the symbolic feature is ignored. Spiro like Bellah turns away from the affective emphasis of Weber, James, Lowie, and Radin. There is in fact no mention of feelings in his definition, which gives primary emphasis to religious action ('culturally patterned interactions'). The choice of the word 'institution' is perhaps unfortunate, since one tends to think of an institution as something that has been consciously instituted.

Anthony Wallace, *Religion: an Anthropological View* (1966: 107): 'A set of rituals, rationalized by myth, which mobilizes supernatural powers for the purpose of achieving transformations of state in man and nature.' Wallace goes beyond Spiro in assigning priority to religious behavior (ritual); so much so that he seems to be implying that belief (myth) exists mainly for the purpose of legitimizing action (ritual). Apart from this, the rather ornate language puts me in mind of Groucho Marx's 'there's less in this than meets the eye.' It becomes clear, reading further on, that 'mobilizing supernatural powers for the purpose of achieving transformations of state' really amounts to no more than 'getting the gods to do something.' But a great deal of ritual is performed not to cause something to happen but to prevent it from happening; to maintain the status quo just as it is. This is the whole essence of Navajo religious practice.

Clifford Geertz, *Religion as a Cultural System* (1966: 90): 'A system of symbols which acts to establish powerful, pervasive, and long-lasting moods and motivations in men by formulating conceptions of a general order of existence and clothing these conceptions with such an aura of factuality that the moods and motivations seem uniquely realistic.' The characterization of Geertz stands apart from most of those quoted above in two important respects. First, it lays emphasis specifically on the symbolic element in religion; second, it identifies the cognitive rather than either the behavioral or the affective dimension as the most important.

It is, nevertheless, a characterization and not a definition. Like much of the work of Geertz it is a kind of intellectual Chinese dinner: tasty and filling at the time, but not satisfying for long. What kind of moods? Motivations to do what? What kind of conceptions? Why do moods and motivations only 'seem' realistic? To do the author justice, he attempts to answer those questions in the essay that follows this statement, though not to my complete satisfaction.

An
assessment

An initial problem with nearly all the definitions cited above is that they are nominal definitions. To say that religion consists of myth or ritual or some combination of the two presupposes that we have a clear idea what myth and ritual are. As I will suggest in a moment, this is far from the case, because both myth and ritual overlap the boundary between the religious and secular domains. At the very least we would have to say that religion consists of certain kinds of myths and certain kinds of rituals; but then: what kinds? If we answer that they consist of religious myths and rituals, then we are back to where we started.

It will be evident in any case that, in saying that religion consists of myths and/or rituals, most of the authors have attempted to define religion by its content. Such statements are acceptable *as characterizations,* but they are unsatisfactory as definitions because none of the elements named is unique to the domain of religion. There are plenty of purely secular myths and rituals, and the special feelings of awe or reverence that we feel toward the deities we may also feel toward certain ordinary mortals. Even those myths that are normally identified as religious, because they deal in part with supernatural beings, also may have a lot of purely secular scientific or historical fact mixed in. In short, religion really cannot be defined in substantive terms, either by its content or by its boundaries.

Some authors, like Wallace and Geertz, have attempted to answer the question, What kind of myths and rituals? by specifying myths and rituals that perform certain functions. ('Achieving transformations of state' in Wallace's definition.) This throws the problem of definition into a whole new domain: that of defining religion by the functions it performs. I will suggest in later pages (especially Chapter 12) that this also is not possible, because religion simply has far too many and diverse functions, and they are different for different individuals.

The outstanding failing of all the definitions cited above is that of reductionism; they lay stress on one of the dimensions of religion as its defining feature, at the expense of the others. Tylor and Geertz emphasis cognition, Spiro and Wallace emphasize action, and James, Lowie, and Radin emphasize feelings as the most salient features. Weber speaks of actions and feelings, but not beliefs, while Durkheim speaks of both belief and behavior, but places primary emphasis on the social dimension of religion. I am convinced however that each of the different domains of religion is its most salient feature for certain individuals and for certain societies, but not for others. Any attempt at a universal definition must therefore embrace them all, and cannot assign saliency to any one.

9

In Search of a Definition

Some years ago, in an excellent book on Egyptian folk religion, my colleague and former student Edward Reeves wrote that "... 'religion' is a folk category, not a scientific one. It has become increasingly clear that religion is a subject that must be decomposed before scientific analysis can begin" (Reeves 1980: 3). I agree wholeheartedly with the second part of that assertion, and will take the same position in several later chapters. I will nevertheless try to suggest, in this chapter, that the first part is wrong: religion can be understood as a scientific category. At the same time, as I've already indicated, it is a category that cannot be defined either by its substantive content, by its boundaries, or by its functions. That means in effect that it cannot be defined on the basis of ethnographic data; it can only be defined conceptually.

The cultural factor

Let us take, as a starting point, a statement that I hope will be non-controversial. Whatever else it may be, nearly everyone will agree that religion is a cultural phenomenon—an essential one, most people would say. Of the various definitions of religion discussed in the previous chapter, only that of the psychologist William James neglected to mention the cultural aspect.

But then, what is culture? There have been at least as many attempts at definition as there have been in the case of religion—some 154 of them, according to a survey complied by Kroeber and Kluckhohn (1952: 77–274). So completely has the word 'culture' passed into everyday discourse that we are apt to forget that its use, in the modern sense, goes back less than two hundred years. It originated (as *Volksgeist*) within the context of German Idealist philosophy (see ibid.: 30–53), later became *Kultur*, and was introduced into English discourse almost single-handedly by E. B. Tylor, in the latter half of the nineteenth century. His *Primitive Culture,* published in 1871, was the first work in English to employ the word in its title, and the first to attempt to define it.

The liberating effect, in the social sciences, was enormous; in fact it made possible the entire discipline of cultural anthropology. Previous social philosophers from Greek times to the Enlightenment had been obliged to use a single term, 'society,' to describe both a people and their mores, as though the two were inseparable. The resulting ambiguity is very evident, when we return to the work of such luminaries as John Locke, Adam Ferguson, or even Lewis Henry Morgan. (Note that Morgan's *magnum opus* has the title *Ancient Society,* although it is at least as much about behavior patterns and beliefs as it is about human groups.) The term 'civilization' came a little closer to what today we call culture, but it too tended to be applied to human groups as well as to their beliefs and behaviors.

The concept of culture as an independent variable made it possible to recognize for the first time that culture can move without people moving. That is, it gave rise to the concept of diffusion. Prior to that time culture changes, whether recognized historically or archaeologically, were always attributed to the migration of peoples. More importantly for our purposes here, the independent culture concept made it possible to 'factor out' religion from society, and recognize that the two, though intertwined, often have quite separate histories. Some modern religions are shared by many societies; within other societies there are many religions.

The first attempt at a formal definition of culture, in English, was in fact the opening sentence of Tylor's *Primitive Culture* (1974: 1): 'Culture, or civilization ... is that complex whole which includes knowledge, belief, art, law, morals, customs, and any other capabilities and habits acquired by man as a member of society.' This definition was repeated with variations by a great many later scholars (cf. Kroeber and Kluckhohn 1952: 81–88), and it includes a number of features that are worthy of remark. First, it states unequivocally that culture is a 'complex whole,' an idea dear to the heart of anthropologists from that day to this, though it is currently challenged by deconstructionists. Second, it is based on the enumeration of content: knowledge, belief, art, law, etc. The idea that any culture can and should be analyzed into a set of discrete categories was not original with Tylor, but thanks to his approach it became a central feature of anthropological analysis for more than a hundred years. Third, his list places overwhelming emphasis on the cognitive rather than the behavioral aspects of culture, as in fact does nearly all of Tylor's writing. The author did not wholly ignore the domains of activity ('customs, capabilities, and habits') or affect, insofar as it is implied by the existence of art. But, following in the tradition of German Idealism (by which he was heavily influenced) he always thought of culture primarily as ways of thinking rather than as ways of doing.

But the most essential features of Tylor's definition are contained in its last eight words: 'acquired by man as a member of society.' In short, culture is *learned* ('acquired') and it is *shared.* Every discussion of culture from that day to this has reiterated those two points, to separate culture from idiosyncratic or instinctual beliefs and behavior.

Many other early definitions or discussions of culture followed Tylor's lead. With the rise of functionalist schools in the twentieth century, however, emphasis shifted from the cognitive to the behavioral aspect of culture, in the case of sociofunctionalists, and to the affective aspects, in the case of psychofunctionalists. Regardless of emphasis, however, just about all anthropologists have agreed that every culture, like every religion, has a cognitive dimension (beliefs), a behavioral dimension (customs) and an affective dimension (feelings). All would also agree that it has a social dimension; every culture is the belief and action system of a particular society. In later discussion of religion, I will refer to these dimensions as Believing, Belonging, Behaving, and Feeling (cf. especially Chapter 13).

The functionalists did what Tylor did not do: they attempted to answer the question 'what is culture?' by asking 'why is culture?' Going beyond the mere recognition that it serves a variety of human needs, they introduced the basic organizing concept of adaptation. Quite simply, culture is mankind's adaptive mechanism, and almost its only one. It takes the place of claws, fangs, thick hide, heavy fur, wings, night vision, and all the other genetically inherited properties that enable our animal cousins to survive. Lacking claws and fangs, our ancestors had to invent cutting tools (the earliest of all human manufactures) and weapons; lacking a heavy coat, they had to invent garments and other ways of keeping warm; lacking a natural nesting instinct, they had to invent ways of housing themselves and their goods; when they began to depend on seasonal plant foods, they had to invent a rodent-proof way of storing them (pottery), and so on and so on. And they very soon learned that those things could be better achieved through collective efforts than individually. These insights were not original with anthropologists; in embryonic form they can be traced all the way back to Democritus, in the fifth century B.C. But it was anthropologists who placed them within a coherent analytical frame of reference.

Recognizing that culture is adaptive, and that it has essential dimensions of cognition, behavior, and affect, I here offer my own definition:

Culture, generically, is the sum of mankind's collective efforts to understand, to exploit, and to enjoy his environment. The culture of any specific people is the sum of that people's collective efforts to understand, to exploit, and to enjoy their environment.

I have couched my definition in this shorthand form for the sake of simplicity, but obviously it requires some amplification. In my usage, 'understand' involves all forms of ideation, mystical as well as rational. 'Exploit' involves all forms of utilization and coping. 'Enjoy' refers not only to feelings but to the actions undertaken to evoke them. Be it noted that, within the context of this definition, both 'exploitation' and 'enjoyment' have negative as well as positive aspects; they may involve prevention or avoidance as well as causation or evocation. For example a great many laws (among the most cultural of all phenomena) exist not to make people do things but to prevent them from doing things, and that is surely adaptive from the standpoint of society. Likewise some religious ceremonies exist not so much to evoke good feelings as to prevent or minimize bad ones; enjoyment is increased when bad feelings are dispelled.

It is important to notice that, in my definition, I say *their* environment, rather than *the* environment. One of the common ethnocentric fallacies of much materialist anthropology is the assumption that all peoples are trying to adapt to the same environment that we perceive, whether they realize it or not. Marvin Harris (one of the worst offenders in this regard) was at pains to argue that Hebrew, Arab, and Hindu food tabus are really adaptive in a purely ecological sense, even though they seem illogical on the surface, and even though the people who practice them explain them in quite other terms. The term adaptation is thus, for Harris and other materialists, a purely etic concept.

The nature of adaptation

But I intend to employ the concept in a more nearly emic sense. The environments of many peoples, as perceived by them, do not include a lot of the things and a lot of the forces that we have come to recognize, while at the same time they include a wide variety of forces, or powers, that we don't recognize, but that are totally real to them. If the single most dangerous threat in your environment is not trichinosis, but a stern and unforgiving Yahweh/Allah, then it is surely more adaptive to avoid pork because it is abomination to him than to avoid it because of the possibility of illness. Peoples everywhere strive to come to the terms with the world as they perceive it, not as we perceive it.

Harris (1968: 168–9) argued that there are really no 'stupid customs,' because if we look at them carefully we will find that they are really adaptive, no matter how illogical and even maladaptive some of them may seem on the surface. They would not otherwise survive (apparently because they would be offensive to the Great Ecologist in the Sky). I agree with Harris, but not for his reasons. I think all customs and beliefs are indeed adaptive in the eyes of those who hold them, and would not survive if they were not. Our ethnographic literature provides plentiful examples of customs that have been discarded because they were no longer found to be efficacious, or useful. I am suggesting in other words that religion is much more intelligible from the perspective of ethno-logic than it is from our particular Western conception of logic. For people like the Navajos, who live amid a myriad dangerous powers, religion is the most critically important of all adaptive strategies.

The composition of the environment

Let us, then, pass on to a second non-controversial proposition, and couple it to the first. Culture is man's adaptive mechanism, and religion is part of culture. Religion must therefore in some sense be adaptive, though perhaps not totally so. The question then is, adaptive to what? The short answer, as I have just suggested, is that it must be adaptive to something or things in the environment of those who practice it, as seen by them. Can we then identify any features that are common to the perceived environments of all peoples, and that therefore result in common adaptations?

I would suggest to begin with that all peoples divide the visible and tangible environment into two basic classes, which for convenience I will call Things and People. This is surely one of those binary oppositions dear to the heart of structural anthropologists

Things are usually though not invariably inanimate, and insensate. The exceptions are certain classes of animals, and, in the most extreme instances of chattel slavery, certain human beings. They have feelings, but not feelings that we have to consider. The defining characteristic of Things is not that they are always insensate, but that we treat them as though they were. We therefore feel free to use, abuse, and even destroy them, without worrying about how they feel about it. We may admire the beauty of a thing or take pride in its possession, but our relations with Things are usually without affect, and always without mutual affect. For that reason, those domains of culture that are concerned with the ownership or manipulation of things have been called, collectively, the Technical Order, in contrast to the Moral Order. And since things are mostly non-sentient, we have to deal with them by physical manipulation rather than by communication.

People, by contrast, are animate, sensate, and sentient, and the awareness of that fact is involved in all our dealings with them. No matter how asymmetrical may be the relationship between two people, there is always a recognition of an interest on the part of both parties. It is not, much of the time, a mutual interest. I may cite, as an example of an asymmetrical relationship, my dealings with students. My primary interest is to try and make them learn as much as possible; their primary interests are to get a good grade and to gain three hours of credit, while how much they actually learn is of secondary importance. But I understand their position and try to help them to their goals, while they understand mine. In my dealings with excavation laborers my primary interest is to get something dug, while theirs is to please me so that they won't get fired, and perhaps will get a bonus. Again though we recognize one another's interests, and in our interaction we try to see that both interests are served.

In addition to mutuality, our relations with people usually involve some degree of affect, and sometimes it is their most salient feature. Because of this, those domains of culture that involve relations with people are called, collectively, the Moral Order. It remains to add that, since people are sentient, we deal with them mainly by techniques of communication rather than by physical manipulation.

(**Animals** represent an intermediate, or bridging category between Things and People. At one end of the bridge, household pets are clearly People. We give them names, we talk to them, we teach them behaviors; we may even make them the subject of religious rituals. At the other end of the bridge, many kinds of wild animals, and in particular vermin, are clearly Things. This is not quite so true in the case of preliterate, and especially pre-agricultural peoples, who often see the animals in much more human terms that we do. Among ourselves it is mainly farm animals and draft animals that occupy a genuinely intermediate position—not quite things and not quite people. However, I don't know of any culture in which animals occupy a formally demarcated third category, separate from both Things and People.)

Forces. No people's environment is confined to the realm of the visible and the tangible. Everywhere there is evidence that unseen forces are at work, making the things and people what they are, and causing them to do what they do. They make the sun rise and set, the tides ebb and flow, and the seasons change; in fact, they cause just about everything that is not attributable to the will of a living human or animal. And as they are so conspicuously and so importantly a part of our environment, even though invisible, we seek to understand, to exploit, and to enjoy them just as we do things and people.

It is necessary to reiterate that my discussion here refers only to the unseen portion of the environment. There are of course a great many forces or powers in the visible and tangible environment also—those exerted by humans and by animals and by running water, for example. We don't have to try and develop special techniques, either religious or scientific, for dealing with them, because we can identify and deal with them at the source. Unseen forces on the other hand require special techniques.

Unseen forces, as we conceive them, fall into the same two categories as do material entities. Some are conceived to be sentient, and to act in accordance with a will of their own; others are non-sentient, and act purely automatically. Not surprisingly, those forces whose actions are unpredictable or erratic are usually thought to be willful, like people; those that operate predictably are thought to be will-less, like things. Sentient forces are agents, or possessed of 'agency' as the modern jargon has it; non-sentient forces are not. For convenience in the remainder of this discussion I will refer to willed forces as Powers, and to forces without a will as Forces. I will capitalize the two terms to emphasize the special sense in which I am using them here.

In the experience of preliterate peoples, the number of happenings that can be absolutely predicted is very small, and the number of unpredictable happenings very large. Not surprisingly, then, those peoples recognize few if any Forces, but a wide variety of Powers. I think perhaps the only force that is universally recognized as non-sentient is gravity; I'm not aware of any people who have deified it, or who require a myth to explain it.

We rarely if ever see the Forces or Powers themselves, but only the effects of their action. Yet we tend to think that anything possessed of a will, and anything that can cause action or motion, must somewhere and somehow have a concrete form. In the absence of any kind of empirical evidence, that form is supplied by human imagination. And since the creative possibilities of the human imagination are unlimited, so also is the number and variety of forms that have been attributed to Powers. It is often the case that 'man makes god in his own image,' and it is therefore not surprising that a great many of the Powers are conceived to have not only a human form or forms, but many human traits of personality. Powers however may also be conceived in the form of animals, of part-man part-animals, or of animate creatures that are neither human nor animal. Their one truly defining characteristic is that they have a will, and can therefore act as they see fit.

Any willed being is obviously a sentient being, and any sentient being is accessible to communication. Virtually all of our interaction with Powers, be they gods, goddesses, saints, or demons, is through techniques of communication—most commonly verbal but sometimes also artistic, musical, architectural, or through other forms of symbolic expression. Since symbols are the basic building blocks of all communication, it is not surprising that all religions are rich in symbolism.

Because they are much like people, but also because they have power, our dealings with the sentient beings are almost never lacking in affect; indeed it is often their strongest component. We may interact with them only intermittently, but we have feelings about them all the time. In short and in sum, our relations with the Powers are an extension, and often an exaggeration, of our attitudes and behavior toward People. Those relations are part of the Moral Order, and they are what I call religion.

The case of Forces (non-sentient powers) is different. Because they act automatically at all times and places, they can not be ascribed to any particular locus. Since they are absolutely predictable, they evidently don't have a will. Consequently we don't conceive of the non-sentient forces as being in any way human, either in form or in other characteristics. And, as they're non-sentient, we can't communicate with them; we can only deal with them through some kind of manipulation. Our relations with Forces are an extension of our relations with things, and are part of the Technical Order. They are what I call science.

Religion, in sum, is the informing ideology of the Moral Order, and Science is the ideology of the Technical Order.

Taken together, Things, People, non-sentient Forces, and sentient Powers make up the four quarters of our environment, and the relations among them can be diagrammed in a kind of four-cell matrix, shown in Figure 1. Let me, then, offer four definitions:

*Four
definitions*

THE VISIBLE ENVIRONMENT

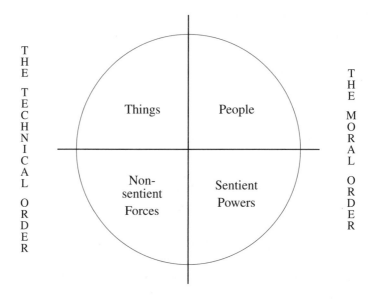

THE UNSEEN ENVIRONMENT

FIGURE 1

Religion is the sum of mankind's collective efforts to understand, to exploit, and to enjoy unseen Powers, largely through techniques of communication. The religion of any given people is the sum of their efforts to understand, exploit, and enjoy the Powers in their environment.

Science is the sum of mankind's collective efforts to understand, to exploit, and to enjoy non-sentient Forces, largely through techniques of manipulation. The science of any given people is the sum of their efforts to understand, exploit, and enjoy the Forces in their environment.

The same amplifications must be offered as in my definition of Culture. 'Understanding' means all forms of ideation, mystical and rational; 'exploitation' means all means of utilizing and coping;' 'enjoyment' involves acts as well as feelings. Once again, exploiting and enjoying must be understood to have negative as well as positive dimensions; to involve prevention as well as causation.

One might, conceivably, take exception to the word 'collective.' There are said to be individuals who have formulated their own, highly idiosyncratic conception of the supernaturals, and have devised their own rituals for dealing with them. Those conceptions and actions would minimally satisfy my definition of religion. But they are neither learned nor shared, and thus are not aspects of culture. I will argue in Chapter 12 that belonging, in addition to believing and behaving, is one of the necessary components of religion as any anthropologist would understand it.

The distinction between religion and science that I have drawn here is strictly a distinction in theory, and as such might be regarded as trivial or irrelevant in practice; not least by the peoples whom I have attempted to characterize. Religion and science are both about the harnessing of power, and most peoples attempt to deal with a wide variety of forces and/or powers by a wide variety of techniques, without stopping to consider whether the forces are sentient or not. The distinction is more apparent and more useful in the behavioral than in the cognitive realm, because of the wholly different technologies that are employed in the cases or religion and science. Forces are controlled or affected by manipulation, and Powers by communication. In practice, then, *communication* is the single most salient feature that defines the behavioral domain of religion, and distinguishes it from science. To this extent I agree with the structural and semiotic theorists, whose ideas will be discussed in Chapter 11.

It is important to notice, before concluding, that I have defined religion only in the abstract or generic sense. My definition implies nothing about the specific content of religion among any given people. The problem of defining any specific religion is a wholly different one from that of defining 'religion' in the abstract. Since my concern in the next chapters will continue to be with *religion* in the singular and generic sense, I will not take up the question of *religions*, in the plural and specific sense, until Part 3.

10

RELIGION AND SCIENCE

In this chapter I want to pursue further the often tendentious and often misunderstood relationship between religion and science. I need to make the obvious point, before going further, that these two together do not comprehend by any means the whole sum of human thought and action. Between them there lies an enormous area of everyday, practical knowledge, acquired through centuries of experience with the tangible world, that does not involve ideas about either Powers or Forces. Much of technology falls into this category, as also do many of our economic institutions. For want of a better term I will refer to that part of culture that involves neither religion nor science as the lay domain. It is not however my concern in the present chapter.

In Chapter 9 I stated a set of neatly logical definitions, which make clear *in theory* the distinction between religion and science. But they are purely nominal definitions, and it remains to see how they play out in the real world. In that context we have to consider the extent of overlap, if any, between religion and science, the question of whether the two together encompass all of our dealings with forces, and how and why religion and science are able to co-exist.

The problem of boundaries

The great anthropologist A. L. Kroeber wrote that

> In anthropology there is little to be gained by pushing conceptual distinctions very far, and some risk of sterility, because phenomena intergrade endlessly, especially in so highly plastic a thing as culture. A broad definition, centering on the core of meaning involved rather than aiming at hairline logical definition at its edges, is therefore ordinarily the most useful (Kroeber 1964: 234).

Whether or not this is true in the case of religion and culture is the issue I propose to explore here.

With respect to the lay domain, Kroeber is surely right. That is, there are large areas of overlap between religion and science, and between both and the lay domain. The practice of medicine may serve as an example. In the case of Navajos it falls mostly within the realm of religion, but also includes a good deal of practical knowledge (not all of it correct from our perspective) about the curative powers of various substances, that has come through experience and not through divine sanction. Medicine as practiced in America falls mainly within the realm of science, but here again there is a lot of practical knowledge, acquired through experience and experiment, for which there is no clearly understood scientific explanation. Let me, then, reiterate the point that my concern in the present discussion is exclusively with the much narrower question of whether there is, in practice as well as in theory, a clear boundary between religion and science.

We have to recognize to begin with that the great majority of human societies have no word for either religion or science, and would surely regard as foolish or incomprehensible any attempt to distinguish them. The Forces and the Powers are out there, for better and worse, and we deal with them as best we know how. Much of the time, I believe, our dealings involve combinations of religion and science. Let me here consider some examples.

Science in religion

The ultimate logic that underlies both religious belief and scientific belief is the same: we find it necessary to conceive of, and to believe in, things that we can't see in order to explain the things that we can see. From that perspective, the Navajo's belief in Changing Woman, the Arab's belief in the village saint, and the Christian's belief in God are no different from the physicist's belief in neutrons or the astronomer's belief in quarks. They are unseen things that help to explain the observable and measurable. For the true believer, the proof of their existence lies in the visible evidence of their actions; actions that would otherwise be unintelligible. As my Arab friends were thinking long ago, how could I be an unbeliever in Allah when every day brought fresh evidence of his existence, in the form of happenings that could not be understood in any other way?

That way of thinking found its outlet in religion long before there was such a thing as science, and its basis was then, as it is now, a wholly rational one. The way in which the unseen Powers/Forces were conceived in the religion of primitive tribesmen may have been fantastic, but there was a logical reason for believing in them: the evidence of their action could be seen everywhere in daily life. Science later deprived some of the forces of a shape and a will, but it did not deny their existence, for it found them as necessary to believe in as did religion. To that extent I am inclined to suggest that primitive religion was—in part—a kind of proto-science. Science did not develop in opposition to religion, but rather grew out of it.

In practical as well as in theoretical religion we can observe a good deal of science, or scientific thinking. A clearcut example is furnished by the immutability of ritual. Again and again we find the survival of archaic forms of language, archaic forms of dress, archaic forms of architecture, on the very sound principle that 'if it works, don't fool with it.' That is good, sound empirical science. The gods should in principle be able to respond to any language; after all, it was they that gave it to us. But if we're sure they understand Latin or Sanskrit or Sumerian, it's better to keep addressing them that way to be on the safe side. And if there are mechanistic performances that always seem to work, even though we don't know why, that is typical of science, which can always predict far more than it can explain. Some religions are rich in explanatory myths; others have very few, and in that respect they simply leave a great deal unexplained. Contrary to the suggestion of Anthony Wallace, there are many rituals that are unsanctioned by any myth; they are simply things that have been found to work.

It should be noted too that religion is not wholly lacking in experimentation. Provisionally borrowing other people's gods or rituals is one kind of experimentation. Claude Levi-Strauss is responsible for the insight that the shaman, in tribal societies, is often a *bricoleur*; that is, a do-it-yourselfer. There are recorded instances, from both Egypt and Jordan, of Muslim village women who have taken their babies to a Christian priest to be baptized, in the hope that it may confer some additional protection.

Then there is the whole problematical area of divination. Practically all peoples before modern times employed some kinds of divinatory techniques, intended to discover a future that has already been pre-ordained. The techniques themselves were and are purely magical and mechanical, and involve no direct appeal to any supernatural power, yet it must have been the powers that pre-ordained the future. Shall we decide therefore that divination represents another case of science within religion? I will take up this problem again a little later.

On the other side of the coin, many scientists are passionately attached to explanatory propositions (so-called scientific laws, though they are often only the fashionable theories of the moment) that are very poorly supported by empirical evidence, simply because they must have something to believe in. Thomas Kuhn, in his theory of dominant paradigms (1962) has shown in effect that unexamined convictions are essential to the progress of science. They allow us to leave aside difficult and at times unanswerable questions, so that we can concentrate our attention on a limited, and manageable, number of questions. The paradigms persist, in Kuhn's analysis, until the weight of evidence piles up to the point that we can no longer ignore it. We then realize that we have been believing something untrue, essentially because we needed to. If Montesquieu said that 'religion, though false, is necessary,' Kuhn might have said that 'scientific untruths, through false, are necessary.' Kuhn's analysis clearly suggests that most scientists, no less than most religious people, need something in which they can place unquestioning faith. Indeed I have often been told by both scientists and religious people, in very nearly the same words, that 'you've got to believe in something.'

The great unresolved problem in all of natural science is that of teleology: the assumption that phenomena in nature must serve some purpose, which is not attributable to man's conscious will. That assumption is basic to all religions, in which the regularity in nature is attributed to one or more divine wills. But the notion of purpose is also woven all through natural science, as it is also in Aristotelian philosophy. In modern science we find it embodied for example in the doctrines of adaptation and natural selection. We are told that if human and animal traits didn't serve some purpose, they wouldn't have survived. And when traits cannot be shown to serve any other purpose, it is said that they must serve the purpose of 'sexual attraction.' It is the naturalist's residual category of the unexplainable, just as is 'religion' for the archaeologist.

But—how can there be a purpose except in relation to a will? That is the question that naturalists have yet to answer, at least to my satisfaction. Who has decreed that the most fundamental need of each species is to survive, when in fact thousands of them haven't, and when the creatures themselves are unaware of such a need? Looking beneath the surface of natural science theories, I can nearly always find, disguised in some form or another, the concept of 'nature's purposes.' In such cases, Nature has been deified as surely as in any primitive religion. The god whom scientists have banished from the heavens turns up in all sorts of unlikely places, including, for sociobiologists, in our genes.

To conclude, thinking is hard work, and thinking that involves decision-making is also stressful. Most people, including the most learned of scientists, would like to avoid it some of the time, and some who are not so learned would like to avoid it all of the time. Scientific doctrines, no less than religious ones, save thinking and may provide an automatic basis for decision-making, providing one can accept them as articles of faith.

The bottom line, I think, is that the line between religion and science cannot be wholly sharp because the dividing line between Powers and Forces is not wholly sharp. Within religion, some Powers are nevertheless susceptible to mechanical compulsion; within science, some Forces are nevertheless conceived as having purposes. It is partially for this reason that there is room for an overlapping category of belief and behavior, not quite religion and not quite science, that I will discuss in the next section.

A third category?

Do science and religion encompass, between them, all of mankind's interaction with Forces and Powers? Or is there some knowledge and behavior that does not readily fit into either category? Those questions have most commonly been debated by anthropologists with reference to magic, sorcery and witchcraft, and different scholars have answered them in different ways. Tylor 1874: 112–159) and Frazer (1922: 11–82) likened them to 'primitive science;' Lowie (1924: 151) included them in religion; while Durkheim (1915: 42–45) and Malinowski (1954) saw them as forming a distinct third category.

Witchcraft and sorcery, as I define the terms, are overt and motivated human actions, while magic is the technology they both employ. Witchcraft nearly always refers to evilly intended action, while sorcery is a broader category that includes witchcraft but also actions intended to be beneficial. Both clearly involve the invocation of special power; the question is, what kind of power? Are sorcerers mechanically invoking non-sentient forces, comparable to electricity, simply because they have mastered a special technology? Or are they capturing and applying power derived ultimately from sentient beings? Or does the power reside entirely within the practitioners themselves?

Magic itself can be dismissed from the discussion, since it is a technology that can be employed in either case. It is worth making the point, however, that the technology of magic itself lies somewhere between religion and science. It involves no direct address to Powers, and is accompanied by little or no affect; to that extent it belongs to the technical order. Moreover, it involves a belief in what can only be called pseudoscientific principles: that the future has been preordained, and therefore is susceptible to discovery through techniques of divination; that like produces like (as when a person is harmed by damaging a replica of the person, such as a voodoo doll); and that the part stands for the whole (as when a person is harmed by placing a curse on articles of his or her clothing). At the same time however magic involves the mechanical manipulation of symbols that have communicative power, and that may at times be intended to compel sentient Powers to action. The practitioners themselves don't, obviously, make any distinction as regards the powers they're exercising, and sometimes they may believe the power resides wholly within themselves. They are merely aware that they are able to command special powers.

The difficulty in deciding where to place witchcraft and sorcery lies in the fact that witches and sorcerers are not usually either addressing or manipulating supernatural powers external to themselves. They are merely making use of supernatural power that has come to lodge within themselves, sometimes from a source that they themselves can't identify. To that extent the witches and sorcerers are themselves supernaturals. And since they are definitely possessed of will, they fall in the broadest sense within my category of religion, even though their practice lacks many of the usual characteristics of religion.

There is, to my thinking, no logical resolution of this problem. Witchcraft and sorcery involve the application, by otherwise ordinary persons, of power that derives ultimately from a supernatural force, using a technology that is largely manipulative rather than communicative. The best I can suggest is that witchcraft and sorcery do not constitute a category wholly distinct from religion and science, but rather a hybrid of the two. They offer further proof that, in practice, there is simply no sharp boundary between religion and science.

The two minds

Although there are areas of overlap between religion and science, it is also apparent that there are large areas in which they directly contradict one another. This is especially true in the modern world, where science has advanced to the point that it explains a great deal that was formerly attributed to God, yet people continue to believe in an omnipotent God who can do as he pleases. How, then, can religion and science coexist not only within every society, but in the minds of nearly every individual? More specifically, how can individuals hold religious beliefs and scientific beliefs that are directly contradictory?

I am going at this point to venture onto very speculative ground, and suggest that every human individual is possessed of two minds. For convenience I will call them Rational and Mystical, but it must be clearly understood that the two terms as I use them have neither positive nor negative loading. I do not simply equate the rational mind with reasoning, for that would imply that the mystical mind is an unthinking mind. But in my conception there is mystical as well as rational reasoning; it simply obeys different rules of logic, and does not demand empirical confirmation. Since they co-exist in every individual, I have to assume that both the rational and the mystical mind are natural and adaptive. Both contribute, if not to physical survival, at least to the improvement and enrichment of life. They are of course the *logos* and *mythos* of the ancients.

The rational mind, as I define it, is our animal mind. It reacts to external stimuli, and holds beliefs based on sensory experience and memory. It puts two and two together, and always gets four. It makes decisions and prompts actions that are either wholly instinctive, or are based on a clear calculation of self-interest The mystical mind is uniquely human; we have no evidence that anything comparable exists in any other animate species. It is able to hold beliefs not based on any empirical evidence, and indeed to hold beliefs that are directly contradicted by empirical evidence. It is able to put two and two together, and come up with an unlimited number of answers. It can conceive of Beings that have human form and yet are simultaneously in two or more places, simultaneously alive and dead, and simultaneously their own fathers and sons—all features characteristic of the Christian Trinity, for example. Unlike the rational mind it is enormously imaginative and creative, and is able to picture all kinds of things that no one has ever actually experienced. Like the rational mind it is often a searching mind, but it is able to search beyond the world of experience, and to venture into areas inaccessible to the rational mind. Although the matter remains highly speculative at this point in time, I suspect that the two minds are seated respectively in the left and right cerebral hemispheres.

The mystical mind, untrammeled by the limitations of observable reality, is often highly creative, and the great bodies of mythology that we find in so many religions are surely the products of that creativity. Still, mysticism should not simply be equated with creativity, or vice versa. Creativity can be found in rational as well as in mystical thought, the quintessential example being perhaps the theory of general relativity. At the opposite extreme, there are plenty of scientists and plenty of religious persons whose beliefs are simply those taught to them, and involve no component of personal creativity. And there are artists, composers, and poets—probably the majority of them in today's world—whose creativity is unrelated to any belief system; they simply have creative minds. It seems evident nevertheless that religion offers more scope for creativity than does science, and to that extent it is likely to have greater appeal for naturally creative persons.

Though the rational and the mystical mind are present, I believe, in every human, they may be very unequally developed. To some extent I suspect that this is a matter of heredity: some people I know in our own society seem to be naturally mystical, without belonging to any of the overt mystical sects, and some seem naturally rational, even though they may have little formal education. To a far greater extent however the two minds are obviously developed through conditioning, either personal or, more often, cultural. Some cultures are clearly far more mystical than others. India has for millennia been a fountainhead of mysticism, and has been the originator of mystical belief systems that have spread eastward and westward over much of the Old World. Europe and China have both been fountainheads of rationalism, and have generally been resistant to mystical movements. My own very poorly developed mystical mind is partly a consequence of that tradition, and partly a result of personal conditioning in my own family. There might even be a factor of heredity: all the Adamses that I know about have been hard-headed and coldly logical.

It would be tempting to solve the problem of the coexistence of science and religion by suggesting that science is seated in the rational mind, and religion in the mystical mind. I think that to a considerable extent this is true in the modern world of the West, where thought tends to be highly compartmentalized. However, the matter is not nearly that simple, especially when seen in historical perspective. Science does indeed reside entirely within the rational mind, but religion involves both minds. Moreover, it finds its earliest development in the rational mind, both in individuals and societies, as I will suggest in later chapters. That is, it is in the beginning a quite logical attempt to understand the experienced

*Mysticism
in religion*

world, within the context of available information. This theme will be much further pursued in Chapter 16. I will suggest also, at the end of this chapter, that a great deal of religion finds its locus neither in the rational nor in the mystical mind, but in a third, basically unthinking domain that I will call the accepting mind.

As I suggested a little earlier, both religion and science find it necessary to conceive of unseen Powers/Forces in order to explain what is actually seen. And there is in the beginning a logic, based on childhood experience, in attributing sentience and a will to the Powers. But in seeking to discover and define the sentient Powers, and in figuring how to deal with them, we have to go far beyond the world of practical experience, which is to say beyond the capabilities of the rational mind. It is here that the imaginative and creative powers of the mystical mind find full play. If mankind had not the mystical mind, there would be no religion in the full sense that we encounter it in all societies.

But while there is no religion without a component of mysticism, the different religions of the world vary enormously in the extent of their mystical content. This is explainable partly, but not wholly, on evolutionary or adaptive grounds. The most primitive tribal religions of which we have knowledge are some of the least mystical, partly because they are so largely and so necessarily practical. My impression is that mysticism in religion grows side by side with, and yet as a reaction to, the growth of scientific and technical knowledge. As more and more things are explained without reference to the gods, it becomes necessary to think of the gods in more and more supernatural terms, as remote, miraculous, and perhaps even unknowable. Religion thus becomes more and more the province either of the mystical or of the merely accepting mind, as it seems to be in modern America and Europe. This should be evidence enough that religious mysticism does not represent the survival of childlike thinking, as some atheistic thinkers have suggested. I will explore these themes further in Chapters 14 and 16.

I do not want to suggest however that the religion of modern Americans and Europeans is always highly mystical. As I will argue a little later, there are many reasons for being religious, not all of which require very much in the way of either rational or mystical thought. The 'makers' of religion, if I can use that term, are usually mystical; the 'consumers' may or may not be.

I do not want to suggest either that evolutionary theory provides a complete explanation for the varying mysticism found in different religions. I know of no logical reason why India should for so long have been a fountainhead of mystical religions, while the Near East has just as conspicuously been a fountainhead of legalistic religions. There are regional traditions in religion, as there as in other aspects of culture, that probably trace back to remote and undiscoverable antiquity, and that simply 'go their own way' once they get started.

I have to conclude by acknowledging that while the distinction between mystical and rational thought is easy to make in theory, it is much harder to make in practice. The thought of most people in most societies is not compartmentalized; mystical and rational ideas are all mixed up together, as are religion and science. Moreover, no belief is inherently mystical or inherently rational. It depends on whether it is or is not in conformity with the experienced world, and conformity exists to a considerable extent in the eye of the beholder. Thus, beliefs that are rational in the mind of one person, because they seem to have been confirmed by experience, may be mystical in the mind of another, because they are contrary to experience. The therapeutic powers of a particular saint are empirical realities to someone who, in his own mind, has been cured by them again and again; they are mystical beliefs to someone who doesn't believe in saints. I will suggest in later chapters that a great deal of practical religion resides in the rational mind, while most mythology engages the mystical mind.

The rational and the mystical mind as I conceive them are not simply the reciprocals of one another, for they are both, in their different ways, actively reasoning minds. But between them there lies a very large area of human cognition that is accepted not on the basis of active reasoning, but simply on the authority of other persons. That area, for many persons, may include large parts of religion, but equally may include large parts of scientific knowledge. I would suggest that such knowledge resides neither in the rational nor in the mystical mind, but simply in what I would call the accepting mind.

*The
accepting
mind*

There are many possible reasons for accepting religious beliefs and practices on the authority of others. To begin with it saves the trouble of thinking; something that most people would like to avoid some of the time, and some would like to avoid all of the time. Religious thinking, no less than scientific thinking, involves tackling tough questions. But unquestioning acceptance may also be motivated by a desire for social respectability, or simply by a desire to conform. In any case it seems clear to me that for a great many people in every society, a large part of religion is to be found simply in the accepting mind.

It does not automatically follow, then, that persons with highly developed rational minds have poorly developed mystical minds, or vice versa. Just as it is possible for persons to hold two or more religions simultaneously, as I will suggest in Chapter 13, so also it is possible for them to hold religious and scientific beliefs simultaneously, by compartmentalized thinking. In some individuals—perhaps even the majority—neither the rational nor the mystical mind is very highly developed; most of their knowledge and understanding reside in the accepting mind. At the opposite extreme are individuals, exemplified by Isaac Newton, in which he rational and the mystical minds are equally highly developed.

11

The Problem of Explanation

The word 'religion' is of Latin origin, but the word, and indeed the entire subject of religion as we understand it today, figured very little in ancient or medieval discourse. Just about everyone before modern times took for granted the existence of one or more sentient Powers; there was consequently no need either to question why religion existed, or to try and define it. Debate was almost entirely over the nature of the Powers; that is, essentially theological. It was not until the rise of scientific agnosticism in the seventeenth century that people began to ask the most basic questions that we ask today: what is religion, and why does it exist?

It is not my purpose here to review the history of thought about religion, which would require not a single volume but an encyclopedia (for a very brief overview see Cain 1987). I will be content in this chapter simply to identify the different basic approaches or schools of thought that have emerged since philosophers and scientists first began to ask the questions that concern us today, and I will try and suggest how much they do and don't answer. I have listed and classified the different approaches in Table 1.

Until the middle of the nineteenth century there were only two recognized disciplines concerned with the human spiritual condition: history, and philosophy. Between them they embraced nearly all of what today are sociology, psychology, anthropology, political science, and economics. When thinkers first began speculating about religion, therefore, it is not surprising that they turned either to history or to philosophy, or occasionally to a combination of the two, for their answers. Generally speaking history explained everything in terms of antecedents, and philosophy explained everything in terms of some kind of logic. The historical schools were, and still are, best able to account for the forms of religion, and the philosophical schools were and are best able to account for its functions.

After the differentiation of the social sciences in the latter half of the nineteenth century, much of the historical theorizing about religion was absorbed into anthropology, and most of the philosophical theorizing was absorbed into sociology and psychology. There is still a separate discipline called History of Religions (*Religionswissenschaft* in Germany, where it is mainly pursued), independent of anthropology, but there is no longer a viable, distinct discipline of Philosophy of Religion. Nearly all recent books with that title have been written by true believers, pursuing the subject from a theistic point of view.

TABLE 1. Approaches to the explanation of religion

I. Developmental
  A. Evolutionist
  B. Historical

II. Functional
    A. Sociofunctional
    B. Political
      1. Marxist
      2. Ecological-Marxist
    C. Psychofunctional
      1. Pathogenic
      2. Normative
        a. Preventive
        b. Curative
    D. Semiotic

III. Substantive
    A. Structural

Theology, which largely occupied the thinkers of earlier times, is omitted from consideration here, since it starts from the apriori assumption that a god or gods exist, and therefore finds no need to account for the existence or the functions of religion. It is a search for understanding *within* religion, not *about* religion.

Developmental theories

Personality theory in psychology takes it for granted that every person is the product of shaping influences in his or her background. History makes the same assumption about social and cultural institutions; that is, it attempts to explain them in terms of antecedents. In the study of religion there have been two main historical approaches, the evolutionist and the culture-historical, each attempting to explain the religions of today by tracing the process of their development.

The major theoretical concern of anthropologists, in the latter part of the nineteenth century, was to develop a single grand theory of social and cultural evolution, which should embrace religion along the way. Contrary to a common assumption, this was not inspired by Darwin; it built upon a much older body of thought that had been quite fully developed by moral philosophers of the French and Scottish Enlightenments a hundred years earlier. With the exception of Herbert Spencer, most of the early anthropologists (as we now retrospectively call them) used the term 'progress' rather than 'evolution,' and none of them avowed any debt to Darwin.

Be that as it may, the evolutionary perspective was applied quite specifically to three domains of culture: those of technology, kinship (and social organization more generally), and religion. Rather surprisingly, the early anthropologists made little attempt to connect up the latter two. Theories of social evolution, as propounded especially by Lewis Henry Morgan and John McLennan, were essentially materialistic, and paid little heed to the domain of religion. Theories of religion, propounded by E. B. Tylor and James Frazer, were highly mentalistic, and assigned no determining role to kinship institutions.

It was Tylor who first propounded an evolutionary stage theory, involving a progression from animism to totemism, to a belief in anthropomorphic spirits, to generalized polytheism, to a belief in high gods, to a belief in a supreme deity. The scheme, like much of Tylor's evolutionist thinking, was based on a belief in the progressive maturation of the human mind from age to age; it was not significantly connected with either technological or social developments. Thanks perhaps to its concreteness and the appeal of its classificatory nature, Tylor's scheme has been adopted, with variations, by a great many students of religion from his own day to this. It remains the basic conceptual framework of *Religionswissenschaft,* exemplified for example in the works of Mircea Eliade. Scholars however disagree as to whether the progression should end with monotheism, where we currently are, or whether it should proceed to a logical conclusion in atheism, as Marx and Durkheim believed, and Freud hoped.

The theories of Tylor and his contemporaries carried at least the implied recognition that 'man makes god in his own image;' that is, man models his conception of the supernaturals after his understanding of himself. Yet by and large the early theorists failed to recognize how changing conceptions of the supernaturals—Tylor's evolutionary stages—mirrored changes in the sphere of human socio-political organization. We can recognize now that, to the extent that the evolutionary approach to religion still has power (and it certainly has considerable, as I will suggest in Chapter 14), it is largely because of the connection between religion and socio-political organization.

Although both Tylor and Frazer marshaled enormous masses of ethnographic data in support of their theories, their approach was essentially logical rather than empirical, differing in no important respect from the 'conjectural prehistories' constructed by Enlightenment moral philosophers a hundred years earlier. That is, data collected from present-day societies at various levels of cultural complexity was adduced to support a preconceived scheme based largely on logic. According to this conception, the primitives of today are fossilized survivals preserving, for our inspection, the original forms of human culture and society. This was what Auguste Comte had designated as the 'comparative method;' it became and still largely remains the basic empirical prop for evolutionary anthropology. In fact, as Evans-Pritchard pointed out (1965:11), 'It is a remarkable fact that none of the anthropologists whose theories about primitive religion have been most influential had ever been near a primitive people.'

A curious flaw in many of the early evolutionary theories of religion, both developmental and functional, resulted from the authors' preoccupation with, and misunderstanding of, 'totemism,' which was perhaps the hottest single topic in anthropology at the end of the nineteenth century. At that time the ethnographic data from Australia was just beginning to appear in print, and it came as a kind of revelation to anthropologists. Here were, as it seemed, by far the most primitive people yet encountered anywhere, and they immediately displaced the native North American as everybody's model for the original Primitive Man. And since Australian religion was essentially totemic, with different tribes or lineages worshipping different Powers whom they regarded as ancestral, this was taken to be the primordial form of all religion. Within a span of seven years (1911–1918) Frazer, Durkheim, and Freud all published books based on that assumption.

But the Australian ethnographers, Fison and Howitt and later Spencer and Gillen, offered no emic insights; they made no attempt to suggest what was going on in the minds of native Australians when they practiced their totemic rituals. That left the armchair ethnologists, who had never seen an Australian, free to recreate the cognitive dimension of totemic religion from their own imaginations, or logical perspective. Tylor saw it as merely one of the common expressions of animal-worship; Freud supposed that the participants in totemic feasts were eating the slain father-figure, an idea always dear to his heart. The authors, with the partial exception of Durkheim, failed to recognize that the belief in tutelary deities, each responsive to a particular social group, is a very pervasive one in many religions. It is exemplified by Yahweh in relation to the ancient Hebrews, by patron saints in medieval thought, and by the village saints about whom I have written in Chapter 3. Instead, under the compelling logic of early evolutionism, totemism came to be seen as a fixed evolutionary stage common to all the earliest peoples. I will return to this topic in Chapter 14.

*Culture
history*

To a considerable extent, the neatly logical theories of the evolutionists were destroyed by the field-work revolution of the early twentieth century. Observed on the ground, the religion of so-called primitives turned out to be far more complex and more diversified than had been assumed, often combining elements from several of the supposed evolutionary stages. There was at the same time a strong reaction against evolutionist theory in general, partly because its most ardent proponents demanded too much from it, and partly because of the excesses committed in its name by eugenicists, social Darwinists, racists, and others. Both anthropologists and historians, impressed by the complexity and seeming lack of order in their material, retreated to a belief that history proceeds mostly by unplanned accidents, in response to local and unpredictable circumstances. According to this view there is no coherent pattern in history; it is what Lowie called an 'unplanned hodgepodge; a thing of shreds of patches' (Lowie 1920: 441). The assumption in regard to religion was that, once originated, it was carried along by the weight of tradition, and diffused from one people to another and from one age to another. Along the way it acquired accretions through contact with other religions, as well as through human ingenuity.

The culture historians were mainly diffusionists. They did not have a great deal of respect for human inventiveness, preferring to believe that most peoples' culture traits were borrowed from other peoples. In the study of religion, their principal endeavor was to try and reconstruct the historical development of particular religions, by identifying within them the accretions that could be traced to contact with different peoples or circumstances. Within Judaism and Christianity, for example, it was possible to identify elements that are clearly the legacies of pre-Judaic Sumerian and Babylonian belief; others that reflect Egyptian influence; accretions from Zoroastrianism at the time of the Babylonian captivity; influences from Indian-derived salvationism; and still later influences from Greek thought. In the study of Navajo religion it was possible to factor out what are surely post-contact beliefs and practices inspired by Christianity; a great many beliefs and practices borrowed from the Pueblo Indian neighbors; and a small core of beliefs that are evidently part of the Athabascan heritage, carried south by the Navajos from their original sub-Arctic homeland.

Although the diffusionist approach has been dismissed out of hand as 'unscientific' by modern evolutionists like Marvin Harris, it actually had a much more substantial ethnographic basis than had the theory of the evolutionists. The diffusionists were able to point out, in the modern world, how religions are continually borrowing from one another, and how every religion is recognizably a mass of accretions from all kinds of sources. For that very reason religion has often been treated by the culture historians, no less than by the early evolutionists, as an autonomous domain of thought of and activity, uninfluenced by developments in other areas of culture.

The problem of origins

The limitation of both diffusionist and evolutionary theories of religion lay in their inability to account for its ultimate origins. To address that question—which became one of the major preoccupations of early anthropologists—both diffusionists and evolutionists were forced to turn from history to philosophy; that is, to purely logical explanation. Tylor's view, which had many followers, was that religion arose from mankind's need to explain the unexplainable in everyday experience: he had reference specifically to sleep, dreams, trance, death, and the like. These, he believed, led to the belief in a detachable soul in each person, which led in turn to the belief that there must also be a detachable soul in everything else. Such was the general character of religious belief that Tylor attributed to all the earliest human societies, and which he designated as 'animism.' Others took a less intellectualized and more affective approach to the problem of origins, supposing that religion arose because it was necessary to find something concrete onto which to project the feelings of awe, adoration, inspiration, and fear to which we are all subject. All such theories, as Evans-Pritchard (1965: 25) has justly observed, can never be anything but 'Just-So Stories,' logically clever but beyond any possibility of verification, because we cannot get inside the heads of primordial men and women.

Both evolutionary and historical theories have a great deal of explanatory power, retrodictively, but practically no predictive power. In the case of evolutionary theory, the problem is: where do we go from here? Evolution, as applied to cultural institutions, is seen as a process of unidirectional development. It is a conception peculiar to the West, and its proponents have unhesitatingly placed their own Euro-American civilization at the top of the evolutionary ladder. In the case of religion, this places monotheism at the top of the ladder. There are, then, only two logical possibilities as to what comes next. Either we stay forever where we are, which is contrary to the basic assumption of evolutionism, or we pass on to atheism. The latter idea was attractive to rationalists of the eighteenth and nineteenth centuries, and even the early twentieth, but since that time most social scientists have backed away from it. A third possibility of course is that we revert to one of the earlier forms of religion, but that idea runs counter to the basic linearity of evolutionary theory.

Unpredictability is of course taken for granted by diffusionists. Since religion offers a virtually unlimited field for the human creative imagination, there is no telling what it will come up with. As Harold Ross once predicted about the future of the New Yorker Magazine which he had founded, 'it will go its own goddam way.'

Functional theories bypass the question of origins and ignore altogether the question of specific content, suggesting that religion is sufficiently accounted for by identifying the obvious and, seemingly, necessary functions that it performs in every society. They disagree however as to which are the most salient of is functions, as will be evident from the discussion that follows.

According to one interpretation, the word 'religion' is derived from Latin *religio,* 'to bind.' If true, the most basic premise of sociofunctional theory is embodied within the etymology of that one word: religion is that which binds people into communities. The idea is certainly an old one, and is quite clearly suggested in much social and political writing of the seventeenth and eighteenth centuries. However it was two thinkers of the nineteenth and early twentieth centuries, Emile Durkheim and Max Weber, who gave both shape and theoretical power to the sociology of religion as we understand it today. They combined two much older ideas, that society is necessary for human survival and that religion is necessary for the functioning of society, with a new, organic model of society as an organism having needs of its own to survive, independent of the needs of its individual members. It can survive and function only if, in many circumstances, the members subordinate their individual interests to those of the group.

Durkheim and Weber also gave to sociology of religion two of its most basic organizing concepts: solidarity (from Durkheim) and legitimation (from Weber). Solidarity is the collective sentiment, transcending both morality and personal self-interest, that we share with other members of a community. It makes us willing to act on their behalf even when it's not in our own self-interest. It finds perfect expression in the famous toast offered by James G. Blaine: 'My country: may she always be in the right, but right or wrong, my country!' Durkheim believed however that in nearly all pre-modern societies it was religion rather than patriotic nationalism that provided the ideological basis of solidarity.

Legitimation is whatever gives moral authority to the demands society places on us, in its own interest, so that we are willing to obey. It is a conspicuous fact that the only authority humans are normally willing to obey, without some form of external justification, is parental authority. 'You'll do what I say, because I'm your father,' carries sanction enough. But any command from another person is likely to elicit the response: 'Why should I obey you—you're not my father!' In short, all authority apart from parental authority requires some form of external legitimation. Therefore, according to the view of Weber and Durkheim, society casts itself in the role of a kind of super-father, by inventing gods who speak its wishes. Society deifies itself in order to legitimize the demands that it places upon us, in its own interest rather than in ours.

The great strength of Durkheim's and Weber's approach is that it clearly links religion to the question of moral authority, which every society must have if it is to survive and to function. This makes it possible to understand also the factor of inertia, so conspicuous in all religions. They are not simply carried along by the weight of tradition, as the culture historians supposed; they are slow to change because legitimation requires a degree of constancy. People are slow to accept new voices of authority, even when the world is changing around them. 'Give me that old-time religion' is a cry continually heard.

Durkheim was a dedicated evolutionist, and to a much greater extent than other thinkers of the time he was able to link religious evolution to social evolution. Since the gods are society deified, they have to be periodically reconceptualized as the forms of society change. Animism (the belief in spirits dwelling in everything) is appropriate to the egalitarian society of the most primitive folk; anthropomorphic deities emerge when man achieves a greater degree of mastery over nature; high gods emerge when hereditary rulers appear in human society. Like all early evolutionary theories, that of Durkheim rested more on logic than on ethnography or history; indeed it was wrong in many of its ethnographic specifics. It did nevertheless place religion firmly within the broader context of culture and society.

The most serious weakness in Durkheim's theory, as stated by him, is simply its dogmatic reductionism and determinism. Society *causes* religion, and all other explanations for religion are false, as he categorically asserted at one point. Weber, whose intellectual background was in German Idealism rather than in Enlightenment Rationalism, was somewhat less deterministic. Although his basic theoretical outlook is not easy to distill from the enormous and disparate mass of his writings, he seems to have envisioned a kind of feedback relationship between religion and society, without finally according primacy to either.

There was, of course, a politico-economic dimension in Weber's work that is not found in Durkheim, and for which he is chiefly remembered. He was able to show that modern European Protestantism was more conducive to the development of capitalism than were the religions of China and India, because of its emphasis on the individual rather than the group as the main focus of religion. Weber viewed this difference in evolutionary terms, but he was an evolutionist (actually a progressivist) in the mentalist tradition of German Idealism rather than in the sociofunctional tradition of the French Enlightenment. Evolution as Weber conceived it was mainly a mental process, involving the progressive maturation of the human mind, which he called 'rationalization.' His conception of primitive society was purely a 'type concept' (his term), based on logic rather than on ethnography. This is undoubtedly one reason why he is much less read by anthropologists than is Durkheim.

We owe to Weber nevertheless the important concept of charisma: the extraordinary quality possessed by some people, that makes others want to follow them. It is nearly always attributed to a divine or supernatural source. As we saw in Chapter 8, this concept is really at the heart of Weber's definition of religion itself.

The sociological approach of Durkheim and Weber, further developed by many later scholars, remains a powerful force within anthropology, especially in Great Britain. In later years, structuralists have added an interesting new dimension to it, showing how structural regularities in myth and ritual are adaptable to the needs of society. The specific contribution of the structuralists will be considered in later paragraphs.

The sociological approach is unique among functional theories of religion in its ability to predict something about the specific content of religion. Starting from the premise that man makes god in his own image, it predicts that conceptions of the supernatural will reflect in a general way the current organization of society. The predictive possibilities in this regard have been quite extensively explored by Guy Swanson in *Birth of the Gods* (1964).

Political theory

Karl Marx's view of religion, as of much else, was basically a conspiratorial one. His approach was not very different from that of Durkheim, except that for organic society he substituted the state: a conscious and self-directing entity. The state, or its rulers, invent gods in order to get people to obey them, because they would not obey a purely human authority. Marx's theory is certainly not entirely wrong, or even inconsistent with Durkheim, provided one can accept (as Marx could not) that leaders are not always conspirators. But it lacks altogether the optimistic voluntarism characteristic of Durkheim and his school. According to Durkheim, people have the religion that they want or need to have; according to Marx they have the religion that's forced upon them. But Marx's evolutionary scenario envisioned a final, utopian stage in which there would be no religion because there would be no leaders.

In defense of Marx it must be acknowledged that when society submits itself to a human ruler, it also submits to a conscious and self-directing will, which thereafter may or may not act in the interest of the society that has created it. Among other things, the ruler may be able to shape the development of religion, in his own interest. This perspective resonates in the work of many present-day archaeologists, despite their otherwise strong dedication to ecological models. Since their excessive rationalism and materialism requires a rational and a causal explanation for everything, and since religion is not well explained on ecological grounds, the next best thing is to explain it in Marxist terms. Thus, we find a continuing explanation of religious phenomena on the presupposition that they serve the interests of elites.

For all its hyper-materialistic deficiencies, Marxism stands alone in one important respect. It captures, more articulately than any other approach, one of the central truths about religion: that it is fundamentally about power.

*Psycho-
functional
theories*

As a field of theory, the psychology of religion is not nearly so unified as is the sociology of religion, mainly because it has been developed by psychologists as much as by anthropologists and sociologists. There is, as in nearly all psychology, an insistence on explaining religion in terms of individual rather than of group needs, and theories about individual needs are themselves highly diverse. The two major bodies of psychofunctional theory have been called pathogenic and normative, but there are also two versions of the latter.

Pathogenic theories. This conception of religion, no longer fashionable among scientists, was a byproduct of eighteenth and nineteenth century scientific atheism. It starts from the presupposition that religion is not merely a mystery to be explained, but an aberration, because it is anti-rational. What, then, is the etymology of this disease?

The philologist Max Müller sought to answer the question in historical and philological terms. If we accept that man has always been a rational being, where and why did he go wrong? Müller believed that all humans have a 'consciousness of the infinite,' by which he meant an undifferentiated, unseen power. But primitive man lacked the conceptual vocabulary to think in abstract terms, so he was forced to point to concrete beings that have power, to symbolize his understanding of the 'infinite.' In the beginning those beings were recognized to be mere symbols, like words, but later people mistook the symbol for the thing symbolized, and men and animals became deified in their own right. Thus, according to Müller's rather idiosyncratic view, religion is 'a disease of language.'

Much more commonly, psychological thinkers of the nineteenth and early twentieth centuries conceived of religion as a kind of neurosis, which could be linked to specific physiological or psychological disorders. This approach reached its fullest development in the works of Sigmund Freud and his school. In his typically dogmatic and aggressive style, Freud linked everything to sexual neuroses. '... the fantastic re- pressions, denials, displacements, reaction formations, and other defen- sive maneuvers institutionalized by religion are a necessary but painful discipline imposed on an immature humanity incapable, for the time be- ing, of rational ego control of sexual and aggressive instincts' (Wallace 1966: 14).

The strain of apriori atheism is very evident in Freud's thinking. He had his own version of evolutionism, in which man would eventually learn to control his sexual and aggressive instincts, and religion would disappear. On that point at least, Freud shared the same utopian vision as Marx.

Normative theories. In addition to his rather murky theory, which is now out of fashion, Freud also invented a whole new conceptual vocabu- lary for the analysis of personality, which has proven valuable to anthro- pologists as well as psychologists. To that extent many anthropologists have been influenced by Freud, especially in America. On the other hand only a few have been willing to follow down his theoretical path. For one thing his evolutionary schema, based on an odd combination of classi- cal mythology and misunderstood ethnography, is simply unacceptable. More to the point, though, the notion that any of the basic, recurring features of culture is 'abnormal' is anthropological heresy. To anthropol- ogists, culture *is* norm.

Anthropologists, as well as some psychologists, therefore developed psychofunctional theories based on the assumption that religion is nor- mal and necessary—the 'religion of healthy-mindedness,' as William James called it. Most anthropologists favored a theory of religion as a kind of preventive medicine, to reduce or displace anxieties. That view, which obviously places primary emphasis on the cognitive domain of religion, was advanced by several of the most distinguished American anthropologists of the mid-twentieth century, including Irving Hallow- ell, John Honigmann, Clyde Kluckhohn, Weston LaBarre, and Morris Opler. Its most articulate exponent however was the British anthropolo- gist Bronislaw Malinowski.

Some psychologists, including William James and C. G. Jung, pre- ferred to think of religion as a kind of curative medicine, relieving stress rather than preventing it. This view, which places emphasis more on ritual than on belief, did not find a great deal of favor among anthropologists, although echoes of it are found in the work of Paul Radin. However, a study of Navajo religion would seem to provide more support for the curative theory than for the preventive one. On one hand, Navajo ideas about the supernaturals seem more calculated to engender than to relieve neuroses. On the other hand, a very large part of Navajo ritual is devoted quite specifically to the healing of conditions caused by the supernaturals.

A fundamental weakness of most psychofunctional theory is its assumption that the gods are benevolent—an ethnocentric fallacy reflecting the Abrahamic conception of God. For most peoples, many of the gods are anything but benevolent, and they contribute not comfort but anxiety to the human condition. A great deal of ritual is intended merely to allay their evil actions. In this regard I'm often reminded of the line spoken by the young Jewish Prince Herod, in Robert Graves' *I, Claudius*. The Emperor Augustus says to him, 'I've never understood how you Jews can have only one god,' and Herod replies, 'If you knew how cruel our god is to us, you wouldn't want any more.'[22]

Semiotic theory

Among functional theories of religion, the semiotic approach places the most complete stress on the cognitive domain. Its most articulate, and frequently eloquent, spokesman has been Clifford Geertz, whose 'definition' (read: characterization) of religion was cited in Chapter 8. Because it serves as an introduction to the semiotic approach, it is worth restating here. Religion is 'a system of symbols which acts to establish powerful, pervasive, and long-lasting moods and motivations in men by formulating conceptions of a general order of existence and clothing these conceptions with such an aura of factuality that the moods and motivations seem uniquely realistic' (Geertz 1966: 4). The extraordinary thing about this rather high-flown 'definition' is the absence of the word 'meaning,' which is really at the heart and core of semiotic theory (and is contained within the etymology of 'semiotic' itself). The essence of the semiotic theory is that language gives names to things, but religion gives them meanings, which make it possible for us to deal with them. It enables us to make decisions we could never make on our own, by telling us which things are good to do or to have or to see or to eat, and which are bad. Religion is first and foremost a way of knowing—a kind of language—but at the same time a system of evaluation.

Semiotic theory, like much linguistic theory, starts from the presumption that humans can only think with the aid of symbols, which are mostly

---

[22]The above is paraphrased from the televised version of *I, Claudius*. I don't have an actual transcript.

but not entirely words. There is a further assumption, as in linguistics, that the meanings assigned to symbols are wholly arbitrary: any word in any language can mean whatever the speakers want. Consequently semiotic theory (like psychofunctional theory) ignores as unimportant the specific content of religion. The deities themselves are symbols, and there is no way of predicting how they will be conceived by particular peoples. They are in a certain sense dependent variables, created out of our need to symbolize. The symbols themselves are the ultimate datum and the first cause of religion, as is made evident in Geertz' characterization.

There is, consequently, no possibility of developing a general theory in regard to the content of religion. Since all symbols are completely arbitrary, knowing one religion will not necessarily tell you anything about any other. Semiotic analysis can only be particularistic with respect to each religion; i.e. emic. As Geertz (1966: 4) has further remarked, 'The notion that religion tunes human actions to an envisioned cosmic order and projects cosmic order onto the plane of human experience is hardly novel. But it is hardly investigated either, so that we have very little idea of how, in empirical terms, this particular miracle is accomplished .... the theoretical framework which would allow us to provide an analytical account of it ... does not exist.' It probably never will exist, until we know far more about what goes on within the 'black box' of the human mind than we do at present.

Because it is quintessentially particularistic, and can predict nothing, the semiotic approach has sometimes been characterized by both its adherents and its opponents as humanistic rather than 'scientific.' Be that as it may, it is the only functional theory of religion that starts with the horse rather than the cart. That is, it gives primary attention to the cognitive sphere because cognition must precede action.

*An
assessment*

Most functional theories of religion have both explanatory and predictive power, though not as much as their most ardent champions have claimed. Sociofunctional theory predicts that religion will continue to go where society leads, modeling the supernatural order on the existing social order. Political theory predicts that religion will go where leaders direct it to go. Psychofunctional theory predicts that many aspects of religion will remain constant, because stresses and strains will always be with us. Only semiotic theory asserts that there can be no prediction, since the content of religion is wholly arbitrary.

With the exception of Malinowski, British anthropologists, who are very susceptible to French influence, have generally opted for sociofunctional explanations of religion. Americans, who have historically been more susceptible to German influences, have opted more for psychofunctional theories. As readers may have gathered, however, I do not share the latter preference. While I find explanatory power in both approaches, the sociological seems more compelling because it recognizes the social embeddedness of religion. The trouble with all of the psychofunctional theories, as I suggested in Chapter 7, lies in their ethnocentric assumption about the primacy of the psychological function.

The major deficiency of all the functional theories, as they are usually presented to us, lies in their reductionism. It is the result of a basic tautology: that of letting explanation serve as definition. If we presuppose that the collective function of religion is more important than the personal function, we can define its center and its boundaries in such a way that many of the non-social aspects are left out of account, or downplayed. This is evident in the work of Durkheim, and even more so in that of Marx. If we presuppose on the other hand that the individual functions are most important, we can dismiss the social functions as aspects of social organization rather than of religion per se, as some anthropologists have done. But ethnography has shown that both individuals and societies vary enormously in the relative importance that they attach to the collective and to the individual domains of religion. I will add here that the same is true as regards the purely cognitive domain. Although I agree with the semioticists that religion is quintessentially a way of knowing, it is one that provides far more complete and valuable knowledge to some peoples than to others.

This points up another deficiency of most functionalist theory: that of 'one theory fits all' universalism. There is an underlying assumption that the same basic needs, social or psychological, are salient in all societies. The Navajo and Arab cases alone are sufficient to show how wrong such an assumption is.

In explaining religion by identifying the needs that it serves, the functionalists have really solved a non-problem. No one ever doubted that religion serves needs, and no one ever doubted what at least some of those needs are. Functionalism, as I have indicated more than once before, bypasses the most difficult of all questions, to anyone interested in the processes of human thought: 'how can people believe *this stuff?*'

As I have just suggested, the specific content of any particular religion is by far the hardest part to account for. The psychofunctional and political schools ignore it as irrelevant, the sociofunctional school predicts it only to a limited extent, while the semiotic school insists that it cannot be predicted. Nevertheless there has arisen since World War II one school, that of structuralism, that attempts to account at least in part for the substantive content of religion. It shares with the semiotic school an emphasis on religion as a symbolic system, closely intertwined with language, but disagrees with the proposition that symbols are totally arbitrary and unpredictable.

Setting aside both historical and materialistic perspectives, structuralism attempts to account for commonalities in religion, both in form and in function, in terms of universal, built-in features of the human mind, sometimes called 'mental templates.' Structuralists share with evolutionists the conviction that there is a lot of cross-cultural regularity among peoples, which cannot be explained simply by history, or accidental contacts. Their doctrine however is more nearly universalist than that of evolutionists, finding cultural regularities at all times and places, which are the consequences of an unchanging human mind.

Structural anthropology derives from a fairly solid foundation in linguistic theory. Most scholars accept that the ability to communicate by means of symbols—to create as well as to learn and use them—is uniquely human, and that all humans create and use them in broadly similar ways. The thousands of extant languages sound enormously diverse but, considering all the possibilities for symboling, they exhibit a remarkable degree of similarity. They all originate in the same area of the brain, and they all communicate by means of a finite number of sounds, produced by a fairly limited number of muscles. There are also basic features of grammar common to them all. The structuralists carry that understanding beyond language and into other domains of culture, which also, in their view, involve symbolic communication in broadly similar ways. It is no surprise therefore that much of their attention has been devoted to the domain of religion, or that they have achieved their most generally recognized successes in this domain.

Perhaps because of its universalism, structuralism had an enormous vogue shortly after World War II, particularly among anthropologists in France and Britain. Many different domains of culture have been subjected to structural analysis, but the domain of religion, pervaded as it is with symbolism, has proved especially susceptible. The three most original thinkers on this subject have been Claude Lévi-Strauss (often identified as the founder of the school, though he sometimes denies it), Mary Douglas, and Victor Turner.

Lévi-Strauss and Douglas have concentrated mainly on the analysis of myth, in which they find a great many recurring features. Douglas interprets this regularity in terms of Durkheimian sociofunctional theory: the recurring features help to legitimize society and its organizational features. Lévi-Strauss takes a more autonomist view, suggesting that the regularities in mythology, like regularities in language, are expressive of a common inherent logic, not dictated by material needs. Both Douglas and Lévi-Strauss have, like the semioticists, stressed the close interlinkage between religion and language. For that reason they approach mythology from a static perspective, as something whose purpose is to create and to maintain society in a steady state. Theirs is an analysis of a world-in-being.

Victor Turner, who has concentrated mainly on ritual rather than on myth, has conceived of religion from the perspective of a world-in-becoming rather than a world-in-being. The world is always changing, and ritual serves to channel the course of change through desired, ritually sanctioned transformations. Ritual in this view is fundamentally a process. For that reason, Turner's version of structuralism is less intimately connected with language than are the approaches of Lévi-Strauss and Douglas. All three however have found enough recurrences to confirm, to their satisfaction, the view that all human minds are programmed to create and to use symbols in the same ways, and that this is exemplified in their religions.

The anthropological structuralists are not of course building on wholly new ground. Both Freud and Jung, with their concept of the 'collective unconscious,' were arguing in essence that there is an inborn mental template in all of us, which religion comes to occupy.

Structuralism stands alone in its ability to account for the origin not only of religion but of specific religious forms, which it does on the same basis as the origin of linguistic forms: on the pre-programming of the human brain. Of course, this only carries the mystery back a step further into the past. The question then becomes: how did the mind come to be so programmed, given that this feature is unique to the human species? The structuralists can only fall back on the same logical explanation offered by all materialists: it must have been necessary for survival.

Anthropologists and sociologists, seeking to explain the reasons for religion, have often put me in mind of John Saxe's six blind Hindoos, who went to 'see' the elephant. One took hold of the trunk, one took a tusk, one grabbed an ear, one seized a leg, one took the tail, and one held a hand against the animal's side; each then offered a characterization of the beast based in whatever appendage he had taken hold of. In the case of religion, some social scientists have seized upon its sociological functions, some on its psychological, some on its dramaturgical or mythological or historical elements, and we have been assured in each case that this is what religion is 'really about.'

In short, explanations of religion suffer from the same deficiency as do definitions: that of reductionism. They are not wrong; they are simply incomplete. None of them explains more than one appendage of the elephant. Developmental theories account to some extent for the current forms of religion, but not its reason for being, while in the case of functionalist theories the reverse is true. There is a reason for this disconnect: namely that there is no deterministic relationship between function and forms. The functions of religion don't determine its forms in any very definite way, and the forms certainly don't determine the functions.

It is useful to recall, too, the distinction that I made in Chapter 5, between pure and applied religion. The functionalists, in the tradition of modern Western thought, are simply too pragmatic; they have tended to treat all religion as though it were applied religion. They ignore the importance of religion simply as a system of knowledge.

After a lifetime of studying religion, E. E. Evans-Pritchard wrote that 'I no not deny that peoples have reasons for their beliefs—that they are rational; I do not deny that all religious rites may be accompanied by emotional experiences, that feeling may even be an important element in the performance; and I certainly do not deny that religious ideas and practices are directly associated with social groups—that religion, whatever else it may be, is a social phenomenon. What I do deny is that it is explained by any of these facts, or all of them together . . . .' (Evans-Pritchard 1965: 111). The author, who had converted to Roman Catholicism, was speaking from a theistic point of view, but I find it possible to agree with him provided that for 'explained' we substitute 'sufficiently explained.'

12

A CATALOGUE OF NEEDS

The various functional approaches to religion have established what was never in doubt: that religion exists in large part because it satisfies common human needs. But functional theories, by identifying religion as a response to needs, make it a kind of dependent variable, while needs themselves emerge as the ultimate datum or prime mover. In our search for an adaptive understanding of religion, it then becomes necessary to explain why we have the needs that religion satisfies, many of which are not found in other animal species.

What needs? The only possible answer, in light of ethnographic knowledge is: a great many needs—intellectual, social, psychological, creative, and aesthetic. But needs, if by that we mean imperatives, don't provide a full explanation either. Religions respond also to a great many desires that are common to much of humanity, but are less than imperative. They are much more compelling for some persons than for others, and for some may be absent altogether. I will employ the term 'needs' throughout the analysis that follows, but it must be understood to include desires, of varying strength, as well as imperative needs.

The best way to escape from the reductionism that is inherent in both sociofunctional and psychofunctional theory is to recognize that needs vary enormously not only from individual to individual but from society to society. We can then begin to appreciate that there are some societies, like those of the Pueblo Indians, in which the most important function of religion is social, others, like our own, where it is primarily psychological, and others again, like that of ancient Egypt, where it was primarily political. But religion in all of them is multi-vocal; it satisfies a great many needs besides the most basic ones.

In this chapter I will try to do two things: to identify, as specifically as I can, the different needs that are met by religion, and to consider why those needs exist. In the next two chapters I will consider how those needs are satisfied by specific features of content, in different religions. My premise is simply that religion is adaptive because the needs it satisfies are adaptive. My approach to that extent is teleological, as in fact is all adaptive theory.

Readers should note that I disavow any suggestion of causality. Religion did not create any of the needs discussed here, now was it necessarily created by them. I merely suggest that it persists because it meets all of these needs, to some extent and for some people.

Cognitive needs

I have to insist once again that any attempt to understand religion must begin with its cognitive domain , because cognition must precede action, or reaction. Cognitive needs, as I conceive them, are individual and at the same time collective. They are individual because thinking can go on only in individual human minds; they are collective because society, if it is to function effectively, requires all its members to think pretty much the same way, in many circumstances. That means also that the individual members must need or desire pretty much the same things. It is often religion that conditions them to do so.

The need to know

It is hardly necessary to consider why there is a need for knowledge, in a species as poorly endowed with instinct as is *Homo sapiens*. Nearly all of our dealings with the world have to be based on the stored information we possess, derived from our own or from other peoples' experiences. Every religion is quintessentially a system of knowledge; not necessarily an all-embracing system but nevertheless, for most peoples, a very extensive one. It embodies nearly all the information that people possess about the unseen Powers, apart from those few powers (i.e. Forces) that don't seem to be sentient.

To begin with it endows the Powers with form, without which it is almost impossible to think about them in any concrete way. We know they're out there and watching us, but we can't see them, so as a cognitive necessity we have to imagine them. Imagination has conceived them as humans, as animals, as partly both, and in a variety of shapes that seem neither human nor animal. One of the clearest evidences of their specialness lies in the fact that they are rarely confined within the normal morphological boundaries found in the everyday world. They can be in impossible shapes, can readily change shape, and can be in several places at once.

Religions usually define also, quite explicitly, the powers that each of the sentient beings possesses. This is vitally important practical knowledge, because it tells us what to expect and what to fear from each of them. Some of the loftiest of the Beings can do anything; many of the others are much more restricted in what they can and can't do. Knowledge about specific powers helps us to decide which ones to address and which ones to avoid in specific circumstances.

In addition to defining their powers, religion usually endows the Beings with a fairly well-defined personality, which may or may not be human personality writ large. Some are mainly or entirely benevolently inclined; some are malevolent; many are capricious, and many are vengeful. Ideas about their personality help us to understand not only what they can and can't do, but what they might or might not be inclined to do. This again is helpful in deciding which ones it is worthwhile to address, and which ones are more likely to be annoyed than to be pleased by our attention.

Finally, many of the deities are endowed with a biography which further helps us to understand them, just as biographical information does in the case of living persons. We may be told how the deities came into being, what adventures they have subsequently had, and what feats they have performed. Very often it is the biography that helps us to understand the extent of their power; we judge what they can and can't do on the basis of what they've done in the past.

A great deal of knowledge about the supernaturals is embodied in formal mythology, but there is also a vast amount of folk wisdom that is simply based on peoples' personal experiences with the powers. In the Roman Catholic world, much of the enormous folklore about particular saints falls into this category. The dwellers in a Spanish valley, where there are fourteen different shrines to the Virgin, have discovered that the Virgins at different localities can bring quite different kinds of benefits (see Christian 1972). This is widely shared folk wisdom, but it is not formal mythology (and is condemned as false by the priests).

Religious knowledge is not of course confined to the realm of the otherworlds. It may provide definition for just about everything in the everyday world as well, including the nature of man himself. For Navajos, nearly every feature of the physical landscape is the focus of some amount of religious knowledge, which tells how and/or why it acquired its shape, and whether it is beneficial or harmful to go near.

People everywhere vary in the extent of their religious knowledge, just as they do in their secular knowledge. It may be a question of how much they have been taught, or how much they have sought to acquire on their own, which may reflect in turn how personally important it is to them. In many societies, like the Navajo, the total sum of knowledge is far too great for an ordinary person to master, because of the investment of time and effort that is required. In such cases it may not be necessary for the average person to have extensive knowledge , as long as he or she can have ready access to someone who has. Hence the vital importance of religious sages and practitioners, who are libraries of the unwritten knowledge that everyone needs to access at times.

The need to believe

Since most religious knowledge cannot be verified empirically (i.e. through observation and experience), it must be accepted on faith. However, few people in any society are what we would call fundamentalists, accepting every tenet and every myth with equal faith. Individuals vary in the extent of their faith, as they do in the extent of their knowledge, and the two are quite often correlated. The more you know, the more you believe, just because the more you know, the more questions religion answers for you.

Regardless of the extent of doubts, however, most people need at least a few things in which they can place absolute and unquestioning faith: an anchor point or points in the turbulent sea of knowledge. Usually, the most complete faith is placed in those Beings, or in those tenets, or in those rituals on which people have to rely in life-threatening situations; the situations in which purely existential decision-making is unbearable. The Beings or their dicta take decision-making out of our hands at the critical moments when we most need them to do so. It goes without saying however that not all persons place absolute faith in the same Beings or tenets. Within polytheistic systems, there is a wide range of possibilities.

I have the impression that, in our own and most other societies, people are apt to profess publicly more belief than they entertain privately. To express doubt nearly always brings a measure of social disapproval, and for good reason. It may sow the seeds of doubt in others; a doubt which, if it continues to spread, will undermine the central moral authority of society. The abhorrence of heresy that is so conspicuous in the Abrahamic religions is not because heresy threatens the damnation of the individual heretic; it is a potential infection that threatens the whole fabric of belief. The doubter is always the potential bad apple in the barrel. Hence the medieval Inquisition, to take one obvious example.

Language gives names to things, say the semioticists, and religion gives them meaning. Nothing in the universe, as most peoples see it, is there purely by chance. It was created, or came into being, for a purpose, and therefore must have some meaning. But the meaning can only be understood with relation to the purpose, and this is what religion supplies. To know how to think about a thing, we need to know what the supernaturals had in mind when they created it. From that perspective, religion tells us not merely which things are good or bad, but also which are important, which are interesting, and which are unknowable.

The need to understand

As I have just suggested, religion defines not only what is true but what is good, and for many people (and indeed for many theorists) this is its most important function. The practical value of our religious understanding is that it enables us to evaluate: what is good to do, what is good to have, what is good to eat, what is good to see, even what is good to think. That knowledge in turn forms the basis for much of our daily decision-making. By suggesting the proper course of action, religious knowledge may make easy a process of deciding that is otherwise very stressful.

The need to decide

Materialist theories of adaptation take it for granted that whatever is physically labor-saving is adaptive. Labor freed from one task can be devoted to others, thus increasing and diversifying the number of tasks that can be undertaken in any given period of time. It might likewise be suggested that religion is adaptive to the extent that it saves mental labor, which, just like physical labor, can be hard work. The mind can then be set free to concentrate on those innumerable problems of everyday existence that religion doesn't address.

The kinds of knowledge that I discussed in the previous sections are basically ontological; they give definition both to the supernatural and to the natural sphere. Definition however is not explanation. The human mind is endlessly curious, and demands to know not only what things are but why they are. It wants a solution to mysteries. This propensity also, if not an adaptive necessity, is at least an adaptive advantage. It is what leads us to seek more knowledge, and knowledge is the most valuable of all our possessions in dealing with the world around us.

The need to explain

Much of our religious knowledge and understanding is seated in, and appeals to, the mystical mind, but explanation is the rationalist dimension of religion. Many things can and must be accepted on faith, which the mystical mind permits, but faith can be enhanced if beliefs can also be supported by rational arguments, or information. A great deal of mythology in fact helps to explain how the supernaturals came to be as they are.

Among the most widespread of myths, therefore, are those that explain why things are. Such myths (just like theories of religion) are of two types: those that explain things by telling how they originated, and those that explain things by showing how they serve necessary functions, which may not on the surface be obvious. Take for example the question of sexuality, which is one of nature's must absorbing mysteries. Why did the gods choose to make all beings in different male and female forms, for purposes of reproduction, when they could just as easily have made all the members of each species in a single form, capable of reproducing itself? The latter choice would have been the more parsimonious, and hence the more intuitively logical. Therefore nearly all peoples have a myth to account either for the origin of sexual division, or for its function, or both.

One of the most intriguingly rationalistic myths known to me is the Navajo myth that accounts for the existence of cold, hunger, pain, death, and a few other ills. The great Hero Twins, who had set themselves the task of slaying all of the ills besetting the *Diné*, encountered and menaced each of those things in its turn, but each was able to persuade them, on wholly logical and pragmatic grounds, that it was necessary for human good. Without cold people would freeze to death without knowing it; without hunger people would not eat, and would die of malnutrition; without pain they would not know they were hurt, and might bleed to death; without death the world would become overpopulated, and so on.

The need for renewal

Religious beliefs serve above all to create and to maintain a status quo, by identifying it as the will of the gods. And yet society and technology inevitably change, in spite of our best efforts (and indeed often because of them), and when that happens the old beliefs are often seen to be out of step. They don't provide adequate explanation or understanding of the world of our own making that now confronts us. When that disjuncture occurs the most dedicated of fundamentalists may try to repair it by halting or even reversing the course of social change. Their efforts however are never successful for long, and as a result, sooner or later, it is religion itself that has to change. But while the need for change is generally recognized, there is a continual dialectic between those who want to throw out the old and those who want to throw out the new.

Revitalization movements of one kind or another are as common and as predictable as is social change. They vary in their degree of drastic-ness, from minor reforms to total replacement. Christianity as envisioned by Jesus was a movement for reform within the system; as envisioned by his apostles (particularly Paul) it was a movement for total replacement of the system.

The phenomenon of Jesus and other messiahs raises one of the most intriguing problems in the study of religion, and the most inexplicable in purely rational terms. For at least the last twenty-five hundred years, individuals have come forward with extraordinary frequency to assert that they have received a message from on high, that will offer a new road to salvation for those that follow. The person thus favored is rarely if ever content to keep the new dispensation to himself; he (very occasionally also she) is duty bound to share it with others, and thus to become a teacher and a leader. Reformers and messiahs of this kind, who go by a variety of names, continue to appear regularly both in the Islamic world and in India, and occasionally also in the Christian world.

Although the need to keep religion in step with a changing world is understandable enough, why is it met so frequently in this particular fash-ion? I can offer only a very partial explanation, for in fact I am still in many ways mystified—not by its occurrence but by the frequency of its recurrence. First, I'm sure it has something to do with the nature of the mystical mind, which to me is a total 'black box.' The mystical mind, I guess, is ever receptive to the possibility of messages from out beyond. Second, and more rationally understandable, any change in religion can only be sanctioned by a new message from on high. An attempt for man to change religion on his own initiative is heresy.

I will discuss messianic movements, and their relationship to salva-tionism, much more fully in Chapter 14.

Social needs

Social needs are instinctual needs that we have because we are social animals. In the broadest sense they are the needs of society itself. We as individuals have them because society could not exist if we did not have them.

The need to belong

The origin of society, as envisioned by early rationalist theories, lay in man's recognition that he could not survive in a hostile world except through collaborative efforts. Division of labor between males and fe-males was necessary if children were to be raised at the same time when food was being procured; collaboration of males was required initially to bring down large game, and for defense against rival groups. Since it was an adaptive necessity, this social bonding was assumed to have begun in the very earliest days of prehistory.

In the recent past, the researches of primatologists have suggested that the origins of human social bonding may lie much farther back than that; in our pre-human days. The social bonding among animals and even insects, often quite elaborate, has of course been recognized for a long time, but it has always been attributed to pure instinct, while human bonding was explained as a consequence of rational decisions. But forms of social grouping similar to those among humans, including even rituals of incorporation, have now been recorded among chimpanzees, bonobos, and gorillas. Like the bonding propensities of other species, they can only be ascribed to instinct. It seems then that human social bonding also may be a matter of instinct as much as of reason.

Whether by instinct or by reason, we all clearly have a need to join. To join what? In the beginning it may have been, as in the case of our primate cousins, no more than a foraging and a food-sharing group. But our grouping and joining instinct has long since carried us beyond that elementary level, to create groupings much larger than are needed to provide nutrition, or to meet the other simple needs for physical survival.

The fact that humans always bond into groups larger than are physically necessary has long been noted by evolutionary theorists, and would seem to call for some kind of adaptive explanation. Various rationalistic theories have been suggested, usually involving the control of food resource areas. That is a good explanation as far as it goes; it recognizes that people bond out of a conscious or unconscious need for security, which in this case is security against starvation. But there are other threats to collective security as well. There is the threat from wild animals, the threat from enemy humans, and very importantly the threat from the gods. I would suggest that we bond instinctively, not in response to any conscious threat, but simply from a feeling that 'there's safety in numbers.' In effect, the human herd instinct is no different from the herd instinct of many animals.

For analytical purposes, it is useful at this point to distinguish between the need to join and the need to belong. The vast majority of us are born into social groups; we don't have to join them. We all have a need to belong, but the only people who have a need to join are those who either have no group (who are practically non-existent) or those who are dissatisfied with the group they're in. In the latter case, they nearly always join some other group as a matter of calculated self-interest, which does not often involve religion in any conscious way. So, I would say, religion is involved in belonging but not ordinarily in joining. Your religion comes to you automatically, as a consequence of your group membership.

What holds together the groups into which we bond? What makes us willing to give away food that we have collected, to rush to the defense of others, and in other ways to engage in activities from which we as individuals can expect no personal benefit? Early anthropologists, having 'discovered' kinship in the last third of the nineteenth century, decided that this was the original answer. The earliest human groups were extended family groups held together purely by bonds of kinship. But there was, and still is, no very clear understanding of why kinship bonds have such binding force, beyond the limits of the immediate household. It has been treated implicitly, and probably correctly, as an instinct. We now know however that even chimp and gorilla groups are not held together by kinship ties alone; there are formal rituals though which outsiders can be incorporated into the group. Because of their evident need for bonding, isolated primate males continually seek for such incorporation.

It was Durkheim who correctly recognized that what holds social groups together is that powerful collective sentiment that he called solidarity. It is not at all based on a rational calculation of self-interest, for it is embodied in much more deep-seated feelings. In many parts of the world, but especially in the Middle East, there are members of religious minorities who suffer lifelong disadvantage and sometimes persecution because they are Copts or Druze or Jews. The option of converting to a mainstream religion, and thereby escaping persecution, is always open to them, and yet few take it. Their sense of ethnic identity exists independently of any consciousness of a need for collection action or collective defense. Their solidarity in the most basic sense simply defines 'we' as versus 'they,' carrying with it the conviction that we are what matters, and they are not.

The single most powerful component of solidarity, and more particularly of religious solidarity, is an ultimate sense or rightness, transcending any rational or ethical considerations. We are not right because of the things we do; we are right because of who we are, and the gods have made us this way. That sentiment justifies whatever our society does, and it also justifies whatever the society demands of us. It convinces us of the 'rightness' of our group so completely that we are willing to submerge our individual interests and even our sense of identity within that of the larger group, and are willing and even eager to perform acts on its behalf from which as individuals we can derive no benefit.

Materialists, who seem unable to see the world except through the lens of self-interest, often pooh-pooh the idea that men will die for an idea. Yet everyone who lays down his life for his tribe or for his country is in effect dying for an idea; the idea that *our* group is more important than I am as an individual. It is not necessarily because we are better than other people (though we would always prefer to think so), but just because we are us. 'My country: may she always be in the right, but right or wrong, my country!' in the famous toast of James G. Blaine.

Why is solidarity necessary to hold groups together? Because large human groupings exist most of the time as a response to a latent threat rather than an active one. As a result, most of the time, there is no practical need for the group to function as a group. But there must be the sense of commonality that allows it to mobilize and to function, more or less as an instinctual reaction, when an actual threat arises.

Durkheim also correctly observed that the sentiment of solidarity extends automatically to kin, and seems to require no external legitimation or ideology. In the case of the nuclear family, with its totally interdependent members, this is understandable enough, but we don't really know why more distant kin relationships have such compelling force. They clearly do, though: 'Me against my brother; me and my brother against my cousin; me, my brother and my cousin against the world,' as an Arab saying has it. Durkheim's explanation, no longer very convincing, was that when social bonds are not based on interdependence, they must be created artificially because society needs them in order to exist. He referred to this as 'mechanical solidarity,' in contrast to what he perceived as the 'organic solidarity' of modern society, in which all people are truly interdependent. Such an explanation, for most of us today, carries teleology too far, imputing a rational will to society when it dictates how its members shall organize themselves.

In the earliest stages of human society, then, the formation and functioning of groups can be explained in purely ethological terms, and without reference to religion. It is a response to instincts inherited from our primate past. But the problem of explanation arises when bonding extends beyond the limits of kinship—as it does in nearly all societies—and therefore beyond the limits of animal instinct. Solidarity beyond the kin group has to be based on ideology rather than on instinct, and it is at this point that we part company from the apes. Here, then, religion enters the picture. It is not an automatic consequence either of the human bonding propensity or of the sense of solidarity, for both are rooted in instincts far older than religion itself. Religion comes into the picture when solidarity requires an ideological basis.

The ideologies that underpin solidarity are of course not always and necessarily religious. The secular ideology of the nation-state, which has its own mythology and rituals, has more compelling force than has religion in much of the modern world. When it comes to rightness, however, the nation-state itself must still usually claim divine ordination. America is the greatest nation that God ever created (and therefore entitled to bully smaller states), as we often hear it from conservative politicians. But Durkheim was surely correct in the assumption that in earlier societies solidarity was nearly always based in religion.

Religion, in sum, is not what makes us want to join; it is what makes us want to belong and to participate, even when it is clearly not in our self-interest. Its role is thus ancillary rather than primary. We don't, usually, join a specifically religious group for the sake of safety. We join a social and a political group, which relies on religion to sanction its existence and its actions.

We also don't, ordinarily, join a group for the sake of enjoyment, but we nevertheless enjoy the consciousness of belonging. That consciousness is one of the important psychological rewards that religion provides.

The need to follow is pretty much implicit in the need to belong; both are consequences of society's need to exist and to function. There can be no effective group without leadership, and there can be no effective leadership without followers. Even in the most democratic of groupings, decision-making must be relegated to one or a few persons, whose decisions the others are willing to accept. Yet, when we act in rational self-interest, we often see no reason to obey the decisions of another person; rather the opposite much of the time. It is society that needs us to obey, and it is our inherent propensity to follow that makes that possible. In this respect too we are not wholly unlike sheep, for whom safety lies in following.

In the interest of society, something has to motivate us to follow its leaders, and that something has very commonly been religion. Weber's concept of charisma becomes important at this point. Charisma, which all of us have encountered at one time or another in certain persons, is that indefinable quality that gives us an instinctive trust in their judgment, and makes us willing to follow them. Often it makes us not only willing but eager to follow. Charisma may be acquired through circumstances of birth or accomplishment, but in some people, who can claim neither one, it is simply an unaccountable quality; a gift. I think it is often something that shines forth from the eyes.

Up to this point, once again, we can explain leadership without reference to religion. Charismatic leaders can be recognized in animal as well as in human groups. But among humans charisma, like solidarity, seems to need ideological sanction, and it is usually seen as a gift specifically from the gods. When we follow a charismatic leader who has no divine sanction we are conscious of 'playing a hunch;' very possibly of placing too much faith in our own fallible judgment. When we follow a divinely ordained leader we are following someone whom the gods have chosen to lead us.

Above all, it is the divine sanction that allows authority to become institutionalized, as it must be if society is to function effectively for any length of time. A purely charismatic leader, with no divine sanction, will cease to be followed as soon as something happens that calls his judgment into question. In the case of a divinely sanctioned leader it is less likely, though not impossible, that the approval of the gods will be withdrawn. In the meantime people will follow him through thick and thin; something that effective leadership absolutely requires.

The belief in supernatural sanction becomes especially critical when leadership must be transferred. The power of a purely charismatic leader dies with him, leaving a power vacuum that is dangerous for any society. Mythology however dictates in one way or another a rule of succession to avoid that danger. Power is very often inherited, on the assumption (which often turns out to be wrong) that charisma is inherited, but there are many other recognized ways in which the mantle of leadership can be passed. The important thing is that the candidate or candidates for succession are identified through religious sanctions, just as was the fallen or deceased predecessor in his own time.

Weber's most important insight was the recognition that the institutionalization of leadership, usually though not always through religion, allows it to be transmitted and perpetuated in the absence of personal charisma—the process that he called routinization. Charisma becomes a quality of the office rather than of its occupant. Genuinely charismatic persons appear only sporadically and unpredictably; all too often they are not there when society needs them. Religious belief, in earlier societies, takes its place, in designating who is to lead us. There is always the possibility however that a genuinely charismatic person will appear and will overthrow the routinely designated leader, because more people will follow him than his opponent. When this happens, it is usually because the usurper claims a special divine sanction. It has happened over and over in history.

The need for collective action

I have already suggested that society exists most of the time, especially at its simpler levels, as insurance against latent threats rather than manifest ones. Consequently, most of the time it has no need for overt action. But if the members do not get together for collective activities with a certain degree of regularity, their sense of solidarity gradually erodes. The longer the time between mobilizations of society, the harder it is to mobilize when need arises.

It is here that religion performs what many sociofunctionalists regard as its single most vital function. Ritual brings the members of society together with great regularity: at the very minimum annually, much more often monthly, and for all the Abrahamic religions weekly. Each such occasion involves collective action, and reknits the bonds of solidarity.

Many people in many societies see the need for ritual in quite pragmatic terms, both as a response to a threat and as an opportunity. The gods are always there, and consequently the need to deal with them is also always there. In a pessimistic scenario, they can at least be kept off our backs by constant propitiation, leaving us in peace to pursue our worldly ends. That seems to have been the general outlook of ancient Sumerian religion, and it has come through at least to some extent in all of the legalistic religions of the Near East that have succeeded it. I am reminded of the rabbi's prayer for the Tsar, in *Fiddler in the Roof*: 'May the Lord protect and keep the Tsar—far away from us!' In a more optimistic scenario, exemplified in Pueblo Indian religion, the gods can be induced by enough propitiation to come among us, and make the crops grow. In sum, then, it is ritual that keeps the community in a state of readiness, to mobilize for collective action when needed.

Psychological needs

The satisfaction of psychological needs represents the personal dimension of religion. As I have suggested before, this seems to be the main remaining function of religion in the modern, secularizing world, but it was not always so. In the discussion that follows I will have to indulge somewhat more in pure speculation than in the preceding section, because I am much less versed in psychological than in sociological theory.

The need to enjoy Any people that spends as much time, energy, and money in the pursuit of pleasure as do modern Americans, should need no convincing about the need to enjoy. In spite of psychofunctional theories about reassurance and stress reduction, I think the need to enjoy is the single most common psychological need that religion satisfies. Many people would probably say that, after sex, it is the most enjoyable of all pastimes.

There are all kinds of religious enjoyment. There is the comfortable sense of belonging and participation, with the social approval that it brings; there is the excitement generated by hearing the thrilling and hair-raising myths; there is the aesthetic enjoyment from listening to beautiful poetry and witnessing spectacular pageantry; there is the sense of mastery that comes from the performance of complex rituals; and there is the pride that comes from contemplating the mighty monuments that we have raised to our gods. But the greatest of all enjoyments, for those who can attain it, is surely ecstasy, when we are seemingly transported out of our bodies and into another realm of consciousness. This, as I take it, is possible only for persons with well developed mystical minds; I have never experienced it myself.

The achievement of altered states of consciousness is the overt objective of much ritual. It may be aided by the use of drugs, by trance-inducing rituals such as hyperventilation, or by ordeals such as fasting or self-mutilation. Considering that the use of drugs in ritual is fairly widespread, it has always surprised me that the use of alcohol, at least to achieve altered states of consciousness, is emphasized in only a few religions, and is disparaged in many. Yet I have always suspected that its mind-bending power is one of the explanations—certainly not the only one—for the alcoholic problems besetting American Indians. For them drunkenness may bring a mental state that, in traditional religion, is devoutly to be wished. I have the impression that alcoholic problems are most acute in precisely those tribes, especially on the northern Plains, in which ecstatic experience was most prized in traditional religion.

The need for security One of the most prevalent psychofunctional theories of religion insists that its main function is the reduction of anxiety in an uncertain world. There can be little doubt that, in the minds of the poor and the weak, religion provides the best insurance against the misfortunes with which they are continually threatened. And yet the case of Navajo religion offers an interesting paradox: most of the misfortunes that people fear also originate within religion. Religion seems to embody within itself both anxiety and anxiety reduction.

The key to this riddle lies in the concept of embodiment. The evils that people have to fear—especially disease and natural disaster—are real enough, and yet without religion they have no identifiable source, and no form. Religion embodies them in the form and in the actions of sentient beings, and thus makes it possible to deal with them, as one would with any sentient being, through techniques of address, manipulation, or compulsion. This is clearly an important dimension of Navajo religion. It does not provide very sure means of averting disaster—Blessingway and many personal rituals are about the only possibilities—but it provides the comforting knowledge that, when disaster strikes, there are concrete ways of dealing with it.

The provision of security is even more clearcut in the case of Arab village religion, where *baraka* is nothing if not insurance.

The need for comfort

This is perhaps the need most stressed by adherents and by students of modern Christianity. 'Jesus loves you' or 'somebody up there loves you' are continually reiterated slogans. The need for comfort is not so conspicuous in the case of Navajo religion, where among all the Powers only Changing Woman is wholly benevolent, but it is very conspicuous indeed in the case of Arab village religion. In contrast to Navajos, villagers at the best of times do not lead particularly happy lives, and they have a proportionately greater need to know that 'somebody out there loves them.' The presence of the nearby saint, a generally benevolent being, is a continual source of comfort. This is especially important to Arab women, whose lives are deprived in so many respects. Allah, on the other hand, provides only the coldest of cold comfort.

In all the salvationist religions, the ultimate comfort is of course to be found in the contemplation of a happier life to come. It is no surprise that these religions sprang up in bad times, and that they had their earliest mass appeal among the dispossessed classes.

The need for help

Everybody needs help at one time or another, and most are inclined to ask it from the gods, in circumstances that are beyond human aid. I think that the possibility of asking for divine aid is probably envisioned within all religions. However, the extent to which this feature is emphasized varies a great deal. At one extreme, practically all Navajo ceremonies are in the broadest sense attempts to gain divine help. Christians are urged to ask for it through individual prayers, and in the Catholic denominations there are also masses to aid the distressed. Arab villagers also continually ask for help from their saint. On the other hand, asking for divine help plays only a small part in the practice of orthodox Islam; one should not bother almighty Allah with personal troubles.

Perhaps the single most common circumstance in which divine help is sought, in nearly all societies, is in the case if illness, for it is the circumstance in which men and their lay knowledge are most helpless. Lacking other explanation, most people attribute sickness to supernatural causes, and therefore assume that it can only be cured or alleviated by supernatural Powers. This may be sought through intermediary practitioners and formal ritual, as in the case of Navajos, but just as often it is sought through individual appeals. Even among people who do not attribute disease to God's will, and who are familiar with scientific theories of disease, there remains the assumption that God can cure it if he chooses, a fact that is reflected in the prayers of many Christians.

Individuals also vary in their felt need for divine help, and their faith in the possibility of obtaining it. In one Navajo community, Kluckhohn and Leighton (1946: 159–60) found no one over the age of thirty who had not had at least one sing, while fully half the younger adults had never had one.

The desire for favors

Asking the gods for presents, or other purely personal benefits, is a very different thing from asking their help in times of need. Religions seem sharply divided on this issue. The Pueblo Indians may represent one extreme view: to perform a religious act without asking for something in return is simply wasting an opportunity, something like throwing away money (Parsons 1939: 313–15). Christians are urged to ask for personal favors; indeed no differentiation is made between asking for help and asking for favors. 'God grants all wishes.' This is certainly the view also of Arab villagers, in addressing their saint. Many religious amulets are worn quite specifically to bring wealth or other forms of success. At the opposite extreme, asking God for personal benefits is very much frowned on in orthodox Islam, as it is also in ascetic Christian and Indian sects. In the Navajo case, all the major ceremonies are performed to secure help, not favors, but some individual rituals are meant to bring a successful outcome to personal endeavors.

The need to venerate

The evident need of humans to venerate someone or something is surely linked to the sociological need to follow, discussed earlier. In order to follow, we must respect, and the more we respect the more ready we are to follow. In situations where society places extreme demands on us, it is almost necessary that we should venerate either its human ruler, or the gods who speak for it. It is the feeling that makes us willing to sacrifice.

Psychofunctionalists have suggested that the veneration of deities is a projection in adult life of our childhood feelings toward parents. We have, they suggest, a lifelong subconscious need for a father and/or a mother. My own feeling is that this theory has limited explanatory value. To begin with, it involves the ethnocentric fallacy of taking the patriarchal Abrahamic deity as a model for all gods. It may be that there is someone like a father figure and a mother figure in every pantheon—the Sun and Changing Woman in the case of Navajos—but in many religions there are other deities, bearing no resemblance to a father or a mother, who are venerated as much or more.

Moreover, if the psychofunctionalists mean to suggest that veneration of deities has its origin in childhood feelings, I think they may have got the wrong end of the stick. My hunch is that the need to venerate, like nearly all other needs, is part of our inborn makeup. In childhood it finds its first outlet in feelings toward parents if they seem worthy, which is surely not always the case. The feelings of Arab children toward their parents, as described by Hamed Ammar (1966: 125–143) convey hardly a hint of veneration. In the case of boys, their situation of total subordination breeds not respect or gratitude but resentment. In later life, our need may find its outlet in the veneration of all kinds of beings, human and divine, who may or may not have any father-like qualities. Sports figures and military heroes are obvious examples. In short, I think we venerate because we need to venerate, and our imagination seeks for suitable objects.

This brings me back to my original point about the connection between the need to venerate and the need to follow. It is, nevertheless, a rationalistic and functionalistic explanation that does not fully account for the emotional high brought on by veneration. There can be no doubt that, in looking up to others, we seem to lift ourselves up at the same time—so much so that exaltation, in extreme cases, becomes a kind of out-of-body experience. To that extent, veneration may be counted as one of the enjoyments of religion.

Sharing is, I believe, the supreme human virtue, by which I mean that it is the one act most consistently approved in all moral systems. We are surely equipped from birth onwrd with a desire to give, and perhaps it is

The need to
give

strong enough to call it a need. Once again, of course, it is one of those things that society depends on, since a society is nothing if not a system of interdependence.

It is a curious paradox, at least to my mind, that we seem to feel conscience-driven to give to the poor, while we have a positive desire to give to the rich and powerful. We feel, at best, a fleeting self-righteousness when we give to charity, while we feel a positive exaltation when we give to a ruler—especially if we couldn't afford it. Gifts and favors flow unasked to leaders, even when there can be no expectation of anything in return. I am sure this is because we need some concrete way of expressing our feelings of veneration.

Religion, obviously, offers the supreme outlet for our need to give. Offerings to the gods, of one sort or another, play a very large role in all our dealings with them, even though no one could need them less.

The need for self-justification

At least in the modern world, everyone's conception of an ideal society is a totally democratic one, in which all men and women are exactly equal. That is the vision of heaven held out by all the Abrahamic religions, where all are equal in the eyes of God. I think it is also true in the egalitarian world of tribal societies; certainly the Navajo conception of *hozhoni* applies with equal force to everyone. Equality of persons is therefore seemingly a divine ideal.

That being the case, conspicuous differences of wealth, or any other measure of earthly success, may be seen as violations of what the gods intended. I think that must be the reason why so many successful or fortunate people feel it necessary to attribute their success to divine help; to allay any suggestion that their wealth or success is contrary to divine will. A great deal of wealth and success has been achieved at other people's expense, at least as seen by them, and to claim that you have gained it through your own unaided efforts is to risk envy and resentment. It shows that you have deliberately set out to put yourself above others. But to attribute it to divine favor shifts the burden of blame from you to the gods. From that perspective, the rich man's or the politician's acknowledgment of God's help is less a gesture of humility than of exculpation.

The need for self-justification is found in whole societies no less than in individuals, but it takes a different form. No individual in the modern world wants to claim that he was created superior to others; his success has come through divine favor in his lifetime rather than through creation. It is just the opposite in the case of tribes or nations; they are likely to attribute their sense of superiority over others to creation, rather than to achievement. The most conspicuous case is of course that of the Hebrews, who conquered Canaan and dispossessed its inhabitants because Yahweh had promised them the land. But in our own day we still hear conservative politicians referring to America as 'the greatest nation God ever created.'

The important point, in the case of both individuals and nations, is that they must attribute their success to God's will to avoid the suggestion that it is against his will.

The need for self-identification

I noted in a previous section how important it is for most persons to have a sense of collective identity, shared with their fellows, and how often this is provided through religion. It is sometimes the case also that individuals feel a need for an enhanced sense of personal identity; particularly in complex and differentiated societies where there are many alternative possibilities. This has been noted by psychologists as a major reason for acts of religious conversion. The convert much of the time is less concerned about joining a congregation or worshipping new gods, than about simply acquiring a new and more self-satisfying identity. For many African Americans, who adopt Arabic names but don't regularly say prayers or fast, the new identity is surely the main motivation for their conversion to Islam, as they conceive it.

The need to execrate

We are all born with a capacity to hate, and most of us have at least one or two persons whom we hate with good reason. But many people's capacity to hate seems to exceed the number of legitimate targets; they must hate someone (usually plural) from whom they have suffered no harm. Again and again, this 'unearned hatred' falls upon people who are different, just because they are different. There seems to be a feeling that we are as the gods or nature intended, and therefore those who are not like us are accursed. To that extent, the need to execrate may be the "flip side" of the need for self-justification.

I am sure that kind of hatred, like most other kinds, must be rooted partly in fear. It is, for better or worse, a nearly inescapable feature of human thought that to compare is to judge. The existence of people who are not just like us, but who think they are just as good, and who may be getting along with the world as well as we are, is thus a kind of standing affront our sense of our own rightness. We cannot allow the thought that they are better than us, which would undermine the very fabric of society, so we are obliged to find a way of believing that they are worse.

It is hardly necessary to point out that religion offers many sanctioned outlets for that kind of hatred—we can see examples of it in the newscasts just about every night. Within the context of exclusivist religion, it becomes possible (and for many even necessary) to hate all of those who don't adhere to our own faith, or even to our own narrowly sectarian version of it. In the case of scriptural Islam, hatred is something demanded toward apostates and *kafirs* (roughly, pagans). For Navajos and for Arab villagers, the belief in witchcraft provides a sanctioned outlet for feelings of hatred toward individuals.

Many religions provide overt rituals of execration. There are rituals of execration for individuals, as in the case of excommunication, and others in which whole peoples are execrated, as in the case of interdiction. Often, a single individual is sacrificed, and is made to stand symbolically for a whole people whom we despise. One of the most extreme examples known to me (from literature) was the eastern American Indian practice of torturing a captured enemy to death, while every kind of verbal abuse was heaped on him by the bystanders. Lynchings in the American South are another clearcut example, though not one officially sanctioned by religion. I am often reminded of the line, spoken by an English priest in G. B. Shaw's play *Saint Joan,* that 'it feels grand to throw oil on the flaming hell of your own temper.'

The need to atone

This feature is heavily emphasized in Judaeo-Christian religion, but much less so in other religions that I know of. Nevertheless we are all conscious of having done wrong at times, and we need to rid ourselves of the burden of guilt that comes with that knowledge. The quickest way is by some form of restitution, which makes things all right, but there are many harms that cannot be made right in any material way—they have caused irreparable damage. In those cases we probably cannot ask for human forgiveness, so we have to ask for divine forgiveness. Religion may provide quite specific ways of doing that, through procedures of atonement that allow us to lay down the burden of guilt. Apart from church-imposed penances, there are all kinds of self-imposed penances we can do, in the belief that they will bring divine forgiveness. If nothing else, we can continually beg God, or the gods, for forgiveness.

The need to create

The connection between religion and every kind of artistic creativity is so obvious as to hardly require mention. Every religion is from the start a work of creative imagination, giving shape and personality and history to all of the unseen powers. And it is a work that is never finished; creative persons can continue to embroider it or build on it or work variations on it, ad infinitum. In the modern world there are also many secular outlets for creativity, but for most peoples at most times religion was the principal or even the only one. The artistic creativity of the Navajos and Pueblos, which is enormous in the case of both peoples, is expressed very largely through religion.

Why is the artistic creativity of the Navajos and Pueblos so much greater than the religious artistry of Muslims and of Protestant Christians? I think the answer lies in the severe restraints on creativity that are imposed by the claim of monotheism. Not only is there a major reduction in the pantheon, but we (if we take the Second Commandment seriously) are forbidden to make representations of the only god who remains. Catholic and Orthodox Christians have gotten around the problem by abandoning anything but a lip-service pretense at monotheism. The great church paintings are crowded with the Virgin, the Christ child, all kinds of saints, and clouds of angels and archangels—everything but God himself. Puritanical Protestants have dismissed all that as idolatry, and are therefore back under the same restraints as Muslims and Jews. I'm sure that the great florescence of secular art in post-Reformation Europe was a direct result of the constraint that Protestantism placed on religious art.

Reprise

After the foregoing catalogue of needs, I hope it is apparent that no single need, or kind of need, can begin to account for the endlessly complex phenomenon that is religion. This is the ultimate failing of just about all functionalist theory. I would say instead that religion is the way that imagination has found to supply nearly all of mankind's non-material needs. But those needs vary enormously from society to society and from person to person, and religion varies accordingly.

PART 3

THE PRACTICE OF RELIGION

13

THE ANATOMY OF RELIGION

We come now to the most difficult part in the study of religion: the problem of specific content. Given the virtually unlimited creative potential of the human imagination, it is possible for peoples to think up all kinds of gods and spirits, all kinds of myths, and all kinds of rituals. A world survey of ethnographic literature will confirm that they have in fact done so. How far can we go, then, in understanding and perhaps even predicting anything about the specific content of any particular religion? This is the question that I will attempt to answer, in the present chapter and the next. In this chapter I will consider broad general features of content that will be found in most if not all religions, because they are responsive to universal needs. Collectively, these constitute what I call the anatomy of religion. In the following chapter I will consider much more specific features of content, responsive to human needs in particular environmental or evolutionary circumstances.

I have suggested earlier that religion, in the abstract, cannot be defined by its content, and the reverse is equally true. That is, none of the dozen definitions that were reviewed in Chapters 8 and 9, including my own, says or implies anything specific about content. Myth, ritual, and veneration, which are mentioned repeatedly in the definitions, are all enormously variable, and all have secular as well as religious aspects. Even those myths and rituals that we identify as religious usually turn out to have a lot of secular content as well. Conversely, there is virtually nothing found outside the domain of religion that is not also found within one religion or another.

The question of content has often been addressed by culture historians and by evolutionists, applying either diffusionist or evolutionary theory. At the same time it has been almost wholly ignored by functionalists, who have treated the content of religion as a kind of free variable. Their attitude (epitomized above all by Durkheim) has been that 'it doesn't matter what peoples believe as long as they all believe the same thing.' And yet, for all that, I think that a functional approach does offer our best hope of understanding the content of each religion, insofar as each is responsive to the particular needs of its time and place. Universal human needs account for those features of content that are common to most or all religions, and situational needs are responsible for the features found in, for example, tribal religions and those of the early states. We have to ask: what are the things that each religion has to define, to explain, and to regulate, in the context of its own time and place? By dealing with each religion as a system of adaptation to its own special environment, we can escape from the universalism and the reductionism that are inherent in so much functionalist theory.

When I talk about commonalities and basic features I am, as always, thinking in terms of the whole broad spectrum of the world's religions, without regard for the number of their votaries. In any attempt to understand religion in all its wonderful variety, the religions of the Bushmen and the Andamanese have to be accorded equal importance with the religions of Christianity and Islam.

Religious symbolism: the language for the gods

According to my definition (Chapter 9), religion is our way of dealing with sentient Powers, mainly through techniques of communication. Any review of the content of religion must therefore begin with a consideration of religious symbols, for they are our language of communication with the gods, as well as our way of sharing our religious feelings with one another. As such they are involved alike in all the different domains of religion: cognitive, social, ritual, and affective.

Religious symbols are not conceptually different from other symbols; they are utterances, actions, or material creations that convey an enormous amount of meaning in a single word or act or thing. However, they employ a larger and a richer vocabulary than does most lay discourse, including all kinds of actions and material creations as well as verbal utterances. The words used in prayer, the actions of censing or prostrating, hand-held fetishes and gigantic statues are all heavily loaded religious symbols.

What mainly distinguishes religious symbols from other symbols, insofar as they are distinct, is the extreme complexity of their meaning-loading, and above all its highly mystical component. For those who most fully 'comprehend' them, they may convey many different levels of meaning simultaneously. A whole philosophy of life and death may be encompassed within a few words or acts. The word *hozhoni* and the icon of the crucifix are both examples of highly multivocal symbols. It is clear that the creation and use of religious symbols has provided a fertile field of creative expression for the mystical mind. So also their study has provided a fertile field for mystically-minded scholars, who have sought and found a vast array of arcane meanings in religious symbols.

More pragmatic scholars, like the structuralists whose work was discussed in Chapter 11, have found a number of recurring features in religious symbolism, which they relate to innate human 'mental templates.' There is, in this view, a kind of basic 'deep grammar' that is common to most if not all religions. Important and interesting as is this theory, however, it accounts for only a small part of the total domain of religious symbolism. In the vast majority of cases, the relationships between religious symbols and the things symbolized are as arbitrary as they as in the case of words in any everyday language. As the gods can be imagined in a nearly infinite number of shapes and characters, so also we can conceive an infinitely varied vocabulary for communicating with them. For purposes of this chapter, it is enough to suggest that every religion has, of necessity, its own rich and distinctive vocabulary of symbols, while at the same time we have to recognize that very little can be predicted about their specific form.

As I've said many times before, the cognitive domain of religion is to my mind the most important, since it tells people how and what to think, and therefore, secondarily, how to act. Following conventional practice, I will here refer to the whole cognitive content of religion as mythology, although, as I've also suggested in earlier chapters, there is a great deal of informal folk wisdom about the supernaturals that is not embodied in formally codified knowledge.

*Believing:
the cognitive
dimension*

It should be noted, before going further, that the style of mythology is rarely didactic. As a field of literature, no less than of information, it is frequently ambiguous, self-contradictory, full of 'double-think' and mystical allusions that are never clarified. It has been, through the ages, one of the important functions of priesthood to interpret the myths so as to make them clear to the pragmatic-minded. The following then are some of the important categories of information that peoples have to deduce from their mythology, even though they are often far from explicitly spelled out.

If cognition must precede action, then obviously the first task of any religion must be to give definition to those Powers that are recognized to be out there. There's no way we can deal with them until we have formed some conception of what they're like. To state the obvious, that supernaturals are defined by the possession of power, is to miss the essential point. From the emic perspective, the supernaturals *are* power. It does not define them; they define it.

I will suggest here that the formation of pantheons involves initially three processes of the human creative imagination: those of embodiment, of set-extension, and of elaboration. By embodiment I mean that Powers are conceived to have some kind of physical shape, which usually but not always reflects the shape of things we have encountered in the everyday world. By set-extension I mean that once a particular kind of deity has been conceived, it becomes easy and indeed logical to conceive or other deities in the same general category. Once there is a lion or a jaguar god, it is logical to add other animal deities; once the existence of an Arab saint is admitted, the door is open to the recognition of a lot more saints. By elaboration I mean that once a Power has been conceived, it 'grows in the telling,' so to speak. Successive generations may invest it with more and more miraculous qualities. It may acquire a wholly fantastic shape, or, often enough, a whole series of alternative shapes into which it can 'morph.'

At a later developmental stage, especially if the pantheon has become over-elaborated, there are likely to be processes of reduction, syncretism, and redefinition. I will discuss those processes more fully in the next chapter.

The name of the Powers. If the process of getting to know the Powers parallels the normal processes of human cognition, as I suspect it does, then the very first step when we become aware of their existence must be to find a name for them. Only then can we share our perception with others, and, just as importantly, only then can we address them. Sometimes the name given to a deity has an obvious derivation, as when an animal god is named for the earthly representatives of the species: Coyote, or Lion. Far more often though the names of the gods, like the origins of other basic words, are lost in the remote mists of prehistory. All the Semitic languages, back to earliest Babylonian times, have a name for a high god derived from El or Al, but who knows how that began?

The name of a deity becomes, along with its shape and its character, one of its essential attributes, and as such may have enormous power in its own right. Whenever it is spoken the deity hears it, and therefore it has to be used very carefully. Inserted as an invocation, it may give added strength to any statement. All Arabic statements of any consequence should be prefaced by 'in the name of God, the Merciful, the Compassionate,' just as medieval Christian statements were prefaced by 'in the name of the Father and of the Son and of the Holy Spirit.' The name of a deity may also be invoked to confer either a blessing or a curse on a person or thing.

The shape of the Powers. The next step after naming must be to endow the Powers with some kind of form in which our mind can picture them. A few—mainly the celestial bodies—can actually be seen at a great distance, but most are not directly visible to us. How then do we go about giving form and substance to the unseen Powers? Most of the time, we do it by projection from the seen; by imputing to them the same shape and qualities that we have observed among persons or things in the natural world. The form in which we conceive of the supernaturals mirrors, much of the time, the form of powerful or active or mysterious things we have encountered in the world around us.

Celestial bodies: the visible Powers. There are a few Powers which, though remote, are not unseen. These are the celestial bodies which all peoples observe, and which most of them study, at least to some extent. There are relatively few religions in which the Sun does not play a prominent role, for reasons that are too obvious to require discussion. In the religions of stratified societies he (the Sun is almost invariably male) is apt to be at the top of the celestial hierarchy. He may be a creator and he may be a progenitor, as in the Navajo case, although these are not universal attributes. On the other hand his actions are so unvarying and predictable, from day to day and from season to season, that he is not generally thought of as amenable to human appeal. He is, as a result, the subject more of veneration than of supplication.

There are probably few if any religions that include a Sun god that do not also include a Moon god or goddess. The idea that she is a female consort of the Sun is a common and a logically appealing one, though it is certainly not universal; there are a number of religions in which the Moon is male. When female she is often associated with fertility, presumably because her monthly cycle recalls the human female menstrual cycle. The moon seems to have an especially honored place in the religions of pastoral nomads, who (since they have no fixed horizons) must use the moon rather than the sun to mark the passing of the seasons.[23] Like the Sun, and for the same reasons, the Moon is not usually much invoked in practical religion.

Most peoples have a substantial body of 'ethnoastronomy' (star-lore), and it is commonly intertwined with mythology, as in the ancient Greek case. On the other hand the stars and planets are not often thought of as Powers in and of themselves, and they are rarely subjects of veneration. The constellations are in a sense art-works created by the gods rather than gods in their own right. The Arabs of the pre-Islamic era were an exception in this respect; the special veneration that they accorded to meteorites was rooted in their belief that these immigrants from space were messengers from the stars.

I think this pretty well exhausts the list of visible things that actually *are* Powers, in any direct way. Many other visible things, including both animals and humans, may sometimes or at all times have power dwelling within them, but it is power the proceeds from an external and an invisible source. Similarly, natural phenomena like the winds and weather are attributable to a supernatural origin, but they are not deities in and of themselves: they are evidence of the action of unseen deities. A great many peoples, including the Navajos, have weather gods, who more often than not are conceived in human form.

Zoomorphs. The most powerful beings encountered by most pre-agricultural peoples were not fellow humans, but animals. Lions, jaguars, and bears could and did kill humans with their unaided natural weapons and abilities, while humans could only kill the great predators by stealth and strategy, and usually by group efforts. In everyday life humans had considerably more to fear from the great predators than vice versa. It is no surprise therefore that important deities of pre-agricultural peoples were very often conceived in the form of the giant felines, bears, crocodiles, or some other especially fearsome beast. Those deities embody pure power, and the danger that inevitably attends it. For that reason they are rarely seen as benevolent, or answerable to human wishes. They are likely to need regular propitiation just to keep them in check, but they are not asked for favors.

But if there is a single animal deity, there is apt to be a multiplicity of them. If power is symbolized by powerful animals like the jaguar, other qualities in nature, such as capriciousness or malevolence, may be

---

[23] Hence the prominent place given to the crescent moon in Islamic holy symbolism.

attributed to other animal deities, like the coyote or the snake, which have those qualities of personality. Animals having seemingly miraculous powers, such as the ability to live both above and below ground, or on land as well as in water, are often thought to be endowed with supernatural power, emanating from an unseen deity in the same shape as themselves.

In many religions, all of the earthly manifestations of an animal god— i.e. actual lions or coyotes—are thought to be under the protection of their tutelary god, and therefore may at times be immune from killing by humans. It seems to be the case, at least most of the time, that these Powers have no sex; they are representatives of and for the entire species. Perhaps this is because, when hunting or otherwise exploiting their earthly representatives, humans do not differentiate between the sexes.

Animal deities are invoked very often as explanatory phenomena, and they may require propitiation to mitigate their evil potential, but I don't think they are usually viewed as benevolent toward mankind. American Indians commonly regarded animal deities as a main source of human illness—it was their way of revenging themselves on the humans who hunted them. A conspicuous exception occurs however in the case of totems or guardian spirits, which are very often animal deities that serve as tutelaries of one particular individual or group. The guardian spirits sought by individual North American Indians were usually spirits in animal form, as were and are the clan totems worshipped by native Australians and many others. These human groups often claim mythical descent from their animal-deity ancestor, who must therefore look after them.

Societies vary greatly in the extent to which they conceive of the animal deities as having human characteristics and human institutions like society, law, and language. I think it can be said as a generality, however, that techniques of appeal to the animal deities are more often imitative and mechanistic than verbal.

I suspect that most zoomorphic pantheons have grown by the process of set-extension, especially when mythology becomes elaborated as literature. As a result, there are apt to be far more animals mentioned in myth than are actually venerated or propitiated in any practical way. For all their miraculous deeds and powers, I am not sure in these cases that the animals should be regarded as actual deities, rather than merely as literary figures.

Anthropomorphs. Humans, far more than animals, are endowed with a clearly perceivable will, and they act in accordance with it rather than by instinct. For that reason, I think that Powers that seem to act in accordance with a will—rather than more or less automatically—are apt to be conceived in human form. There may be religions that include no anthropomorphic deities, but there are surely not many of them.

In the pantheons of most peoples there are, to begin with, recognizable father figures and mother figures, the one embodying the stern but benevolent authority of society, and the other embodying the principles of reproduction and nurturance. On the other hand it is surely a mistake to suppose, as Freudians have done, that these are the most basic of deities, or that all religion grows out of a projection from our feelings toward human parents. Religion grows from many sources and many felt needs, among which the lifelong need for parental figures may or may not be important.

Other commonly recurring deities in human form are great warriors, saviors in one sense or another, treacherous malefactors, and the deities responsible for sex. It is conspicuous that, in contrast to animal deities, the anthropomorphic Powers nearly always have clearly specified sex, and the traits of character associated therewith.

Because they are endowed with a human-like character and will, anthropomorphic deities are much more responsive than are animal deities to human verbal address. Human-like, they are amenable to all kinds of flattery: verbal praise, pictorial and sculptural representation, and imitation in costume and drama. They can also be entertained with song and dance.

It is hardly necessary to make the point that the importance of anthropomorphic deities has grown, and that of animal deities declined, as power and command passed from animals to humans. Animal domestication, occurring at the beginning of the Neolithic age, marks a significant turning point in this respect. Man was given dominion over the beasts in the field, by a god in human form, as the book of Genesis has it. But anthropomorphic gods grew even more in importance as humans acquired power over other humans, with the onset of chiefdoms and stratified society. The higher gods took on the character of the human emperor or, as in the case of Arabs and early Jews, the tribal sheikh. Eventually, for many peoples, there emerged a clearcut hierarchy of deities, reflecting the complex stratification of human society.

Obviously, the anthropomorphic pantheon has also grown by set-extension. Nature is full of quirks and caprices, and imagination finds it possible and logical to attribute each of them to the action of a different willful deity.

Deities of hybrid or fantastic form. I suspect that deities having partly human and partly animal form, like many of the Egyptian gods, or those that have separate human and animal manifestations, like Zeus and other Greek gods, are probably deities in a process of evolutionary mutation, if I can put it that way. They are legacies of older mythology, in which they had a purely animal form, but are undergoing reinterpretation in and for a man-dominated world. On the other hand purely fantastic creatures, like the Chinese Dragon and Phoenix, I can only see as products of the human playful imagination.

Formless Powers. Many peoples believe in powers that have a name but no specifiable form, or an infinite multiplicity of forms. Such are for example the *ch'indi* of the Navajos and the *jinni* of the Arabs. I have the impression that these are likely to be quite localized Powers, and also that they are more often than not malevolent, or at least mischievous. During World War II, U.S. Air Force pilots invented the concept of Gremlins, to account for glitches that defied rational explanation, but that seemed too trivial to attribute to a high god. I think that belief in *jinni* and other such formless local spirits may have arisen under similar circumstances. Once conceived and given a name, they become a convenient scapegoat for all kinds of mysterious, and often unfortunate, occurrences.

Although the Polynesian *mana* is often cited in the literature as an example of a generalized (rather than localized) formless power, I am not sure that *mana* is really an ultimate source, or that it is possessed of a will. I suspect that, like *baraka,* it is power that flows from an embodied source external to itself.

The power of the Powers. Obviously, in attempting to deal with the Powers, it is important to know what they can and can't do. The deities in different religions vary greatly in the extent of their powers. The Abrahamic supreme deity is said to be omnipotent, but omnipotent Powers are decidedly rare in other religions. More often, there are deities having control over specific domains of nature: the seasons, the weather, the tides, the growth of plants, and so on. In more advanced societies there are likely also to be gods having control over different spheres of human activity, like agriculture, hunting, and warfare.

How far the actual power of the deities extends, geographically, is also variable. Most peoples have at least a few 'world-gods' whose control extends over the whole of the known world, and a larger number who operate only within specific regions. In addition to localized spirits, there are also tutelary deities who have power only with respect to specific individuals or groups of people, and others that have power only with respect to a particular animal species.

The will of the Powers. The question of what the deities are *willing* to do is a separate issue from what they are *able* to do. Most if not all Powers are endowed with a will, which means that they may or may not be inclined to act in every situation where they are able to do so. It is in this particular aspect of theology that our human capacity for mental projection becomes most evident. The principal will that we experience in the world around us is a human will, and so the will that we attribute to the deities is likewise a human-like will, even when they have the outward form of an animal or a monster. They are thinking, calculating creatures, with purposes of their own that we try to divine as best we can.

Above and beyond the simple question of will, most deities are conceived as having well defined, human-like characters, or personalities. They are anthropophysic even when they are not anthropomorphic, to use the theologians' terminology. Among them we can recognize projections from the familiar personae of human experience: father figures, mother figures, autocrats, heroes, bullies, mischievous ones, temptresses, evil persons, and the like.

Whether or not we choose to deal with a particular deity will depend on what we think he or she is able to do. *How* we go about dealing with the deity will depend on our estimate of his or her character: what is the best form of address, what are desirable gifts, what are appropriate things to ask for, what may give offense, and so on.

Explanation

One of the peculiarities of the human mind, in contrast to that of animals, is its endless curiosity. It is dissatisfied with ignorance, and seeks explanation for all kinds of phenomena, whether or not the explanation is of any practical importance. Science provides the sought-for explanation for most modern peoples, but for earlier peoples explanation was found very largely within the realm of mythology. Religion, like science, filled empty spaces in the human mind. The following are a few of the categories of experience for which nearly all pre-modern peoples have, or had, explanatory myths.

Origins and etiology. The world is full of extraordinary phenomena, and just about everyone wonders how they came to be. The explanations, for the majority of peoples, are found in what are called creation myths and etiological myths. The Abrahamic religions attribute everything to the will of a single creator deity, but they are unusual in this respect. It is much more common to find that phenomena are attributed to multiple creations by a variety of Powers, often over a long period of time, as is true in Navajo mythology.

It is also the case, for many peoples, that things are attributed not to acts of deliberate creation but to accidental developments in the mythological past. The Navajo Monsters, slain eventually by the Hero Twins, were born from women who practiced sexual aberrations during a time when they were separated from men. For Puebloan peoples, water-dwelling creatures are sacred because they are the spirits of the tribe's children, drowned when the people were crossing a river in an earlier existence. Etiological myths are often notably ingenious, and can be an entertaining literary form.

Celestial phenomena. The sun, the moon, and the stars are among the most intriguing and mysterious phenomena observed by all peoples, and there are nearly always myths that give them shape and personality, and frequently a biography.

Weather and seasons. Partly because of their seeming capriciousness, these have been subjects of human fascination since time out of mind. It is only necessary to observe how much time is devoted to the weather forecast in today's news broadcasts, to appreciate how important they still are. Most peoples have attributed weather phenomena not to one deity but to several of them, who are responsible for specific features such as lightning, wind, rain, and ice. There is often an extensive mythology to explain how and why these beings act as they do.

Illness, misfortune, and death. These are for all peoples the great mysteries and the great levelers. They can come unexpected at any time, and strike down the richest or most powerful along with the humble. Despite the frequency and indeed the inevitability of illness and death, the great majority of peoples regard these things as unnatural, and attribute them to the action of malevolent beings. There is usually an extensive mythology surrounding them, which at the same time often suggests what can be done to allay them.

Sex. Why did the gods choose to make all living things in separate male and female forms, when they could as easily have created each species in a single self-reproducing form? It is an endlessly intriguing mystery which nearly all peoples have pondered, and for which most have sought an explanation through mythology.

The foregoing are the most nearly universal features of explanatory mythology, but they by no means exhaust the genre. All peoples have additional myths to account for special features in their particular environments: natural formations or volcanism or earthquakes or tides, for example.

Justification

All of us at times need reassurance that our way of doing things is the right way—especially when we are conscious that other peoples have different ways. Justification comes, for nearly all peoples including ourselves, in the form of divine ordination, as expressed in mythology. The following are some aspects of cultural practice that are regularly sanctified through mythology.

Kinship and the family. The gods created man and woman, and ordained that they should live together, collaborate, and procreate. That much is specified in just about every known body of mythology. For many, however, mythology provides justification as well for much more extended bonds of kinship, and it may provide the rationale for rules of residence (patrilocal or matrilocal) and of inheritance. For Navajos and many other peoples, the kinship relations that exist among the *Diné* are a reflection of the kinship relations that exist among the gods. For Muslims the *Sunna,* the central mythology of Islam, is very specific about a wide range of kinship obligations.

Political authority. The exercise of power, beyond the context of the immediate family, always requires legitimation, and that legitimation comes ultimately from on high. Rulers in the early empires claimed to be living gods, or to be descended from gods, or to have the Mandate of Heaven; medieval European kings also claimed Divine Right. Modern democracies still cite the principle *vox populi vox dei*—the voice of the people is the voice of God.

Cultural practices. Most peoples are very conscious that there are neighboring peoples different from themselves, and they seek to justify through mythology their own distinctive practices. Traditions of housing, of dress, of diet, and just about every other aspect of culture may be explained as a gift or as a decree of the tribal gods, while at the same time the different traditions of other peoples are seen as the gift of other gods. The culture-bringer or culture-giver is a very common figure of mythology.

Warfare. Many and perhaps most peoples have war gods, whose very existence provides justification for the practice of warfare. It is also true that warlike activity is often glorified in mythology, as it was for Greeks and Romans. Some peoples have 'hereditary enemies,' and the relationship of enmity is explained and justified through mythology.

Regulation

Among its many gifts to humanity, religion always provides law. Basic ideas of what is right and wrong are fundamental to the functioning of every society, and they are nearly always attributed to divine decree. Society deifies itself in order to legitimize the demands that it places on its members, as the functionalists have insisted. The lawgivers of antiquity—Hammurabi and Moses, for example—were not lawmakers; they were simply handing down decrees from on high.

Law in the widest sense is present in all societies, nonliterate as well as literate, and there are all kinds of myths to explain how it has been transmitted from the divine to the human realm. Sometimes it has been handed down to a messiah or prophet; sometimes it has been revealed through divination; sometimes (as in Confucian thought) it is simply immemorial custom which is accepted as divinely ordained, because whatever endures must reflect the will of the gods. To Navajos the law has not come to be known through specific revelations, but mostly through trial and error; that is, through observing the consequence of transgression.

Instruction

Although it is by no means always the case, mythology may provide quite specific guidelines as to how acts of worship are to be carried out, and how votive objects are to be made. This is conspicuously true in both the Navajo and the Arab village cases. Each of the major Navajo ceremonies has its own defining myth, telling how and when it was given to the *Diné* by the *Dighini*. Similarly, the *hadra* ritual of each of the Arab brotherhoods is specified in the mythology surrounding the founding *wali*.

Remembrance

A sense of history is one of the universal human characteristics that is not shared with animals. A desire to remember the past is common to nearly all peoples, and for most of them remembrance is embodied in mythology. Myths tell how the people came to exist, what adventures and misadventures they suffered in earlier times, and how they came to be where they are now located. Migration tales, telling how the people wandered until they found 'the center of the world,' are common among North American Indians and many other peoples. Historical myths may contain, incidentally, a great deal of explanation and a great deal of justification, but they do not exist just to serve those purposes. First and foremost they satisfy mankind's longing to know about the past, and they are a highly prized literary form as well.

Eschatology

No review of the content of religion can ignore the subject of eschatology, and yet, contrary to what is often supposed, it is not an important feature of most religions. Beliefs about supernatural Powers are found among all peoples, and some kind of belief about an afterlife is also found among nearly all of them, but the connection between the two areas of belief is often far from close, and may in some cases be absent altogether.

E. B. Tylor and some other early evolutionary theorists believed that religion had its origin in man's attempt to cope with the mystery of death (Tylor 1874). If this were true, however, we should expect to find eschatology highly developed in the religions of the simplest societies today. In fact, the reverse is true. Not only are ideas about the afterlife very imprecise, but they are wholly unconnected with ideas about the deities, or with any kind of formal mythology. This is true even in the case of the Navajos, whose culture is far from primitive.

Religion in tribal societies, as the armchair scholar Tylor did not realize, is quintessentially practical. It has to concern itself with the uncertainties of this world, not with those of a world to come. To the extent that the rather vague eschatology of tribal peoples can be called a religion at all, it is virtually a religion unto itself, without deities and without mythology. (I will take up this issue again at the end of the chapter.)

Archaeologists have sometimes cited the evidence of burial ritual in Paleolithic graves (flowers or red ochre covering the body) as the earliest evidence for the existence of religion in human society—thereby lending support to Tylor's theory. However, I think this is debatable on two grounds. We have to ask not only whether primitive eschatology is really religion, but whether burial ritual necessarily betokens a belief in an afterlife. Much of our funerary ritual today has nothing to do with any eschatological beliefs; it is simply a way of giving expression to our grief, and at the same time a final expression of affection or respect for the deceased. I see no reason why we should not assume the same in the case of our stone-age forbears.

In the evolutionary development of religion (discussed in the next chapter) eschatology seems to become more important as human mastery over the immediate natural environment increases, leaving people freer to address the uncertainties of a life to come. By the time of the earliest state-level societies (i.e. civilizations) we find that eschatology has definitely become integrated with the other domains of religion; that is, with beliefs about the gods. Ideas about the nature of the next world are now highly specific, and are embedded in mythology. And finally, with the coming of the salvationist cults, they become, at least nominally, the central focus of religion. Far from being the beginning point of religious evolution, eschatological beliefs are much more clearly associated with its later stages of development.

Descriptive information

Along with everything else, mythology is for many peoples an encyclopedia of miscellaneous information. It may provide descriptive detail not only about the supernatural world, but about the unseen parts of the natural world and the world of the hereafter as well. Mythology often tells what is on the other side of the mountains or across the seas, and above and below the earth surface. It may also provide practical information about lucky and unlucky times and days, dangerous substances, and the like.

Belonging: the communal dimension

This aspect of religion can be dealt with fairly quickly, since it is essentially implicit in the definition of religion itself. Durkheim (1915: 45) was surely incorrect in his assertion that religion necessarily involves a church, if by that we mean a formally organized body of worshippers. On the other hand he was correct in the assertion—basic to his entire theory—that religion always involves community. Every religion has a self-recognizing body of votaries, to whom it 'belongs' and who belong to it. In some cases it is religion that actually creates the community, though more often religion merely provides ideological sanction for a social grouping that already existed.

There are, it is true, individuals who espouse highly idiosyncratic bodies of belief about supernatural powers, which they refer to as 'their' personal religion. However, these do not satisfy my definition of religion, for three reasons. First, they are usually systems of belief only, having neither a communal nor a behavioral (i.e. ritual) aspect. Second, since they are not shared, they are not properly cultural phenomena, while religion as I view it can only be understood as an aspect of culture. Third, they have no component of tradition; neither ancestry nor posterity.

Segmentation, solidarity, and religion

One of the most important conceptual insights that we owe to Emile Durkheim is the recognition that human societies, when they grow to a certain size, will predictably break up into smaller units which tend to replicate one another in terms of their size, composition, and characteristics. They then exist in a state of 'balanced opposition' to one another, as Durkheim put it. He referred to this process as segmentation. (He could have included many kinds of animal bands or troops under the same theory, had his interest extended that far.) Among humans, the segmentary units thus formed may be nations or city-states or tribes or lineages or villages or simply nuclear families. They are not necessarily in active opposition or conflict with one another (though they often are), but they are in competition in the sense that each strives to have all the things that the others have.

Each segmentary unit, in Durkheim's conception, is in the broadest sense a community, held together and at the same time differentiated from rival communities by a sense of solidarity. And that sense of solidarity is very commonly rooted in, or at least reinforced by, religion, which is always at least slightly (and consciously) different for each community. Tribes have their tribal gods; lineages have their ancestral tutelaries; villages have their patron saints and/or special rituals.

If religion is essential to the solidarity and the functioning of many communities, the reverse is even more true. Communities are essential to the existence and the functioning of religion, because each religion is a body of *shared* beliefs and practices. At the cognitive level, most people are 'other-directed' or 'tradition-directed,' to use David Riesman's (1961: 3–5) terms. The strength of their faith rests not on direct revelation or personal conviction, but on the fact that all their fellows believe the same things. Similarly, at the behavioral level, they follow the religious practices of their neighbors, and indeed often join with their neighbors in collective ritual activity. In dealing with the gods, as in most other adaptive activities, there is a feeling that collective action is more effective than individual action, and I don't know of any religion that does not involve collectively performed rituals.

Religious communities

Navajo religion and scriptural Islam share in common the fact that they are catholic, in the lower-case sense of the term. That is they are, and are meant to be, universal (within tribal limits in the Navajo case) and without internal differentiation. They are unsegmented because they are the religions of unsegmented communities. To be a Navajo is, a priori, to be a follower of Navajo religion; there is no priesthood, no church, no local level of organization, and no ritual of enrollment. The same is true in theory of orthodox Islam, in which there is only a single worldwide community of the faithful. A Navajo readily attends a sing in any part of the reservation, without any sense of special belonging or not belonging, and an orthodox Muslim worships in any mosque that is handy, from Morocco to Java.

In this respect however the two religions are decidedly atypical. Much more commonly, religions are associated with specifically delimited segments of society, which may be localized but may also be differentiated on the basis of descent, or even of belief itself. We have seen that in village Islam there are distinct, enrolled brotherhoods, and this is typical of religion in complex societies. When there are competing sects, commitment to a specific community of worshippers is required. Even among nonliterate peoples there may be competing, esoteric religious communities, like the different ritual, curing, and hunting societies of the Pueblo Indians. The following are some of the more recognizable types of religious communities.

Nation-states and city-states. The modern nation-state is, in theory, a purely secular conception, having its roots in the secularist philosophy of the Enlightenment. Although a fair number of modern nations still have an established (i.e. state-supported) church, the only modern nation which still has anything like a unifying national religion, so far as I know, is Japan. On the other hand, religion was one of the most important differentiating and unifying features of the city-states of earlier times. Each city-state of the Sumero-Babylonians, of the Greeks, and of the Maya was possessed of, and possessed by, its own tutelary deity, whose worship was the central feature of civic ritual.

Tribes. It is one of the consistent features of the tribal world-view that every people has its own religion, because every people has its own gods. Religion, especially in the form of mythology, provides the basis for a sense of identity among tribal peoples. At the same time, the extent to which ritual serves to reinforce the sense of solidarity is highly variable. Among the relatively individualistic Navajos, there are no tribe-wide or even locality-wide rituals; every ceremony is privately sponsored and is held because of a situational need. Among the neighboring Pueblos, at the other extreme, there are village-wide and even multi-village ceremonies at which attendance is compulsory, and which are definitely meant to reinforce community solidarity.

Lineages. In many tribal societies, segmentation involves the splitting off not of local residential groups but of widely ramified kin groups (usually called lineages; sometimes clans), each claiming descent from its own common ancestor. It is these groups in which solidarity is rooted: one turns for support and protection not to near neighbors but to kinsmen, near or far. Kin group solidarity is very often reinforced by the possession of a special, esoteric body of myth and ritual, which may focus on the worship of a divine common ancestor. Religious differentiation of this sort is especially prevalent in Australia and in Africa, but is certainly not absent in other parts of the tribal world.

Villages. Villages represent the single most common form of social segmentation, both in the tribal and in the peasant worlds, and they are usually foci of religious segmentation as well. At this localized level, ritual is likely to be more important than mythology, as a basis for differentiation. It is rare to find any village that has beliefs markedly distinct from those of its neighbors, but each has its patron saint or its special rituals, that help to reinforce village solidarity. While nations, tribes, and lineages may or may not have collective rituals involving all the members, villages nearly always do: the saint's days of Roman Catholic villages and the *mulids* of the Arab villagers, for example.

Sodalities. Esoteric ritual societies, charged with the performance of particular ceremonies, were widespread among North American Indians, and the *turuq* (brotherhoods) of the Arabs represent something comparable in the Near Eastern world. These formally organized and enrolled groups are not properly sects, since they do not hold tenets antithetical to one another; they are simply aspects of religious segmentation. In anthropological literature they are usually called sodalities. Each forms a solidary group united by the possession of its own esoteric body of myth and ritual. The mystery cults of classical antiquity probably also fall into this category.

Sects. Sects are segmentary divisions of Christianity, Islam, or any other religion which are differentiated by conflicting tenets. Since their basis is fundamentally cognitive (i.e. a matter of belief), they do not always and necessarily have a communal basis. One may be an isolated Baptist

or Druze or Nestorian, living far from co-religionists and never participating in collective worship. Since sects always exist in active competition with other sects, however, they require a strong organizational basis to survive. Consequently, wherever possible the sectarian members
are gathered into formally organized congregations, for the performance
of collective ritual. In the Middle East, especially, religious sects have
played a very large role not merely in the maintenance but in the creation
of communities.

Mythology tells us what the Powers are like, and also, directly or by
inference, suggests how to deal with them. This is the behavioral domain
of religion; what has sometimes been called the 'business end.' I will
here follow conventional practice in referring to all kinds of religious
activity as ritual, although it must be remembered that many religious
acts are individual, spontaneous, and not dictated by tradition. The more
complex religious performances, involving a series of individual rituals,
should properly be called ceremonies, but most of the time I will use the
terms ritual and ceremony interchangeably.

*Behaving:
the commu-
nicative
dimension*

 The single most nearly universal feature of all religious acts is that
they are, in the broadest sense, acts of communication with the Powers.
Such communication may take a wide variety of forms, and it may be
undertaken for a wide variety of purposes, just as in the purely human
sphere. Much of it is verbal, but paintings, sculpture, drama, monumental
architecture, gifts, and acts of imitation may also serve to communicate
with and to influence the gods.

As religion may serve a wide variety of needs, so, obviously, religious
activity may be undertaken for a variety of purposes. It may be intended
to cause things to happen, as several of the previously cited definitions
(Chapter 8) have suggested, but it is just as often intended to prevent
things from happening, or simply to evoke and to express feelings. In
normal times a great deal of ritual activity is meant simply to maintain
the status quo: to keep things running as they are. Much of the time this
is the manifest purpose alike of the Navajo Blessingway (*hozhoji*), of the
Arab villagers' *hadra,* and of the weekly worship in all of the Abrahamic
religions.

*The functions
of ritual*

 Of course, religious activity has latent as well as manifest functions,
to use Ralph Linton's (1936: 401–421) terms. It is the latent functions
that have chiefly engaged the attention of functional theorists: those of

providing integration for society, and psychological comfort for individuals. But I will be concerned here mainly with the manifest functions: those that motivate the votaries themselves. Viewed in that light, I think that nearly all religious activity can be glossed under four broad headings, which I will call veneration, propitiation, supplication, and compulsion. The boundaries between the categories are of course far from sharp; many rituals involve a combination of two, three, or even four of them.

Veneration. Much ritual activity, both individual and collective, is not meant to achieve any specific end, but simply to let the gods know how we feel about them. We need a way of expressing our feelings, irrespective of any expected consequences. Psalms of praise and of thanks are the single most important features of worship in the Abrahamic religions, and they are important in many other religions as well. Thanksgiving ceremonies of one kind or another are among the most common of rituals. Veneration may be expressed also by acts of physical obeisance, such as prostration, by making pictorial or sculptural representations of the gods, by imitating them in drama and dance, and by building architectural monuments to them.

Propitiation. By propitiation I refer to acts that are meant to have a specific influence on the gods, in either a positive or a negative sense. That is, they may be undertaken in the hope of causing the gods to act in beneficial ways, but also to dissuade them from acting in harmful ways. Aztec and Maya blood sacrifices, for example, were meant to prevent the gods from destroying the world, the way they had destroyed three previous worlds. For many God-fearing Christians, acts of worship are meant not so much to achieve heavenly salvation as to avoid damnation.

Acts of propitiation commonly involve gifts, a category that, in the broad sense, includes also sacrifices. Offerings of food are probably the most common propitiatory gifts, but many acts of personal or collective self-denial are also gratifying to the Powers. So also are various ritual observances that the deities have specifically ordained for us, either through mythology or through direct revelation. Jews (and most Christians) have been commanded to observe the Ten Commandments; orthodox Muslims have been commanded to perform the Five Pillars of the Faith. Dietary tabus, observed by Jews, Muslims, Navajos, and a host of other peoples, are among the most common acts of propitiation; they are meant not to achieve benefits but to avoid divine displeasure.

Supplication. Rituals of supplication are those in which we seek for specific benefits, like rain or recovery from an illness or success in war. When asking for personal favors we nearly always use verbal address, but all kinds of flattery—verbal, pictorial, or imitative—may be employed in major communal rituals which seek for collective benefits.

Compulsion. A great deal of ritual is meant not so much to beg the deities as to compel them to act, through the performance of minutely prescribed ritual formulas. These may involve repeated verbal recitations, like the Navajo *hozhonigo*, but they also may involve imitative magic, such as blowing tobacco smoke to imitate the movement of clouds, or whirling a bull-roarer (noise-maker) to imitate the sound of thunder. Compulsive rituals are more prevalent among preliterate peoples than in more complex societies, but Tantric Buddhism, found in the relatively complex societies of Tibet and neighboring countries, involves a great deal of compulsive magic.

Human groups have conceived of a seemingly endless variety of supernatural beings, having an equally endless variety of personality traits. The number of acts that may be propitiatory or pleasing to one god or another is vast in proportion. A detailed review of ritual practices among different peoples would require a book several times the size of this one. I will do no more here than to suggest some of the most regularly recurring features of ritual practice. As I have already suggested, all of them are in the broadest sense acts of communication.

Respect. Power demands respect: I think we can take that as a first premise in any general consideration of the nature and content of ritual. Like human rulers, the gods require veneration at times, praise at times, and offerings at times, but they require respect at all times—in language, dress, and deportment. We speak to them in elevated, poetic, and sometimes archaic language; we cleanse ourselves and if possible 'put on our Sunday best' before addressing them; and we behave in a suitably reverent manner, like obedient children, in their presence.

Verbal address is surely the most universal way of communicating with the Powers, as it is with living humans. It may be involved equally in rituals of veneration, propitiation, supplication, or compulsion. It differs from normal human discourse in that it is mostly formal, and formulaic. In speaking to the gods we employ formulas to which they have become accustomed; sometimes indeed formulas which they themselves have prescribed, as in the case of both Muslim and Navajo prayers.

The three most common themes that are likely to be sounded in verbal address are admiration for the power of the gods, adoration for their kindness, and thanks for their gifts. Also very common are supplications, which may also be formulaic when they are more or less routine requests for good weather or success in warfare, for example. They may also be highly personal requests for success in enterprises or for relief from illness, but even these individual supplications are likely to be couched in a set formula.

In a slightly different category from those discussed above are verbal formulas that are designed to compel rather than to persuade the gods. They generally involve no words of supplication or praise, but rather are likely to be rendered in a kind of impersonal imperative: 'let there be peace,' or 'let me win.' Much of the supposed power of these invocations comes through endless repetition of the same formula. I am inevitably reminded of the doctrine espoused by many professional advertisers, that effective salesmanship may require continual hammering on the same slogan.

Gifts. Reciprocity is one of the most fundamental requirements in the maintenance of social equilibrium: when we receive gifts or services, there is an equal return obligation. The same principle applies in our relations with the Powers. As we are continually receiving their gifts, in the form of abundant game or good weather or health, so we owe them gifts in return. The making of offerings is probably, next to verbal address, the single most common ritual activity. And of all the offerings given to the deities, food is probably the most common, as it is also in the case of gifts to humans. 'First fruits' of the hunt or of the harvest are returned to the gods; offerings of cereal cakes or mush are placed on the holy altars by farming peoples; animals (and occasionally humans) are ritually slaughtered by those who have them in sufficient number. But of course gifts of money or jeweled objects, donated to the church, mosque, or synagogue, are especially prized in complex and monetized societies. Surely the most precious of all gifts are great architectural monuments raised to honor the gods, most often by a community but occasionally by a single individual or family.

Sacrifice and self-denial are particular and uniquely human kinds of gift-giving, when we mortify ourselves, literally or figuratively, to signalize our submission to the gods. We deliberately give them something we can't afford, or go without something we need or would like. Sacrifice very often involves destroying the thing sacrificed, so that it could no longer be of use to humans.

Pilgrimage. Gifts, sacrifices, and rites of worship take on added value when we travel for a distance to present them. The journey itself becomes an act of worship, and is often surrounded by all kinds of ritual. I mentioned earlier the importance of pilgrimages to the shrines of saints, in Arab village religion. The most extreme examples or ritualized pilgrimage are probably to be seen in the 'inchworm' progressions of Indian and Tibetan votaries, who travel very long distances to reach a holy shrine, by a series of prostrations.

Imitative art. The gods, with the notable exceptions of Yahweh and Allah, love to see themselves depicted, and the making of representations of them is one of the most common of votive acts. In addition to figurines, paintings, and statues, there are also ritual dramas and dances in which they are impersonated, and songs in which their voices are imitated. Imitation may have compulsive as well as propitiatory power, as in the case for example of Pueblo Indian dances and Navajo sandpaintings, in which the deities are portrayed. At the same time imitative art also and conspicuously represents an aesthetic dimension of religion, and as such will be further discussed in a later section.

There is no sphere of human experience from which ritual activity is wholly absent, among all peoples. It is obvious however that the help of the gods is most urgently needed in those situations over which humans have the least control: situations of uncertainty. The following are some of the most common situations, or spheres of activity, in which ritual performance is regularly involved.

Ritual occasions

The food quest. Most people in the modern industrial world have a luxury enjoyed by very few of their predecessors: they can take their food supply for granted. For people in the pre-industrial world, and indeed among many peasant peoples today, the daily and the year-around provision of food was a source of recurring anxiety. As a result, there is probably no sphere of human activity that is more consistently surrounded by ritual than is the food quest. Hunting peoples have a wide variety of rituals to insure the continued appearance of the game, to bring success in the chase, and to thank the animal deities (or sometimes apologize to them) for the gift of their kind. Agricultural peoples have especially to appeal to the weather gods, to bring the right amount or rain at the right time, and to thank them when they do so. Harvest festivals of thanksgiving are widespread even in the modern industrial world. Devout votaries of all the Abrahamic religions ask a blessing or offer thanks before each meal. It is no surprise therefore that the most frequent of all gifts offered to the gods are gifts of food.

The seasonal cycle. In most parts of the world, the weather is just variable enough from year to year to be a source of anxiety. Even for non-agricultural peoples, early snows or a late thaw or torrential rains can bring disaster. Communal rituals to mark the passing of the seasons, and to insure their continued orderly passing in the future, are therefore common. They occur perhaps most commonly at the spring and fall equinoxes, but also in mid-winter. For Americans, Easter and Thanksgiving are the vestigial survivals of equinoctial rituals, while Christmas is the survival of an old mid-winter renewal rite.

Natural disasters, in the non-industrial world, are nearly always seen as the work of malevolent or at least offended deities. To some extent these misfortunes can be avoided by propitiatory rituals addressed to the appropriate Powers. Ancient Mesopotamians prayed to the river gods to prevent floods; Andean Indians have, or had, rituals to propitiate the deities responsible for earthquakes and avalanches. After a disaster has occurred, there may be rituals of atonement to appease the deities who have brought destruction.

Illness and misfortune. Many peoples, like the Navajos, do not differentiate sharply between illness, injury, and other unexpected misfortunes such as the death of valued animals. All are seen as the result of malevolent supernatural forces. There are, as a result, a vast number of rituals intended to insure against these misfortunes, and an even greater number to allay them once they have occurred.

Travel in earlier days was often fraught with dangers, and even today it is not without its hazards. Ritual preparation before undertaking a trip is therefore common, as are special ritual observances while on the road. Devout Navajos will have a Blessingway both before and after an extended trip; Arabs will recite the Profession of Faith, and may also seek out and give alms to a beggar at the start of a trip. Many Catholics still carry St. Christopher medals for protection while traveling.

Warfare is always a hazardous proposition, not only for the combatants but for non-combatant populations as well. Most warrior peoples undergo extensive ritual preparation before beginning any offensive operations, and may have to submit to ritual purification afterward as well. Victory celebrations may thank the war gods for giving victory, and lamentation ceremonies may help assuage the feeling of defeat. In a sense, activity of this kind serves to legitimize the practice of warfare, which otherwise might appear problematical at best. There are also appeals to the war gods which may help to protect non-combatants against surprise attacks by enemies.

Politics. In chiefdoms and early states, the rulers depend heavily on ritual to legitimize their authority, through rites that in one way or another affirm their connection with the gods. Their reign begins with an elaborate rite of investiture and ends with an elaborate funeral, and in between they are likely to have a prominent part in annually recurring ceremonies. But, as Max Gluckman (1955, 1963) and other British anthropologists have pointed out, there are also rituals of rebellion against the established order of things, which serve to relieve social tensions.

Games and gambling are uncertain by design; there would be no fun in them if the outcome were assured. They are, as a result, surrounded by a considerable amount of ritual, designed to bring success. In modern casinos, surviving folk rituals can be observed especially at the craps table. The actual performance of games or gambling may itself be highly ritualized, as is true in the Navajo case.

Craft activity. Even the most skilled potter, weaver, or cabinetmaker cannot be certain of success every time. These various crafts often have patron saints, or in earlier times tutelary deities, who should be propitiated with prayers or offerings in order to assure success.

Rites of passage. Every society is a network in which each person has one or more recognized statuses: as a male or female, as a child or adult, as a kinsman, as a member of a clan, as a member of a social class, as a follower of a particular occupation, and so on. Social stability depends on the maintenance of the network, so that each persons knows what to expect from each other person. The transition of any person from one status to another is therefore potentially upsetting to the system, and it very often requires ritual validation through what are called rites of passage (sometimes also 'life crisis rites,' though this is a misleading term).

Rites of passage are among the most common of all ceremonies, and are found in nearly every society. In the normal course of physical maturation there may be ceremonies to mark birth, naming, circumcision, puberty, adulthood, marriage, and death, but there will probably also be ceremonies of investiture to mark advances in social status. Very frequently these ceremonies involve a kind of ritual death and rebirth, in which the subject person acquires a new name and/or titles and new forms of dress or adornment.

Scheduled worship, occurring at fixed intervals and without reference to external events, is obviously an exception to the general rule that ritual finds its place in situations of uncertainty. The weekly church, mosque, or synagogue service is the prescribed form of ritual in all the Abrahamic religions, and the major ceremonies of the Maya and other Mesoamerican peoples also were driven more by the calendar than by events. Rituals of this type may be referred to, for want of a better term, as routine renewal ceremonies, since they are meant to replenish our faith and at the same time to remind the gods that we are still thinking of them. Weekly ceremonies are decidedly rare, except in the Abrahamic religions, but many peoples have seasonally recurring rituals, corresponding to the passage of the seasons.

Feeling: the affective dimension
Power always evokes feelings in us, and the stronger the power, the stronger the feelings, both positive and negative. Inevitably, there is no religion without a very important affective content, for some if not all of its votaries.

Feelings toward the Powers, like those toward human objects, may be quite complex, sometimes involving veneration, love, and fear toward the same individual. Good Christians are supposed to be at once god-loving and god-fearing, as we find expressed in the names Amadeus or Gottlieb (God-loving) and Timotheos (God-fearing). In polytheistic systems, the various deities are the objects of a very wide range of feelings, including hate and contempt as well as more positive feelings. Even for nominally monotheistic Christians, different feelings can be apportioned among different beings. Fear and respect are likely to be felt toward the Supreme Being, love toward the Virgin, familiar affection toward patron saints, and hate toward the Devil.

But religion does not merely invoke feelings incidentally. A great deal of religious performance is undertaken with the specific intent of invoking feelings, heightened above the levels that we normally experience in everyday life. Persons during or at the conclusion of great ritual dramas may be seen with tears streaming down their faces, while at any other time they would seek to avoid any such display of feeling. At their most extreme, rituals may induce altered states of consciousness, during which individuals may believe that they are physically possessed by spirits, or are in direct communication with a deity. The *dhikr* of the Arab villagers are rituals of this type, as are the rituals of Christian charismatics, Hindu yogas, and many peoples who use drugs in religious performance. These can be moments of high exaltation for persons whose everyday life is likely to be dull and monotonous.

Some psychofunctionalists have identified the affective as the single most important dimension of religion, ignoring the fact that a great deal of routine worship is carried on without invoking any very strong feelings. Moreover, this is probably the single most individually variable dimension of religion. Within any community, most people may be believing the same things and performing the same ritual acts, but some will do so with a high sense of emotional involvement, and others with a sense of almost total detachment. I think it would be accurate to say that religion invokes some of the most powerful feelings that people are able to enjoy, most of the time, in their lives, without at the same time suggesting that this is the main reason for being religious. But the hope of enjoying exalted feelings may indeed be one of the most compelling reasons for participating in particular rituals, or even for witnessing them.

The feelings deliberately invoked in religion are not always and necessarily positive. There are also rituals designed to invoke fear, like the Katcina performances of the Pueblo Indians, and even rituals of execration, in which the flames of hatred are fanned to a state something like exaltation, as in the victory dances of eastern American Indians. Hate, as well as love, can be a compelling self-indulgence permitted and encouraged within religion.

Of course, not all religious feelings are heightened feelings, nor do they always find outward expression. The sense of security that comes from reduction of anxiety, about the food supply or disease or death, is an important kind of religious sentiment. So also is the sense of comfort that comes from knowing that one's own people are the chosen people. So, again, is the pure aesthetic enjoyment that comes from contemplating works of religious art, or performances. But when all is said and done, perhaps the most pervasive of latent sentiments is the continual fear of the gods, which is never far from the minds of those who recognize their own powerlessness. As I will suggest at the end of the book, religion is not so much the force that impels us to be good, as it is the force that stops us from being bad.

Creation: the artistic dimension

Religion is, in my view, both a product of the human creative imagination, and at the same time a great stimulus to the creative imagination. Through the ages it has given rise to a very large part of the world's art, literature, music, drama, and monumental architecture. The results, in the case of our own Western civilization, are too familiar to require enumeration, but there is probably no religion in the world that has not also served as a source of aesthetic inspiration, at least for some of its votaries. Artistic inspiration cannot, obviously, be identified as one of the essential functions of religion, in spite of its universality. It is simply one of religion's many gifts.

Representational art

The gods, always excepting Yahweh/Allah, love to see themselves depicted, and mankind obviously loves to oblige them. Figurines, presumed to represent deities, are found already far back in the Stone Age, and with the advancement of technology they are joined by life-sized and ultimately by heroic-sized statues, not to mention paintings and mosaics. Indeed it is not until Greek times, at least in the Near East and the West, that we begin to recognize any significant development of non-religious art, apart from purely decorative designs found on pottery and other utilitarian objects.

Verbal art

It may be noted to begin with that the entire corpus of mythology is for many peoples a great and highly entertaining art form. In the case of tribal peoples it is virtually the whole of their literature. Many myths have no real connection with any kind of religious performance; they are simply perpetuated from generation to generation, and frequently recited, because of their entertainment value. Marvels, miracles, grotesqueries, and various kinds of humor have a prominent place. This is not true only of tribal peoples; there is much in the Old Testament that has been retained mainly for its entertainment value. The Song of Solomon is one obvious example.

More formal verbal art is found in the flowery poetic addresses in praise or in supplication to the gods, which are a part of a great many rituals. They are equally evident in the Navajo case and in all the Abrahamic religions. But there are also many religious psalms, lamentations, and other forms of literary art that have been composed not for ritual recital, but simply for aesthetic expression of our feelings. It is pleasing to the gods just to know that such works have been composed. The religious poetry most familiar to us in the West is that contained in the Old Testament, which actually derives from a much older tradition already highly developed in Sumerian and Babylonian times. Among tribal cultures, a good deal of mythology is also embodied in elegantly poetic forms.

Music

Music, like poetry, is woven into a great deal of ritual, for it is evident that the gods enjoy the sound of it. More than that, though, many peoples, including most North American Indians, believe that there is special power in songs. But in this sphere also, there is a great deal of religious music that has not been composed specifically for ritual performance, but just for the aesthetic enjoyment of the composers and performers, and presumably the supernatural hearers. The great oratorios and cantatas of the Baroque age fall into that category, but so also do Christmas carols, and the impromptu songs that are prized by many American Indians.

Performing art

Ritual dramas, popular throughout the Christian middle ages, have virtually died out in modern times, and they are expressly forbidden in the worlds of Judaism and Islam. Among non-Abrahamic peoples however they remain one of the most popular and elaborated of art forms. Throughout the tribal world, as well as in India and neighboring countries, costumed impersonations of the gods, in drama, song, and dance, are the great ritual events of the year. Masks are especially elaborated among native American groups, as they are also in Africa and Melanesia, and as representations of the gods they are believed to possess great ritual power.

Architecture

Mankind's supreme artistic expressions, in the name of religion, are surely to be found in the field of architecture. Nearly all of the world's high civilizations have sought to glorify their gods, and coincidentally themselves, through monumental buildings, which far outstripped any other constructions of their time. In major cities and in peasant villages alike, the temple or the church or the mosque is almost certain to be the largest, the most ornate, and the most permanent of structures. Most tribal societies do not possess the technology to build on so grand a scale, but in them also we may find that great collective efforts have gone into the rearing of earthen mounds, or temporary structures of wood for the performance of ceremonies. It is only among nomadic peoples that we find no emphasis on religious building, and it is the legacy of a nomadic past that accounts for the lack of imposing religious buildings both among Navajos and among many Arab groups.

Pure and applied religion

Enough has been said in earlier pages to drive home the point that every religion has both a pure and an applied aspect, analogous to the relationship of pure and applied science. The explanatory dimension, contained largely in mythology and folk wisdom, represents pure religion. Religious practice intended to make things happen, or to prevent them from happening, is applied religion. Much of ritual, though by no means all of it, falls into this category. The two dimensions are, obviously, very differently developed in different societies, and also to some extent in different persons. The extent of pure religion depends on how much people feel a need or a desire to explain the supernatural; the extent of applied religion depends on how much they feel they need to control it, or try to. Pure religion consists of whatever people find they can believe in; applied religion consists of whatever seems to work. The fact that all religions have both aspects is one reason why so few of them are really integrated systems of thought and action. It should be clear of course that most religious persons do not make this distinction in their own minds.

The problem of plurality

The foregoing discussion does not, obviously, exhaust the possibilities for religious thought and action, for there is no limit to those possibilities. I would only suggest that most of the world's religions, past and present, have cognitive, communal, behavioral, affective, and aesthetic aspects, and most involve some combination of the more specific elements I have discussed. But the number of possible combinations is without limit, given the capabilities of the human creative imagination.

At this point, finally, it becomes necessary to take up a problem that I have thus far avoided: that of defining and describing religions in a specific rather than a generic sense. It is easy to say that all peoples have religion, as I have defined it, but can we always say that they have 'a' religion? Or may it not be the case that some individuals, and some whole societies, are holding and practicing several different religions simultaneously? This was the problem hinted at by Edward Reeves (1980: 3) when he wrote that "... 'religion' is a folk category, not a scientific one. It has become increasingly clear that religion is a subject that must be decomposed before scientific analysis can begin." Durkheim was clearly incorrect in defining religion as a 'unified system,' but is it, among specific peoples, necessarily a system at all?

The problem is most clearly illustrated in the case of eschatology, a category that encompasses both beliefs about the afterlife, and funerary beliefs and practices that may or may not be connected with them. Some kind of eschatology is found in nearly all societies, yet it rarely connects in any coherent way with other aspects of religion, as we saw in the Navajo case. It may even be that beliefs about the afterlife on one hand, and funerary practices on the other, do not correlate with each other, as is the case in our own Judaeo-Christian society. There is nothing in scripture that sanctions our elaborate funerals and tombstones, nothing that even specifies how the body is to be disposed of, nor are such practices held to contribute in any way to the salvation either of the deceased or of the mourners.

The most extreme disconnect that I have encountered between funerary practice and the rest of culture can be seen in Kazakhstan and Kirghizia, where Marxist indoctrination has expunged just about all other traces of religion among the elites, yet they continue to bury their dead under elaborate monuments (often constructed like the tribal *yurt*) adorned with the traditional Muslim star and crescent.

One way of dealing with this problem would be to say that mortuary practices are not religion, but merely cultural tradition. This is perhaps true in the Kazakh case, but for most other peoples the mortuary practices are in fact overseen by religious practitioners, and the names of the gods may be invoked in the burial ritual. It could also be argued that beliefs about the afterlife are not religion when, as in the Navajo case, they do not connect with any mythology or any specific ideas about the gods. Yet in the broadest sense the eternally persisting souls in the afterworld are themselves supernaturals; among other things they have the power to revisit earth. Despite its separation from the rest of religion, therefore, I do not think that eschatology can ever be eliminated altogether from the domain of religion as I have defined it. It is simply, for many peoples, a second religion.

Setting aside the question of eschatology, the most clearcut example of religious plurality known to me is that of the Pueblo Indians of New Mexico. They are equally sincere in their devotion to Roman Catholicism and to their aboriginal religion, while at the same time keeping the two rigidly distinct. On their own initiative, and without prodding from the church, they appoint *fiscales* whose job it is to see that people attend the major Catholic ceremonies, just as it is the job of the traditional religious societies (usually the Clown on the Warrior Society) to see that people attend the native ceremonies. Lip service or even sincere practice of Christianity side by side with some continuation of native religion is fairly common among peoples under colonial rule, where adoption of Christianity may have been enforced, but the Pueblos have kept this up on their own initiative for more than a hundred and fifty years after the end of the Spanish/Mexican colonial regime.[24]

Plurality of another kind is exhibited in the Arab village religion, described in Chapter 3, in which orthodox Islam and the worship of local saints constitute virtually separate religions (although the villagers do not think of them that way), while the *zar* cult stands wholly apart from both. The latter cult exemplifies the fact that curing rituals and beliefs among many peoples stand rather sharply apart from other domains of religion, and involve their own set of supernaturals. This of course is distinctly not true in the Navajo case, but it is true among their Pueblo neighbors.

I think we are forced to conclude that, as there are many kinds of supernaturals having many kinds of power, so there may be many different bodies of belief and practice connected with them, that may not connect in any coherent way with one another. The religion of any people is thus likely to be a congeries, not a system, and it is one that has developed through ages of accretion and deletion. It is also one in which individuals can and do make choices, in what they believe and in what they do. There is a normative and officially approved body of religious beliefs and practices in most societies, but it is probable that the religion of no two persons is ever exactly the same.

On this point it is clear that the anthropologist's conception of what is 'a' religion differs from that of the theologian. To the latter any religion is an idealized body of beliefs that may exist apart from what people actually practice. Its defining basis in ideological, not behavioral. To the anthropologist on the other hand 'a' religion, in the broad sense, is whatever a recognized social group can be observed to believe and practice, however internally inconsistent it may be. In the most specific sense, 'a' religion is whatever any one individual believes and practices.

---

[24]I think that anthropologists like Leslie White, who have dismissed the Pueblos' devotion to Catholicism as superficial, have simply failed to appreciate the complexity of the Pueblo religious mind.

14

The Evolution of Religion

In the last chapter I was concerned chiefly to enumerate the features that are common among all religions. Here, I want to consider much more specifically the differences between them, mainly though not entirely from the perspectives of evolution and adaptation.

The theories of social and of biological evolution that are so often associated with the discipline of anthropology were not actually originated by anthropologists. Social evolutionary theory was already very fully developed by Enlightenment moral philosophers, a hundred years before the birth of anthropology, while biological evolutionary theory was propounded by three pioneers, Darwin, Wallace, and Huxley, who made no claim to be anthropologists. Nevertheless the evolutionary theory of religion, propounded initially by Tylor and Frazer, has been a uniquely anthropological achievement, and it is one of the discipline's most valuable and most widely accepted contributions to human understanding. For all the naive simplicity of the early evolutionary schemes, their basic approach still provides the most coherent theoretical foundation for understanding the similarities and differences among religions. To a considerable extent it is still accepted by most latter-day scholars of the subject.

The evolutionary perspective

The great and lasting contribution of the original, nineteenth-century formulations was their inclusiveness. Discarding the common and long-accepted distinction between religion and 'superstition,' they sought to include all the world's religious beliefs and practices, ancient and modern, within a single definition and a single evolutionary schema. The weakness of the schemes, like other nineteenth-century evolutionary theories, was their unilinear simplicity. All the world's religions were ranged in a single, linear scale of development, beginning with animism and progressing through various stages of polytheism, to a culmination in monotheism. The explanatory principle was strictly mentalistic: the progress from stage to stage was viewed not as adaptation to changing circumstances, but as evidence of the progressive maturation of human thought.

The oversimplification so obvious in the early theories of religion resulted from the fact that they were spun out by armchair scholars who had never been near an actual 'savage,' to use their own favorite term. Consequently, logic played a good deal larger part in their formulations than did actual ethnographic knowledge. Their 'savage' was in the beginning an ideal type that included everything from the marginal hunters of Tierra del Fuego to the complex horticultural societies of New Guinea to the great chiefdoms of West Africa. Such an outlook could take no account of the enormous ecological differences among nonliterate societies, and their inevitable effect on religious belief and practice.

*The
Australian
delusion*

A little later the problem—that of basing theory on logic rather than ethnographic facts—seemed to be corrected when a whole generation of scholars adopted the native Australian as their model of the primordial savage. However, this proved to be a delusion of another kind. Social evolutionists, going back at least to the time of John Locke, had taken the North American Indians as their model for the earliest form of human society; the 'zero of human society' as Lewis Henry Morgan called them (1851: 348). When ethnographic data on the native Australians began to appear near the end of the nineteenth century, however, these Aboriginals immediately displaced the Indians as everyone's original savage. Here were people not only without agriculture, but with virtually no clothing, no form of shelter, no pottery, and only the simplest of tools and weaponry. In the eyes of materially-minded Europeans and Americans, these must surely represent a survival of mankind's earliest forms of society and culture. Accordingly the native Australian religion, with its heavy emphasis on totemic worship, was taken to be the oldest form of religion. In the early twentieth century, Frazer, Durkheim, and Freud all published books based on that assumption.

It was a fundamental mistake, and one that in time contributed to the general discrediting of evolutionary theories of religion. Notwithstanding their lack of interest in things material, the native Australians actually had quite complex forms both of social organization and of religion. Population pressure had forced some Aboriginal tribes into marginal, desert areas, where they were obliged to scatter in small and nomadic groups, but most of the tribes lived in large, regularly interacting groups in areas with abundant food resources. In everything except the material sphere, their culture was at least as complex as that of California Indians, for example. In terms of social evolution as we now understand it, they had progressed beyond the band level, and as far as the tribal level of organization. This was equally true as regards their richly complex religion. We now know in fact that totemic beliefs are not highly developed in the simplest of societies, because they lack widely ramified kin groups.

The early, linear view of religious evolution lives on in the discipline of History of Religion (*Religionswissenschaft*), as it is taught chiefly in continental European countries. Among its outstanding proponents are Mircea Eliade and Åke Hultkrantz. Among anthropologists, however, the simplistic theories of the armchair logicians went out of fashion when ethnographers actually began studying 'primitive' societies at first hand, in the early twentieth century. The field workers soon concluded that the course or religious evolution has been a good deal more complex than the early proponents supposed. Some tribal peoples did indeed have simple religions in which animism and/or totemism played a major part; others had enormously complex religions and huge communal ceremonies. Since there seemed to be no clearcut order of progression, evolutionary theory gave way to purely historical explanation. Each religion was seen as the outcome of a unique set of historical circumstances, usually involving culture contacts and borrowing. When Lowie (1920: 441) referred to culture as '... that planless hodgepodge, that thing of shreds and patches ...,' I suspect that he had religion especially in mind.

The historical reaction

Social evolutionary theory was revived after World War II, when it was realized that the evolutionary baby was far too big to go out with the bathwater. The neo-evolutionists added a critical understanding that was missing from earlier theory—that of cultural ecology. They recognized that, while all the world's peoples were indeed progressing along roughly similar paths, they were at the same time adapting to all kinds of enormously dissimilar environments, which dictated specific, localized forms of cultural adaptation. The richness or poverty of environmental resources allowed for much larger co-resident and interacting population groups in some areas than in others, and this in turn largely dictated the amount of social and cultural elaboration that could take place.

Early evolutionary stage theory, articulated by social philosophers of

The rise of neo-evolutionism

the Enlightenment, had assigned all peoples to one of three evolutionary stages based on their made of subsistence: pre-agricultural, agricultural, and 'civilized' (i.e. industrial). But ecologists were able to observe that some peoples, like the fishing tribes of the American Northwest Coast, had succeeded in developing enormously complex cultures without benefit of agriculture, while farmers in marginal areas like the Amazon rainforest had much simpler cultures. In place of an evolutionary schema based on modes of subsistence, therefore, the neo-evolutionists proposed a classification of peoples based simply on the size and complexity of regularly interacting social groups—which in turn were largely determined by factors of ecology.

One of the foremost neo-evolutionists was Elman Service, who propounded a series of evolutionary stages which he called band, tribe, chiefdom, and state (Service 1978). The new schema was eagerly seized upon by a whole generation of anthropologists, and it remains today the dominant paradigm in social evolutionary theory, at least in America. Like all dominant paradigms it became dogma in the minds of the unthinking. Archaeologists in particular are apt to treat it as theoretically prescriptive, rather than as a set of classificatory pigeonholes into which actual societies can be fitted with varying degrees of appropriateness. If however we can accept it as no more than a heuristic device, without prescriptive value, it remains the most useful framework for an evolutionary understanding of most aspects of culture, including religion.

The limits of neo-evolutionism

But the limitation of neo-evolutionist theory is that it is overwhelmingly materialist. As a consequence, while the neo-evolutionists have revived and improved upon the nineteenth-century theories of social and material evolution, they have almost wholly ignored the topic of religious evolution. Strongly influenced as they are by Marxist materialism, the neo-evolutionists have tended to brush religion aside as epiphenomenon, or merely a reflection of the existing social order. As a result, theories of religious evolution are still pretty much where Tylor, Frazer, and Durkheim left them a century ago.[25]

A further weakness of the Service schema, as of most other anthropological theories of evolution, is that it ends with the establishment of the earliest civilized states. From that point onward, the theory seems to im-

---

[25]This is less true in the discipline of historical sociology, where both Guy Swanson (1960) and Robert Bellah (1964; 1970) have produced evolutionary formulations which, although basically linear, have departed considerably from the 19th century model.

ply, 'we lived happily (or unhappily) ever after.' This is unsatisfactory for a complete understanding of any aspect of culture, and doubly so in the case of religion. It is only necessary to point out that some of the most profound developments in religion, like exclusivity, nominal monotheism, and salvationism, have all arisen subsequent to the emergence of the early states. In fact they were all, in one sense or another, reactions against the complex state religions developed in the earliest civilizations.

Although I think the time is ripe for a comprehensive re-examination of religious evolution, such an undertaking is beyond the intended scope of this book. I want here only to reopen the topic for discussion; to see how some of the ideas I have developed in earlier chapters play out in the context of religious history. In order to carry forward the discussion beyond the limits of the Service scheme, however, I am obliged to add several additional developmental phases to Service's original four. These are nomadic chiefdoms, secularizing states, peasantries, and industrial civilizations. I do not suggest that they all represent stages in a continual, one-directional course of development; they are, rather, adaptations to specific social, political, and economic conditions, in an increasingly complex and diversifying world.

I have also to point out that not all the changes and differences that I will discuss here would fit the definition of 'evolution,' as it is currently employed by theoreticians—nor are they readily explainable in terms of any other theory known to me. Some historical changes, like the rise of salvationism, I am unable to see as adaptive, and I am still far from understanding them. There have also been changes, like the alternation between ages of faith and ages of reason, that are at least somewhat cyclical in nature, and thus do not fit the usual conception of evolution. I am, therefore, using the term 'evolution' throughout this chapter in a very loose sense, to discuss processes of change in which a certain pattern can be discerned, but which are only explained in part by current evolutionary theory. In the end I would have to say that the historical development of religions, as I have traced it here, may serve to illustrate both the strengths and the limitations of evolutionary theory.

Religion in band-level societies

Band-level societies are those in which people are forced to live a mostly nomadic life in small groups, united mainly or entirely by bonds of kinship and marriage. This was true of all or nearly all human groups before the Neolithic revolution of ten to twelve thousand years ago, and it has remained true of certain groups, living in environmentally marginal areas, down to the present day. Band-level societies are found in three kinds of environments where agriculture is not possible: in high latitudes (especially in the Americas), in dense tropical forests, and in deserts. In all these places the people are forced to live by a combination of hunting such game as there is, and collecting wild food products. Hunting provides almost the whole subsistence for dwellers in high latitudes, while gathering is proportionately more important for dwellers in tropical forests and in deserts. During most of the year the band is likely to consist of no more than 25 persons, although at times and in areas where food is plentiful, bands may come together in temporary aggregations of up to 200 to 300 persons.

Students of the !Kung (Kalahari Bushmen) of southern Africa found that they did not have to devote more than two or three days a week to the food quest, and therefore had a great deal of leisure time on their hands. One student was even tempted to call them 'the original affluent society' (Sahlins 1972: 1–39). However, this interpretation has been challenged by others (esp. Wilmsen 1989), and in any case it is certainly not typical of band-level societies. An examination of their mythology and folklore will show that the theme of starvation is very frequently repeated. There may indeed have been good years, when there was ample leisure time, but there were inevitably and predictably bad years when the rains failed, game did not appear, or plant food was scarce. Among native North American hunters, late winter snows were particularly disastrous, and March was sometimes referred to as 'the moon of starvation.' An Inuit (Eskimo) woman, at a conference I attended, remarked that 'we'd rather be dependent on Government checks, because they're more dependable than the herring'—the food resource on which her people had traditionally relied. A recognition of the unpredictability of food resources is surely a factor influencing the content of all the earliest religions.

The fullest descriptions of religion among band-level societies are those from the South American tropics, the North American Great Basin, and the North American Arctic. Native Australians are omitted from this list because, as I have already suggested, their religion is much more nearly like that of tribal societies than like that of other band groups.

The super-
naturals

There seem to be two main kinds of supernatural beings: 'high gods' who dwell in remote places, and local spirits who live all around the human sphere. The latter are primarily animals, but there may also be spirits in plants and even inanimate objects. There are also demons of vaguely defined form.

The high gods. There is a limited number of remote deities, usually including the sun and moon as well as vaguely anthropomorphic beings. They figure in mythology but, because of their remoteness, are rarely the foci of ritual. They may be identified as creators or culture-bringers, though this is by no means always the case. There is usually no deity connected specifically with fertility, and none associated with war. The most important activity of the high gods is to control the weather, the seasons, and the movements of game. Their appearance and character are seldom very sharply delineated in mythology, again presumably because of their remoteness.

Local spirits. There is usually a spirit for every species of animal and bird, dwelling within each representative of the species as well as in a more abstract power that is tutelary to the species as a whole. The spirit of an especially powerful species, such as bear, wolf, or jaguar, is likely to be particularly exalted, and there may be a prohibition against killing those creatures. The animal spirits dwell in the earthly environment, and are the cause of all kinds of everyday phenomena, including disease. None is purely evil, but many animal spirits are ill-disposed toward humans because humans live by hunting them. Animal spirits are the foci of a great deal of practical ritual, connected with hunting and with curing. The indwelling spirits in plants and in inanimate objects are usually less important in mythology and in ritual.

The mythology of even the simplest societies is fairly extensive, if only because it is virtually the whole of their literature. However, it exists mostly as informal folk wisdom, passed on from elders to children, since there are no learned religious practitioners who are its recognized keepers. Consequently, there is nothing like a canonical form of any myth; every teller has his own version. For the same reason, the mythology of band-level societies does not constitute anything like an integrated corpus; there are all kinds of individual myths that do not connect to one another. Many of them also do not connect with ritual in any direct way.

Mythology

Myths are most often tales about the doings of the supernaturals. In comparison with more complex societies, however, the mythology of band groups is relatively weak in cosmogony and cosmology. There may be myths explaining the origin of this or that custom or phenomenon, but creation is not a major theme. Viewing themselves as just another species of animal, with only the most limited control over nature, people in band societies seem inclined to take the world as they find it, without speculating much about the origin of things. However, mythology may explain in some detail the origin of diseases.

Ritual

Ritual practice is overwhelmingly magical and mechanistic; there is little effort to appeal to the deities through verbal supplication or through visual art. However, formulaic songs are considered to have special compelling power. All ritual is devoted to practical and immediate ends; there are no ceremonies of worship for its own sake. Because all the band members are united by bonds of kinship or marriage, there is no need for rituals to reinforce the solidarity of the group. The daily family meal is sufficient for that purpose.

Collective ritual, involving groups larger than the single migrating band, is for obvious reasons rare. For nearly all band societies however there is at least one season of abundance, when many bands may come together for a period of a few days or weeks. On these occasions social rituals and dances are common, but they are likely to have little specifically religious content. However, there may be collective rituals to mark in some way the passing of the seasons. These will usually be conducted by a shaman.

Individual rituals, rather than collective ones, are the norm in band societies. They have two principal foci: on the food quest, and on the treatment of illness. The hunter, as well as his wife and other members of his family, must undergo extensive rituals and observe many tabus in connection with the killing of game and its preparation as food, and there are rituals connected with the gathering of plant foods as well. Disease is treated by shamans, using a wide variety of techniques involving either imitative or contagious magic.

Rites of passage are generally little emphasized, because these is little formal differentiation of statuses. The main exception occurs in the case of initiation rituals, in which boys are formally graduated to the status of hunters.

Eschatology

Eschatology is little developed. Ideas about the afterlife, if any, are vague and unimportant, and material objects are not often buried with the dead. There may however be fairly elaborate and formal rituals of mourning.

The shaman, usually but not always male, is the sole religious practi- *Practitioners*
tioner, whose power has come from a dream or vision, or some other
out-of-body experience. He is not necessarily learned in myth, but must
at least be able to give the mythical rationale for his shamanistic practices. Most of his activity is involved with the treatment of illness. However, as the person most able to contact the supernaturals, he may in times
of need be asked to use his powers to bring a break in the weather, or the
return of the game. Since there is often no clearcut body of precedents
on these occasions, he may have to improvise a great deal. Most of his
practice involves some kind of imitative magic.

Fetishes, or portable objects having a special connection with the super- *Sacred*
naturals, are important; they take the place of the statuary, paintings, and *objects*
other religious images found in more advanced societies. The shaman
will have a sizable collection of especially powerful paraphernalia, but
individual hunters also regularly carry amulets or fetishes that bring luck
and protection.

There is usually no place specifically designated for the performance of *Sacred*
ritual, and no place that is specially beneficial to visit. There may how- *places*
ever be places that are tabu, because of their association with events in
mythology.

Man is generally viewed as just one more species of animal, more pow- *The human*
erful than some and less powerful than others. All are pretty much at the *condition*
mercy of nature, and man is in no way especially favored by the supernaturals. It is commonly assumed that all animals have their own societies
and language and religion.

Three things can be said in summarizing the religion of band-level soci- *An overview*
eties. First, like all other aspects of culture, it is relatively simple and limited, in comparison to the religions of tribal societies and chiefdoms. The
pantheon, mythology, and ritual are all limited. Consequently, it seems
safe to say that the overall role of religion, in the daily lives of people, is
not as great as in the case of more complex societies.

Second, the cognitive role of religion is more important than the social
role, as reflected in the fact that mythology is considerably more developed than is ritual. Mythology is needed to explain the universe, insofar
as it is explained, but ritual is not needed to reinforce the solidarity of the

social group, united as it is by bonds of daily interaction and interdependence. The psychological role of religion in band societies is difficult to judge, and probably varies greatly from individual to individual.

Third, religious practice, like everything else in culture, is devoted overwhelmingly to practical and immediate ends. For that reason the mystical component of band-level religion is relatively small, in comparison to more complex societies. The social component is also relatively small; there is no ritual for ritual's sake.

Religion in tribal societies

Tribes, in the Service formulation, are at an evolutionary stage between bands and chiefdoms. They are societies made up of several different bands or family clusters, often spread over a considerable area but regularly interacting with one another. They definitely have a sense of common identity, based usually on the possession of a common language and common religion, and often of a common territory. There is however no central political authority, and society remains egalitarian, without ranking or hereditary leadership. Politically, each of the member bands or settlements is autonomous.

Because tribal groups are larger than bands, their social organization is necessarily more complex. Kinship is still the main basis of group membership and interaction, but larger and more ramified kin groups—lineages or clans—now serve to knit together the members of different villages or resident groups in a single tribe-wide network of kin. There may at the same time be groupings (especially of males) based on some principle other than kinship: hunting or curing societies, age grades, or age sets.

The majority of tribal peoples are sedentary, and the majority are farmers, but neither of these things is universally true. On the North American Plains, once the horse was introduced by Europeans, whole tribes (who had formerly been settled farmers) were able to lead a nomadic life, following the bison herds. In California and Australia, there were sedentary, village-dwelling peoples who were able to live without agriculture, because of the abundance of natural food resources. Most tribal peoples lived by a combination of farming and hunting or, in the Californian and Australian cases, of hunting and gathering.

Aboriginally, tribal peoples occupied most of North America and lowland South America, excluding the high latitudes; large parts of central and southern Africa; the sub-Arctic areas of Asia; and large parts of highland and insular Southeast Asia. It should be noted however that the category of 'tribes,' thus defined, does not include the numerous pastoral nomad groups of Africa, the Near East, and Inner Asia; peoples who are often called tribes but who in fact are, in an evolutionary sense, chief-doms.

The religion of tribal societies is more complex in nearly every respect than is that of band societies, both because it has more ground to cover and because people have more time to devote to it. As peoples increase their control over the material world, through advances in technology and food production, they seek to increase their control over the world of the supernaturals as well, through increased knowledge and through new techniques of address. However, a distinction must be noted between tribal religions in the New and Old Worlds. Even the most sedentary of New World farmers kept no food animals of importance, and therefore continued to rely heavily on hunting and fishing for their meat supplies. Consequently, hunting ritual and animal spirits remained important for these peoples. By contrast, all Old World farmers also kept, and keep, food animals, and hunting and its attendant ritual are of almost no importance to them.

In characterizing the pantheon of tribal peoples I can do no better than to quote the words of Robert Bellah (1964: 364):

The super-naturals

> ... mythical beings are much more definitely characterized [than in band societies]. Instead of being great paradigmatic figures with whom men in ritual identify but with whom they do not really interact, the mythical beings are more objectified, conceived as actively and sometimes willfully controlling the natural and human world, and as beings with whom men must deal in a definite and purposive way—in a word they have become gods. Relations among the gods are a matter of considerable speculation and systematization, so that definite principles of organization, especially hierarchies of control, are established.

What Bellah is saying, in sum, is that the mystical component is much more conspicuous in tribal than in band-level religion.

The pantheon of the Navajo Indians, described in Chapter 2, is fairly typical of tribal peoples, at least in the New World. It includes a considerable number of anthropomorphic deities, related to one another by kinship or marriage, but there are also deities in the form of animals and birds, and some having no distinct form. The deities are associated very specifically with the weather, with fertility, and with various craft activities; somewhat less so with disease, and much less so with warfare. The belief in animistic spirits, dwelling in the nearby environment, remains highly developed among Navajos and most other tribal peoples.

Because tribal pantheons are large, a certain amount of selective worship may be a practical necessity. Nobody can worship all the different powers. Hence we find, for the first time, the appearance of tutelary cults. There are collective tutelary deities for clans or villages, and also individual tutelaries—the guardian spirits so often sought by North American Indians.

Ancestral
spirits

Ramified kin groups, which are highly developed in many tribal societies, often derive a sense of solidarity through the worship of a deified ancestor or ancestors. There are both individual and collective rituals addressed to the ancestors, and there may also be extensive bodies of clan or lineage mythology. The worship of ancestral spirits is especially highly developed in South America, Africa, Southeast Asia, and Melanesia.

Mythology

The mythology of tribal peoples is far more extensive and more systematized than is the case among band peoples; it begins to resemble a comprehensive system of knowledge. All the same kinds of myth that were present in band societies are still found among tribesmen, but there are many new kinds as well. Cosmogony and cosmology are well developed; it seems that tribal peoples are simply more curious about the nature of things than were their more primitive forebears. Fertility is likely to be a major theme: there are myths to explain the origins and meaning of sex, and the deities that are responsible for it. The whole history of the people, from the time of their creation to the present, is also likely to be embodied in a cycle of myths. There are in addition cultic myths relating the origin and history of clans or lineages, others relating to the origin and function of secret societies, and others again relating to the performance of specific rituals.

To a much greater extent than earlier, knowledge of mythology becomes the province of learned religious practitioners—either shamans or priests or persons who are partly both. As a result, myths begin to take on a standardized or canonical form.

Ritual

Collective rituals, usually involving whole communities and sometimes the whole tribe, are highly developed and are one of the main sources of social cohesion in tribal societies. Virtually all agricultural peoples have a calendric cycle of rituals to mark the passing of the seasons, and the farming activities associated with them. Hunting rituals, similar to those found in band societies, also remained important for New World tribal peoples, who still obtained most of their meat by hunting. And because many tribal peoples are warlike, war ritual too is often highly developed. Collective rituals are often elaborate and highly expressive, involving masks, costumes, and a great deal of music and dance in addition to verbal formulas of address. Sacrifice, though not wholly lacking in band societies, becomes a more important feature of collective ritual in tribal societies.

Cultic rituals are those belonging to and performed by particular segments of society, such as clans and secret societies. Among North American Indians, where medicine societies were common, curing ritual was very often a cultic practice. Initiation ceremonies, especially for boys, are also commonly of this type.

Individual rituals. Where medicine societies are absent, the treatment of disease continues to be the province of the shaman, whose practice differs in no way from that of the shamans in band societies. There are of course innumerable personal rituals connected with just about every sphere of daily activity: farming, pottery making, weaving, and travel, as well as with the more risky activities of hunting and warfare.

Rites of passage are somewhat more developed than in the case of band societies, and this is true in particular of the girls' puberty ceremony, which is often a major collective affair. So also, in some tribal groups, are funerals. Weddings on the other hand are usually relatively simple and private affairs, reflecting the fact that marriage partners continue still to belong to their natal kin groups, and hence the marriage bond does not effect a major social transformation.

Eschatology is considerably more developed than in band societies, though it varies markedly from society to society, as it does in most later ages as well. The afterlife is more concretely envisioned, and is likely to be conceived as pretty much a continuation of life in the present world. It is not a place of rewards and punishments. There is a definite belief in a corporeal afterlife, with the result that useful objects as well as prized possessions are very often likely to be buried with the dead. Often too there are cemeteries—places demarcated exclusively for the burial of the dead. Burial rituals and mourning rituals may both be fairly elaborate.

Eschatology

Practitioners	The shaman continues to be an important figure, with primary responsibility for the treatment of disease. However, among most tribal peoples there are also learned religious practitioners—essentially priests—whose job it is to conduct the major ceremonies. They are the main 'library' of the tribe's extensive mythology. Much more than shamans, they may be looked up to as informal community leaders. They do not however constitute a sharply differentiated class; most are part-time religious practitioners who at the same time are still farmers. Many combine shamanistic and priestly functions.
Sacred objects	Fetishes and amulets continue to have the same importance as in band societies. There are usually no large carved or painted images; their place is taken by masked and/or costumed dancers who impersonate the gods. In many societies, masks have enormous supernatural importance, and are surrounded by all kinds of special rituals and tabus.
Sacred places	Specially designed religious architecture is rare but not wholly lacking. However, the places where major communal ceremonies are performed are usually consecrated as sacred places, at least for the duration of the ceremony. Under those circumstances, only ritually certified individuals are allowed to enter them.
The human condition	Peoples who are able to produce their own food, or who can count on natural abundance, can face life—and the supernaturals—with more confidence than can nomadic hunters and gatherers. This is clearly reflected in the elaboration of both mythology and ritual in tribal societies. There is among most tribal peoples, especially in the Old World, a sense of human superiority over other species of animals. At the same time there is still a sense of relative weakness in relation to the gods, who may at any time send droughts, floods, or other disasters against which humans are powerless.
An overview	As peoples achieve a greater control over their fates, through advanced technology and the domestication of plants and animals, they seek also for a greater control over the Powers in their environment. This must inevitably begin with a clearer and more comprehensive definition of the Powers themselves; something reflected in the enlarged and clarified pantheons of tribal peoples. There is at the same time increased curiosity about the world, and in particular about the relationship between the supernaturals and man, which leads to the development of cosmogenic and

cosmological mythology. These circumstances allow ample play for the mystical element in tribal religions.

On the basis of increased knowledge, new and more effective ways are devised of communicating with the supernaturals, through collective and cultic as well as individual rituals. At the same time, magic remains important especially in individual ritual.

While the cognitive function of religion has increased importance, the social function also becomes for the first time highly important. In the absence of formal structures of leadership, collective rituals are the chief mechanism that maintains a sense of solidarity within the tribe. Ramified kin groups and secret societies also have their supporting mythologies and rituals.

We may notice too that, in tribal societies, religion emerges for the first time as a highly expressive art form. Music, dancing, costumed pageantry, and poetry all become major foci of interest and excitement. Some of the great tribal ceremonies performed, for example, in New Guinea and in the American Southwest, are as elaborate and expressive as anything found in state-level societies.

In many tribal societies, we can perceive the embryonic beginnings of a division between collective and personal religion. Collective religion involves the great ceremonies just described, and is the province of learned, priestly ritual leaders. Personal religion remains essentially the same as in band societies. Insofar as it requires the services of a professional, it remains very much the province of the shaman.

In sum, tribal religion represents a quantum advance over the religion of band societies, in terms of quantity, elaboration, and specificity. People simply have far more time and energy to devote to it, and they are able to expect more from it. All the original elements found in band societies are still present, and many new elements have been added to them. The cognitive function is very much enlarged, into something like a comprehensive system of knowledge, and it involves a considerably higher component of mysticism. At the same time, both the social and the artistic functions also become important. What is still missing at this stage of development is the political function of religion.

Chiefdoms are tribes having a formally established central authority, in the form of a hereditary ruler. Mostly, they have arisen under conditions of endemic tribal warfare. Nearly all tribal peoples appoint a temporary war leader, with specific coercive powers, in times of military emergency,

*The religion
of
agricultural
chiefdoms*

and when the emergency becomes more or less permanent, so also does the coercive leader. But while the temporary war leader owed his position to common consent, the chief owes his to divine ordination or descent. A whole new mythology arises, connecting the ruler with the gods, as religion acquires for the first time a specifically political dimension.

The presence of a central authority obviously makes possible the mobilization of people and of resources much more rapidly and effectively than was true among tribes and bands, and this capacity finds expression both in warlike activity and in ritual. All chiefdoms are warlike, and many are expansionist. That is, they have used their coercive power to incorporate, against their will, what were formerly autonomous bands. But because of their military basis, chiefdoms tend also to be unstable. Only in areas rich in resources, where energy can be spared from the food quest for the maintenance of a non-productive elite, of monumental ritual, and of continual warfare, do they achieve a degree of permanence.

There are actually two quite distinct kinds of chiefdoms: those found in wealthy agricultural societies, and those among nomadic pastoralists. Only the first kind will be dealt with in this section; the religion of nomadic pastoralists will require separate, if brief, treatment later.

In agricultural chiefdoms we witness the beginnings both of social stratification and of economic differentiation. At the top of the social scale, the ruler and members of his family represent a distinct class, having divine origin or ordination. At the bottom of the scale, slaves are found in most chiefdoms, though they are usually personal servants rather than food or craft producers. Between those two extremes there are no sharply differentiated classes, but people may be ranked according to their descent or their occupation. The majority of people are still food producers, but there may now be specialists in various trades such as pottery making and metal working. Importantly too there is often a specialized class of priests, who conduct the special rituals surrounding the ruler, who himself may be the high priest. In the absence of a market economy, economic differentiation requires a certain amount of economic management by the chief; it is he who must ensure, through some form of redistribution, that the potters and metalsmiths and priests receive the food that they need.

But chiefly authority does not supplant the older system of social organization based on kinship. Chiefdoms are still, in the broadest sense, tribes, knit together by tribe-wide webs of kinship as well as by the possession of a common language, culture, and religion. The authority of the ruler is simply superimposed over the top of the tribal system.

Agricultural chiefdoms were found most abundantly in the Old World, where population pressure and advanced technology led to endemic warfare. They were prevalent among the island dwellers of Polynesia and Melanesia, the hill peoples of Southeast Asia, and in Central and West Africa. In earlier times they also preceded the rise of the first state-level societies in China, the Near East, and parts of Europe. In the New World, chiefdoms were found mainly on the Northwest Coast and in the Southeast of North America, and on the fringes of the high cultures in Central America and the Andes.

The religion of agricultural chiefdoms is similar in most respects to that of tribes. The main innovations are the emergence of a kind of royal cult, including a special priesthood and rituals, surrounding the ruler. Very often, worship of the ruler's ancestors is involved, and is mandated upon the whole population. The ruler and his priests will usually assume responsibility also for the performance of the major collective rituals; especially those connected with agriculture. On these occasions the ruler himself may act as high priest. Meanwhile however other specialized rituals may be performed by priests who are not under chiefly control, and shamanistic practice continues as before.

The super-naturals

Anthropomorphs become proportionately more important, and animal spirits less so, than in tribal societies. The anthropomorphic pantheon reflects the condition of human society: it is likely to be formally stratified, with a single supreme god (often the ancestor of the chief) at the top of the heap. Male deities are usually accorded more importance than female deities, as a warlike society places heavy emphasis on physical strength.

Animal spirits remain present but decline in importance, as most (not all) chiefdom societies have domesticated food animals, and hunting becomes economically unimportant.

Ancestral spirits are likely to be as important, or more so, than in tribal societies, as the worship of the chief's ancestors provides sanction for the worship of other group ancestors as well.

Evil spirits. There seems to be a considerable degree of paranoia among warlike peoples; there is a kind of feedback cycle among hate, fear, and conflict. In consequence, illness and misfortune are proportionately more likely to be attributed either to witchcraft or to some malevolent power, and exorcistic action or else retribution is required. As there is a supreme god, there may also be a supreme demon figure.

Mythology	Mythology remains elaborate in chiefdom societies, and retains all the basic features found among tribesmen. There is however more emphasis on the actions of anthropomorphic deities, and relations among them, and less on animal deities. On top of the generalized mythology there is an extensive mythology supporting the institution of chiefly rule, by connecting the chief directly with one or more supernatural Powers. It may be the special duty of certain priests to know and to recite this body of mythology.
Ritual	**Collective ritual** in chiefdom societies is always highly developed, reflecting the ruler's ability to mobilize collective action on the part of a large number of his followers. Calendric agricultural rituals, war rituals, and rituals celebrating the chief's ancestral cult are all important. Some ceremonies, with elaborate pageantry and sometimes temporarily built structures, may require weeks of preparation. Massive feasts are likely to be featured on these occasions. The preparation and conduct of collective rituals is under the direction of a recognized class of priests. Sacrifice is practiced on a larger scale than in earlier societies, and may include human sacrifice, especially on the occasion of the chief's funeral.
	Cultic rituals. Clan or lineage ceremonies, ritual society ceremonies, and age-grade rituals, found already in tribal societies, are likely to persist, and to be somewhat more elaborated than in earlier times. Again, the greater availability of leisure time is a major contributing factor.
	Individual rituals are little different from those in tribal societies, and as always they include most curing ritual.
	Rites of passage remain important, and weddings and funerals in the chiefly class now become major public ceremonies.
Eschatology	Eschatological beliefs are much the same as in tribal societies. Funerary ritual however is considerably more elaborated. Graves are likely to be marked by some kind of memorial structure above them, which may at times be fairly large and ornamental, and those of the nobility may contain a wealth of material goods. They may also contain animal sacrifices and, occasionally, human sacrifices. The funeral of the chief is usually a great public ceremony, and his tomb may also be the society's most imposing monument.
Practitioners	**The shaman** continues to be an important figure, primarily responsible for curing and for other aspects of personal and practical religion. His

role is however more restricted than in band and tribal societies, as he is no longer a leader of group ritual, and is less likely to be looked up to for leadership in other situations as well.

Priests now emerge for the first time as a distinct class of full-time specialists. They have official responsibility for knowing and reciting the myths—particularly those connected with the chiefly office—and for the conduct of major ceremonies. Their power has come not as a direct gift from the supernaturals but through study as well as, often, inheritance from a priestly predecessor. There is always a close association between the priesthood and the chiefly family. Between them they form a kind of collective aristocracy, and the chief himself may be the high priest.

These remain much the same as in tribal societies, but artistic representations of the chief, in the character if a divinity, may be added.

Sacred objects and art

Chiefdoms have generally possessed the labor resources but not the technology to build large and permanent temples. However, the beginnings of distinctive religious architecture can certainly be observed at the chiefdom level of society. Such are the very ornate ceremonial houses of Melanesia and New Guinea and, in another sense, the great earthen mounds erected by eastern North American Indians. In Africa, especially, the tomb of the chief, and sometimes also his relatives, likewise became a major religious monument.

Sacred places and structures

While tribes grow out of bands mainly through advances in subsistence practices and technology, the same is not true in the case of chiefdoms. They emerge from tribes mainly through advances in human organizational capacity, associated with strong and institutionalized leadership. There is not yet a sense of total mastery over nature, and therefore the various nature gods still figure importantly in ritual, but they are addressed with more confidence than in earlier times, through larger and more elaborate ceremonies. At the same time the human world is a more threatening one than before, thanks to institutionalized warfare, and the war gods may assume much more importance than they had among tribesmen.

The human condition

But the most important feature of the human world is the existence of a formally stratified society, divided between a small group of rulers (chiefs and priests) and everyone else, with slaves sometimes constituting a distinct third class. From this time forward until the beginning of modern times, social stratification was to be accepted by all human groups as a fact of life, and a decree of the gods.

Up to this point, both the total content and the variety of religion have grown by steady accretion. The cognitive function, already important among band societies, has become significantly more so among tribes and chiefdoms through the elaboration of pantheons and mythology. And as stratification emerges in human society at the chiefdom level, so also hierarchy appears among the deities, often with a single high god at the top of the pantheon. Moreover, as man's understanding of the natural world increases, so also do his attempts to control it, both through secular technology and through religion.

The social function of religion, relatively minor in band societies, has become important with the emergence of collective rituals in tribal societies, and the political function has been added in chiefdoms. And while a great deal has been added at each step of the way, comparatively little has been lost. There is however increasing focus on the worship of the higher deities, and less concern with animistic and localized spirits, in the case of tribes and chiefdoms. In particular, we find that the importance of animal spirits consistently decreases. In tribes and especially in chiefdoms, illness and bad luck are more likely to be blamed on malevolent human witches than on animals.

The religion of pastoral chiefdoms

Contrary to a long-popular evolutionary belief, pastoral nomadism does not represent a distinct evolutionary stage, intermediate between hunting/gathering and agriculture. All evidence now suggests that it is a specialized adaptation to arid environments, that did not develop until long after the emergence of the first agricultural societies. The first pastoralists were perhaps failed farmers, who lost their land or crops but were able to hold onto their animals. In fact, pastoral nomadism probably emerged at about the same time as did the earliest agricultural chiefdoms.

All nomadic pastoral societies are chiefdoms, but of a kind quite different from agricultural chiefdoms (a fact not commonly recognized by modern evolutionary theorists). They are found in a single wide swath of desert or semi-arid territory in the Old World, extending from Inner Asia across the Near East, the Arabian Peninsula, and sub-Saharan Africa. These are regions with few permanent rivers, and even fewer small streams, but where the combination of winter snows and summer showers produces lush stands of grass in the best years, and adequate grass in most other years. However, sooner or later there are always years when the rain and the grass are not adequate.

Pastoral nomadism is a far more specialized and more vulnerable ecological niche than is agriculture. Humans are wholly dependent or animals, which are wholly dependent on grass, which is wholly dependent on rainfall, which is not wholly dependable. Thus, pastoralists must accept uncertainty, and the potential threat of starvation, as an inevitable fact of existence. They can do nothing to allay it as can agricultural peoples, with their irrigation schemes and their stored surpluses. The only thing they can do when pastures fail is to move on to other pastures, which they may have to wrest from other peoples already in possession, or else to raid the settlements of farmers in the oases. As a form of insurance, most pastoral peoples have attempted to hold the nearby oasis dwellers in some kind of vassalage, often through sheer military coercion.

Pastoral societies are chiefdoms because without a powerful leader they would not survive. But far more than in agricultural chiefdoms, the leader must always be a wise, experienced, and active person. Throughout the year there are almost daily decisions to be made about when, whether, and where to migrate; whether and how to split the tribe up into smaller units when pasture is scanty; how to deal with other groups attempting to encroach. There are also continual disputes to be resolved among the member families, resulting from the loss or theft of animals, failure to collaborate in herding activities, and a host of other matters. And the chief must in addition be an effective war leader, because pastoral nomads are almost of necessity warlike, and frequently expansionist. Power and safety are found in numbers, and numbers come from increased pasturage.

For all those reasons, nomadic pastoralists cannot rely on a rigidly hereditary rule of succession. They cannot afford an immature leader or a half-witted one, as sometimes happens in agricultural chiefdoms where the leader is propped up by the priesthood. The chiefly office is likely to be hereditary within a 'noble' clan or lineage, but within that group it is always elective, as it is today, for example, in the Saudi royal family. Because there is no fixed rule, there is very often a fight for the succession among rival claimants, and this may actually be regarded as salutary, as Fredrik Barth found among the Basseri nomads of south Persia (Barth 1961: 135–153). The winner of the contest for succession has in the process qualified himself as the best man to lead. But he may always be overthrown by an upstart from his own or a rival lineage, who has by that act shown himself to be the best leader.

These circumstances probably explain why the chief (most commonly called *khan* or *sheikh*) among pastoral nomads is a purely secular leader, not a divine one. Less easily explained is the fact there does not seem to be a great deal of religion of any sort among the nomads, in contrast to either tribesmen or agricultural chiefdoms. It is a commonplace among urban Muslims, for example, that 'the Islam of the bedouin is only skin deep.' Barth (ibid.), viewing the matter from the perspective of British social anthropology, argued that the dramatic circumstances of daily life provide all the solidarity and all the sense of fulfillment that in other societies is provided by religion, but this has been disputed by other scholars. It is a notable fact that, despite being at the mercy of unpredictable rains, nomad groups do not seem to have had weather gods, or any sense that they could affect the annual precipitation through ritual activity, as sedentary farmers habitually do. For whatever reason, the abundant surplus energy that the nomads enjoy at certain seasons of the year seems to be directed almost wholly into warlike rather than to religious activity. And because there is little or no organized ritual, there is also no instituted priesthood, in marked contrast to the case in agricultural chiefdoms.

Four patterns of religious activity and belief have been observed among the nomads. The Turco-Mongolic peoples of Inner Asia, before the coming of Buddhism and of Islam, followed a kind of shamanic practice not very different from that found in band-level societies. Not very much is known however about the extent of their mythology or pantheons. The tribes of the Arabian Peninsula were worshippers of the stars and the moon, and by extension of meteorites, but again not much is known about specific rituals. Since the coming of Islam, both the Turkic nomads and the Arab bedouins have adopted a version of it most nearly like that of village peasants, with a primary emphasis on the worship of local saints. Because of their migratory life, however, they generally do not have any special tutelary saint; they make offerings and perform prayers at whatever saintly shrines they pass by in the course of their movements. The only religious practitioners among them are *fekis*, hired when needed from nearby settled villages. Most nomads do not attempt to perform the Five Pillars of Islam, other than the Profession of Faith.

Mongols have adopted a unique form of religion by surrogate. Most families who can afford it have attempted to place a son in one or another of the innumerable Buddhist monasteries scattered throughout the country, and to support him for life with gifts of food and other needs. His prayers and observances then serve as the ritual life for the whole family, whose other members are thereby absolved from religious duties.

The earliest state-level societies grew out of chiefdoms through increasingly complex and institutionalized systems of control, over both man and environment. The organization of labor on a large scale made possible the development of extensive irrigation works, vastly increasing agricultural productivity. Usually at the same time there were quantum advances in technology: the extensive use of animal power (in the Old World), metallurgy, and above all the development of written communication. These developments facilitated both the division of labor among specialists and the growth of long-distance trade, both contributing to the growth of cities. Indeed the earliest state societies are often referred to in popular literature as 'civilizations,' a word deriving from the Latin for 'city.'

All the earliest states of which we have knowledge were theocracies, headed by an autocrat who was considered personally divine, divinely descended, or divinely appointed. He was at the head both of an extensive civil bureaucracy and a priesthood—two elite classes that were closely interlocked. Both could become vast royal patronage networks, although when the ruler was weak the offices might become hereditary. Below them was a hierarchy of commoners ranked, at least in an informal way, on the basis of their occupations, with peasant farmers at or near the bottom of the scale. The latter, living necessarily in villages rather than in the cities, still made up the bulk of the population, and it was they who produced the food on which all the city-dwelling artisans and traders as well as the priests and bureaucrats depended. At the absolute bottom of the scale were slaves, now clearly recognizable as a hereditary class although not a large or an economically important one. To a very large extent, social status for all classes was hereditary rather than achieved.

Despite the extensive economic specialization, free trade was limited and localized, and there was no money in the modern sense. Most economic exchange took place within centrally controlled systems of redistribution, which assured that the state and its elite classes got an ample share of the goods and services produced by others. Thus the surplus of the peasants was extracted through legally instituted serfdom or peonage or obligated service, often leaving them with just enough to subsist on. These redistribution systems largely took the place of taxation in the modern sense, which did not emerge until the development of monetized economies.

In a rigidly stratified society there was little or no opportunity for individuals to improve their lot, except through the largesse of higher-status individuals to whom they might attach themselves as clients. Thus, patron-client relations became an important feature of the social structure in early states. In ancient Egypt, the entire state bureaucracy was a huge royal patronage network.

Although religion and the state were not wholly synonymous, they were so closely intertwined that each reinforced and legitimized the other. Thus religion, like most other aspects of life, was much more centrally controlled than before, and like other aspects it was controlled by and in the interests of the state. Priests told the people what gods to believe in, what ceremonies to perform, and what monuments to build; they also decided which myths were to be recorded in writing. Control of course was not total; there was a continuation of private and personal religion and of local cults that were not under state control.

On the basis of archaeology and history, we can recognize the first of the early states in China, India, Mesopotamia, and Egypt in the Old World, and in upper Mesoamerica and the Andes (including their Pacific littoral) in the New World. Later, and to a considerable extent by imitation, other early states developed on the fringes of the original ones, in Japan, Southeast Asia, Persia, the eastern Mediterranean, and Nubia.

From the standpoint of anthropological analysis, the difficulty we face in describing the religion of the early states is that we must mostly employ the past tense. Bands, tribes, and chiefdoms can all be described on the basis of modern or recently extinct exemplars, but nearly all of the original state-level societies disappeared long ago. That is, they were supplanted by secondary civilizations, which I will describe in a later section. The only exceptions that I know of were the petty kingdoms of Indonesia and Southeast Asia, which, though nominally Islamic or Buddhist, retained some of the features of early state society and religion (see especially Geertz 1960). Otherwise, the nearest thing that we have to ethnographic documents relating to early states are the accounts left us by Spanish chroniclers, of the civilizations of Mesoamerica and the Andes—the two which survived until the most recent times. These documents are indeed of great value, but they are of course both incomplete and biased.

For the rest, we must rely on what the civilizations have told us about themselves, through their inscriptions and their monuments. That record is at least as incomplete as is the Spanish ethnographic record, and it is also at least as biased, though in a positive rather than a negative sense. Scribes in the early civilizations were self-aggrandizing rather than self-critical; they have told us about themselves only what they wanted the world to know. Added to the problem is our very imperfect understanding of their pre-alphabetic systems of writing. One has only to read through the enormous literature on ancient Egyptian religion to discover how many different interpretations have been placed by modern scholars on the same hieroglyphic texts. Ethnographic studies even of modern religions involve a good deal of subjective interpretation on the part of the observer, but the problem is proportionately greater in the case of the ancient religions. This caveat must be kept in mind by readers of the paragraphs that follow.

Finally, the records that have come down to us were produced by elites, for elites. What is missing from all the accounts of ancient religions is any information about the commoners, and above all the peasants. We are left to assume that the religion of ancient peasants was much like that of modern peasants, and as such I will consider it in a later section.

The super-naturals

There was still a plethora of gods, nearly all surviving from earlier times but now often invested with new powers and personalities. In the Old World the great majority of deities were anthropomorphic, or part-human and part-animal, but in the New World (where the hunting of wild animals was still important to the diet) animal deities remained common alongside the anthropomorphs. Among these latter both males and females were important, and the kinship and sexual relations among them were often complex and convoluted. There was not, curiously, a great deal of differentiation along sexual lines: either males or females could be war gods, hunting gods, or the principal tutelaries of cities.

Like tribal gods, those of the early states had thoroughly human personalities, and few if any of them were either totally benevolent or totally evil. The god-emperor however was (in theory) wholly benevolent toward those who obeyed him, and devoted to the welfare of his people. He was from that practical standpoint the most important of all deities, even if not the most powerful. The goodwill of other deities could be cultivated through tutelary attachments, much as the early Hebrews secured the favor of Yahweh through their covenant, but they were never wholly reliable.

The differentiations of power and function among the deities were a mirror of those obtaining in the human sphere. There were at least three bases of differentiation. First, there was a recognized hierarchy, with those deities ancestral to or tutelary to the ruler rating the top spot. Second, there was a differentiation of local tutelaries. Among the Sumero-Babylonian and the Maya city-states each city had its own tutelary deity, drawn from the common pantheon that they all shared, and the same was true of the Egyptian nomes (rural districts). Third, there were tutelaries for the different crafts; for metalsmiths, potters, masons, and so on. There were almost certainly also special tutelaries for women, whose status in the early states was very much depressed, in contrast to earlier times. In these tutelary cults the patron-client relations, so important in the human sphere, were reflected also in the relations between humans and their gods.

Mythology

The mythology of early states differed relatively little from that of chiefdoms except that parts of it were now formally codified by the priestly class, who more than ever were its official custodians. The most important myths, from the standpoint of the state, were set down in writing, and thus achieved a much more immutable form from generation to generation than was true earlier. As in chiefly societies, the most important myths were those that validated and explicated the divine status of the ruler. According to the central state myth, the ruler alone was responsible for prosperity, order, and justice among the people, in a world in which none of the other gods could be trusted. He thus became the linchpin of religious thought and practice: the people worshipped him, and he in turn conducted or orchestrated the worship of the other gods.

Not all the myths were state myths, however; all the older kinds of myths survived as well. We know especially from the cases of Mesopotamian, Egyptian, Hebrew, and Mesoamerican mythology that cosmology, cosmogony, and etiology all remained important elements.

Ritual

Among the advances in technology that took place in the early states, advances in what might be called religious technology were among the most conspicuous. Public ceremonies were performed on a far larger scale than ever before, and involved a greater diversity of elements.

State ceremonies. The principal rituals of which we have evidence, from texts and mural depictions, were the great state ceremonies, which often lasted over many days. They were carried on in and around the temples, which were the principal architectural monuments as well as the foci of religion in all the early states. The most sacred parts of the ceremonies were rites of adoration, offering, and sacrifice, conducted by the professional priests within sacred precincts from which the laity were often excluded. But there were also public parades, pageantry, and feasting. Costumed religious pageantry, already well developed in tribal societies and chiefdoms, undoubtedly reached its peak of elaboration in the early states.

Since all the early states had an agricultural basis, it is not surprising that most of the major ceremonies were calendric, occurring at a fixed season each year. Typically, each ceremony was focused on the worship of a particular god, though other deities might also be honored at the same time. Other major state ceremonies, not calendric, were those associated with the investiture of the divine ruler, and with his funeral.

Cultic ceremonies. Local deities continued to play an important role in the early states, and they too had their temples and their priesthoods, which were usually but not always under state control. Rituals in honor of the local deities tended to mirror those of the state deities, on a smaller scale. At least in the New World civilizations there were also cultic rituals associated with lineage or clan groups (*calpulli* and *ayllu*).

Individual ritual. We know relatively little about personal religion in the early states, where the surviving records are those produced by the state and for the state. Since individual rituals and personal tutelaries remained highly developed in the later (and better documented) civilizations, however, we can safely assume that they were important in the early states as well. People may have chosen to worship one or another of the state gods, but it is probable that there was also a class of 'lesser' deities that were involved primarily in personal and family religion. Ancestral spirits, important at least in China and in South America, were in this category. In ancient Egypt, the little bandy-legged god Bes seems to have been mainly a household deity.

Pilgrimage, essentially a form of personal worship, seems to have emerged for the first time as a major feature of religion in the early states. Individuals and families traveled for considerable distances to pray and make offerings at the temples or shrines of deities who were thought to be especially beneficial to them. The act of travel was itself considered a major expression of obeisance and sacrifice.

Sacrifices. Like many other aspects of religion, the practice of sacrifice reached its apogee in the early states. Along with other forms of sacrifice, that of living humans—already found occasionally in chiefdoms—was practiced on a very large scale in most if not all of the early states. It took place most commonly in the context of royal and noble funerals, with the victims placed in or around the tombs, though this was not the case in Mesoamerica. But were these meant to propitiate the powerful and bloodthirsty gods, or were they meant simply to assure the noble dead a retinue of family and servants in the next world—or were they an instrument of terroristic control by the state? Scholars continue to argue all three positions.

In all of the early states of the Old World, the practice of human sacrifice died out after the earliest centuries, for reasons that are not fully understood. Clearly, some kind of evolution of thought, either about the state or the gods or the afterlife, was involved. The practice however still existed in the early states of the New World at the time of Spanish conquest, for these civilizations were still, relatively speaking, in their infancies. On the basis of Old World parallels, it is a reasonable assumption that human sacrifice would have been abandoned in time in the New World as well.

The abandonment of human sacrifice was not accompanied by a diminution in other forms of sacrifice. Animals, as well as all kinds of inanimate goods and wealth, continued to be sacrificed extensively through the whole history of the early states.

Rites of passage, except possibly for funerals, seem to have lost a good deal of their importance in the early states. This was probably due to two factors. First, ramified kin groups tended to atrophy under the conditions of urban life, as membership in an occupational class replaced kinship as the primary basis of social identity. Thus marriages, in particular, no longer created an alliance between lineages or clans, but only between two individuals. Second, within the framework of rigidly stratified society, most statuses were hereditary rather than achieved. There was consequently little opportunity for advancement in status, which might have been celebrated by a rite of passage.

Eschatology   Thanks both to ancient texts and to archaeology, we know perhaps as much about eschatology as about any phase of early state religion. Ideas about the afterworld were now a good deal more explicit than formerly. If not precisely a place of rewards and punishments, there were at least more and less desirable conditions of existence in the afterworld, depending partly on personal virtue but partly on how one died, and the extent of funerary preparations and ceremonies. There were special deities associated with the world of the dead, and special rituals for propitiating them. The volume of goods buried in royal and noble tombs, including animal and human sacrifices, was nothing short of prodigious, but even the lowliest of commoners hoped to be buried with a goodly supply of tools, weapons, containers, and provisions of food. And since the deceased body was translated to the afterworld in the flesh, there were elaborate efforts to protect it from decomposition after burial—a practice sometimes seen earlier in the case of chiefly burials, but now much more widespread. Grave monuments on the ground surface were more consistently employed and more elaborate than in earlier times, reflecting, among other things, an effort to see that the burial was not disturbed.

Priests. The priesthood was now institutionalized and extensive; it was a major arm of the state bureaucracy. There was both a hierarchy of offices and a differentiation of functions. The high priest within each temple took the leading role in acts of worship, but he (occasionally she) also orchestrated the activities of lesser priests who might be responsible for specific aspects of ritual as well as for collecting offerings, curating paraphernalia, or writing texts. The priests were an educated elite who through long apprenticeship had mastered a prodigious mass of myth and ritual, as well as the arcane arts of reading and writing. For this reason the divine ruler, though nominally at the head of the religious establishment, was not usually the high priest in a literal sense. Each temple cult had its own high priest, and rulers occasionally found it expedient to play off different temple priesthoods against one another. Although priests were overwhelmingly male, as they were in all earlier societies, there were some deities who were served mainly or even exclusively by female priests.

Practitioners

Shamans. In both Sumero-Babylonian and Egyptian texts we catch glimpses of 'doctors,' whose practice evidently included a considerable amount of shamanistic procedure. Their presence and activities are somewhat better attested in the case of the Aztecs and Incas, where they were observed by Spanish chroniclers. It seems fairly clear that, at least among the urban classes, shamans were not very highly regarded, in comparison to priests, and we sometimes find them condemned by the latter as quacks. Shamanistic practice for the city-dwellers was probably pretty much confined to the medical sphere, although in the peasant villages it probably continued to play a larger role.

Sacred objects and art

Small, portable fetishes, icons, and amulets certainly continued to be important; we often find them buried with the dead. A great deal of elaborate paraphernalia was also used in the major public ceremonies, as they are depicted for us in mural paintings and carvings. However, the great innovation found in nearly all the early states was the life-size or monumental cult statue, which might be a representation of the living ruler or of any of the other gods. The most sacred of cult statues normally resided within the 'inner sanctum' of a temple, but might be taken out and paraded in the course of major ceremonies. Other statues frequently adorned the temple exterior.

Sacred places and structures

Sacred places, like so much else in religion, attained a degree of specificity and also of monumentality in the early states, far beyond anything found in earlier societies. The temple is the major surviving monument of nearly every one of the earliest states, and it became the focal point of nearly all organized religious activity. Temples were of widely varying size, depending largely on the degree of their importance in state ritual. However, they exhibited everywhere three recurring features. First, they were made as everlasting as possible; not infrequently they were the only buildings of stone where all other construction was in mud brick. They were also kept in repair century after century, while the secular buildings around them crumbled and were replaced. Second, their plan was bilaterally symmetrical, mirroring the bilateral symmetry found in all animate beings, which was obviously seen as a reflection of divine intent. Third, they reached upward toward the heavens as far as technology would allow, either through towering walls or because they were built on top of high artificial mounds. In addition to temples there were many other, lesser shines or simply sacred localities, like caves, where minor deities dwelled and were worshipped.

A second major type of religious monument found in most if not all of the early states was the royal tomb, which proclaimed the majesty of the ruling family. It was always the focus of an enormous funerary ceremony, including sacrifices and special mourning rituals, but there might also be annual commemorative celebrations at the tomb in after years.

The human condition

People in the early states probably saw themselves differently in relation to the gods, according to their position in the social order. At the top of the hierarchy, the ruler was himself a god, and this status might extend to other members of his family as well. Immediately below him were the priests, who had convinced the masses (and presumably themselves) that it was through their continual votive efforts that the unpredictable gods were kept in line, for the benefit of the whole society. As long as the rains came and the crops were abundant, therefore—as they usually were in these agriculturally rich societies—the priests might feel a certain smug confidence about their command over the gods. In bad times however their lot was an anxious one, for the populace might accuse them of failing in the duty for which the whole elaborate and costly priestly establishment was maintained. In China they might be killed at the order of the emperor, if he was not killed first, at their command.

The illiterate lower orders of society, who could follow but not lead in ritual activities, were conscious of their dependence on the priests who stood as intermediaries between them and the deities. The extent of their confidence or anxiety in relation to the gods was therefore pretty much a reflection of their confidence in the priesthood. Few if any people doubted the efficacy of the rituals themselves; what they might doubt, especially in times of misfortune, was the competence of the priests to perform them. The wrath of the gods was seldom attributed to transgressions by the people as a whole, as it was later seen to be by the Hebrews.

Peasants, dwelling in their villages beyond the towns and cities, also stood pretty much outside the whole panoply of state religion, except that they might be laborers on temple-owned estates. They were not usually conscripted to take part in the great state ceremonies, except to perform ancillary labor, and they rarely made pilgrimages to the urban temples. Their religious life focused on local Powers, as it had done since tribal times, and as it has continued to do down to the present.

An overview

In many respects, the earliest states represented a revolutionary turning point in human social and political history. However, this was not true in the domain of religion. Nearly all aspects of the pantheon, of mythology, and of ritual were continuations and elaborations of long-held beliefs and practices. The differences from tribal and chiefdom religion were mainly quantitative, not qualitative.

They were, nevertheless, enormous, for the early theocratic states witnessed the apogee of power, wealth, and sheer elaboration in the evolution of religion. From its beginnings as an organizing political force at the chiefdom level, it had now become an all-embracing one, affecting the lives of every individual. Rituals, supported by the mobilizing power of the state, were numerous and elaborate as never before; a great deal of the surplus wealth collected through state redistribution systems was devoted to their performance. A great deal more of it went to the construction of temples and tombs. If the character of early state religion were to be described in a single word, it would surely be 'monumental.'

The early states proved to be remarkably durable, and it was religion that provided the main basis of continuity. Dynasties were overthrown, barbarians invaded and seized power, but the temples were kept in repair and the basic theocratic framework was not disturbed. Each new ruler was able to co-opt the priesthood and to claim divinity on the same basis as had his predecessors. While various aspects of technology and of the economy changed over the centuries, religion itself changed hardly at all. The theocratic states and religions of Mesopotamia and Egypt endured for three thousand years—more than half the total span of recorded history.

*The later
stages of
religious
evolution*

Evolutionary theorists have tended to conclude their developmental schemes with the emergence of the early states. This is acceptable only in the sense that all subsequent polities have had, in the broadest sense, a state form of government. But in the years since the emergence of the first states, specific institutions of government have changed radically, economic organization has changed even more, and religion has changed most of all. Indeed in the later stages of religious evolution there have been changes more profound than anything that occurred between tribal times and the earliest states.

It is clear therefore that we cannot leave the story of religious development where the evolutionary theorists customarily do. The later stages of religion may nevertheless be dealt with rather more briefly here, since they are all thoroughly familiar from the history of our own Western civilization.

*Religion
in the
secularizing
states*

Secularization of government was reflected in the emergence of rulers who were not divine, of governing councils, and of man-made laws. These developments did not take place initially within the territory of the old theocracies, where divinely ordained government remained firmly entrenched. We observe them rather in some of the barbarian chiefdoms that lay on their frontiers—most notably at the eastern end of the Mediterranean. Secularization is most clearly recognizable in the early Greek polities, but it may simultaneously have occurred among Phoenicians and other Levantine peoples. There are suggestions of secularization even within the Persian Empire, for all its continuation of the theocratic traditions of Mesopotamia.

Two major factors contributed to secularization. One was the monetization of the economy, beginning around the sixth century B.C. It freed a great deal of economic activity from state control, and led to the emergence of a prosperous, wholly secular mercantile and landowning class. It was the members of that class who in time overthrew the early Greek monarchies, and replaced them with councils of wealthy burghers (the *polis*). The second factor was the development of alphabetic writing, which made literacy far more accessible than before, and broke the age-long monopoly of the priestly class on the transmission of written knowledge. Literacy became general in the mercantile class, and it was the wealthy, idle sons of merchants and landowners who pioneered in the development of Greek secular science and philosophy.

These developments led to a reduction in the once-pervasive role played by religion in the life of the community. It was not wholly separated from government: the *polei* and the empires that succeeded them continued to build temples to the city gods, though they were never quite as monumental as some of those of the Egyptians and Babylonians. The citizenry were still required to worship at the state temples, and those who failed to do so might be severely punished, as the earliest Christians were to discover. But the size and influence of the priesthood was much reduced, and its activity was confined to the religious sphere; priests no longer played any significant role in civil or economic administration. What we witness, then, is the beginning of a process of compartmentalization, in which religion no longer pervades all of culture.

Public ceremonies in the secularizing states were less frequent and much less elaborate than before. They no longer had a major political function, in that they played little part in legitimizing the rule of the councils or, later, the emperors. (Some of the later Roman emperors tried to claim personal divinity, after the fashion of their theocratic predecessors, but this was treated as a joke by most of the citizenry.) At the same time, at least among the educated, secular science and philosophy began to cut into the huge explanatory role that religion had once played.

Religion adapted to these altered circumstances, so to speak, by a reduction and a systematization of the pantheon, making it more intelligible to an increasingly critical-minded population. No gods were formally repudiated, but, without state support, the worship of a great many died out, while a limited group of deities (the Olympians, in the Greek and Roman case) were accorded elite status and received the bulk of public attention. In the process some syncretization took place, as the characters and the history of several earlier deities were collapsed into the personae of Zeus, Hera, Athena, and other Olympians. At the same time the Greeks were always eager to identify their own deities with those they encountered among Egyptians, Persians, and other neighboring peoples. There was however no comparable attempt to reduce or to systematize mythology, in which a great many other deities besides the Olympians continued to be mentioned. But to an increasing number of the educated, mythology came to be appreciated as literature rather than as religious truth.

In time the secularizing philosophers of Greece and Rome (and also in China) became a more important ideological force than were the priests. They were by no means atheists, but they viewed religion, or at least religious morality, in a light entirely different from that of earlier times. They began insisting that personal virtues of honesty, generosity, and self-sacrifice were more gratifying to the gods than were ritual performances. In effect, they were saying that social morality is more important than is sacral morality, as it was usually conceived at the time—an idea that I will pursue at greater length in a later chapter. Although it originated earlier, it was an idea that came to fullest expression in the works of Plato and Aristotle, and in the whole school of Stoic philosophy. A similar idea can be found in the Chinese philosophies that developed during the Warring States period, more or less contemporaneously with the great age of Greek moral philosophy.

Eschatology remained as important as before, and funerals were often elaborate, but there was decreasing ostentation in graves, and especially in the amount of goods buried within them. The Romans in fact preferred cremation to inhumation, which eliminated altogether the need to bury offerings with the dead. The concept of a corporeal afterlife was beginning to give way to the doctrine of transmigration of souls.

Personal religion, especially among the less educated, appears to have been little affected by these changes. There was continued worship of a host of localized and household gods. There were almost certainly still quack 'doctors,' whose practice retained a good deal of shamanism.

Peasant
religion

Within the compass of both the theocratic and the secularizing states there continued to live rural, village-dwelling peasants who lay largely beyond the reach of the urban religious systems, and whose religious beliefs and practices retained many features dating back to tribal times. Like the religions of tribesmen they were religions of the weak, who felt little of the confidence in relation to the gods that the city dwellers enjoyed.

The religion of Arab peasants, described in detail in Chapter 3, may serve to exemplify peasant religion in general. The outstanding feature of all such religions is their overwhelmingly local focus. Peasants have been, all through history, 'earthbound;' they are tied to their ancestral soil by instruments of serfdom or peonage or taxation that make it virtually impossible to leave. Their religion therefore reflects the importance of deities that they can access within the compass of their limited worlds: the *awlia* of the Arabs, the village saints and the local manifestations of the Virgin in the Roman Catholic and Greek Orthodox worlds; the village gods of India and China. The villagers give what obeisance they can to the high gods of the city dwellers, but it is those within reach of their voices that matter.

Salvationist religions place overwhelming emphasis on personal virtue, in preparation for a life to come. They arose out of the eschatological beliefs of earlier times, but involve a dramatically altered vision of the afterlife, and of the relation between this world and the next. They seem to have originated in India in the last millennium B.C., and from there spread both eastward and westward. In the West they became increasingly popular in the later years of the Roman Empire, and then, within an extraordinarily short time, took the whole of the Western and Near Eastern worlds as though by storm. At the same time the salvationist doctrines of Buddhism and, for a time, Daoism, had almost as powerful an influence in eastern Asia.

The rise of salvationist cults

The rise of salvationism was not associated with major changes in society, polity, or economy, and therefore cannot be identified as an evolutionary stage in the same sense as can tribes or chiefdoms or states. Within the domain of religion itself, however, salvationism must certainly be regarded not merely as an evolutionary but as a revolutionary change—more so than any other in the entire history of religion. It cannot however be explained any of the currently known laws of evolution.

What all the salvationist cults did was to adopt the same doctrine espoused by the secularizing philosophers: that personal virtues are more gratifying to the gods (or the single god) than are ritual performances. I am not necessarily suggesting that the prophets of salvationism were influenced by the philosophers; it may have been the other way around, since the two trends of thought both become visible at just about the same time in history. But the salvationists went beyond the philosophers in linking personal virtue quite explicitly to the expectation of rewards in a life to come—a domain that the philosophers had almost wholly ignored. In the salvationist cults, then, social morality became also the essence of religious morality.

Not all salvationist religions were, or are, overtly dualistic, in the same way as are the Abrahamic faiths. That is, they did not necessarily hold out the threat of eternal damnation side by side with the hope of eternal salvation. For Buddhists and Daoists salvation is not an escape from the flames of hell, but simply from the eternal misery of everyday existence, and I think this was true as well of the early Isis and Mithra cults. In the Near East and West, however, salvationism seems to have been associated from the beginning with dualism, although this feature has been stressed more or less at different times and in different sects.

The salvationist religions thus introduced for the first time the concept of sin, coupled explicitly with a fear of damnation. The concept was, and is, very poorly defined, but it is at least clear that it involves a great deal more than just sacrilege in the old sense; that is, blasphemy and the failure of ritual duties. Sin encompasses at the same time a great deal of social immorality, like selfishness and cruelty and sexual license. Just as social morality became, for salvationists, a major component of religious morality, so social immorality became religious immorality.

The historical context of salvationism

In explaining the origin of Islam, one of the most successful of salvationist religions, A. L. Kroeber wrote that

> ... Islam arose in the very region of that first hearth of all higher civilization—in the Near Eastern area of the Neolithic Revolution, of the first farming and towns and kings and letters. But it arose at a time when constructive impulses had long since moved out from that hearth, and had begun to move beyond Greece and Persia even; yet at a time when the Near East still lay covered with a detritus of forcibly imposed and presumably uncongenial Hellenic and Iranic civilization—a detritus that had long since become heavier and deader with each generation. There was apparently no longer any hope, in our seventh century [i.e. A.D.], for a really creative new great civilization ... to spring up in this Nearer East, among the palimpsested, tired, worn societies of Egypt, Syria, or Mesopotamia. For that to happen would have been, so to speak, to burn over again the ashes of the past. But there was a chance for a reduced, retractile civilization, an anti-Hellenic, anti-Sassanian, anti-Christian civilization ....
> (Kroeber 1952: 381–2).

Although Kroeber's reference is specifically to the rise of Islam, his words seem applicable much more generally to the rise and the success of salvationist religions. Unlike any previous religious developments, they did not evolve out of the past but were repudiations of it. They were reactions against the legacy of outworn tradition: of overelaborated pantheons and mythology and ritual, and the influence of a bloated and an increasingly irrelevant priesthood. In that respect they were also reactions against the state, which supported the priesthood. They were not only revolutionary in an ideological sense, but subversive in a political one.

But the salvationist religions were not just reactions against the established politico-religious order; they were in the beginning reactions against a whole world that appeared fundamentally flawed, and incapable of reform. They espoused the pessimistic doctrine that humankind was naturally and inevitably corrupt, but that individuals through personal virtue (as well as correct ritual) could escape to a happier world in the next life. At the same time those who were not virtuous could expect dire punishment in the hereafter, although this feature of eschatology was not so much emphasized in the earliest salvationist cults as it was to be later. The whole of this life should in any case be devoted primarily to a preparation for the life to come, which would be eternal. Eschatology thus took on an entirely new dimension, as the central focus of religion. But the afterlife would be for the soul only, for all things material were corrupt, and would be left behind at death.

In the making of religion, then, the salvationist cults virtually swept the ground and began anew. They discarded all earlier ritual and most of the mythology, and they dismissed as irrelevant the great religious monuments of earlier times. The rituals of worship were very much simpler than those of earlier times, with a heavy emphasis on verbal address, and they were conducted initially in private. Although not rigidly monotheistic in the beginning, they focused attention entirely on one or a very few deities, insisting that worship of them alone was sufficient to attain salvation. The deities they chose were exotic ones—the Egyptian Isis or the Persian Mithra or the god of the Hebrews. For their votaries, these deities were not part of a previously worshipped pantheon, which was tainted by its association with the state and with the priesthood. The adoption of new gods was evidently a necessary feature, for the salvationist cults did not prosper among those peoples for whom the focal gods were already familiar. The Graeco-Roman Isis and Mithra cults were not accepted by Egyptians or Persians, Christianity was rejected by the Hebrews, and Buddhism was rejected in India.

A radical innovation of the salvationist cults, and a vitally important one for later religious history, was the concept of the messiah. Many though not all of the cults were founded by a divinely inspired individual, to whom the tutelary god of the cult had sent a special message, to discard old religious practices and to institute new ones.[26] Although some of these individuals, like Buddha and Jesus, probably saw themselves only as reformers, they were in fact revolutionaries who founded whole new religions, and were worshipped as such by the votaries. The belief in the messiah past, and the possibility of future messiahs to come, remains a feature of all salvationist religions down to the present day, and it has led to the emergence of any number of self-proclaimed messiahs and of new, though usually short-lived, salvationist cults.

The salvationist religions were in the beginning cults, which existed in opposition to one another as well as to the state religion. Because they did not coincide with any previously existing social or political entity, they had in effect to create communities of their own. They thus introduced, for the first time in the history of religion, the concept of formal enrollment with its attendant rituals. Out of those circumstances there emerged the church, as we know it today. And because the cults were in competition with other cults and with the state, they were also evangelistic, seeking actively to recruit and to indoctrinate new members. These were to be powerfully important features of religion in all future generations.

Perhaps the most revolutionary, and in the long run the most subversive, feature of salvationism was its emphasis on the individual rather than the community. Salvation could be achieved only by individuals, through their own personal virtue. The collective performance of ritual, though virtuous in its own right, was never necessary for salvation. The immemorial function of religion, in creating or reinforcing solidarity within existing social and political groups, was thus lost—until such time as the salvationist cults of Buddhism, Judaism, Christianity, and Islam became themselves the established religions of states.

The salvationist religions were far more restricted in scope than anything that had preceded, for they did not pretend to be comprehensive systems either of government or of knowledge. In turning their back on

---

[26]These individuals are often referred to in literature as prophets, but the term is an unsatisfactory one, for many of the so-called prophets of the Old Testament and of the Quran were mere prognosticators, not religious innovators.

the things of this world they (with the nominal exception of Islam) surrendered to the civil authorities the job of regulating society ('Render unto Caesar ...'). At the same time they surrendered to secular philosophy and to science the job of explaining the world, which had been so important in all earlier religion. This development marks the first major reduction in the cognitive function of religion. Within the broad context of culture, religion became far more compartmentalized than in any earlier time, and at least in the world of Christendom this has persisted to the present day.

The salvationist cults in the beginning represented the apogee of mysticism in Western and Near Eastern religious thought. There had been plenty of mysticism in all the earlier religions, but the cults in their original form were religion stripped of nearly everything except its mystical element. It is not inappropriate that they are often designated in literature as mystery religions.

In sum, the salvationist religions represented a revolutionary new beginning in the history of religion. They at first ignored and before long repudiated over 90% of the content of religion as it had existed up to their time, and those parts that they retained, like the belief in the afterlife, were reinterpreted in a new light. From ignoring the existence of all gods but their own tutelary, they proceeded in time to a denial that any other gods existed, and their votaries defaced or destroyed many of the great temples that their predecessors for centuries had carefully maintained. From that simplest of beginnings, however, they began a process of growth and elaboration that in time rivaled that of the older religions they had replaced.

Medieval civilizations were those in which salvationist cults, from their humble beginnings, had grown with startling rapidity into world religions. In the process they had supplanted and then suppressed their rivals, had been accepted as state religions, and had then spread far beyond the borders of the states where they first arose. In both a moral and an intellectual sense they provided the chief source of unity in the medieval world. They did not however provide any semblance of political or economic unity. The medieval world was divided among kingdoms or emirates, many of them petty, which warred fiercely with one another even while they professed the same faith. For the first time, therefore, we are obliged to recognize religion as a mainly ideological force, independent of polity and economy.

Medieval civilizations: the triumph of salvationism

The medieval civilizations that we can most clearly recognize are those of Western Christendom, Eastern Christendom, and Islam. The Buddhist states of Southeast Asia and the Buddhist dynasties in China might perhaps also be included, though these polities retained a good many of the characteristics of early theocracies.

Whether the medieval civilizations should be regarded as representing an evolutionary stage in the usual sense is debatable, given the diversity of their political and economic institutions. The polities of Western Christendom were rival dynasties, while the economy was an agrarian one, based on a complex, hierarchical system of land tenures and obligated services.[27] Church and state were here very clearly separated. Eastern Christendom however was a remaining fragment of the Roman Empire, administered mostly under prebendial grants from the emperor. Cities and trade remained highly important, though with a considerable degree of state control. Church and state, though separately organized, were closely integrated, and both were under the emperor. The domains of Islam, far more extensive and ecologically diverse than those of either Western or Eastern Christendom, embraced a variety of economic and political systems adaptive to different conditions. In theory there was no law but the law of Islam and no government but that of the Prophet's successor, the Caliph; in practice there were not only warring dynasties along the Mediterranean rim, but short-lived, powerful nomad empires in the hinterlands. Trade however was a vitally important activity throughout the Islamic domains, and it remained almost wholly free from state control.

The two political concepts found most consistently among all the medieval polities, Christian and Muslim, were those of dynasticism and of legalism. The allegiance of people was not to ethnic groups or territories, or even to any particular governing institution, but very specifically and personally to whoever was the hereditary ruler of their territory. But complex systems of law existed independently of the various warring polities, and they were continually referred to for guidance in an otherwise unstable world, where the moral authority of rulers was weak. Systems of courts were extensive in both the Christian and the Islamic

---

[27]Orthodox Marxist theory identifies Feudalism, as practiced in medieval Europe, as a distinct evolutionary stage, but this is an ethnocentric fallacy. Feudalism is a mode of production found only in agrarian societies, and it develops in times when central government is weak. It was not very highly developed in the domains either of Eastern Christendom or of Islam, although it was at times in China.

worlds, and legally established contracts played a much larger role in the organization and regulation of society than in any earlier time.

If the medieval civilizations do not represent a clearly marked evolutionary stage in the political or economic sense, they most assuredly do in the domain of religion. They witnessed a marked reaction against the secularizing tendency of the preceding centuries, and have been characterized by modern scholars as an Age of Faith. Though religion did not provide political or economic unification, it provided a remarkable degree of intellectual unification, and it wholly co-opted the intellectual classes. The secular philosophy and science of Greek and Roman times were either repudiated or, much more commonly, were reinterpreted to make them consistent with religious scripture. Lay scholars no less than clergy contributed eagerly to this enterprise, especially in the cities of the Byzantine and Islamic lands.

At the heart and core of the medieval religions was scripture: the recorded teaching of the messiahs, which endured eternally after the founders themselves had passed away. This feature was not present in the original salvationist cults, whose the sacred mysteries were transmitted mostly in oral form. The holy texts were compiled later, after the cults had acquired an organized church and a degree of state recognition. Christianity and Islam (and also Manichaeanism and Buddhism) each possessed a limited body of sacred texts that directly or indirectly was considered to have come from God.

In the evolution of the medieval religions from their salvationist beginnings, the first step was one of rationalization. The founders and the earliest votaries of both Christianity and Islam were mystics, content to live with ambiguity and uncertainty as mystics always are. But when the two became established state religions, it was necessary to establish a certain degree of orthodoxy. At the same time, authority on matters religious passed from the humble and illiterate into the hands of learned scholars and clerics, who for the most part were rational-minded, and who sought to resolve the ambiguity in the original doctrines. The result, in Christendom, was a series of ecumenical councils which propounded such sophisticated doctrines as the virgin birth, the Trinity, and the dual nature of Christ—ideas that would surely have astounded Jesus, and I think in some cases would have appalled him. As a result of this process of deliberation and resolution, the Christianity of today is a mystical doctrine that has been refracted through a lens of Greek rationalism.

Since the Quran either embodies or implies a good deal of law, it is no surprise that its interpretation, and the explication of Islam more generally, passed into the hands not of speculative thinkers but of learned jurists. In the eighth and ninth centuries they promulgated the four recognized codes of *Sharia* law, which are much more nearly at the heart of Islamic practice than is the Quran. Thus, the Islam of today is a mystical, or at least a utopian, doctrine that has come to us refracted through a lens of Near Eastern legalism.

In a way, the scriptures and their importance give further evidence of the essential legalism of the Middle Ages. They stood apart from and above the religious establishment in the same way that legal codes stood apart from and above the individual polities and the courts. They were subject to endless interpretation and reinterpretation by the priesthoods, but the original words could not be changed, added to, or subtracted from; they could not even be translated from their ancient languages. Not only all religious practice but all philosophy and science—virtually all thought—had to be conformable with those sacred texts.

Since the scriptures were preserved in alphabetic scripts, in the beginning they were widely accessible to the educated classes, who could hold both priesthood and rulers accountable for the orthodoxy of their actions. Over time however spoken language drifted farther and farther away from that of the texts, until the language of scripture was left in effect as a second language that had to be separately learned. In those circumstances familiarity with scripture became once again a near-monopoly of the religious clergy, as it had been in the time of the early states.

Once it attained the support of powerful and wealthy states, as it did in the late Roman Empire and in the early Islamic Caliphate, salvationist religion regained many of the trappings of earlier state religions. The concept of a separation between religion and the state, so insisted upon in the early salvationist cults, was for a time entirely lost. In the worlds of Islam and of eastern Christendom the church and the state were nominally one, while in the politically divided world of western Christendom the Roman church became virtually a state in its own right. The priesthood, whom we now usually call clergy, became extensive and hierarchically differentiated, and was headed by a high priest (pope, patriarch, or caliph). Religious buildings proliferated, and became once again the civilization's most conspicuous architectural monuments, culminating in the magnificent late medieval cathedrals and the great mosques. Religious establishments were provided with landed estates to support them, and became in many cases enormously rich. This situation, in western

Europe, allowed them to hold their own against the secular rulers, with whom their relationship was often tendentious.

In the Christian world, the priesthood came to control religion as wholly as it had in any theocratic state. People were compelled to attend services, to undergo the prescribed sacraments under priestly supervision, and to pay tithes, and might be severely punished if they did not. Heterodox beliefs and practices, not sanctioned by the clergy or by scripture, were considered especially heinous. There was a separate system of ecclesiastical courts and a hierarchy of religious judges, who in the western Christian world were wholly outside state control.

In the process, salvationist religion moved farther and farther away from its original emphasis on personal virtue, and back toward the earlier insistence on ritual duty and performance, as the approved road to salvation. The same thing happened in time in nearly all the salvationist cults when they became world religions: in Buddhism, Daoism, and Manichaeanism, no less than in Christianity. That is, they all became increasingly ritualized. It was as if the mass of followers was not yet ready for a doctrine that placed such a heavy load of responsibility and decision-making on the individual.

Eschatology remained, in theory, at the heart and core of medieval religion, but in the hands of the church it acquired a considerably more sinister emphasis than in earlier years. Instead of the hope of eternal bliss, the preachings of the clergy laid heavy emphasis on the innate wickedness of man, and therefore on the ever-present threat of damnation. It was the doctrine of a time dominated by law-and-order mentality, and was also an instrument of control by the church itself.

In its totality, nevertheless, medieval religion was much more worldly, and less otherworldly, than were the early cults from which it sprang. The church sought to glorify itself through elaborate rituals and monumental buildings that had little to do with any preparation for the afterlife. There was also little of mysticism in the great masses and the individual sacraments, with their mechanistic recitations and censing. The mystical mind however continued to be thrilled by hagiographies, recounting the marvels and miracles of the saints, which were an important part of the lore of medieval religion.

In the world of Islam, the influence of religion was in theory even more pervasive than in Christendom, because the four orthodox law codes regulated virtually every aspect of life, down to minute details of dress and diet. Means of control however were not very well developed, since there was, by the Prophet's design, neither a church nor a clergy in the Christian sense. As Kroeber observed, Islam arose in reaction not only against the old state religions but also against Christianity, which by the time of Muhammad had long been the established church of the Byzantine Empire. The Prophet, himself illiterate, aimed to keep his new religion simple and accessible to everyone; to create a single, universal community of the faithful, who would be naturally virtuous once they had surrendered to God.[28] But that utopian vision did not long outlive the Prophet, and by the ninth century it was found necessary to compile the comprehensive law codes and to create the system of religious (*Sharia*) courts that still exist today. In the absence of a supervising clergy, however, there was and is more religious heterodoxy and more laxity of performance than existed in the medieval Catholic or Orthodox Christian worlds.

Nativistic religions

The salvationist religions were in the beginning religions of the oppressed. Once they became the established religions of states and empires, however, their votaries became oppressors in their own right, as they imposed both their political rule and their religions upon the pagan peoples beyond their borders. Just as they had in their time been reactions against an oppressive older order, so they in their turn provoked reaction against themselves.

The years between 1492 and 1922 witnessed one of the most extraordinary developments in political history: the spread of European imperial domination over just about every part of the globe, except for east Asia. A very high percentage of the world's non-European peoples then found themselves subject to new and frequently oppressive colonial masters, who at the very least disrupted and frequently destroyed their traditional lifeways. Under those circumstances there arose, among the subject peoples, a whole series of reactive religious movements which have variously been called nativistic movements, messianic movements, and millenarian movements. So ubiquitous have these movements been that they might in the broadest sense even be regarded as an evolutionary development.

Nativistic religious movements have significant features in common with the salvationist cults of much earlier times. They have usually, though not always, been founded by a messiah, who proclaimed a new revelation from a god or gods. The new revelation is then combined with

---

[28]The word Islam means, literally, 'surrender.'

elements from older mythology, as well as with borrowed elements from Christianity or Islam, to create a highly syncretic new religion. There is a very explicit rejection of certain aspects of the existing situation, and especially of colonial rulers and their imperial regimes. There is at the same time a promise of final salvation or liberation, at some not too distant time in the future. (Since this text was first written, there have even been glimmerings of such a movement among the Navajo—see Schwarz 1998.)

The most salient feature of nativistic movements, that distinguishes them from the cults of earlier times, is their ethnocentrism. They are movements not for individual salvation but for the liberation of a whole people from the control of the colonial masters. At the same time there is a deliberate emphasis on preserving, or in some cases reviving, traditional cultural practices that are disappearing under the colonial regime. To the extent that personal virtue is stressed, it is likely to be defined mostly in terms of adherence to newly developed rituals and to old cultural ways, rather than of the universal virtues of generosity and self-sacrifice.

Although freedom from the oppressive yoke of colonial masters has been the common denominator of all nativistic movements, liberation is conceived in quite different ways by different cults. Movements like the Taiping and Boxer rebellions in China and the Tupamaru movement in Peru were as much military as religious; they aimed at driving out the foreigners by organized military force. Millenarian movements like the Smohalla and Ghost Dance religions of North American Indians and the cargo cults of Melanesia left the job of expulsion to the gods; the votaries prayed and sang and danced in order to bring on the millennial time when the gods would intervene and remove all the foreigners. Introversionist movements like the Handsome Lake religion of the Iroquois and the Ringatu Church of the New Zealand Maori place primary emphasis on withdrawal; they seek simply to maintain ethnic separatism and to give their followers a distinct and respected identity within a plural society that they cannot control.

Because their focus is on collective rather than individual redemption, very few of the cults lay much stress on the afterlife. The hoped-for salvation will come in this world, often at some millenarian moment in the future when a great miracle will occur.

Nativistic movements of the first two types, militant and millenarian, are essentially foredoomed to failure. They are either actively suppressed by the colonial authorities, as has happened many times, or they die out in the second generation when the promised miracle of redemption does not occur. Withdrawal movements have a better chance of survival, since they offer less threat to the authorities but also less exaggerated promise to their followers. The Handsome Lake Religion and the Peyote Religion of American Indians are two such movements that have survived to become established syncretic religions.

Religion in the modern industrial democracies

Today, most of the nations of Europe and North America are characterized by wholly secular and nominally democratic systems of government, by (relatively) free market economies, and by an industrial technology, in which fossil fuel power has largely replaced human and animal labor. Nations in other parts of the world are seeking, with greater or less success, to follow suit. A number of Latin American and some Islamic and Asian countries, conspicuously including Japan, have done so. This is clearly a spreading phenomenon which gives evidence of becoming worldwide, and by any measure it deserves recognition as a distinct stage in human cultural evolution.[29]

It is important to notice at this point, as Max Weber (1930) so cogently did, the influence of the Protestant ethic, with its emphasis on the individual, throughout the modernizing world. It is observable not only in the nominally Protestant countries of northern Europe and North America, but to a degree in all other countries that are striving to develop capital institutions and an industrial economy.

The Protestant Reformation was in the beginning, like the original salvationist cults two thousand years earlier, a reaction against ritualism, placing a renewed emphasis on personal virtue as the road to salvation. This meant once again a repudiation both of the state and of state-sponsored religion as sources of moral authority, while still accepting, however grudgingly, the legal authority of the state. The resulting separation of church and state—not yet total but far more complete than in any earlier age—has become the most salient feature of both religious and secular life in the modern world.

All of the dominant modern institutions, political, economic, and technological, are secular; they lie wholly outside the domain of religious control or influence. As a result, while the salvationist world religions

---

[29]Marxist theory identifies this evolutionary stage as Capitalist, failing to recognize that it is industrial production, not capital financing, that has so transformed the world of our times. The transformation is just as great in socialist countries as in capitalist ones.

survive from the Middle Ages with almost no doctrinal change, they have had to accept a vastly reduced role. They have, to begin with, surrendered government and also law entirely to the secular authorities. Gone are the religious courts, and with them a great deal of the fear of damnation that was so emphasized in the Middle Ages. Gone too are the theocentric systems of science and philosophy, except insofar as they survive among certain ordained clergy. Among the mass of laity, modern science commands as much faith as does religion. The saintly miracles that so stirred the imagination of the Middle Ages have been supplanted by the scientific and technological miracles that daily arouse our wonder. The compartmentalization of religion that began in Greek times continues, while at the same time the size of the 'compartment' occupied by religion is very much reduced.

Under these reduced circumstances, one might have expected a degree of reunification, as the custodians of religion banded together to defend what ground was left to them. Instead, in the Christian world, the opposite has happened: there has been diversification and heterodoxy as never before, as the splinters of a once unified church vie for control of what moral and intellectual ground is still left to them. This condition of diversity, still unacceptable to Roman Catholics, has nevertheless come to be accepted as a fact of life by the majority of Christians. In the Islamic world heterodoxy, in the proliferation of the numerous Shi'a sects, has existed since much earlier times, but it is only recently that their peaceful co-existence has come to be accepted.

The dominant trend within Christianity, responsible for the proliferation of sects, has been what I would call the secularization of the church. The belief that the church and religion are synonymous, so dominant in the Middle Ages, has come to an end for Protestants and even for an increasing number of Catholics. Scripture and a great deal of dogma (for example the Trinity) remain sacrosanct, while at the same time there is a widespread recognition—dating back initially to the Reformation—that the church itself is not sacrosanct. It is more often recognized today as a man-made institution, and consequently subject to reformation and even to a degree of control by the votaries.

However, ideas about how much power should still be accorded to the clerical hierarchy have differed widely. All the Protestant sects have done away with the pope, nearly all have done away with the archbishops, many have done away with the bishops, and the most radical of sects have done away with all governance above the local level. These developments reflect varying degrees of anti-clericalism, which has been a consistent if not always an acknowledged theme in Protestant Christianity since the Reformation. There are certainly doctrinal differences among the various Protestant denominations, but the most conspicuous differences have to do simply with issues of church governance, and the role that is allowed to the laity.

Diversification has led to a situation of active or latent rivalry between the sects, which at times fulminate against one another, tending further to undermine respect for the church as an institution. There are still many devout Christians who have unlimited faith in the scriptures, but few have unlimited faith in their churches or ministers, and many are openly critical. Most Americans today place more unquestioning faith in the word of their doctors than in that of their preachers. Church attendance remains high, but not many people regard it as a sacred duty.

Although Christianity remains at heart a salvationist creed, it seems to me that the eschatological element is pretty much in abeyance, as indeed are all other aspects of mysticism. Ours is a worldly and for most people a comfortable age, when the hope of escape to a happier life to come has less appeal than it formerly had. I think most Christians feel that, if they regularly attend church, they can fairly confidently count on a blissful afterlife, and they need not otherwise give it a lot of thought. Outside some of the hell-and-brimstone sects I don't see very much fear of damnation, to judge from the acquisitive and self-seeking way in which most people behave.

There are in Christianity today, as there have been in many earlier times, two views in regard to the current erosion of faith. One view blames it on the church, and seeks to reverse the trend through 'modernizations,' including simplification of the liturgy and updated translations of the scriptures. The other view blames it on the times, and insists that the church should stand fast in preserving 'that old-time religion.' It is a curious fact that these modernizing and archaizing tendencies sometimes go hand in hand in the same Protestant sects. That is, in simplifying the liturgy and reducing the role of clergy they claim that they are at the same time going back to the earliest forms of Christian worship, ordained by the Apostles.

What role, then, is left for religion in the secularized industrial democracies? In considering that question I think we have to maintain the distinction between religion and the church. With regard to religion itself the answer seems clear: its role is the provision of moral authority, an issue that I will pursue much more fully in a later chapter. This is the one domain of religion that has not been seriously undercut either by modern science or by secular law, and it probably never will be. The lives of everyone today are regulated by the enacted laws of the state, but no one accepts these as defining right and wrong in any absolute sense. The laws are recognized as man-made, and humans are fallible. There is recurring debate over the justice or injustice of particular laws, and they are continually being changed as new views or new factions become ascendant. It is only scripture that defines right and wrong in a way that the whole of the Christian community accepts. Not all people feel equally the need for moral authority in their lives, but those who do so continue to find it in the doctrines of salvationist religion. And for everyone, the scriptures are a rock of permanence and reliability in a turbulent sea of change.

Psychofunctionalists have stressed also the extent to which religion provides comfort and solace among the uncertainties and trials of everyday life. As I have suggested before, I'm not certain that this was always the case with earlier religions, but it probably is indeed one of the important functions of modern-day Christianity. For those who can believe that Jesus sees them and loves them, that belief probably brings more solace than does any amount of human commiseration.

As a non-member, I'm less certain about the present-day role of the church. I think it probably differs as between rural and urban communities. In the former, collective worship and village rituals may still make an important contribution to community solidarity, something that is much less likely to happen in urban churches with their dispersed congregations. But I don't think in either place that the fulminations and behavioral exhortations of preachers have the same influence that they once had. It is only the words of scripture and not the words of preachers that carry moral conviction, and in today's world of mass literacy the scriptures are accessible to nearly everyone.

For both urbanites and rural dwellers, I suspect that the most important present-day function of the church is educational. Very little religious instruction now takes place in the home, and none at all in the public schools which the vast majority of children attend. There are probably still Bibles in most homes, but they are not read with anything like the regularity that they once were—there is too much available television in the evening hours. It is through Sunday schools and weekly sermons that people learn the scriptures that are meant to be their moral guides through life.

The church may of course also organize social and recreational activities that are valuable to the community—perhaps compensating for its loss of spiritual power by increasing its secular attraction. These activities help to keep up membership and Sunday church attendance, but I am not sure that they do very much toward reinforcing the faith of the votaries. However, they serve to bring people together in the venue where religious instruction takes place.

Unlike some earlier theorists, I don't assume that this is the end of the story of religious evolution. On the contrary, I'm quite sure that it isn't. I will consider, at the end of the next chapter, the question of where we go from here.

15

THE DYNAMICS OF RELIGIOUS CHANGE

Peoples want for obvious reasons to think of their religions as eternal; they are, for most, the one rock of stability in a changing world. And yet, as a system of adaptation, religion like everything else in culture must change to fit the changing times. As we come to know better both the seen and the unseen worlds, religion has somehow to accommodate that altered and enlarged knowledge. In the process religion itself creates new knowledge, in the form of new deities and new myths.

I have dealt *in extenso* with religious change in the last chapter, under the heading The Evolution of Religion. And yet it should be apparent, from the data presented, that not all religious change can be fitted within the compass of evolutionary theory. Some change has not been an outcome of existing social and political conditions but a reaction against them: a revolutionary rather than an evolutionary development. There have in addition been dialectical changes, stylistic changes, and changes brought about simply by the accidents of history, that do not show any obvious directionality. In this chapter I will consider briefly some of the different processes of change that are observable in the history of religion, and that are still going on in the world of today. I will conclude the chapter with a few speculations about the future of religion.

Social evolutionary change

This is the easiest kind of religious change to account for, within the context of conventional theory. If we accept the Durkheimian and Weberian premise, that man makes god in his own image, and that the deities are basically Society deified, then the character of the deities must necessarily change as the character of society changes. Whatever else they do, the mythologies of band, tribe, chiefdom, and early state societies must legitimize the existing social and political order of their times.

We can observe, in the course of human social evolution, the suc-

Processes of change

cessive development of sedentary life, of food production (as opposed to hunting and gathering), of widely ramified kin groups, of economic differentiation by occupation, of hereditary leadership, of hierarchically ranked society, and of divine rulers. Each of those developments was reflected in a redefinition of the supernatural, and in a new component of mythology. At the same time, the increasingly productive food quest allowed more time for religious activities, and the increasing size of co-resident groups (from bands to villages to cities) permitted the staging of more and more elaborate collective rituals. Religious complexity increased as a consequence and as a reflection of social complexity.

This theoretical approach takes us comfortably up to the emergence of the early, theocratic states, but no further. As I have noted, the next major changes, in the time of the secularizing states, were revolutionary rather than evolutionary, and they could not have been predicted on the basis of anything that had gone before. They must be understood from the perspective of reactive change rather than of linear development, and will be discussed as such in a later section. But then, once the revolutionary, salvationist cults were firmly established and politically legitimized, there began a second evolutionary process, in which the cults once again became increasingly complex. Nevertheless, religion from this time onward was at least partially compartmentalized, and separated from a direct connection with the state. As a result, religion and society increasingly went their separate ways; the course of religious development was never again simply a mirror of the contemporary social and political order. At a very general level, however, we can notice that the strict and literal adherence to scripture in the medieval religions was in keeping with the essential legalism of medieval society.

The Protestant Reformation was then a second reactive change, albeit one that took place only in a limited part of the Christian world. If Max Weber was right about its relation to the growth of capitalism, then we can certainly link this religious change to an important simultaneous change in the economy, if not in society or polity more broadly. But Weber himself seemed to think that in this case it was religion that led, rather than followed, the change in the secular realm, which would represent a reversal of the usual evolutionary reasoning.

Cognitive evolutionary change

Some of the earliest theorists of religious evolution saw it as a matter not of adaptation to evolving society, but simply as a reflection of the increasing maturity of the human mind. Primitive religion was presumed to reflect childlike thinking, while the religions of our times were seen as those of the fully mature mind. This view has been highly unfashionable since the beginning of the twentieth century, inasmuch as it seems to disparage the mental powers of band-level and tribal peoples. Yet I think the theory, if properly understood, is not wholly without merit.

It is not a question of reasoning capacity; it is a question of available information. I am not convinced that the reasoning capacity of children, in the abstract, is that much inferior to our own. Indeed all parents know that, within the compass of their very limited information base, the logic of their children is unanswerable. What they lack, in comparison to us grownups, is information and experience. Like the rest of us they attribute everything to a cause, but, lacking both science and religion, they are likely to attribute causality to those things that they can see and understand. A table has attacked them when they stumble and hit their head on it; the house is evil when it is silent and cold. Children, in short, are primitive animists, until such time as they are indoctrinated into the systems of knowledge and belief created by grownups. (This theme will be much more fully explored in the next chapter.)

Band-level and tribal peoples, in comparison to ourselves, are possessed of rather limited experiential information about the world they live in. But they have, like the rest of us, a hunger for knowledge and understanding, and at the same time fertile creative imaginations. Out of that combination of inexperience and creativity come religions, which can supply knowledge and explanation where direct experience cannot. But as experiential knowledge of the world increases, and as our purely technological capacity to exploit it increases, bodies of secular knowledge are built up alongside religious knowledge. For a time the two systems of knowledge increase together; greater scientific knowledge makes it possible to conceive of bigger and more powerful gods, and new technologies of communication are developed to deal with them.

There comes a time however when religion begins to retreat as science advances, and the process accelerates over time. And as the amount of ground it has to cover diminishes, religion can be, and usually has been, refocused on those areas where it still has a role to play. Both mythology and pantheons are reduced and systematized, giving them greater intelligibility to the secular mind. All in all, then, I think this process of cognitive evolution is not unlike the maturation of the individual human mind, as it grows in knowledge and experience.

What we observe, in the course of cognitive evolution, are periodic re-definitions of the three-cornered relationship between men, gods, and nature. In the process, the mystical element in religion comes increasingly into play. In the beginning the gods and nature are one, and man is surrounded by them in the immediate environment. He is relatively powerless to control them, but deals with them as best he can through religious technology that involves a great deal of imitative magic and compulsive formulas. But as purely technical control over the physical environment increases, attention shifts more and more away from the immediate and toward the more remote deities, who are seen as the causal forces behind the phenomena of the immediate environment. There is, at this point, the beginning of a separation between the gods and nature, and also between man and nature. Concurrently there is an increased confidence in man's power, in relation to nature, but not in his power in relation to the gods.

The next step, when human technology advances, is a fuller separation between the gods and nature, along with a vastly increased sense of human control over the latter. At this point the gods, although still all-powerful and beyond human control, become ever more remote from involvement in everyday activity. They may still be remembered through routine worship services, but they are no longer continually invoked in the course of planting, weaving, traveling, and other daily activities. They are much more likely to be invoked and propitiated in special, out-of-the-ordinary circumstances that call for out-of-the-ordinary measures.

The gods dwell in those domains that humans cannot understand or control through experience and rational understanding, but that has been over time a continually shrinking domain. Thus, as man's control over his immediate surroundings increases, his attention turns to more and more remote deities. In the process the number of deities decreases, as the gods of the immediate world disappear, until finally (in the Abrahamic religions) only a few very remote beings are left. But this is true only for the privileged classes that really do enjoy a sense of confidence in relation to the world around them. There remain vast numbers of peasants and the poor, whose sense of mastery is very limited, and who still feel a need to deal with the many Powers that are within reach of their voices.

The issue of cognitive evolution will be considered again, from a more personal perspective, in the next chapter.

Reactive change

In the history of religion there was one revolutionary change that surely involved a major cognitive shift, yet that cannot be fully understood from either a social or a cognitive evolutionary perspective. This was the rise and then the incredibly rapid triumph of salvationist religion, over a large part of the Old World and within a span of no more than a thousand years. As I have said before, I regard this as the single most revolutionary development in the entire history of religion. It was in most respects a reactive change, on so comprehensive a scale and over so wide an area that it seems to represent a reaction against just about everything in the then-existing world.

The salvationist cults did not, of course, involve a total break with older religious tradition. Their most salient feature, the belief in an after-life, had already been around for a very long time, although in the case of band-level and tribal societies it is hard to see any very direct connection between eschatology and other aspects of religion. By the time of the early states however there certainly was such a connection, and eschatology had even become one of the prominent features of religion in Egypt and China. There are also hints, in the eschatological beliefs of Egyptians, Chinese, and a good many other peoples, of a differentiated afterlife, with greater rewards for some individuals than for others. Those rewards might depend in part on personal merit, although the manner of death and the extent of funerary preparations and ritual could also play a part.

The salvationist cults also were not, in their origins, equally revolutionary and rejectionist. Buddhism, Manichaeanism, and Christianity were all conceived by their founders as internal reform movements rather than as new beginnings, and, notably, each of them accepted the authority of older scriptures. But these three movements did not 'take' among the populations for whom they were originally intended. Instead, they were accepted by alien peoples for whom they, including both their gods and their scriptures, were truly revolutionary.

The novel features of salvationism were both positive and negative. It was the negative or rejectionist features that so alarmed the established political authorities, and led to active persecution of Buddhists, Manichaeans, and Christians alike. In repudiating the worship of long-extant gods, and even denying their existence, the salvationist cults were at the same time undermining the authority of the state that had closely associated itself with those gods, and had commanded their worship. In their egalitarianism, the cults were at the same time repudiating the hierarchically ordered society that had existed since the earliest beginnings of state society, and had been accepted as part of the god-given order of things. And in denying any importance to the material things of this world, they were in some sense undermining the commercial economy as well.

But these negative features did not, in the end, have a lasting impact, apart from the denial of the older gods. Once the political authorities realized what they were up against, they adopted the age-old stratagem, 'if you can't beat 'em, join 'em.' From that point onward religion came once again to be closely identified with the interests of the state, and it re-acquired a good many of the characteristics of earlier state religions, including the performance of elaborate rituals and the erection of monumental structures.

It was the positive features of salvationism that endured, and have become basic to nearly all the religions that have emerged in the world in the last two thousand years. Those features include the messianic tradition, the emphasis on personal virtue rather than ritual performance as the road to salvation, the dualistic conception of the afterlife, and the doctrine of the transmigration of souls. They can be found not only in all of today's world religions, but also in the innumerable messianic cults that have sprung up among tribal peoples, and are still doing so.

The messianic tradition is, up to a point, the most easily explained feature of salvationist religion. A wholly new religion obviously requires a new revelation from the gods or god, and someone on earth must be found to proclaim it. On the other hand, why such a revelation should be given to one and only one person instead of to several persons, or to all mankind at once, is less easily explained. We can only observe that the idea of the specially favored person, who can receive messages from the gods that others cannot, is a common one that goes all the way back to the days of the shaman.

The ideals of personal virtue to which the salvationists attached such importance were of course not new. The qualities of generosity, self-sacrifice, charity, and other aspects of what I call social morality (see Chapter 18) have been admired among all peoples, probably since the dawn of society. Nevertheless, they were not prominently stressed in the pre-salvationist religions, which laid primary emphasis on ritual duty rather than on personal virtue as the thing which the gods demanded. The impulses toward social morality came from the approbation of friends and neighbors, rather than from the gods.

What the salvationist religions did in effect was to add their voices to that of society, in stressing the importance of personal virtue. This was clearly seen as necessary by the founding messiahs, who were convinced that the power of public opinion was no longer enough to keep people behaving as they should. All the cults were reactions against a world which was seen as corrupt, self-seeking, and irresponsible; a world in which the voice of society had lost its moral power. And at the same time when they took over the job of promoting social morality, the cults did what society could not do: they coupled the ideal of personal virtue very explicitly to the promise of a blissful afterlife. Most also coupled the lack of virtue to the threat of eternal torment. This was a much more powerful inducement to behave than was the accusation of witchcraft—the most common punishment of the un-virtuous in tribal societies.

In one respect this new emphasis on personal virtue represents a reversal of the more general course of religious evolution, which has witnessed a diminution of the role played by religion in relation to that played by secular society. But taking over, from secular society, the primary responsibility for social morality involved a very considerable enlargement in at least this one role of religion. At the same time, paradoxically, we can see the new development as evolutionary in one sense: it foreshadowed the emphasis on individual rather than collective responsibility that is characteristic of modern society. Salvation as conceived by the new cults was, and remains, purely an individual matter.

The dualistic feature of so many salvationist religions—the clear and total separation of good and bad deities, and of heaven and hell—appears to be as old as salvationism itself. In a way it might be thought of as a logical corollary to the concept of salvation itself. If there is to be a reward for merit in the world to come, there should be the opposite of a reward for those persons who are not meritorious. Yet not all salvationist religions are dualistic. For Buddhists there are all kinds and degrees of possible happiness or unhappiness in the next life, while the greatest of all happinesses is to have no next life at all. Structuralists like Lévi-Strauss might want to argue that religious dualism results from the human propensity to think of everything in terms of binary oppositions, and yet this leaves unexplained the nearly total absence of dualism in religions before the last millennium B.C.

One final revolutionary feature of salvationist religion was the belief in the transmigration of the soul. We archaeologists who have worked in Egypt and in Nubia have seen the dramatic consequences of that cognitive shift. The graves of the pre-Christian and pre-Islamic eras, extending over a period of thousands of years, are rich in all kinds of material offerings, while those of Christians and of Muslims contain none. The change, as we see it represented in the cemeteries, did not take place gradually; it occurred virtually overnight. It was more than just a change of custom, such as is common in mortuary ritual; it involved the abandonment of a mode of thought that had prevailed for millennia.

An extraordinary latter-day recurrence of religious reaction and of salvationist religion is to be seen in the literally hundreds of nativistic cults that have sprung up among colonized and oppressed peoples, as discussed in the last chapter. They have occurred so commonly in those circumstances as to be virtually predictable. Most have been founded by messiahs, and all of them included some of the same elements found in the earliest salvation cults: rejection of the existing social and political order, emphasis on personal virtue, and the hope of a better life to come. The nativistic cults however differ from those of earlier times in their ethnocentrism: they aim at the salvation or liberation not of individual souls but of whole peoples. They also differ from earlier cults in their attempt to turn back the clock, emphasizing the preservation or revival of old and traditional ways. In that respect they are like the archaizing movements in some Christian and Islamic sects.

The vast majority of latter-day messianic cults have arisen out of the contact between indigenous peoples and colonial powers, and they have been influenced in varying degrees by the messianic traditions of Christianity or Islam. Nevertheless, there are a few well attested cases of purely endogenous messianic movements among tribal peoples, antedating their contact with colonial regimes. They include the Koréri and Taro movements in New Guinea, the Bird-man Religion that sprang up in the eighteenth century among the Polynesians of Easter Island, and the extraordinary series of movements that drove the Tupi-Guaraní tribes of Brazil from place to place.

There are two respects in which the development of the salvationist cults might conceivably be thought of as evolutionary. In the political sphere, they provided the ideological basis for the separation of church and state, although its full realization was to be a long time in coming. In the cognitive sphere, they reflect an increased confidence in man's ability to control his individual destiny with respect to the gods. But while in the above paragraphs I have sought, so far as I could, to find rational explanations for the various radical innovations connected with salvationism, it must be obvious that they fall far short of a full explanation of why this phenomenon was so long in coming, but then triumphed so completely.

I am driven in the end to conclude that, like a lot of evolutionary developments (pottery, metallurgy, and writing, for example) it was simply an idea whose time had come.

Enforced change

Not all religious change has been internally driven. We have only to look at the religious picture throughout Latin America, where for three centuries the Spanish colonial authorities actively suppressed native religious practices and insisted on Catholic worship, to realize how much religious change has taken place under circumstances of duress. Indigenous communities have to varying degrees succeeded in blending some of their earlier practices and beliefs with the overarching Catholic faith, but many older practices (human sacrifice, for example) have been suppressed altogether, and scores of old gods have disappeared.

A certain amount of enforced change undoubtedly took place before the modern colonial era, when empires extended their sway over newly conquered peoples. In those cases the conquerors might demand that the subjects worship the gods of their new masters, as for example the worship of the emperor was mandated throughout the Roman Empire. But there was, at the same time, very little in the way of suppression. Since all the religions were open systems, the gods of the conquerors could simply be added to the existing pantheons. In that sense, the enforced change was all in the direction of religious enrichment.

It is only the exclusivist religions (mainly the Abrahamic faiths) that do not allow of syncretism. In the role of conquerors, they insist not only on the worship of new gods but on the repudiation of all the older ones. As I have suggested earlier, the exclusivist faiths are very much in the minority among the world's religions, but they happen to be the religions embraced by the dominant colonial powers of our time, and the enforced adoption of Christianity or of Islam has been a conscious part of the colonizing effort in many parts of the world. The consequences are evident throughout the whole of Latin America and the Islamic Middle East.

The dialectic of complexity and simplicity

There is virtually no aspect of human culture that does not increase in size and complexity over time, through the gradual accumulation of knowledge, and of practical abilities based on that knowledge. Although in most circumstances this is recognizably adaptive, it is also true that the tendency to make things more complicated has a kind of internal dynamic all its own. Mankind strives always for the better, and there seems to be a general human tendency to think that more is better. As a result, some aspects of culture can in time become maladaptive. We can see many examples in our own time, in the overgrowth of cities and the proliferation of non-productive bureaucracies. Parkinson's Law represents the classic demonstration of this latter phenomenon.

There is no domain of culture in which this is more conspicuously true than in religion. Since it is virtually unconstrained by material or technical considerations, there is no theoretical limit to the growth of pantheons, of mythology, and of ritual. And since, as I have suggested, religion is usually to some extent experimental, there are always the two basic considerations: 'if it works, keep it,' and 'if it works for other people, maybe it will work for us.' So while new elements are being added, old ones are not discarded, and there is a steady increase in the sheer quantity as well as in the complexity of religious belief and practice.

But there comes a time eventually when the towering edifice of religion becomes too top-heavy to stand securely. There is simply too much to know, and too much to do. The problem is alleviated to some extent by the development of a specialized and professional priesthood, who can relieve the populace at large from a part of the burden both of knowledge and of practice. But the priesthood itself is likely to grow in numbers, power, and influence to the point where it is not seen as serving the people's interest.

At this point there is a perceived necessity for simplification, not only among the populace but often among the priests themselves, as they see their influence, and that of religion in general, under criticism. So there have been, all through history (and perhaps even prehistory), periodic moves toward simplification. The original Abrahamic religion of the Hebrews provides one example, as does the unsuccessful Cult of Aten which the Pharaoh Akhenaten attempted to launch.

The most extreme of simplification movements are those, like the early salvationist cults, that would throw out the old altogether, and begin from scratch. However, these are properly movements for replacement rather than simplification, and as such I have dealt with then in an earlier section. My concern here is with reform movements that take place within established religions, and are intended to revitalize them.

Simplification movements are of two basic types, which may be called archaizing and modernizing. The fundamental principle in the archaizing movements is to 'throw out the new,' while keeping that which is hallowed by tradition. The archaizers within both Christianity and Islam seek a return to a purely scriptural religion, eliminating much of the encrustation of ritual and organization that has taken place without scriptural foundation. Christian archaizing movements are often somewhat anti-clerical, insisting that the votaries should go back to the earliest forms of worship, before it was encumbered by the intervention of a church.

The basic principle of the modernizers is to 'throw out the obsolete;' to get rid of language and costumes and ritual that are no longer either intelligible or meaningful to the great majority of votaries. These movements, unlike those of archaizing, assign rather a large role to the church in redesigning the forms of scripture and worship. But if history is any guide, it can be predicted that whatever simplifications are achieved, they will only set the stage for a new dynamic of growth and complexity, leading in time to further demands for simplification.

Diffusion

When, in the early twentieth century, American anthropologists turned their backs on evolutionary theory, they decided instead that religions grow mostly through processes of diffusion; that is, through borrowing elements from one another. The anthropologists found plenty of ethnographic evidence to back them up; especially among North American Indians, where religious traits were widely shared among peoples of otherwise diverse language and culture. The growth of religion was thus seen not as an orderly process but as a more or less accidental one—the result of historical contacts between peoples that could not have been predicted. This paradigm of explanation has in turn gone out of fashion in recent generations, and yet the ethnographic evidence remains substantial.

We have only to look at the present-day distribution of religious traits, from just about any part of the world, to recognize how much of each people's religion has been borrowed from the neighbors. In the American Southwest, to take one example, there are Indian tribes speaking six wholly unrelated languages, which must mean that they came originally from different areas, and probably settled in the Southwest at different times. Yet there are a great many broad similarities of religious thought and practice among all of them, which can only have come about through borrowing from one another. We can also notice, latterly, how many elements can be attributed to the influence of Catholic missionaries.

The Navajo case is particularly instructive. The *Diné* came into the Southwest probably not more than seven centuries ago, from somewhere in the far northwest of North America. Yet very little of their present-day religion can be attributed to that northern origin; most of their very rich body of belief and practice is shared in common with the Pueblo Indian neighbors who were already established in the Southwest when the Navajos arrived. I think this extensive borrowing reflects a very widespread idea about the deities, especially among tribal and peasant peoples: the belief that they are locally rooted. The Navajos therefore presumably believed that, when in a new region, it behooved them to deal with the deities that held sway in that region.

There is an obvious explanation for all religious borrowing. Most peoples, outside the Abrahamic faiths, are well aware that their religions are incomplete and imperfect systems of knowledge and control, as is demonstrated by the fact that they are insufficient to prevent droughts, floods, and all the other disasters visited on mankind by the gods. Unless people are deterred by an entrenched and self-interested priesthood, therefore, they are inclined to try anything new that shows a chance of working. In particular, there is always a hope that the gods and rituals that work for other peoples will work for them also. Within the compass of polytheistic religion, there is always room for new gods

Borrowing can take place in any circumstance where there is active contact between two peoples. It is probably facilitated when there is extensive intermarriage between the peoples, as was true in the Navajo and Pueblo case. But I think borrowing is most likely to occur when there is an asymmetrical relationship; when one people is seen to be more powerful or more prosperous than another. Their success is very likely to be attributed to superior gods, and superior techniques for dealing with them. The underprivileged neighbors will then be anxious to acquire the same gods and the same techniques. This too was true to some extent in the Navajo and Pueblo case. Navajos to this day attribute superior supernatural knowledge and abilities to their Hopi and Zuni neighbors.

The extensive adoption both of Christianity and of Islam, among tribal peoples in the modern world, is clear evidence of borrowing under relationships of asymmetry. The common claim of anthropologists, that the Abrahamic faiths have been forced upon the reluctant natives through the coercion of missionaries, is at best partly true in the case of Christianity, and is hardly true at all in the case of Islam, at least in recent centuries. The colonized peoples have simply observed the vastly superior control over all aspects of nature that is enjoyed by their colonizers, and have sought to obtain the same power for themselves. This process is clearly going on today among the Navajos, as I suggested at the end of Chapter 2. The process of voluntary change was referred to by an earlier generation of anthropologists as acculturative, though the term is now somewhat out of fashion.

Syncretism

All cases of religious borrowing represent syncretism to a degree. At times however so much combination takes place, along with a certain amount of innovation, that an entirely new religion results.

Among the most conspicuous examples of syncretic religion are the various nativistic movements discussed in the last chapter. Most are at the same time messianic; that is, they have been consciously originated by one or a few individuals, usually claiming some kind of divine revelation. They have arisen most often under political relationships of asymmetry, when a weaker people has borrowed religious elements from a stronger one, and blended them with older traditions of their own, in the attempt to improve their position in a changing world. Although most nativistic movements have been short-lived, the Peyote Religion and the Handsome Lake religion among North American Indians are two syncretic religions that have survived and prospered.

Not all syncretic religions have arisen under conditions of oppression. The thoroughly syncretic Sikh Religion of India seems to have resulted simply from prolonged and intense culture contact.

Stylistic change

It is common wisdom that every cultural act and every cultural product has a form and a function, or in other words a shape and a purpose. Less commonly recognized is the fact that just about every act and artifact has also a certain component of style. What I mean is that there are usually two or three or more equally effective ways of doing or making anything, with reference to its purpose, but we do or make them in only one or a few of the possible ways, in preference to the others. Our choice is wholly arbitrary, and is dictated by culture. Often we put it down to aesthetics: we like the way one thing looks better than another, though we can give no rational explanation why. We just say 'it's the American way,' as Navajos say 'it's the Navajo way.' 'There's no accounting for taste,' as the old saying has it.

Style, then, stands in a negative relationship to function: it is that aspect of any act or object that cannot be related to a purpose. The combination of function and style together is what determines the form of any act or product.

For all its lack of a rational basis, stylistic preference has an important functional role in our lives, in a cognitive sense. It saves us from a great deal of arbitrary decision-making, in circumstances where there is no clear choice between alternatives. When meeting someone we don't have to stop and think, 'should I extend my right or my left hand?' When we sit down at table we don't have to wonder, 'should I hold the fork in my right or left hand?' When going out on the street we don't have to wonder, 'should I wear a suit or a bathing suit?' It is style that helps reduce the possibilities in our world to a manageable number.

But style at the same time has an extraordinary, and largely unexplained, feature: it is always changing. It does so in response to one of the most basic characteristics of human mentality, and one that is wholly ignored in rationalistic theory: the fact that in time we grow tired of everything. When we first tasted a new dish, we thought it delicious; after a steady diet we could not face it again. When we first heard a new tune we greatly enjoyed it; after the 500th playing we wanted to hold our ears. And when we grow tired of something, we change it, or search for something else. So strong is the impulse to change that if we can't make a thing better, in a purely functional sense, we'll not infrequently make it worse.

Functional change takes place, of course, along with stylistic change, when we find a better or more efficient way of making or doing things. But functional change is related to the goal of practical efficiency, and is therefore to a considerable extent predictable. Stylistic change on the other hand is not change *toward* something but change *away* from something. Thus while the fact that change will take place is predictable, the direction it will take is usually not.

The compelling power of stylistic change should not be underestimated, for at times it can override even functional efficiency. Fashions in dress provide the most obvious example: they are very often uncomfortable, inconvenient, and at times physically damaging. American automobiles, also, have gone through phases when they were made more uneconomical, more uncomfortable, and more dangerous than before, in the interest of stylistic change. I would say as a general rule about almost anything that, if we can't make it better, we'll make it worse, but one way or another we *will* change it. If we are using the perfect table knife today, in fifty years' time we will be using a less than perfect knife.

To the limited extent that the direction of stylistic change is predictable, it is generally because of limited alternatives. The hemlines of women's dresses provide an amusing example, as was demonstrated by Richardson and Kroeber (1940). There is an obvious practical limit to how far they can go either up or down, and so they keep moving back and forth between the two. It is because of similar considerations that we find a good many pendulum-swings in stylistic change.

There are styles in religion as in everything else. Indeed they are a critical necessity, given the otherwise endless possibilities for belief and performance. Style is most immediately obvious in religious art and iconography, but we can also find elements of style in the choice of words in prayer and in scripture, in the order in which ritual acts are performed, in the choice of things to be offered, and even in the choice of deities to be propitiated. And insofar as there is style in religion, it like everything else in culture has been changing, and will continue to do so. The vast changes in the forms of worship, from the earliest Christian communities to the Catholic masses of today, are more attributable to stylistic change than to any other factor.

Religious conversion

All the processes of change that I have discussed heretofore are, in the broadest sense, collective changes, affecting all the votaries of a religion at once. The religion of individual votaries changed when and as the religion of their communities changed. But we cannot wholly ignore change at the individual level, when persons opt for a new set of religious beliefs on their own initiative.

The phenomenon of individual religious conversion, as we observe it in our times, was pretty much unthinkable in the days before exclusivist religion. People could and did turn their attention to new deities, through new forms of worship, when for example they moved to a new region, or were conquered by outsiders having a religion different from their own. But they were not compelled to give up anything in the process; they could and did simply add to the existing pantheon. Sooner or later they might give up the worship of older tutelaries, as having no longer any practical benefit, but they did not disavow their existence. These changes did not involve a major redefinition of the self.

However, all of the Abrahamic religions demand conversion; that is, repudiation of older gods and older practices along with the adoption of new ones. And the acts of repudiation and conversion must essentially be personal; one cannot simply say 'all right, now I'm a Christian because my tribe is.' To the extent that the change is voluntary and not enforced, it is likely to involve a major, even drastic redefinition of the self. In effect, the convert is acknowledging that everything that he said and did up to the time of conversion was wrong.

Notwithstanding the wrenching psychological shift that may be involved, a great many individuals do undergo conversion in the modern world: from polytheistic religions to both Christianity and Islam, from one Christian sect to another, and very occasionally from Christianity to Islam or Buddhism. Usually, these acts express a strong dissatisfaction with the religion in which the convert was brought up, as for example in the case of African Americans who convert to the Nation of Islam. Such conversion may at the same time reflect a strong dissatisfaction with an earlier self. Occasionally however it may only respond to the superior appeal of a religion that has been newly made available.

All these factors were probably involved in the very rapid and wide spread of Christianity in the late Roman Empire, which came about through successive individual conversions. But, as the historical evidence shows, when enough individual conversions took place, the stage was set for a mass religious change.

The future of religion

Early evolutionary theorists were pretty much united in their linear view of religious evolution, beginning with animism and ending with monotheism. Most however avoided the issue of where we go from here. Those who were religious probably assumed that monotheistic religion, as the loftiest achievement of human thought, would endure from now on, while those who were not religious (like Marx and Freud) assumed, and hoped, that the next logical step after one god is no god. But viewing the course of religious evolution as I have done in this and the last chapter, it becomes clear that the development has by no means been strictly linear. Consequently we are in no position to predict, simply on trajectory grounds, either that 'monotheistic' religion will persist in its present state, or that it will disappear.

I think the single conclusion we can most safely draw from the history of religion is that, since it has always been with us, it probably always will be, in one form or another. It is not, as Marx and Freud insisted, something that the maturing human mind will outgrow, unless that mind should reach a point where it can dispense altogether with moral authority, relying instead on science or on wholly personal judgment. But neither of those can speak of right and wrong with the voice of absolute authority that most people require some of the time, and that some people require all of the time.

The most extreme rationalists of the Enlightenment hoped that in time the mantle of moral authority would pass from religion to pure reason. Robespierre, the French revolutionary, is said to have remarked that in post-revolutionary France the only statue allowed would be that of Reason enthroned. It was in rebuttal of that conception that Immanuel Kant published his famous and influential *Critique of Pure Reason* (1860; orig. 1781). Quite apart from Kant's philosophical objections, however, the difficulty with pure reason is that it is too reasonable, and as such is the antithesis of faith. The mystical mind requires something in which it can place total faith without having to reason.

In the modern, secularizing world, the nation-state has attempted to assume the cloak of moral authority once worn exclusively by religion. This was the fondest hope of Emile Durkheim, who worked for years with the French educational establishment in an effort to devise curricula that would inculcate a purely secular faith. Today however we are in a time of declining faith in the authority of the state. We have seen it make too many mistakes, commit too many outrages, and we are a less law-abiding and civic-minded people than we once were. Moreover faith in the state was never strong in most other parts of the world. I see no reason to suppose therefore that secular authority is ever going to supplant religious authority in any moral sense.

I am sure also that the mystical mind and the creative imagination will always be part of the inborn human makeup. As long as that is so they will seek for, and if necessary create, religion, to provide them with the stimulation and the satisfaction that they can not sufficiently derive from the world of everyday experience and of reason.

At the same time, as I have said, we cannot make linear projections about the future of religion, because there has been no clearcut trajectory of development from cave-man times to the present. From the time of bands to that of the earliest states there was indeed a process of incremental growth and power, reaching an apogee in the great early theocracies. From then on, for a while, it was a story of decline and ultimate repudiation. The power and influence of religion was eroded by secularization of government and of thought in the secondary states, and the beliefs and practices carried over from earlier times came to seem more and more archaic and out of step with the times. Eventually most people no longer believed in them, and the time was ripe for the salvationist cults to sweep them aside.

From that point onward there was a second trajectory of growth and pomp and power, reaching its apogee in the high Middle Ages. Thereafter it has once again been downhill, as secularization of thought has destroyed much of the formerly huge cognitive role of religion, and the secularizing church has split into fragments.

Who is to say that the cycle will not be repeated a third time, or a fourth? The rise and ultimate triumph of the salvationist cults was fueled by dissatisfaction with the then existing religions, which had lost their mystical appeal and had come to seem irrelevant. There are many today who are likewise questioning the relevance of both Christianity and Islam, and are experimenting with all sorts of new cults, most of them once again highly mystical. Among these same individuals there is at the same time a professed lack of faith in secular science; even antagonism to it. If this trend escalates, it may be that we are witnessing the beginning of a new Age of Faith. For the time being I don't think dissatisfaction with the status quo is nearly general enough so that the ground is ready for a revolutionary new religion or religions. I only suggest that, since it has happened before, it is one of the possibilities in the future history of religion.

If new religions should arise and triumph, I would predict three things about them. First, they will be proclaimed by messiahs, for the messianic tradition is so deeply rooted in all the Abrahamic religions that I don't think it will ever disappear. Second, as long as they are proclaimed by messiahs, they must eventually develop a scriptural canon, so that the teachings of the messiah can be preserved, hopefully for eternity, in textual form. Third, although probably not highly ritualistic in the beginning, they will become increasingly so with the passage of time; especially if and when they acquire a church.

I don't think it's inevitable, however, that new religions will be salvationist in the usual eschatological sense. They may instead be utopian, offering a vision of salvation in the present world, but at a future time, as for example Marxism (a religion in many ways) attempted to do. And I think that, like Marxism, they may attempt to compromise with science (or even co-opt it) by incorporating then-current scientific theories as dogma.

The future of the churches is a somewhat different matter from the future of religion in general. As I have suggested before, it is not necessary for every religion to have a church, as we understand it; most tribal religions do not. But it is necessary for religions in an urban and differentiated setting to have an organized church, in order to hold the votaries together in the face of competing possibilities. I would predict therefore that, whatever religion prevails in the future, it will inevitably develop a church or churches, even if it does not have one to begin with. And with a church, it will also have to have some kind of a priesthood.

Whatever religion develops in the future, it must, like all religions up to now, address itself to the reduction of whatever is uncertain in the human condition at that time.

16

THE GROWTH OF INDIVIDUAL RELIGION

I dealt in the last two chapters with religious development and change at the level of whole societies. But religion rests intimately in the minds of each individual, and it remains to consider here how religious consciousness develops in those individual minds. I use the term 'religious consciousness' rather than 'religion' to underscore the fact that I am concerned here almost exclusively with the cognitive domain. As I will suggest, that domain has at its foundation a large component of intuitive belief that is basically rational rather than mystical, and which may be called proto-religion. On the other hand there is little or nothing in the domain of religious action (ritual) that can be attributed to instinct.

I have said that the religion of every person represents an effort to understand the experienced world. It follows that, as the experienced world of no two persons is ever quite the same, so also the religion of no two persons is ever quite the same. Likewise, as the experienced world of each person changes over time, so also that person's religion changes over time. Some people, on the strength of increased information or personal experiences, become markedly more religious, and some less so, but in any case perception changes.

The quest for information

Perhaps the most distinctive quality of the human mind, in contrast to that of animals, is its hunger for information. It is a strongly felt need, without which we feel helpless in confronting the world around us. It is most conspicuous in young children, who from the moment they can talk bombard us with questions, as they seek to understand their experienced world: 'who,' 'what,' 'when,' but above all, 'why?' That is the question that we parents always find most difficult to answer, because so much of the time we ourselves are not sure. And it is, quite simply, the main reason why we have both religion and science.

One of the things that all parents soon discover is that, within the limited compass of their understanding, the logic of their children is in-controvertible. They know very little of the world, but explanations that are given to them must conform to those parts of it that they do know. As that knowledge increases, through experience or instruction, the children are able to accept more and more complex explanations, but they cannot be contrary to observed reality.

Most theory in developmental psychology rests on the assumption that there are recognizable stages in the development of human reasoning power, as the individual progresses from early infancy to childhood to adolescence to adulthood. These stages are assumed by many theorists to be innate or pre-programmed; most or all individuals in all cultures pass through them, usually in the same order. This theory is supported by a great deal of experimental evidence, and I am in no position to question it. I want only to suggest here that, irrespective of developmental stages, reasoning power develops as a consequence of the amount and the kinds of information that must be processed. The difference between the child mind and the adult mind, I suspect, is less a difference in reasoning power than it is a difference in the amount of information possessed. New ways of reasoning are developed when and as they are needed to process more and more complex information. Without added information, more sophisticated reasoning will not be developed, regardless of the age of the individual.

This notion, which I can hardly call a theory, has specific relevance to the development of religious consciousness, as I will suggest in the pages that follow. The oft-suggested resemblance between the religious belief of young children and that found in tribal societies is a consequence not of limited reasoning power, but of limited information in both cases.

The development of religious conscious-ness

The idea that children are naturally religious, because they need some-thing to believe in, is a very old and very pervasive one. Freud and many other psychologists saw religion as an outgrowth ('projection,' in Freud's terms) of feelings toward and dependence on parents, and especially the father. However, the Swiss psychologist Jean Piaget explored the devel-opment of children's religious feelings much more fully, and much more experimentally, than did Freud or indeed almost any other developmen-tal psychologist. In the process he confirmed that children are indeed naturally religious, but not in the sense that Freud understood. In the dis-cussion that follows I will not review the theory of Piaget in detail, but will draw heavily on his work (especially Piaget 1960) in developing my own ideas. I will suggest that, just as the religion of every society is a logical adaptation to its particular environment, so also is the religion of each individual, beginning in infancy, a logical adaptation to his or her particular environment. I have to add however that I am by no means an expert in the field of developmental psychology, or even very widely read, and many of the ideas presented here are highly speculative.

The origins of infant animism

The meaningful environment of the newborn infant consists almost exclusively of fellow human beings. That is, it consists of animate, sensate beings that are possessed of a will, and are activated by it. That will, moreover, is encountered by the child very largely in the form of constraints, or compulsions, unsanctioned by reasoned argument. Parents or siblings or other kin may encourage the child to do certain things, but more of the time they are compelling him or her not to do things. The will of others is exerted in such a way as to suggest that some things are right to do, and others are wrong. In the early stages of childhood, however, there is no attempt to understand *why* things are right or wrong, beyond the fact that they are pleasing of displeasing to parents or siblings.

As the child's consciousness of his or her environment increases, among the first non-human things to become meaningful are very often animals. Their behavior shows that they are animate and activated by a will, and the child is entirely justified in ascribing to them all the same qualities found in humans. Piaget's researches found that nearly all children take it for granted that animals understand human speech, and could respond to it if they wanted to.

But the animism of the young child is not confined to animate creatures; it is all-embracing. Very early in life he or she becomes aware of inanimate things, like doors or walls that constrain him or her, and also things like sharp-cornered tables and chairs, or hot stoves, that hurt when encountered. In the light of previous experience with constraints and with hurts, what could be more logical than to assume that these inanimate things are also activated by a will? This in turn is extended to a belief that will is present in all things, as Piaget's research clearly showed. "Bad table—you hurt me!" is an expression not infrequently heard from toddlers who have bumped their heads.

The Swiss psychologist found that many and perhaps most of his young subjects had very strong and definite beliefs about the sun and the moon, as well as about meteorological phenomena. Again this is no surprise, since these are by far the most powerful and the most conspic-uous non-human forces that the average child will become aware of. Pi-aget found that most children believe that the sun and the moon follow them when they walk or travel, and therefore are keeping an eye on them. Both celestial bodies, but especially the sun, are regarded as benevolent because they give light, and heat in the case of the sun, while no ob-vious harm can be attributed to them. But there is also a marked—and wholly understandable—propensity to attribute a rather perverse will to the wind. (Indeed, in moments of exasperation I am sure many of us are still prone to this feeling.)

But if things are possessed of and activated by a will, rather than by mechanical forces, it follows that they can do as they please; there is no reason why they should behave in any predictable way. The fact that they generally do so is attributed, as it is in the case of human actors, to the fact that they are doing what they are supposed to do. Piaget found in young children the same kind of instinctive teleology that exists in Aristotelian philosophy and in so many of today's adult nature-lovers: the assumption that everything exists for a purpose.

The fact that things exist for a purpose implies that they were orig-inally created by some kind of creative will, an outlook which Piaget referred to as 'artificialism.' Yet children show no real curiosity about how things were created, or about a creator force. Most of them take it for granted that things were created by humans, until such time as they are told about a god or gods—creator forces that they are able to accept as long as they are conceived in purely human form. But children do not, apparently, conceive of a god or gods on their own, for human actions are sufficient to account for everything in their experience. They transfer their belief in causality from human to divine actors only after religious instruction, and then only to a very limited extent. '... the majority of children only bring in God against their will, as it were, and not until they can find nothing else to bring forward. The religious instruction im-parted to children between the ages of 4 and 7 often appears as something foreign to the child's natural thought ....' (Piaget 1960: 353). The psy-chologist also found that, once children were told about a god, a great many of them took it for granted that there must be many gods, just as there were many human actors causing things to happen.

The purpose of things, as perceived by Piaget's subjects, must be for the benefit of man. As the author wrote, '... the child, whose every activ-ity is linked from the cradle onward to a complementary activity on the part of his parents, must during his first years live with the impression of being perpetually surrounded by thoughts and actions directed to his well-being' (Piaget 1960: 245).

It follows, then, that the universe is fundamentally governed not by physical laws but by moral laws. Indeed the child makes no distinction between voluntary and involuntary action, presuming all action to be voluntary. But while will is present in all things, it is most of the time controlled by duty. 'Nature presents a continuum of life, such that every object possesses activity and awareness in some degree. This continuum is a network of purposive movements, more or less mutually dependent on one another and all tending toward the good of humanity' (ibid.: 233). Things that do not work to the benefit of humans are thought to be possessed of an evil will.

A caveat is clearly necessary at this point, however. Piaget's subjects were, so far as I know, well-fed Swiss and French infants, who had every reason to regard life as good. Had the psychologist worked with Arab peasant children, or a good many tribesmen, I am sure that he would have found the same universal animism and teleology, but much less tendency to explain things in terms of benevolent nature.

Religion in later childhood

Piaget found that the instinctive animism of young children began to decline around the age of five or six, although it persisted much longer and much more strongly in some than in others. Several factors can be invoked to account for the decline, but all of them in one way or another involve an increase in the child's information. There is, first of all, a realization that things that cannot move cannot really act, and therefore probably are not sentient. A little later, perhaps, comes the consciousness of life and death, and the recognition that inanimate things are not alive because they are not born and do not die. Thereafter, they are no longer credited with a will, and animistic belief is confined the realm of animals and plants.

Another important factor noted by Piaget is the growth of self-awareness in the individual, which leads to an awareness of personality in other humans as well, but not in things. '... as the child becomes clearly aware of personality in himself he refuses to allow a personality to things. According as he realizes his own subjective activity and its inexhaustible scope he refuses to allow self-consciousness to things' (Piaget 1960: 239). Along with that self-awareness comes a consciousness of human frailty in others as well as himself or herself, and therefore a disinclination to attribute things to a human creator. It is at this point that a logical space is created, so to speak, for the existence of a creator god or gods. '... he transfers to God, of whom he learns in his religious instruction, the qualities which he learns to deny to men' (ibid.: 268). At this point, then, the child may become at least provisionally a true believer in a divinity, rather than merely repeating what he or she has been told.

At the same time, however, there is a decreasing inclination to attribute everything to an act of deliberate creation, and also less inclination to believe that things exist for the benefit of humanity. These tendencies Piaget saw as a consequence of the diminishing egocentrism of the developing child. In place of a willed creator, either human or divine, children begin to develop what Piaget called 'myths of generation,' in which things are attributed to the action of other things. 'The sun is the offspring of the clouds, the lightning and the stars are produced by the sun, the wind has collected together to form a cloud, etc' (ibid.: 387).

It seems clear, then, that at the same time when the child may be experiencing the beginnings of genuinely deistic belief, he or she is also exhibiting the beginnings of what we may call pre-scientific thought; that is, explaining things without reference to the action of a will. Perhaps what is occurring, at this point, is the beginnings of that compartmentalization of religious and scientific thought, that becomes so conspicuous among Europeans and Americans in later life. The child may come genuinely to believe in gods, but at the same time is less inclined to attribute to them things that can be explained in other ways.

To Piaget's list of contributing factors, then, I would certainly add the growth of scientific knowledge and technical mastery. By the time the child is 6 or 7 or 8 he or she has been making various things with his/her own hands, and also causing things to happen, not so much to people as to inanimate things. From those experiences there grows a realization that many things react in absolutely predictable ways when manipulated by humans, and with it comes a sense of command over inanimate things. It becomes increasingly difficult to believe that such things have a will of their own, when they respond so predictably and so unresistingly to the will of the child. They therefore lie outside the domain of religion, which always addresses itself to those things that are not under total human control.

The spontaneous animism of the young child, so convincingly demonstrated by Piaget, satisfies my definition of religion, both in its teleology 'and in its belief exclusively in willed forces. Yet it is at best a proto-religion, for it is a system of belief only. It has no ritual dimension, no so-cietal dimension, and little if any affective dimension. Children certainly address themselves to inanimate things, mostly in the form of reproof ('bad stove—you burned me!'), but it is clear that they do not expect any response.

Paradoxically, the child's proto-religion seems to be located almost exclusively in the rational, not the mystical mind. Piaget found virtu-ally no trace of mysticism in the thinking of his youthful subjects. Their animism, their 'artificialism' and their teleology were all perfectly log-ical deductions from the world of their experience. Even the 'myths of generation,' which children invented to explain the origins of the stars or the weather, were logical ways of explaining observed phenomena, within the limited compass of the child's understanding. Children cer-tainly have vivid imaginations, and are prone to fantasize, but the great majority of them are quite aware when they are doing so, and enjoy fan-tasizing precisely because of that awareness. Few of them really believe in the creatures and events of their imagining, for the simple reason that they are contrary to the experienced world. Make-believe to them is just that.

For that reason, the religious instruction often given to children at an early age is likely to be rejected or ignored, as antithetical to their natural religion. '… the notion of God, when introduced in the early stages of education, is useless and embarrassing. Insistence on divine perfection means setting up God as a rival to the parents …' (Piaget 1960: 381, paraphrasing M. Bovet). The researches of Piaget and Bovet showed that children could accept God, or just as often a plurality of gods, only in the character of ordinary persons.

It is clear, then, that the proto-religion of young children is a reli-gion without a supernatural. While some children are genuinely able to believe in a god or gods by about age 7, these beings are essentially su-permen, not immortals. They are endowed with the same degree of om-niscience and omnipotence formerly attributed to a father or other living male, but are not credited with truly supernatural powers such as caus-ing the weather. Moreover, although the child respondents of Piaget and Bovet could not see the gods themselves, they took it for granted that those beings dwelled somewhere else on earth, where others could see them.

At what point in the individual's development, then, does it become possible to conceive of a genuine supernatural? I think it must be when he
or she becomes fully aware of the limitations both of man and of nature.
That is, when observed natural phenomena can no longer be credited to
the action either of human agents or of known natural forces, and must
be attributed to something at once more powerful and less predictable. It
then becomes possible, and perhaps even necessary, to think of a causal
force or power 'out there' or 'up there,' beyond the realm of the physically knowable.

It is at this point that, in theory, the mystical mind should begin to
find scope. When experience forces one to believe in the existence of
something unseen, and something more powerful than anything directly
experienced, it becomes a cognitive necessity to invest that something
first of all with a name, and then with a shape and other characteristics
by which it may be understood. Those qualities may, but need not necessarily, be an enlargement of the qualities previously observed in living
things. Imagination, or experience in the form of visions or dreams, may
endow them with all kinds of shapes and powers not seen in the everyday
world. But the one thing that the unseen Powers always have in common
with previously conceived human powers is the possession of a will, for
that is what makes them Powers.

Once they are conceived, the extent of power attributed to the unseen
beings is proportionate to the amount that cannot be explained in other
ways; i.e. by attribution to human agents or natural forces. Here, then,
the mystical mind may come into full play, and at the same time begin
to part company from the rational mind. When this happens, empirical
knowledge and religious belief will develop largely along separate lines,
although most individuals in most societies will not be conscious of this,
for the mystical and the rational minds continually interact.

This does not mean that, for the adolescent, religion decreases as secular knowledge increases. In the expanding world of the adolescent, more
and more things are found to be susceptible to purely natural explanation,
but at the same time more and more things are encountered that are not.
For many individuals, therefore, I suspect that religious belief and secular, including scientific, knowledge increase at the same time, as parts of
the individual's overall attempt to understand a rapidly expanding world.
The scientific and the mystical mind are both growing through the input
of information.

It is true that certain domains of understanding are transferred, as it were, from the realm of the mystical to that of the practical. That is, things that were logically incomprehensible, and therefore attributed to the action of a deity, come to be understood in terms of natural and predictable causes, and are no longer encompassed within the realm of mythology. This is likely to be true of animal behavior, for youngsters living in more advanced societies, and even of the weather, for those living in modern industrial societies. Yet for the adolescent the number of things that can not be rationally understood may still continue to increase, and to provide ample scope not only for the existence but for the growth of religious consciousness.

And yet, despite the possibility and even perhaps the necessity of believing in supernatural gods, I see very little evidence of true mysticism in the thinking of adolescents. I have the impression that the majority of them are too self-preoccupied to be much interested in the larger issues of existence. In other words, I suggest, the egocentrism so conspicuous both in the child and in the adolescent is at the very least a hindrance to the development of the mystical mind. Of course there are the well-known adolescent visionaries, like Joan of Arc and Bernadette Soubirous, but I think they are the proverbial exceptions that prove the rule: they claim our attention and admiration precisely because they are so unlike other adolescents. Had Joan of Arc been a woman in her 30s, she would most probably have been dismissed as just another crackpot.

In sum, I am convinced that the mystical mind exists, at least as a latent potential, from birth onward, but also that it finds little play in the earlier years of childhood. Perhaps coming to grips with the world of immediate experience provides mystery enough to satisfy any mystical inclinations. Truly reflective mysticism, I have to conclude, is a quality most developed in reflective minds, and therefore most developed in the more reflective years. It is not at all, as some rationalists have insisted, an evidence of child-like thinking, but rather the reverse. Some mythology can, it is true, be likened to the flights of a child's imagination, insofar as both are a kind of escape literature. But the deepest religious beliefs of grownups represent a sincere attempt to understand the world, not to escape from it.

*Religious in-
doctrination
and the
adolescent*

The development of a general theory of religious consciousness , for persons above the age of 10, becomes increasingly difficult, because from this time onward both religious consciousness and secular knowledge are acquired very largely through instruction, rather than through spontaneous experience of the world. And this is something that varies enormously from individual to individual, and even more importantly from society to society. Any understanding of the growth, or the decline, of religious consciousness in the adolescent and adult can only be relative to specific cultural and social conditions.

For most youngsters in most societies, the ages from 6 to 16 are the time when the largest part of culture is acquired through formal and informal instruction, or indoctrination as we would say in the case of religion. The Navajo child hears the myths recited by elders on long winter nights, and also, after a rite of initiation into ritual life, receives more formal and detailed instruction. The Arab village child attends the *khalwa,* but also is told of the miracles and powers of the village saint. In one way or another, the world of the older child and the adolescent is dominated by instructors and instruction, and they are the principal forces and the principal experiences to which the youngster reacts. Which of us, in thinking about those years, associates them primarily with anything other than school?

A certain amount of what has been taught is confirmed by personal experience, and to that extent is internalized. The boy who prays to St. Agnes for a new toy and later receives it finds empirical confirmation for the existence of St. Agnes; the Navajo girl when she begins to menstruate finds that what she has been told about Changing Woman is true. But there is a great deal more than cannot be confirmed through personal experience, and is accepted—to the extent that it is—simply on the strength of parental or societal authority. The same is of course true of nearly all the scientific truth that is taught to children and adolescents. That which seems to be directly disconfirmed by experience is likely to be rejected by the majority of youngsters, in the case of both religion and science.

As I have suggested earlier, on the authority of Piaget and Bovet, the earliest religious instruction that is given to the very young children is likely to be rejected, because their minds are not prepared for doublethink. Later it may be accepted on the strength of parental or societal authority, but I think for most teenagers the acceptance of religious doctrine is initially provisional rather than unquestioning. Later, it may become internalized through habituation, to the extent that it has not been disconfirmed by personal experience.

The animism of the young child will probably be retained by the adolescent only to the extent that it is part of the religion taught and practiced by the adults in his or her society. This will be true to a considerable extent in tribal societies; less so in more complex societies. Artificialism—the notion that everything was originally created—persists longer, and is likely to be retained by the adolescent insofar as it is a feature of most religions. Teleology—the notion that everything exists for a purpose—is a feature of all religions, but is just as pervasive in scientific thinking. In my view it is an inherent and inescapable feature of all human thinking.

The religion of adolescents, I would conclude, resides partly in the rational and partly in the mystical mind, but above all in the accepting mind. That part which is accepted on the basis of parental or societal authority might be said to reside in the rational mind, insofar as the individual has found it expedient to believe what he or she has been told. At the same time it resides in the mystical mind to the extent that it involves a genuine belief in a supernatural. It certainly does not however reside in a reflective mind, either rational or mystical, for obvious reasons having to do with self-preoccupation. In other words, the religion of most adolescents has not really been internalized

I certainly do not want to suggest that adolescents are unquestioning, for all parents and all teachers know better. But as the ideas they are taught, both religious and secular, rest mainly on the authority of the teachers rather than the demonstrable strength of the ideas themselves, so also it is the authority of the teachers rather than the ideas that they are apt to question. This is a perfectly understandable reaction to a world that is basically teacher-dominated rather than idea-dominated.

*The religion
of adults*

The religion of adults exhibits far too much variability, from individual to individual and from society to society, to permit very much in the way of generalization. We may note that people in every society retire from various kinds of activities at different points in their lives, because the activities become too difficult, because they no longer repay the effort, or because they cause trouble, and this is true of reflective thinking as well as of different physical activities. The religious consciousness of any person who has so retired will retain as much or as little of mysticism and of rationalism as it had reached at the time of retirement.

There are many persons in every society for whom neither the rational nor the mystical mind becomes very much developed; for those persons religion remains lodged all their lives in the accepting mind. Others, particularly in the industrial West, become more scientifically educated and more scientifically-minded in adult life, and for them the extent of religious belief is likely to decrease, or even vanish. But there are certainly other reflective thinkers for whom science fails to answer the fundamental questions that really interest them, or who find that science does not provide the guidance that they need in their personal circumstances. Those persons may become more rather than less religious as they seek for understanding. Persons who suffer some kind of personal trauma will often, in Western society, become more religious because science seems to have failed them. I have the impression that in Navajo society it is rather the reverse; people become less religious because religion has failed them. There are also those like Isaac Newton who may become both more scientific-minded and more religious; they manage through compartmentalized thinking to develop the rational and the mystical minds simultaneously. But I think in any case that the religious consciousness of reflective persons seldom remains static. Like all culture, it has to adapt itself to changing circumstances, both societal and personal.

Far more than in the case of children or adolescents, adults vary both in the quantity and in the intensity of their religious beliefs. For that vast majority of votaries who do not receive direct revelations, the amount of personal religion can only be a measure of how much they have absorbed, through the teaching of others or through personal study. That in turn may be a reflection partly of the desire to learn, but just as importantly of the opportunity to learn.

Intensity of belief however is much more a measure of the development of the mystical mind. Quantity and intensity are not necessarily correlated; the most intensely devout persons are not always very learned, or vice versa. It is easier to be deeply committed to a few fairly simple tenets than to a mass of complex and sometimes conflicting tradition.

Societies no less than individuals vary both in the quantity and in the intensity of their religiosity. These will not always be determining factors as far as the individual is concerned: some people in every society are far more deeply religious than the mass of their fellows, and some less so. Still, the religious mind of no individual can be fully understood without reference to the canons of his or her society.

As I suggested in the last chapter, the evolution of religion in societies, from prehistoric to modern times, has sometimes been compared to the development of religious consciousness in the individual, from infancy to adulthood. This idea was very popular among the rationalistic and mostly atheistic social philosophers of the eighteenth and nineteenth centuries, who saw in religion a persistence of childlike thinking, which dimin-

*Ontogeny
recapitulates
phylogeny?*

ished over time. According to their view, the animism of the most primitive tribal religions corresponds to the animism of the youngest children, while later stages in the evolution of religion can be compared to the thinking of older children and of teenagers. This theory of course bears some analogy to the biologists' old principle that 'ontogeny recapitulates phylogeny'—the evolutionary development of the individual mirrors, in microcosm, the evolution of the species.

The growth of religion in the individual and the growth of religion in societies were both seen by the early theorists as innate processes, reflective of the progressive maturation of the individual and collective mind. They were not seen as adaptations to external circumstances, most importantly including increased information and increased control over resources. At least by implication, the religions of pre-modern peoples were thought to represent various stages of arrested mental development.

As I suggested in the last chapter, I do not think this theory can be dismissed out of hand, despite its obvious lack of political correctness. Somewhere in the bathwater there is a baby of sorts, although the theorists were certainly wrong in equating religion with limited reasoning power. The important thing is to recognize that the animism of tribesmen and the animism of young children both stem from the same source: they are indicative not of inferior minds but simply of limited information and experience. I think that the animistic beliefs of grown-up Inuit, Paiute, and other tribal peoples really do represent a retention of childlike thinking; a retention because they remain the best explanations for a world in which very little is predictable, and even less is controlled. For them, nothing more compelling has come along to disprove or displace these early, intuitive beliefs. Brought up in similar circumstances, with limited technical knowledge and no scientific understanding, I am sure each of us would think in the same way.

In short, I believe there are recognizable stages in the development of thought patterns both in human individuals and in societies, but I do not believe in either case that they represent an innate maturation process, which would take place with or without continual information inputs. I see them rather as reflecting the growth of the mind as it can and must process more and more information.

While recognizing that the view of cognitive evolution espoused by some of the early theorists was both too simplistic and too rationalistic, I think it is worthwhile here to consider briefly just how far one can go with the idea that 'ontogeny recapitulates phylogeny' in the growth of religion. It is necessary to reiterate however that this theory applies to the cognitive domain of religion only, and also that I am no expert in this field.

Religious thinking in band-level societies resembles the religious consciousness of young children in a number of respects, but above all in its basic animism. Even allowing for the fact that the pervasiveness of animism among the simplest tribes was very much overestimated by armchair theorists, it is nevertheless true that there is a good deal more animism in their religions than in those of more complex societies. Another point of comparison involves the relative lack of cosmology and cosmogeny. The original creation of things is pretty much taken for granted, and no great creator deities are envisioned, although there may be culture-givers. Concepts of the more remote supernaturals are extremely vague, and they do not figure in practical religion. Religious belief and action, as in the case of children, is overwhelmingly practical and man-centered, while the lack of any development of eschatology reflects a lack of conscious concern about death. The world-view of persons in the simplest societies, like that of small children, displays an acute sense of helplessness in the face of superior powers.

Band-level societies

The religion of tribal societies can be compared to the religious consciousness of adolescents first of all because there is absolutely more of it, reflecting an increasing experience of the world. The religion is not only more complex, with more and better defined supernaturals, but also more speculative, as the mystical mind begins to come into play. Cosmology and cosmogeny reflect the adolescent's readiness to attribute things to other than human or natural causes. At the same time there is a considerable decline in animism, though it certainly does not disappear altogether. Fertility ritual, relatively little developed in band-level societies, reflects an obvious awareness of, and interest in, sex, while eschatology gives evidence of a new concern about death—both features of adolescent thinking. Finally, the much higher development of communal as opposed to individually-focused ritual reflects the much greater consciousness of group identity that is characteristic of adolescents as well as of tribal peoples.

Tribal societies

The chief evolutionary development in religion that takes place in chiefdoms and early states is the addition of a political and a hierarchical dimension. These developments can be related to some extent to the cogni-

Chiefdoms and early states

tive development of young adults. From the time when they become full participants in adult life (around the time of marriage in most societies), they are drawn into the political processes that are at work in all the more complex societies; they become unavoidably political animals. It is also at this time that they are drawn into a system of hierarchically ranked social statuses, to the extent that they begin to think of themselves first and foremost in status terms. These developments are reflected in their increasingly politicized and hierarchical view of the supernatural.

I suppose that at this point we may say that religion has reached 'adulthood,' and this is as far as the ontogeny analogy can be pushed. The evolution of religion may still have a long way to travel at this point, as I suggested in Chapter 14, just as development of religious thinking in adult individuals may also have a long way to travel, in the years following young adulthood. But in both cases the path traveled—or sometimes not traveled—is far too variable to permit of broad cross-cultural generalizations.

Limitations There are many and obvious limitations to the analogy between individual religious development and the evolution of religion in societies. First of all, it applies to the cognitive domain only, and only to a part of that. The religious cognition of children is almost wholly rational, within the compass of their understanding; it includes little if any mysticism. On the other hand even the simplest of religions have some degree of mysticism, although it is not highly developed in the case of band-level societies.

A fundamental mistake of some of the early atheistic thinkers, notably Freud, was the assumption that mysticism in religion represents a survival of child-like thinking. In fact the opposite is true, as was clearly shown by Piaget. To the extent that mysticism is present in the simplest religions, it is evidence not of childish but of adult thinking. It is not only much more conspicuous in the thinking of adults than of children, but also more conspicuous in the religions of complex societies than of simpler ones.

Probably related to the lack of mysticism is the fact that the religious cognition of children has almost no symbolic content. On the other hand, all religions are rich in non-verbal symbolism.

Most importantly, though, the 'ontogeny recapitulates phylogeny' theory fails altogether to account for ritual—the behavioral dimension of religion. The proto-religion of children is a system of belief only, and has no concomitant dimension of action. But ritual is present and conspicuous in all religions, from band-level societies onward. Its development can only be understood in terms of social, not of psychological processes, and as such has been considered in Chapter 14.

I conclude that, for both individuals and societies, religion has its founda-
tions in the rational mind, as a logical reaction to the experienced world.
With the passage of time it claims more and more of the mystical mind
as well, but still retains a considerable amount of rational content. As individuals and societies acquire further experience and further control of
the world, however, the rational mind is increasingly surrendered to science, and religion becomes proportionately more mystical. This does not
at all mean that the intensity of religion will decline, however; only that
its domain becomes restricted. But for many individuals in every society
there are still vast areas of experience that are better understood through
religion than through science.

Conclusion

17

RELIGIONS IN PRACTICE

I have argued in another place that, at least for me, all scientific understanding proceeds through a continual feedback between data and theory, but beginning always with the data; that is, with empirical experience (Adams and Adams 1991). Certainly this has been true in regard to my attempts to understand religion, and it is the approach that I have followed in this book. I began at the level of ethnography, and moved up from there to the level of theory, or indeed philosophy. I took Navajo religion and Arab village religion, and to a lesser extent several others, as starting points for trying to understand all religions, since to me as a disinterested outsider they are all equally in need of understanding. I have therefore been talking, throughout all these later chapters, about religion in the abstract—about religion rather than religions—since that is the level of understanding that I have sought.

It is not, however, the level on which I wish to end my book. As an anthropologist I do not, like the philosopher, seek for abstract understandings for their own sake. I seek them in order to better comprehend the world of experienced human behavior and belief, which is the end point as well as the beginning point of my interest. It remains therefore to come back in this penultimate chapter to the beginning point—the real world—and to consider how my generalized understandings play out in real life situations.

From the generic to the specific

In almost any field of human thought, the relationship between the generic and the specific is descriptive, not prescriptive. The vast majority of the words we employ are abstractions to a greater or lesser degree, derived from the observation of a multiplicity of concrete cases. Each word serves as a categorical label which makes it possible to talk about things without being endlessly, excruciatingly detailed. Yet we realize, or at least should, that the abstractions we employ exist in our minds rather than on the ground. In the case of biology, neither a genus nor a species exists as a tangible reality; there are only individual creatures that we can actually see and touch. The continual formulations and revisions of scientific definition do not in any way determine or alter the nature of the actual beasts.

This is obviously true in the case of religion—surely one of the most abstract concepts in our vocabulary. We have to recognize that, empirically speaking, there is no such thing as 'religion,' there are only religions. And our understanding of religion in the abstract provides, at best, a necessary but not a sufficient basis for understanding each of the individual exemplars.

What is lacking, as I have suggested several times before, is any specification of content. It has been possible, in the preceding chapters, to define and to explain religion in the abstract with almost no reference to specific content, yet the definition and the understanding of any actual religion can hardly begin or end with anything else. Knowing a particular religion is not achieved through abstract reasoning; it is achieved through empirical discovery.

We thus encounter, at the level of practical reality, a wholly new problem of definition. When we talk about religion in the generic sense we recognize that we are employing a heuristic abstraction; there is no such thing out there to be studied. But what about Navajo religion or Arab religion or Christianity—can they actually be studied on the ground, or are they also mere heuristic abstractions derived form a diversity of beliefs and practices on the part of different individuals? What we have to confront at this point is the problem of essentialism.

The problem of essentialism

Nearly all believers are convinced that there is an ideal or a proper form of their religion—a True Faith, if you will—no matter how imperfectly they as individuals may understand or practice it. But the assumption that there is a basic or essential form of each religion is not confined to the votaries; it is found just as commonly in the thought and the writing of unbelievers. If we consider the various definitions of religion that were reviewed in Chapter 8, we will find that a great many of them are essentialist; in particular those that refer to religion as a 'system.' The anthropologist—who is virtually always an unbeliever with respect to the tribal or folk religion that he or she is studying in the field—speaks unhesitatingly about Navajo religion or Nuer religion, rather than merely detailing the thoughts and actions of individual Navajos or Nuers.

An analogy with language—another cultural domain—may be useful at this point, for I think it is one that most anthropologists consciously or unconsciously make. Nearly all our linguistic theory involves the assumption that there is, somewhere in the unconscious minds of all the speakers in any speech community, a common code of rules and practices that they all share, though no individual speaker knows all of them. The point is not that anyone knows all of them, but that individuals are in agreement as regards the rules and usages that they do know. The great linguist Ferdinand de Saussure formulated the distinction between *langue*—the grammatical rules and vocabulary that shape all the utterances of speakers—and *parole,* their actual acts of speech (see Culler 1976: 22–29). *Langue,* in this formulation, cannot be said to exist in the mind of any one speaker, for no one knows all the rules and all the words; it exists above the level of individual thought and action.

In the case of English and many other literary languages, grammarians and lexicographers have not only presumed the existence of *langue,* but have taken it upon themselves to decide and to set down in writing what it should be. Meanwhile in our studies of unwritten languages, we take upon ourselves the role of grammarians. Operating on the apriori assumption that there is such a thing, we set out to discover, through the study of hundreds of individual speech acts, what is the *langue* of the Navajos and the Nuers. Usually, this endeavor meets the approval and encouragement of the people we study, for they no less than we accept that their language exists on a level above that of individual speakers, and they are glad to be told what its rules are. Albert Sandoval, a Navajo interpreter who in his youth had been an informant for the great linguist Edward Sapir, once told me admiringly that 'Edward Sapir taught me Navajo'—meaning that Sapir had explicated for him the rules of his own language.

Early in the last century, A. L. Kroeber applied the same principle to the understanding of culture more generally, when he referred to it as 'superorganic' (Kroeber 1917). He meant that any given culture may be said to exist as a set of codes, on a level above and apart from actual organisms—i.e. people. The concept was similar in essence to Durkheim's conception of the 'collective mind' of society, of which religion was a 'collective representation' (Durkheim 1899). It was, surprisingly, Edward Sapir himself who challenged Kroeber on this point, asking 'where is the locus of this thing called culture, if not in the minds of individuals?' Arguing from a strictly behaviorist perspective, Sapir maintained that culture could have no other locus, and therefore no other existence, except in the minds of individuals (Sapir 1917). Yet the great linguist was not wholly consistent in this view, for in the study of language he found the essentialist perspective as necessary as did Kroeber in the study of culture.

The question of whether any abstraction like language, culture, or religion can be said to 'exist,' when it has no specifiable locus, raises ontological issues that I am not able to pursue here. My provisional conclusion is that in the study of religions, no less than in the study of languages, it is necessary to think in essentialist terms, even if these is no such thing 'on the ground' as Navajo religion or Nuer religion. This is true because the votaries themselves think in those terms, and it is therefore the only way we can hope to comprehend their thoughts and actions.

And yet the core essence of any religion—the religious equivalent of *langue*—turns out to be far more difficult to elicit than is the basic grammar and lexicon of a language. Ideas about what it is are far less uniform, and in fact are continually disputed. There are, moreover, different ideas about how to discover it.

The canonical approach. Among votaries there are, I think, two basic approaches to discovering the 'true' essence of their religion, which I will call the canonical and the mystical. In the case of scriptural and revealed religions, it is possible for fundamentalists to cite a specific body of scripture and/or revelation, as defining the Only True Faith. There are nevertheless serious limitations to this approach, recognized by all but the most narrow of fundamentalists. In the first place scripture, like other mythology, is rarely clear and straightforward; it is capable of a variety of interpretations for both honest and specious reasons. In the second place, every scriptural religion includes a mass of accretions, especially in the area of ritual, that were not present in the time of its founder. They therefore have little nor no sanction in scripture, yet the adherents have come to think of them as fundamental. The Christian sacraments are examples in this category, as is the mass of detailed Islamic law not found in the Quran.

In search of the essence

The mystical approach. It is in part because of the ambiguity of scripture, and the endless wrangling over its meaning, that persons of a mystical mind are often moved to turn away from it, and to seek some kind of personal revelation as to the essence of a religion: something that speaks to them in a personal way, and moves them to feel 'Yes, this is surely ultimate truth.' I cite at this point two examples from personal experience, that have considerably influenced my thinking about the locus of religious reality.

A few years ago a favorite cousin of mine informed me that she felt strongly drawn toward Buddhism. I was surprised, for I have tended to associate Buddhism with grotesquely ornate temples and with the endlessly mechanistic Tantric rituals that I have observed in Tibet. When I asked her which of the various Buddhist sects especially appealed to her, she answered that she didn't really know very much about the sects, but the question seemed to strike her as irrelevant. Clearly in her mind there is an essential message, or ultimate truth, in Buddhism which lies above and beyond what any one individual or group actually practices.

I've encountered something very similar in corresponding with a colleague who is especially attracted to the African-American version of Islam, and who took exception to my characterization of Islam as a religion of the law. When I pointed out to him that all of my Arab friends regarded it as such, and that it was continually proclaimed as such by the *ulema,* his response in effect was that I should not judge Islam by what most Arabs said about it.

It came to me that both the Buddhism of my cousin and the Islam of my colleague are strongly tinged by the influence of American Protestantism, with its powerful anti-clerical and anti-ritual bias. Yet there are many Buddhists and many Muslims who could not imagine their religion without some kind of clergy and some kind of ritual. Who, then, is more entitled to say what is the immutable essence of Buddhism or Islam? The scripturalists would of course say, 'we are,' while the mystic would perhaps argue, 'no one is.' Scripturalism is the approach of those who think they know; mysticism is the approach of those who seek to know, but are not necessarily convinced that anyone else knows better.

The normative approach. The non-believing anthropologist, while accepting tacitly or explicitly the idea that there is such a thing as an essential form of any religion, obviously cannot accept either the canonical or the mystical approach to it. He or she can only do the same in the study of religion as in the study of any unwritten language: that is, extract the essential core of the religion from the study of innumerable sayings and doings of individuals. Any religion thus conceived is no more than, but also no less than, the sum of its parts. I will refer to this as the normative approach.

The canonical, the mystical, and the normative approaches to the definition of any given religion all have the same limitation: they are inescapably egocentric. Every theologian has his own interpretation of scripture; every mystic is seeking something different because he or she has different needs; every anthropologist talks to a different set of informants and attends a different group of ceremonies, and the different parts add up to somewhat different wholes—if they add up to anything coherent at all. But this limitation holds at the same time the key to a profound truth: that religion at the level of empirical reality is ultimately a personal matter.

To say that religion is ultimately a personal matter is not to say that it does not 'exist,' empirically, on any other level. Such an assertion would deny any legitimacy to the whole field of sociology of religion. There are, in fact, empirically discoverable regularities of thought and behavior at the level of state religion, at the level of sectarian religion, and at the level of community religion, no less than in the thoughts and actions of individuals. Consequently religions may 'exist' as discoverable realities at all these levels; and all of them exist at least at the community and the individual levels.

I have suggested several times previously that the average religion, in practice, is anything but an integrated system, despite what theorists have asserted. It is much more likely to be a congeries of disparate beliefs and practices that originated from different sources and at different times. The various beliefs and practices have come together in considerable part through historical accidents, and have thereafter been retained because in one way or another they were found to serve the needs of the votaries. Nevertheless, selected parts of the total panoply of belief and practice have been brought together in such a way as to serve the needs of individuals, and others to serve the needs of groups, so that they form something which appears to the votaries as a coherent system. It is here, then, that we can begin to speak of a degree of integration in religion, while recognizing at the same time that it is integrated in different ways at the individual and at the group level.

We have to recall that religion—any religion—is not just a cultural phenomenon; it must be understood as a sociocultural phenomenon. It is useful to introduce here Julian Steward's concept of Levels of Sociocultural Integration (Steward 1951). His point was that cultures can be integrated by their human carriers at various levels of organizational complexity: the 'folk' (i.e. village or tribal) level, the regional level, and the national level, for example. The smaller units are embedded in the larger ones, and yet the larger ones are not merely the sum of what is found in the smaller ones. There are aspects of national culture that do not exist at the regional or the local level; they are only discoverable by the study of the nation as a whole.

This concept is clearly applicable to the case of religion, and I think it provides at least one key for understanding the diversity and multivocality that is observable in practice in every religion. It must not only speak to several needs, but must speak on several levels, to communities of different sizes that exist for different purposes. There are at least four recurring levels of religious integration that can be recognized from this perspctive; each has different parameters, and is addressed to different needs.

State religion

So far as I know, the only modern nation that has a state religion in the old-fashioned sense (as distinguished from a state-subsidized religion) is Japan.[30] On the other hand state religion existed in all of the earliest civilizations of which we have knowledge, and in each case it provided the essential legitimation for the rule of an autocrat.

State religion in the early civilizations was not simply fashioned out of whole cloth by the rulers and their priestly minions. The rulers and priests merely co-opted many previously existing elements of local and regional tradition—by no means all of them—re-interpreted them, and added a new layer of mythology which connected the rulers to already familiar gods. The main innovations were in the domain of ritual and religious monuments, which constantly reiterated the connection between the ruler and the gods. Local communities and individuals remained free to practice their traditional cults, and indeed many and perhaps most of them took no part in state rituals.

It is clear, then, that state religion represents one level of discoverable reality, involving beliefs and practices unique to this level, and not found at the local or individual level. It is also clear that the function of religion at this level was overwhelmingly political, rather than social in a broader sense. State religion did not serve to create communities, and except in a few places it did not find expression at the community level.

---

[30] I exclude here the Islamic fundamentalist regimes in Iran and Afghanistan because Islamic scripture does not actually legitimize the institutions of government found in these countries. They claim legitimacy because they support Islam, not because it sanctions them.

All of the major world religions have split into rival sects following somewhat variant beliefs and practices. To a degree this would seem to illustrate the Durkheimian principle of segmentation: that whatever grows big enough will split into smaller units which then exist in a state of balanced opposition. What seems extraordinary in the case of religious sects, however, is that they have split so often over issues of doctrine that to an outsider seem inconsequential, or even incomprehensible. The different Shi'a sects of Islam are divided over the question of how many 'Hidden Imams' (spiritual successors to Muhammad, and commanders of the faithful) there have been. The Coptic, Syrian, and Armenian churches have split off from the remainder of Christendom over the question of whether Christ had one or two natures. Many Protestant denominations in America have split over issues of church governance, that have nothing to do with doctrine.

It is all the more extraordinary, then, that sectarian affiliation has become so strongly associated with ethnic identity, as is clearly illustrated in the case of Copts and Armenians. All of the sects are divisions of exclusivist religions, and therefore are in themselves exclusivist. They are in consequence strongly endogamous; marriage to an outsider is considered heretical. Over time, the practice of sectarian endogamy has served not only to reinforce older ethnicities, as in the case of Armenians and Copts, but actually to create new ones, as in the case of Amish, Dukhobors, and Nestorians.

Another distinctive peculiarity of religion, as we observe it at the sectarian level, is the extent of hostility between sects. Historians have often remarked how much blood has been spilled in the name of religion; I suspect that far more of it has been spilled in conflicts between sects of the same religion than between adherents of different religions. Civil wars are always the bloodiest, it is said.

The sectarian aspect of religion often plays out at the regional and local level, in the formation of residential communities as well as of congregations. There are Amish and Dukhobor regions in North America, Druze and Alawite regions in the Levant, and in the traditional Near Eastern city there were residential quarters assigned to each minority sect. And yet the fine points of doctrinal difference—the original reason for the splitting of the sects—find no expression at the local or the individual level. One can attend a Coptic mass and hear no mention of the Monophysite doctrine (Christ had only one nature, part human and part divine), and many individual Copts of my acquaintance are unaware of the doctrine. I once asked a Coptic friend to explicate a particular point of doctrine, and he replied, 'I wouldn't know; I'm not a religious man.' And yet his Coptic identity determined just about everything in his social milieu: who his friends were, what clubs he belonged to, who he married, and what schools his children attended. So it is, of course, with a great many non-practicing Jews in American society.

It seems clear then that the single most important function of religion at the sectarian level is to provide identity markers—to draw the line between 'we' and 'they.' If this is so, then sectarianism is not so much either a cognitive or a behavioral dimension of religion, as it is a purely social dimension. Many sect members are unacquainted with the doctrinal differences that set their group apart, and many take no part in the distinctive rituals of the group, yet all have the strong sense of identity that comes with it. But why sectarian affiliation—especially when based on abstruse doctrines—should have become a primary marker of self-identity, and even become a killing issue all too often, remains something of a mystery to me.

Community religion

This level of religious integration needs little discussion, since it is the focus of nearly all sociofunctional theory. It is above all at the community level that we observe religion less as a set of shared beliefs than as a system of regularly recurring collective actions, which reinforce the group's sense of solidarity. Indeed at this level the extent and even the content of an individual's belief is unimportant; what matters is participation. The weekly or seasonal rituals and rites of passage that take place in the local temple or shrine or church are unique to this level of religion. Except for a few great seasonal festivals they are not replicated at the sectarian or state level, but at the same time they are also quite different from the rituals performed by individuals when alone.

Communities and congregations provide a classic illustration of Durkheimian segmentation. They feel a need to have the same religion as their near neighbors, yet at the same time to mark a distinction that gives them an identity of their own. This may be expressed in the domain of religious architecture, where no two churches are ever exactly the same, but it is just as likely to find expression in the worship of a special patron saint or deity. Religion at the community level thus has a certain function as an identity-marker, yet it has nothing like the same compelling power as has sectarian identity. Individuals very commonly change churches or congregations within the community, often just for considerations of convenience. They very rarely 'convert' from Protestant to Catholic affiliation or vice versa, for this is looked on as a kind of apostasy.

Both fundamentalists and atheists are apt to think of the world as divided between believers and unbelievers, with no middle ground. In reality, there are all kinds and degrees of belief and unbelief, just as there are all kinds and degrees of religiosity in performance. Very few people know all of the tenets of their faith, and fewer still believe all that they do know. At the individual level, religion varies as much in quantity as it does in quality. It is here, no less that at the higher levels, that we encounter the endless diversity that makes any kind of generic definition of religion—any religion—so difficult.

As I have just suggested, religious people vary enormously in the amount that they know, which means in effect the amount that they have learned. Some have consciously sought religious knowledge; some have had it thrust upon them; some have turned their backs on it; some have for one reason or another had no opportunity to acquire it. An old Navajo told W. W. Hill, 'I have always been a poor man. I do not know a single song' (quoted in Kluckhohn and Leighton 1946: 220).

In addition, even the genuinely devout vary enormously in the amount that they are able to believe. A find that a great many Christians are able to believe in the Flood and Noah's ark; I suspect that fewer are able to believe that Lot's wife was literally turned into a pillar of salt, and probably fewer still believe that Joshua was really able to make the sun and moon stand still, to give the Israelites time to finish off the slaughter of their hapless enemies. This may be partly a matter of whether people have a rational or a mystical temperament, partly a matter of what their personal experience makes believable, and partly a matter of how anxious they are to conform to the expectations of their group. Many people make a conscious effort to believe because they want to feel a sense of commonality with what their fellows believe. I have several times heard Mormon friends say, 'We Mormons don't believe in evolution' (for example), implying that 'I don't believe in it because Mormons don't.'

The extent as well as the nature of religiosity in individuals clearly varies according to their personal need. There are, as I suggested in Chapter 12, an enormous number of different needs that may be met by religion, and no two people have all the same needs, or have them to the same extent.

Finally there is the simple question of what seems to work, which may be different for each individual. Nearly all personal religion is to some extent practical—that is, exploited to attain personal ends—and to that extent it may also be experimental. In polytheistic religions it becomes a matter of practical necessity to discover which deities can be appealed to for which purposes. Roman Catholic peasants, in times of distress, are likely to address their prayers to various saints in an effort to discover which one is responsive to them.

Plurality in individual religion

One of the byproducts of essentialism is its implication that each person has either one religion or none. This assumption runs through nearly all anthropological writing on the subject, and yet I think that both the Navajo and the Arab cases are sufficient to demonstrate that there is no reason why a person should have only one religion. If modern Americans can think of Biology and Astronomy as wholly separate sciences, each complete within its domain, I see no reason why individuals cannot hold separate religions in exactly the same way. Indeed, I am convinced that many do.

I have already suggested that the scriptural Islam and the local saint-worship of the villagers are for all practical purposes two separate religions, and the *turuq* (brotherhoods) with their esoteric mythology and rituals are in many ways still another. There can be no doubt that, in different circumstances, the villagers believe devoutly in all of them. And one could add the *zar* cult, in the case of women, and also the whole complex of beliefs and practices about the evil eye, as additional religions.

In the case of Navajos the whole field of eschatology stands quite clearly apart from the body of mythologically sanctioned religion, as indeed it does among many tribal peoples. So also does a good deal of the belief and practice associated with witchcraft, even though the Holy People (specifically First Man and First Woman) are said to have invented it. And many Navajos today have adopted some aspects of Christian worship, without turning their backs on more traditional beliefs and practices.

Among Christians, and indeed some Jews, the Santa Claus cult, so assiduously fostered among children, illustrates another kind of religious plurality. Note that children are not asked to believe in Santa Claus instead of the Christian and Jewish deities, but side by side with them, and at the same time wholly apart from them. To suggest that 'jolly old Saint Nick' is a Christian deity is regarded as a kind of blasphemy, even while he is given the name of a saint. The elaborate mortuary complex followed by so many Americans might be cited as another domain of religion which is wholly unconnected with Christian eschatological beliefs.

Probably the most clearcut example of religious plurality is found among the Pueblo Indians of New Mexico, to whom I made reference earlier. In their case however religious plurality is not a matter or individual choice; it is not only accepted but even enforced by the community as a whole.

On reflection it should come as no surprise that persons can adhere to separate and even at times conflicting religions, for there is plurality and contradiction *within* most religions as well. As I have suggested earlier, most of them require a certain amount of double-think, as in the case of a deity who is simultaneously on earth and in heaven, simultaneously alive and dead, and simultaneously his own father and his own son. Adhering to two or more separate religions simply involves double-think at a higher level.

At the level of individual belief and behavior, therefore, we have to conclude that Durkheim was absolutely wrong. The religion of most individuals is neither integrated nor a system; it is a congeries of thoughts and actions suitable to the needs and understanding of that person.

In an earlier chapter I offered two definitions:

Coda

Religion is the sum of mankind's collective efforts to understand, to exploit, and to enjoy unseen Powers, largely through techniques of communication. The religion of any given people is the sum of their efforts to understand, exploit, and enjoy the Powers in their environment.

It should be clear now that this does not exhaust the requirements of definition. It is necessary to add:

The religion of any given person is the sum of that person's efforts to understand, exploit, and enjoy the Powers in his or her environment.

And the environment, seen and unseen, is never absolutely the same for any two persons. As there is an infinite variety of religions within the overall domain that we call religion, so also there is also an infinite variety of belief and behavior syndromes within the compass of each of them individually. In that sense we would have to say that there are as many religions as there are persons in the world.

Reviewing the different levels of religious integration I have discussed, and also the different explanatory theories I have discussed, it should be

Back to theory

apparent that the political (e.g. Marxist) theory of religion is most applicable to the state level, ethnicity theory to the sectarian level, sociofunctional theory to the community level, and psychofunctional theory to the
individual level. The explanatory power of those theories, in any real-life
situation, is proportional to the extent that religion is or is not elaborated
at the level in question.

18

RELIGION, MORALITY, AND MORAL AUTHORITY

At least since the time of Socrates, philosophers as well as theologians have asserted that moral authority lies at the very heart of religion. Within the last century, most sociologists and many anthropologists have come to agree with them. It is obvious therefore that I can't conclude my book on religion without considering this most profound but at the same time most elusive of its aspects.

Yet I do so with some reluctance, for two reasons. First, the literature on the subject is vast, and I haven't read more than a tiny fraction of it. More importantly, though, I'm not prepared to consider the cosmic issues of Good and Evil that are expressed or implied in most discussions of morality and moral authority. As a comparative social scientist, I can only consider how ideas about what is right and what is wrong play out in the belief systems of behaviors of actual peoples. What acts do most people think are good, and what acts do they think are bad? To what extent do those ideas derive from religion? What I am doing, then, is the same as I have done throughout the book: taking an empirical and ethnographic approach to a subject that is more often approached philosophically. I have once again to repeat the *caveat* with which I started the book: readers are warned not to expect more than is actually here.

In approaching this discussion I have first of all to consider what is meant by morality, and also what is meant by immorality, for the two are very far from being opposite sides of the same coin. I can then consider how morality and immorality relate to moral authority, and finally, how all three of them relate to religion. To a religious fundamentalist these may be simple questions, but to a social scientist (and indeed to many modern theologians) they are very far from it.

As usual in matters connected with religion, we are confronted at the outset with a problem of definition; in fact, several of them. I will attempt to resolve or clarify them in the course of this chapter, but some kind

Some preliminary definitions

of working or provisional definitions are needed at the outset. Since we cannot get to the question of what is moral authority without first deciding what are morality and immorality, I will be concerned very largely with those things in the next pages. I have to stress that the definitions I offer do not necessarily correspond to those that will be found elsewhere in the vast literature on morality and moral authority. They are simply starting points from which to develop my own ideas, as far as they have progressed.

Theologians, and perhaps most philosophers, would argue that morality and immorality are not basic concepts, but simply corollaries of the more basic concepts of Good and Evil, which must be defined first. My approach however is necessarily that of a social scientist, not a theologian. From that relativistic perspective I will suggest that morality consists of acts (and to a lesser extent feelings) that society specially applauds, and immorality consists of acts (and occasionally feelings) that it condemns. Some qualification is necessary in both cases, but I will deal with it in later pages rather than here. I want here to stress, however, the term *specially* applauds, because I think that purely routine and conventional behavior, however approved by society, is not generally regarded as tantamount to morality. If morality is to be a meaningful concept, with reference to moral authority, it must be something above and beyond the ordinary; above and beyond mere duty.

From that point of departure, I will suggest that there are two basic, though interrelated, conceptions of morality, which for want of better terms I will call sacral and social morality. Sacral morality consists of acts pleasing to the gods (and often specifically demanded by them), whether or not they have any material benefit to society. A great many ritual performances, which are often costly in terms of time, effort, and money, fall into this category. To put it simply, sacral morality consists of the fulfillment of ritual obligations, above and beyond the required minimum. Social morality consists of acts especially beneficial to society, whether or not there is any religious sanction or promise of divine reward. Many acts of generosity and self-sacrifice fall into this category.

It should be evident that these are not wholly distinct realms. Duty to society, in terms of generosity, self-sacrifice, and other personal virtues, was identified in most of the original salvationist religions as the road to salvation; in that sense it was a duty to God as well. Thus, social morality was co-opted within the recognized domain of religious morality. It is for this reason that I cannot simply use the terms sacred and secular, with reference to the two domains of morality. Sacral morality is always sacred; social morality may be either sacred or secular.

The same distinction between the sacral and the social can also be made in the case of immorality. Sacrilege, or sacral immorality, consists of acts forbidden by the gods, even though it's often hard to see how any harm to society could accrue from them. The great majority of food tabus fall clearly into this category. Social immorality consists of acts, like the failure to fulfill kinship obligations, that are clearly detrimental to the functioning of society, even though there may be no divine sanctions against them.[31]

Immorality: the negative case

Of the three categories of morality, immorality, and moral authority, by far the easiest to 'get a handle on' is immorality, and especially sacrilege. Tabus are always among the most clearly and explicitly demarcated areas of culture, and therefore the easiest to identify and study. Ethnologists in the field come to learn them very quickly, for they are forcibly made aware of any transgressions. Tabus are normally expressed in quite explicit behavioral proscriptions: Thou shalt not ... (this or that). They are usually backed up by equally explicit, and discoverable, mythological or scriptural sanctions, and—very importantly—society is prepared to punish their infraction. The violation of tabu is everywhere seen as synonymous with immorality.

But tabus, or in other words absolute and rigid prohibitions, do not exhaust the category of sacrilege. There are also acts, such as neglecting ritual duties, that are widely regarded as immoral, but are not proscribed on every single occasion. Anthropologists since the time of Frazer (1887) have suggested that tabus are a special and frequently an incomprehensible category of culture and behavior (or non-behavior), that does not closely integrate with the remainder of culture, or even with other ideas about immorality. This may be true from our rationalistic point of view, but I don't think the people who actually observe the tabus see it in that light. Tabu violations are simply among the many things that anger the gods—and since when are they rational beings?

As I have already suggested, there are also social immoralities. Certain failures of social duty are very widely regarded as immoral, even though they may not be overtly condemned in mythology or scripture. The repeated transgressor is nevertheless very likely to be accused of

---

[31] I will omit from this discussion the concept of sin, because it is too nebulous to be useful as an analytical category.

witchcraft, which itself constitutes a kind of supernatural sanction. But social immorality tends to be less explicitly defined than is sacrilege, since it is judged mainly in the court of public opinion.

There is obviously, then, a very close connection between religion and tabu, and indeed between religion and immorality more generally. Society is clear about what angers the gods; often enough it has been learned through the bitter experience of floods or famines. When Kluckhohn and Leighton (1946: 139) wrote, with reference to Navajo religion, that 'A very high proportion of the actions which arise out of convictions about beings and powers are negative in character,' they might as well have been speaking of nearly all the world's religions.

Categories of sacrilege

What are the commonly recognized activities that anger the gods? Beliefs on this subject vary widely in different cultures, but there are certain kinds of activity that are almost universally condemned. They are activities that, if permitted, may bring divine retribution not just on the malefactor but on the whole of his society. The following are some of the most nearly universal categories of sacrilege:

Forbidden sex. Sexual libertarians are wont to protest that 'the law has no place in the bedroom,' ignoring the fact that there is no other place where the law has so consistently been, apparently since the dawn of human society. Every religion has specific proscriptions about sexual activity, which refer not only to 'who,' but also in many cases to where, when, and how. According to popular tradition (I'm not sure if it's really true) Christian missionaries assured their Polynesian converts that intercourse in any other position except that with the male on top was sinful, with the result that it has been known ever since as 'the missionary position.'

Up to a point, sexual proscriptions are easy to account for in pragmatic terms. Indiscriminate sexual activity threatens the carefully built-up network of marital and kinship relationships, which assigns exclusive sexual rights, along with other rights, to persons in socially approved relationships. Moreover the much-discussed incest tabu, found in one form or another in all societies, enforces a degree of exogamy, which is essential to the building of social networks extending beyond the biological family. The tabu on parent-child and on brother-sister incest is therefore universal,[32] but most societies forbid sex with various other categories

---

[32] Always excluding royal families, like those of Egypt, Peru, and Hawaii, in which the rulers were considered divine. Gods can do as they please, and incest is very common among them.

of kin as well. Which kin are proscribed depends largely on the specific nature of the existing kinship system, and how it may or may not be threatened.

All this is sufficient to account for the 'who' in sexual tabus, but it hardly explains the numerous proscriptions on where, when, and how the act is performed. We can only conclude that sex, because it is a powerful impulse that may take complete possession of us and override our reason, is everywhere regarded as dangerous, and so in need of strict regulation by the gods. It is also—possibly for the same reason—regarded as being in some sense polluting; hence the numerous proscriptions on sex at holy times and in holy places. Even in the simplest of band societies we are likely to find that the hunter abstains from sex before a major hunt, and while preparing for any important ceremony.

Forbidden food. Scripturally ordained food tabus happen to be absent in Christianity, but they are present in most other religions, conspicuously including both Judaism and Islam. They are much harder to account for in pragmatic terms than are sex tabus, for they often appear contrary to society's self-interest. Nevertheless there is no people, no matter how close to the subsistence level, that does not routinely avoid certain available food resources (human flesh, for example), except when on the brink of actual starvation. Marvin Harris, the arch-materialist, conjured up some rather fanciful explanations to show that the Jewish and Islamic ban on pork, and the Hindu ban on beef, are really adaptive to the long-range needs of society (esp. Harris 1974), but his theories at best account for only a tiny fraction of the world's innumerable food tabus.

Because there are no explicit food tabus in Christianity, Americans and Europeans may tend to think of them as relatively trivial, in comparison with sex tabus. But not all others share that view. There are societies—in India, in particular—in which eating forbidden food is considered a good deal more heinous than having forbidden sex. It is all a question of what is most offensive to the gods.

It might be thought that food infractions are purely personal transgressions, unlikely to bring punishment on anyone but the offender. It is clear however that the Hebrews and many other peoples thought otherwise. Lantis (1950: 328) tells of an Eskimo girl who was banished from her village in the middle of winter, and probably froze to death, because she had eaten seal meat and caribou meat at the same meal.

The nearest thing to a rational explanation for food tabus that can be offered, from an emic perspective, is that the great majority of forbidden foods are animal foods, and eating them may be offensive to the powerful gods associated with those species.

Mary Douglas and other structuralists have offered a slightly different argument: that the human body is in effect a temple inhabited by a powerful spirit. Everything that goes into it is therefore an offering and must be ritually clean, while everything that issues from it is polluting (cf. especially Douglas 1970). For that reason peoples' sense, not only of identity but of virtue, is strongly bound up with what they do and don't eat. Navajos look down on Paiutes because they 'live off the vermin of the desert;' the ancient Nubians despised the Egyptians as 'unclean, and eaters of fish.'

Blasphemy and desecration. The gods demand obedience most of the time, but respect at all times. Words and acts that show outright disrespect are dangerous not only to the person who utters or performs them, but to the whole of that person's society. It is hardly a surprise therefore that blasphemy, and the desecration of holy property or holy performances, are everywhere regarded as immoral. Of course, ideas about what specific acts and sayings anger the gods are highly variable from society to society, as are all other ideas about the gods.

Neglect of ritual duty. In the domain of personal religion, the extent to which people choose to pray or not to pray is pretty much up to them. In most religions however there are certain, mostly public ritual performances in which everyone must participate. There may be an acceptable excuse for missing them once or twice, but continued neglect of ritual duties will certainly be regarded by others as immoral. Like all other moral offenses, it may bring misfortune not just to the offender, but to his whole society.

Witchcraft. It might be argued that witchcraft is a social infraction rather than a sacrilege, in that its victims are always humans rather than the gods. However, the universality with which it is punished by society as a whole, and not just by the victims, is sufficient indication that it is indeed regarded as an offense against the deities. This is particularly conspicuous in the Navajo case, where witchcraft and incest (which pretty much always go together) are the only two crimes that may be punished by anyone.

In most societies, few if any persons will admit to being a witch. Witchcraft is an accusation usually brought against persons who have been conspicuously immoral in other respects. The accusation of witch-craft is in that sense a penalty for other kinds of immorality.

It is necessary to recall again that sacrilege and social immorality are not wholly distinct. The kinds of antisocial acts that are condemned by society may also be condemned in scripture or mythology, though this is not always the case.

Failure of familial obligations. In all societies there are certain actions that are regarded as morally obligatory, with or without the sanction of mythology or scripture. Foremost among these is the obligation toward kinfolk. The duty of spouses to provide support for one another and for their children is universally recognized, but in societies with more ram-ified kinship system there are obligations toward other categories of kin as well.

Religions vary widely in the extent to which they provide sanctions against familial neglect. Christianity is relatively silent on this subject, while Islamic law specifies a long list of very specific familial obliga-tions, and punishments if they are neglected. But whether or not there are specific mythological sanctions, the family in its various forms is ev-erywhere regarded as a part of the divinely ordained scheme of things. Failure to fulfill the basic obligations of kinship is therefore decidedly immoral behavior.

Stinginess. While there is an overt obligation to provide support and assistance toward kinfolk, there is no similar obligation toward non-kin. There may at times be good reason for not doing so. Nevertheless there is a general feeling that the fortunate man ought to share with the less fortunate, when he can do so without detriment to is own position. The miser who consistently refuses to do so is just about everywhere regarded as an immoral person. In many societies he is apt to be branded as a witch.

Breaking of vows. Another commonly recognized moral obligation is the keeping of vows. If they have been made specifically to one of the gods, as is frequently the case, then the breaking of them is clearly an act of sacrilege. But the breaking of vows made to fellow humans (which are often sworn on the name of one of the gods) is also widely condemned as immoral.

Excess. 'Moderation in all things' is at the very least a folk ethic in many societies. Having, or doing, too much of anything is likely to be regarded as immoral, because if everyone behaved in the same way, the world would clearly be a worse place. And in most poor societies, both primitive and peasant, there is very likely to be an 'image of limited good;' a belief that there is only so much of anything to go around. He who has an excess of anything has therefore in effect taken someone else's share.

Cruelty. Cruelty and even torture, of animals and of humans, is permitted in some circumstances, and may even form a part of religious ceremonies. On the other hand repeated or habitual cruelty, outside of specified contexts, is nearly always regarded as immoral. There is surely an underlying belief that all things have been created for a purpose, so that to mistreat them is to violate the intended order. In many religions, including at least by implication Christianity, it is believed that all creatures are under the eye and under the protection of the deity who created them, and mistreatment of them is an offense to their creator. There may at times be sufficient provocation to kill or to assault, but at least in the case of animals there is never an adequate provocation for cruelty.

Violent crimes. Killing, assault, rape, robbery, and other violent actions against persons are condemned to some extent by all peoples, and it has therefore often been suggested that they are acts of immorality. I think however that this requires some qualification, for two reasons. First, their prohibition tends to be highly situational; they are not moral absolutes. Killing is permitted and even applauded in time of war. The Mosaic sixth commandment would seem to be stated in absolute terms, yet if we consider the historical situation we find that Yahweh not only encouraged the killing of Canaanites, Philistines, and other innocents, but at times took a hand in it. What the deity obviously meant was, 'Thou shalt not kill other Jews.' Both killing and bodily assault are regularly inflicted as punishment in many societies, and in most of them a man is entitled to rape his wife. In tribal societies, the stealing of property from other tribes is rarely condemned, and is sometimes applauded.

Second, in the majority of societies (including both Navajos and village Arabs) violent crimes are regarded as wrongs only against specific persons or lineage groups, not against society as a whole. That is, in modern legal parlance, they are torts rather than crimes. They can be expiated by some form of restitution or retribution, and the person who does so is thereafter not considered an immoral person, unless he becomes a repeated offender. Most importantly, only the victim or the victim's family has a right to exact retribution or restitution. If they do not choose to do so, other members of society may not intervene—as they would assuredly do if it was thought that the gods had been offended. Although murder and robbery (but not rape and assault) are proscribed in the Ten Commandments, in the majority of societies they are at most acts of secular immorality, and then only when committed in certain situations.

In sum, I would offer the following observations about immorality, as it is perceived by most peoples:

An overview

1. It consists much more of overt actions than of feelings or traits of character.

2. Tabus (acts of sacrilege) are always quite explicitly spelled out. They are known to everyone, and there is little disagreement about them.

3. Tabus are backed up by explicit mythological, scriptural, or ecclesiastical sanctions.

4. Tabus are moral absolutes. They must be obeyed at all times, by everyone.

5. Although the violation of tabus always risks punishment by the gods, society is usually prepared to step in and punish it also, without waiting for the gods to act. Divine punishment is all too often visited on the malefactor's whole lineage or society, and this may be averted if society steps in and acts first.

6. Apart from tabus, there are other categories of action that are offensive to the gods, but they are somewhat less rigidly spelled out and less rigidly enforced than are tabus.

7. Social immorality is not so explicitly defined as is sacrilege, but there is usually fairly general agreement about it.

8. Social immorality may in some societies be a purely secular concept, but more often it is associated also with some degree of divine sanction. This is conspicuously the case, at least ideally, in the salvationist religions.

9. In non-salvationist societies, acts of social immorality will very often lead to an accusation of witchcraft.

10. In sum, there is nearly always a close connection between religion and concepts of immorality.

But while religions are usually quite explicit about what angers the gods, they tend to be very much less so about what pleases them. Take for example the case of the Ten Commandments, often cited by fundamentalists as the heart and core of Christian morality.[33] We can observe to begin with that eight of the ten are actually proscriptions, or in other words tabus, and (except in the case of coveting) the behavioral expectations are highly explicit.[34] The two exceptions are those of observing the Sabbath and honoring the father and mother, but the first of these is deceptive, because observing the Sabbath is almost entirely a matter of avoiding a long list of forbidden behaviors. We are left only with honoring the parents as a positive injunction, but notice how non-specific this is in terms of behavioral expectations. And we could pass on from the Ten Commandments to the abominations of Leviticus and Deuteronomy: an incredibly detailed list of forbidden foods and acts. Nowhere in the Bible is there anything comparable in the way of positively prescribed behavior.

Given that nine of the Ten Commandments are actually proscriptions, the assertion that they are at the heart of Christian morality would seem to suggest that morality is nothing more than the absence of immorality. But a little reflection will show that this proposition is indefensible, either logically or morally. If any act that is not immoral is automatically moral, then eating pickles is moral, since it violates no known food tabu. To take a more extreme case, so likewise is defecating, anywhere except in the temple, a moral act, since it also violates no tabu.

I think we have to recognize, then, that between immorality and morality there lies an enormous neutral territory of the merely routine, which is neither condemned nor applauded by society, but merely expected. The gap is so wide, in fact, that there is really almost no connection between immorality and morality; neither serves in any concrete way to define the other. Knowing what is considered moral, in any particular society, will not help to predict what is considered immoral, or vice versa. This should not surprise us, if we remember the very human-like character of most of the gods. In the case of us mortals there is very little connection between the things that please us and the things that displease us; why should it be otherwise with the deities?

It is clear, then, that morality must have positive defining criteria, and

---

[33] Although the commandments were actually given to and for the Jews only, modern Jews seem much less insistent than Christians that they are at the heart of religious morality.

[34] My late colleague John Roberts suggested, I think quite convincingly, that the tenth commandment is actually a tabu against casting the evil eye.

not merely negative ones. But what, exactly, are they? Here again we have to notice that there are two kinds, or concepts, of morality; those that I have called sacral and social. The definition of sacral morality would appear at first glance to be easy and straightforward: it is whatever the gods have commanded, just as immorality is whatever the gods have forbidden. But the matter is not quite that simple, for two reasons. First, ritual prescriptions are not moral absolutes in the same sense as are ritual proscriptions. Within the context of most religions, everyone is expected to perform a considerable number of religious duties, but no one of them is mandatory at all times and in all circumstances. And in polytheistic religions, no person could possibly perform all the acts of worship devoted to all the different deities.

Second, ritual prescriptions are things that everyone is nominally supposed to do, on pain of divine or ecclesiastical punishment. Performance is therefore a routine expectation, and a matter of self-interest. Moral acts on the other hand are rarely identified with self-interest, but rather with its absence. The devout, or in other words sacrally moral, person is not just someone who does his everyday religious duty, but someone who performs ritual acts *above and beyond the call of duty.* Viewed from that perspective, the criteria of morality (unlike those of immorality) become more a quantitative than qualitative matter. The person who transgresses even once is immoral; the person who performs only routine religious duties is not singled out as moral. But the more he goes beyond the expected, the more moral he is considered.

The latter point is true also in regard to social morality. It is, however, much more difficult to define than is sacral morality. As I have suggested previously, both society and salvationist religion identify morality with personal virtue, but neither is very explicit about what that consists of. Goodness is apt to be defined much more in terms of traits of character or of feelings, than of specific acts. In the absence of clearcut guidelines, we (at least we anthropologists) are forced to turn to public opinion, to define for us what is moral behavior. What are the acts that are most consistently applauded, in any given society, precisely because they are above and beyond the call of duty?

As in the case of sacral morality, I think this latter point is key. Socially moral acts, like sacrally moral acts, are not tantamount to the performance of duties, because those are things that we do under compulsion. They are things that everyone has to do, and the fear of punishment provides a sufficient self-interest for doing them. What sets the moral man apart from his fellows is that he does good things he is not com-pelled to do, and will not be punished if he does not do them. Providing food and shelter to the wife and children are not moral acts, because they are social obligations, but providing food and shelter to a starving stranger are clearly moral acts.

To begin with, then, we can agree that moral acts, either sacral or so-cial, are voluntary acts, performed in response to the will of the actor and not the demand of either society or religion. But a qualification becomes necessary at this point. Not all voluntary acts that win the admiration of society are moral acts. The achievement of stardom on the stage or on the playing field, or indeed in any kind of personal success, is not generally regarded as moral, because it is undertaken in the hope and expectation of reward—not necessary material but at least in the form of public acclaim.

Here then we come to the second defining characteristic or moral acts: they are not self-interested. They are acts performed for the sake of others rather than of ourselves, and from which we expect no reward, at least in this world. And for those fairly numerous individuals who 'do good by stealth,' personal self-approval may be the only reward.

*Categories of
the moral*

Sacral morality has, I think, been sufficiently considered in earlier para-graphs. It is whatever the gods have prescribed for us, but performed above and beyond the call of duty. What the gods have prescribed in the way of sacral duty, like what they have forbidden, is spelled out very explicitly, and there is little dispute about it.

By contrast the categories of social morality are not very explicitly de-fined for us, even when they are identified as religious duties as well. The following however are general categories of action that are applauded in the great majority of societies. All of them have one feature in common: that of putting the interest of others ahead of one's own.

Generosity. There is probably no single category of behavior that is more universally applauded than is generosity: the giving of goods, time, and effort to others, above and beyond what kinship or society require. There is an obvious sociofunctional explanation in this case for, as Mar-cel Mauss (1954; original 1925) has shown us, the giving of gifts is prob-ably the single most basic action in the building and subsequent mainte-nance of social networks. Ethologists have more recently found this to be true even in primate society: offering food is the recognized way of inviting an outsider to join a chimpanzee troop. From any perspective, either religious or social, the generous man is a moral man, even if the act of giving really involves no detriment to his own interest.

Self-sacrifice. Self-sacrifice is a common form of sacral morality; many acts of worship require a sacrifice on the part of the votary. But a person may also be self-sacrificing in doing things for his fellows that are contrary to his personal interest, like taking time away from his farm to help with communal building projects or with charitable activities. In the broadest sense this kind of self-sacrifice is a kind of generosity, with the difference that self-sacrifice involves a recognizable detriment to the actor's interest, where other acts of generosity may not.

Charity. Charity is again a special kind of generosity, specifically toward the less advantaged. Every society recognizes the existence of individuals who, through one misfortune or another, would not survive without the voluntary help of others. Orphans, who have no kin to fall back on, are obviously in this category, but so are persons with major physical disabilities, and those in need of medical treatment that they can't afford. If people are absolutely unable to feed themselves, literally or figuratively, someone else must provide the food. In our times the state has to a very considerable extent assumed responsibility for these persons; in other times and in other societies they have had to rely on the charitable impulses of other persons, who owed them no formal obligation. Society applauds charity because, with occasional exceptions, it acknowledges the right of everyone, no matter now disadvantaged, to survive.

Kindness. Kindness is a kind of emotional gift: being nice to people when you don't have to, so that they feel better about themselves and the world.

Forgiveness. Forgiveness is a virtue much stressed in Christianity; less so in most other religions. It involves a suspension of the normal rule of equity: that an offended person is entitled to restitution or retribution. A strict adherence to that rule can result in generations-long feuds, or at least hatreds. The best way to hold a society together without internal violence may be through a voluntary agreement, on the part of offended parties, to bury the hatchet.

Impartiality. Social rules require us to be partial toward kin, and sometimes also toward neighbors, fellow townsmen, and even fellow countrymen. Beyond that, though, we are generally inclined to be partial also to those that we like or admire, both in the performance of duties and in the giving of gifts and services. But such partiality may often cause rifts within society, between individuals and between groups. It is impartiality that is everywhere equated with justice—a quality of morality emphasized again and again in both religious and secular texts. 'Act to everybody as if they were your own relatives,' is the Navajo way of expressing it (Kluckhohn and Leighton 1946: 220).

An overview

In sum, I would offer the following generalizations about morality:

1. Concepts of morality include both sacral and social acts.

2. Moral acts involve more than just the performance of duty; they are good deeds performed voluntarily, above and beyond the call of duty. Acts performed under threat of punishment, even though demanded by the gods, are not considered moral.

3. Thus, neither sacral nor social acts are moral absolutes, in the same way as are tabus. It is not essential that they be performed at all times, by everyone.

4. Moral acts are performed without the expectation of reward, at least in this life. Acts performed for hire, even though applauded by society or pleasing to the gods, are not considered moral.

5. Moral acts are those in which the actor puts the interest of the group ahead of his own.

6. Because moral acts are voluntary, morality (far more than immorality) is quantifiable. The more good deeds, the more moral is the person.

7. Acts of sacral morality—as of immorality—are clearly identified in mythology, scripture, or the church. In principle, a person knows clearly what the gods expect, in the way of ritual performance.

8. Acts of social morality are usually not very precisely specified in mythology or scripture. Religion (especially salvationist religion) urges us to be good, while leaving us in a great many situations to decide what that means in practice. Social morality, in other words, does not involve very clear or explicit behavioral guidelines.

9. For the foregoing reason, there is not so immediate or clear a connection between religion and morality, as there is between religion and immorality.

*A brief
history of
morality*

It seems worthwhile at this point to review the historical relationship of the two moralities, something that was touched on but not emphasized in the last chapter. Concepts of sacral and of social morality have coexisted in all societies and in all times, but the extent of interrelationship has varied widely. In most if not all of the earlier societies, from bands to the early states, the two domains were fairly distinct. Sacral morality consisted in a very long list of ritual obligations to the gods. If they were not performed, all kinds of misfortune could be visited on the whole of society. Social morality consisted, as always, in acts of generosity, self-sacrifice, charity, and other personal virtues that were applauded by society, but not demanded by the gods. Non-performance might bring public disapproval, or even an accusation of witchcraft, but there was no divine retribution for being an antisocial character.

That started to change in the secularizing states of the last millennium B.C., when philosophers began stressing the importance of personal virtue, or in other words social morality, as the thing most pleasing to the gods. The salvationist cults went a step further, insisting explicitly that personal virtue is more important to the gods than is ritual duty, and that it will bring guaranteed rewards in the afterlife. Social morality, which had existed in the secular realm since time out of mind, thus became for the first time an essential feature of religious morality as well.

The most extreme of salvationists—those who became hermits or monks or wandering ascetics—sought to distance themselves as far as possible from all the corruptions of the earthly world, in preparation for the world to come, For them therefore religious virtue became almost wholly a matter of self-denial, without the social virtues of generosity and charity. However, this was never the majority view of morality among the salvationists. Most of them continued to feel that duty to one's fellow men was an important religious virtue.

The salvationist cults began as subversive movements against the corrupt established order, both political and religious. As long as they remained so, their emphasis on social as opposed to sacral morality continued to be stressed, and to constitute their strongest appeal. In time however their appeal became so strong that the political establishment had to come to terms with them, and the formerly subversive cults were co-opted by the state. After that happened they acquired more and more the characteristics of the old state religions which they had originally condemned, and there was a returning emphasis on ritual performance rather than on social virtue as the essence of morality. Salvation came to be seen mainly as avoidance of the ever-lurking threat of damnation—something to be averted mainly by attention to churchly duties. Meanwhile social morality came to be encompassed—to the extent that it was—within the newly ramified legal systems of the Middle Ages.

The Protestant Reformation was then a second reforming movement, intended to downplay ritual and to reemphasize social morality as the road to salvation. But the movement was fragmented from the beginning, and the various Protestant sects differed widely in their emphasis on ritual duty as opposed to personal virtue—as they still do today. Some are still relatively ritualistic; others stress mainly the avoidance of immorality, through fear of damnation; others, more in keeping with the teaching of the early church, lay greater stress on the positive virtues. A few insist that the most critical need for salvation is simply to believe in Jesus—an injunction that might appear incomprehensible to votaries of other religions, where belief is taken absolutely for granted. There is thus a continuing, ongoing debate. Is duty directly to God, through church attendance and prayer, the essence of morality, or is it duty to society, through good deeds which are said to be gratifying to God, even if he has not made this very explicit in scripture?

Morality and ethics

Before going finally to a consideration of moral authority, it seems desirable to make a distinction between what I am calling morality and ethics. In doing so I am departing from the usual conception of ethics, as we find it in Aristotle and countless subsequent philosophers, for that conception involves a good deal of what I call morality. I have to stress again, therefore, that the definition I employ here is strictly my own.

In my view three points can be made about ethics and ethical relationships, that serve to distinguish them from morality as I have defined it. First, they are purely secular; the gods are not involved. Ethical relationships and transactions are between humans only.

Second, ethical relationships and transactions are essentially dyadic: between two parties only. Not only are the gods not involved, but neither is society. If the parties involved in any transaction are satisfied, it is no one else's business.

Third and most importantly, ethical relationships and transactions involve the concept of *equity*. An ethical transaction is one in which the two parties come out even, and each is satisfied with the result. An unethical transaction is one in which one party gets the better of the other. In that case the injured party may seek redress, but no one else may do so on his behalf. Within the context of our own legal system, he may file a civil suit, but not a criminal one.

Note by contrast, then, that moral actions are not necessarily *trans* actions; they may be acts (like charitable giving) for which there is no clearly identifiable second party. Still more importantly, though, moral actions are by my definition *inequitable*. They are actions in which an individual deliberately alters the existing balance of things, giving from himself and toward others, or toward the gods. At the conclusion he is poorer, in one sense or another, and others are richer.

From this perspective, the oft-cited Golden Rule is properly an ethical precept, not a moral one. 'Do unto others as you would have them do unto you' clearly involves a concept of equity, not to mention self-interest.[35] The Navajo precept, 'Act to everybody as if they were your own relatives' (Kluckhohn and Leighton 1946: 220) comes closer to genuine morality.

What, finally, about moral authority, and its relation to religion?

The role of moral authority

We can note to begin with that authority of any kind has two aspects: it defines, in absolute terms, and it compels. But if we turn to morality—as opposed to immorality—we find that religion per se does neither of those things. At least in the social sphere the dimensions of moral behavior are not nearly as sharply defined as are those of immoral behavior; in a great many situations we are left to decide for ourselves what are the actions that will bring us to salvation.

We may note too that religion does not offer any clearcut promise of reward for exceptionally moral behavior. We are always told that generosity, self-sacrifice, and charity will be abundantly rewarded in the next life, but it is not clear that the merely dutiful man, who is not generous or charitable beyond the call of duty, will not also be admitted to heaven. A suggestion is sometimes given in church, that there will be varying degrees of eternal bliss, depending on one's virtuosity in this life, but this is very poorly confirmed in scripture.

In the absence of clearcut mythological or scriptural sanctions, it is the church that attempts to exercise the moral authority that we cannot find in scripture, by defining our religious and social duties in precise terms. Preachers tell us, as authoritatively as they can, what the scriptures mean. But the church is not religion; it is, and to a degree always has been, recognized as a man-made institution, and it has never spoken entirely with a single voice. There are undoubtedly those who accept the words of their preachers unhesitatingly as the words of God, but I think they are

---

[35]Ronald Green (1987: 95) has pointed out that a similar precept is found in many societies, but it is usually expressed in the negative: 'Don't do to others what you don't want done to you.'

in the minority.

If religion in and of itself does not clearly define morality, so also it does not compel, because moral acts as I have defined them are voluntary, not performed under compulsion. What religion provides, in relation to moral behavior, is suasion, not compulsion. Here again, religion does not exercise absolute authority.

When we turn to the negative side, immorality, the picture is very different. The nature of immoral acts is spelled out in religions with a high degree of specificity, and the sanction against them is absolute. Even one transgression is forbidden, and there is a certainty of punishment in the afterlife. Moreover, immorality may be immediately punished by society, without waiting for the wrath of the gods.

I am driven to conclude, therefore, that throughout history the essential contribution of religion has been not so much to persuade us to be good, in a positive sense, as to prevent us from being bad. The moral suasion of our fellows has always impelled us to be generous, self-sacrificing, and charitable, to the extent that we are, and later salvationist religion has added its voice to that of society. Yet it is clear, if we consider the many societies with non-salvationist religions, like that of the Navajos, that the good opinion of our fellows is usually sufficient to make us be good. But the opinion of our fellows is not always enough to keep us from being bad, partly because bad acts are often the consequence of antisocial feelings. It is here that religion speaks with an authority that society alone cannot. In relation to our fellow men, religion provides a host of moral absolutes as to what we must not do, but very few as to what we must do. It seems in this respect that the Ten Commandments are, after all, a paradigm of religion in general.

This is not an achievement to be underestimated. Society functions most smoothly when people are generous and self-sacrificing and kind, but it can survive without those things. Indeed we have ethnographic descriptions of societies where they seem to be lacking. But society cannot survive if people are bad, without restraint. We would revert to that pre-social condition of 'war of all against all' that was envisioned by Hobbes (1651). I am reminded of a statement long ago attributed to A. R. Radcliffe-Brown, that 'the one public crime in [tribal] societies is often that of being a bad character' (quoted in Colson 1974: 53).

This brings us back to a very old theory of religion: that it stands throughout our lives in *loco parentis*. Bergson (1935: 1) has reminded us that the earliest injunctions that we encounter as we grow up are wholly negative in character, and they carry the absolute sanction of parental authority. 'What a childhood we would have had if only we had been left to do as we pleased!,' as he observes (ibid.). It is those negative injunctions, 'don't do this' and 'don't do that' that bring our animal impulses under control, and convert us into social beings. But there comes a point in our lives when 'you don't do it because I say so, and I'm your father' ceases to compel, and it is at that point that, ideally, religion takes over. It is the moral authority of denial, first parental and later religious, that makes us humans and not animals. And of all the myriad domains of culture, it is religion that sets us most clearly apart from the rest of the animal kingdom.

But, to conclude on a more positive note, I have to concede that the genuinely religious people I know are usually good people in many respects—law-abiding, civic-minded, and charitable, as well as devout in a more narrowly religious sense. I do not of course include fanatics in the category of the devout, for I see no evidence that the rigorous insistence that everyone do just as we do and think just as we think is regarded anywhere as a moral virtue. Fanatics are not generally regarded as good people, either by society or by the church, for fanaticism is excess. It is the extreme of self-righteousness, disguising itself under the mantle of religion (or, just as often today, patriotism).

Of course, to observe that religious people are good people is true to some extent by definition, in those salvationist societies (like our own) in which religiosity is equated with social morality. But I find it just as true among the Navajos and their Pueblo neighbors, where devout people are generally the best neighbors and the best citizens, by the standards of their own societies. I can only ask: is it religion that persuades them to be good persons, or is it an innate goodness that impels them to be religious? In either case, society is the beneficiary.

BIBLIOGRAPHY

BASIC SOURCES

Adams, W. Y. 1963. *Shonto: A Study of the Role of the Trader in a Modern*   *2. Navajo*
Navaho Community. (Bureau of American Ethnology Bulletin 188.) Wash-   *Indian*
ington: Smithsonian Institution.   *Religion*

Kluckhohn, C. 1944. *Navaho Witchcraft.* (Papers of the Peabody Museum of
American Archaeology and Ethnology, vol. 22.) Cambridge: Harvard University Press.

Kluckhohn, C., and D. Leighton. 1946. *The Navaho.* Cambridge: Harvard University Press.

Kluckhohn, C., and L. C. Wyman. 1940. *An Introduction to Navaho Chant
Practice.* (Memoirs of the American Anthropological Association, no. 53.)
Menasha, WI: American Anthropological Association.

Leighton, D., and C. Kluckhohn. 1948. *Children of the People.* Cambridge: Harvard University Press.

Reichard, G. A. 1963. *Navaho Religion.* New York: Bollingen Foundation.

Wyman, L. C. 1950. The Religion of the Navaho Indians. *Forgotten Religions*,
ed V. Ferm., 341–362. New York: Philosophical Library.

Wyman, L. C., W. W. Hill, and I. Osanai. 1942. *Navajo Eschatology.* (University
of New Mexico Bulletin, Anthropological Series, vol. 4, no. 1.) Albuquerque:
University of New Mexico Press.

Wyman, L. C., and C. Kluckhohn. 1938. *Navaho Classification of their Song Ceremonials.* (Memoirs of the American Anthropological Association, no. 50.)
Menasha, WI: American Anthropological Association.

Ammar, H. 1966. *Growing Up in an Egyptian Village.* New York: Octagon   *3. Arab*
Books.   *Village*

Berger, M. 1970. *Islam in Egypt Today.* Cambridge: Cambridge University Press.   *Religion*

Gilsenan, M. 1973. *Saint and Sufi in Modern Egypt.* Oxford: Clarendon Press.

Kennedy, J., ed. 1978. *Nubian Ceremonial Life.* Berkeley: University of California Press.

Reeves, E. B. 1990. *The Hidden Government*. Salt Lake City: University of Utah Press.

Trimingham, J. S. 1949. *Islam in the Sudan*. London: Frank Cass & Co.

Wikan, U. 1980. *Life among the Poor in Cairo*, trans. Ann Henning. London: Tavistock Publications.

*5. Introduction
to Parts 2 and 3*

Firth, R. 1996. *Religion: a Humanist Interpretation*. London: Routlege.

Lewis, I. M. 1986. *Religion in Context*. Cambridge: Cambridge University Press.

*6. Clearing
the Ground*

Evans-Pritchard, E. E. 1965. *Theories of Primitive Religion*. Oxford: Clarendon Press.

Spiro, M. E. 1966. Religion: Problems of Definition and Explanation. *Anthropological Approaches to the Study of Religion*, ed. M. Banton, 85–126. London: Tavistock Publications.

*8. The
Problem of
Definition*

Asad, T. 1993. *Genealogies of Religion*. Baltimore: Johns Hopkins University Press.

Geertz, C. 1966. Religion as a Cultural System. *Anthropological Approaches to the Study of Religion*, ed. M. Banton, 1–46. London: Tavistock Publications.

Spiro, M. E. 1966. Religion: Problems of Definition and Explanation. *Anthropological Approaches to the Study of Religion*, ed. M. Banton, 85–126. London: Tavistock Publications.

Tylor, E. B. 1874. *Primitive Culture* (2 vols.). London: John Murray.

*9. In Search
of a
Definition*

Durkheim É. 1915. *The Elementary Forms of the Religious Life*, trans. J. W. Swain. London: George Allen & Unwin.

Frazer, J. G. 1922. *The Golden Bough*, abridged ed. London: Macmillan Co.

Kroeber, A. L., and C. Kluckhohn. 1972. *Culture: a Critical Review of Concepts and Definitions*. New York: Vintage Books.

Tylor, E. B. 1874. *Primitive Culture* (2 vols.). London: John Murray.

*11. The
Problem of
Explanation*

Evans-Pritchard, E. E. 1965. *Theories of Primitive Religion*. Oxford: Clarendon Press.

LaBarre, W. 1970. *The Ghost Dance*. New York: Delta Books.

Malefijt, A. 1968. *Religion and Culture*. New York: Macmillan.

Wallace, A. F. E. 1966. *Religion: an Anthropological View*. New York: Random House.

Hoult, T. F. 1958. *The Sociology of Religion*. New York: Dryden Press.
Norbeck, E. 1961. *Religion in Primitive Society*. New York: Harper & Row.
Wallace, A. F. E. 1966. *Religion: an Anthropological View*. New York: Random House.
Yinger, J. M. 1957. *Religion, Society and the Individual*. New York: Macmillan.

Howells, W. 1962. *The Heathens*. New York: Doubleday.
Lewis, I. M. 1971. *Ecstatic Religion*. Harmondsworth: Penguin Books.
Radin, P. 1937. *Primitive Religion*. New York: Viking Press.
Wallace, A. F. E. 1966. *Religion: an Anthropological View*. New York: Random House.
Wallis, W. D. 1939. *Religion in Primitive Society*. New York: F. S. Crofts & Co.

Adas, M. 1979. *Prophets of Rebellion*. Chapel Hill: University of North Carolina Press.
Bellah, R. 1964. Religious Evolution. *American Sociological Review* 29, 358–374.
Bellah, R. 1970. *Beyond Belief*. New York: Harper & Row.
Ferm, V., ed. 1950. *Forgotten Religions*. New York: Philosophical Library.
Freud, S. 1928. *The Future of an Illusion*, trans. W. D. Robson-Smith. London: Hogarth Press.
Krader, L. 1968. *Formation of the State*. Englewood Cliffs: Prentice-Hall.
LaBarre, W. 1970. *The Ghost Dance*. New York: Delta Books.
Lanternari, V. 1963. *The Religions of the Oppressed*. New York: Alfred A. Knopf.
Malefijt, A. 1968. *Religion and Culture*. New York: Macmillan.
Noss, J. B. 1963. *Man's Religions*, 3rd ed. New York: Macmillan.
Rapaport, R. A. 1999. *Ritual and Religion in the Making of Humanity*. Cambridge: Cambridge University Press.
Sahlins, M. D. 1968. *Tribesmen*. Englewood Cliffs: Prentice-Hall.
Service, E. 1966. *The Hunters*. Englewood Cliffs: Prentice-Hall.
Swanson, G. E. 1964. *The Birth of the Gods*. Ann Arbor: Ann Arbor Paperbacks.

Malefijt, A. 1968. *Religion and Culture*. New York: Macmillan.
Swanson, G. E. 1964. *The Birth of the Gods*. Ann Arbor: Ann Arbor Paperbacks.
Wilson, B. R. 1973. *Magic and the Millennium*. New York: Harper & Row.

16. *The Growth of Individual Religion*

Bergson, H. 1935. *The Two Sources of Morality and Religion*, trans. R. A. Audra and C. Brereton. New York: Henry Holt.

Piaget, J. 1960. *The Child's Conception of the World*, trans. J. and A. Tomlinson. Totowa: Littlefield, Adams & Co.

18. *Religion, Morality, and Moral Authority*

Bergson, H. 1935. *The Two Sources of Morality and Religion*, trans. R. A. Audra and C. Brereton. New York: Henry Holt.

Durkheim, É. 1961. *Moral Education*, trans. E. K. Wilson and H. Schnurer. New York: Free Press.

Green, R. M. 1987. Morality and Religion. *The Encyclopedia of Religion*, ed. M. Eliade, vol. 10, 92–106. New York: Macmillan.

Westermarck, E. 1908. *The Origin and Development of the Moral Ideas* (2 vols.). London: Macmillan.

Yinger, J. M. 1957. *Religion, Society and the Individual*. New York: Macmillan.

LITERATURE CITED

Adams, W. Y. 1963. *Shonto: a Study of the Role of the Trader in a Modern Navaho Community.* (Bureau of American Ethnology Bulletin 188.) Washington: Smithsonian Institution.

Adams. W. Y. 1998. *The Philosophical Roots of Anthropology.* Stanford: CSLI Publications.

Adams, W. Y., and E. W. Adams. 1991. *Archaeological Typology and Practical Reality.* Cambridge: Cambridge University Press.

Ammar, H. 1966. *Growing Up in an Egyptian Village.* New York: Octagon Books.

Barth, F. 1961. *Nomads of South Persia.* Boston: Little, Brown.

Bellah, R. N. 1964. Religious Evolution. *American Sociological Review,* 29: 358–374.

Bellah, R. N. 1970. *Beyond Belief.* New York: Harper & Row.

Bergson, H. 1935. *The Two Sources of Morality and Religion,* trans. R. A. Audra and C. Brereton. New York: Henry Holt.

Cain, S. 1987. Study of Religion: History of Study. *The Encyclopedia of Religion,* ed. M. Eliade, vol. 14, 64–83. New York: Macmillan.

Christian Jr., W. A. 1972. *Person and God in a Spanish Valley.* New York: Seminar Press.

Colson, E. 1974. *Tradition and Contract.* Chicago: Aldine.

Culler, J. 1976. *Ferdinand de Saussure.* Harmondsworth: Penguin Books.

Douglas, M. 1970. *Purity and Danger.* Harmondsworth: Pelican Books.

Durkheim É. 1899. De la Définition des Phénomènes Religieux. *Année Sociologique,* 2: 1–28.

Durkheim É. 1915. *The Elementary Forms of the Religious Life,* trans. J. W. Swain. London: George Allen & Unwin.

Evans-Pritchard, E. E. 1956. *Nuer Religion.* Oxford: Clarendon Press.

Evans-Pritchard, E. E. 1965. *Theories of Primitive Religion.* Oxford: Clarendon Press.

Frazer, J. G. 1877. *Totemism.* Edinburgh: Adams and Charles.

Frazer, J. G. 1922. *The Golden Bough,* abridged ed. London: Macmillan Co.

Geertz, C. 1960. *The Religion of Java.* Glencoe: Free Press.

Geertz, C. 1966. Religion as a Cultural System. *Anthropological Approaches to the Study of Religion,* ed. M. Banton, 1–46. London: Tavistock Publications.

Gluckman, M. 1955. *Custom and Conflict in Africa.* Oxford: Basil Blackwell.

Gluckman, M. 1963. *Order and Rebellion in Tribal Africa.* New York: Free Press.

Green, R. M. 1987. Morality and Religion. *The Encyclopedia of Religion,* ed. M. Eliade, vol. 10, 92–106. New York: Macmillan

Harris, M. 1968. *The Rise of Anthropological Theory.* New York: Crowell.

Harris, M. 1974. *Cows, Pigs, Wars and Witches.* New York: Random House.

Harris, M. 1979. *Cultural Materialism.* New York: Random House.

Hempel, C. G. 1952. *Fundamentals of Concept Formation in Empirical Science.* Chicago: University of Chicago Press.

Hobbes, T. 1654. *Levciathan.* London: J. M. Dent & Sons.

James, W. 1902. *The Varieties of Religious Experience.* New York: Longmans, Green.

Kant, I. 1860. *Critique of Pure Reason,* trans. J M. D. Meikeljohn. London: Bohn.

Kenyatta, J. 1938. *Facing Mount Kenya.* London: Secker & Warburg.

Kluckhohn, C. 1944. *Navaho Witchcraft.* (Papers of the Peabody Museum of American Archaeology and Ethnology, vol. 22.) Cambridge: Harvard University Press.

Kluckhohn, C., and D. Leighton. 1946. *The Navaho.* Cambridge: Harvard University Press.

Kroeber, A. L. 1917. The Superorganic. *American Anthropologist,* 19: 163–213.

Kroeber, A. L. 1952. *The Nature of Culture.* Chicago: University of Chicago Press.

Kroeber, A. L. 1964. *Anthropology: Culture Patterns and Processes.* New York: Harcourt, Brace.

Kroeber, A. L., and C. Kluckhohn. 1952. *Culture: a Critical Review of Concepts and Definitions.* New York: Vintage Books.

Kuhn, T. 1962. *The Structure of Scientific Revolutions.* Chicago: University of Chicago Press.

Lantis, M. 1950. The Religion of the Eskimos. *Forgotten Religions*, ed. V. Ferm. 309–340. New York: Philosophical Library.

Leach, E. R., ed. 1968. *Dialectic in Practical Religion.* (Cambridge Papers in Social Anthropology 5.) Cambridge: Cambridge University Press.

Linton, R. 1936. *The Study of Man.* Cleveland: D. Appleton-Century.

Lowie, R. H. 1920. *Primitive Society.* New York: Liveright.

Lowie, R. H. 1924. *Primitive Religion.* New York: Liveright.

Lowie, R. H. 1937. *The History of Ethnological Theory.* New York: Farrar & Rinehart.

Lutfiyya, A. 1966. *Baytin: a Jordanian Village.* The Hague: Mouton.

Mahfouz, N. 1981. *Children of Gebelawi,* trans. P. Stewart. London: Heineman.

Malinowski, B. 1935. *Coral Gardens and their Magic* (2 vols.). London: George Allen & Unwin.

Malinowski, B. 1954. *Magic, Science and Religion.* New York: Doubleday Anchor Books.

Margolis, H. 1987. *Patterns, Thinking, and Cognition.* Chicago: University of Chicago Press.

Mauss, M. 1954. *The Gift,* trans I. Cunnison. New York: Free Press.

Montesquieu, B. 1762. *The Spirit of the Laws,* 3rd ed., trans. anonymous. Edinburgh: M. Donaldson and J. Reid.

Morgan, L. H. 1851. *League of the Ho-De-No-Sau-Nee, or Iroquois.* Rochester: Sage and Broa.

Morgan, L. H. 1877. *Ancient Society.* New York: Henry Holt.

Morgan, W. 1936. *Human-wolves among the Navaho.* (Yale University Publications in Anthropology, no. 11.) New Haven: Yale University Press.

Ortiz, A. 1969. *The Tewa World.* Chicago: University of Chicago Press.

Parsons, E. C. 1939. *Pueblo Indian Religion* (2 vols.). Chicago: University of Chicago Press.

Parsons, T. 1937. *The Structure of Social Action.* Glencoe: Free Press.

Piaget, J. 1960. *The Child's Conception of the World,* trans. J. and A. Tomlinson. Totowa: Littlefield, Adams & Co.

Radin, P. 1937. *Primitive Religion.* New York: Viking Press.

Reeves, E. B. 1990. *The Hidden Government.* Salt Lake City: University of Utah Press.

Reichard, G. 1944. *Prayer: the Compulsive Word.* (American Ethnological Society Monograph 7.) Washington: American Ethnological Society.

Reichard, G. 1963. *Navaho Religion,* 2nd edition. New York: Bollingen Foundation.

Reichel-Domatoff, F. G. 1971. *Amazonian Cosmos.* Chicago: University of Chicago Press.

Richardson, J, and A. L. Kroeber. 1940. Three Centuries of Women's Dress Fashions: a Quantitative Analysis, reprinted in Kroeber 1952,. 358–372.

Riesman, D. 1961. *The Lonely Crowd.* New Haven: Yale University Press.

Sahlins, M. 1972. *Stone-Age Economics.* Chicago: University of Chicago Press.

Sapir, E. 1917. Do We Need a 'Superorganic?' *American Anthropologist,* 19: 441–447.

Schwarz, M. T. 1998. Holy Visit 1998: Prophecy, Revitalization, and Resistance in the Contemporary Navajo World. *Ethnohistory* 45, 747–793.

Service, E. 1978. *Profiles in Ethnology,* 3rd ed. New York: Harper & Row.

Spiro, M. E. 1966. Religion: Problems of Definition and Explanation. *Anthropological Approaches to the Study of Religion,* ed. M. Banton, 85–126. London: Tavistock Publications.

Srinivas, M. N. 1976. *The Remembered Village.* Berkeley: University of California Press.

Steward, J. H. 1951. Levels of Sociocultural Integration: an Operational Concept. *Southwestern Journal of Anthropology* 7: 374–390.

Swanson, G. E. 1964. *The Birth of the Gods.* Ann Arbor: Ann Arbor Paperbacks.

Trimingham, J. S. 1949. *Islam in the Sudan.* London: Frank Cass & Co.

Tylor, E. B. 1874. *Primitive Culture,* 2nd ed. (2 vols.). Boston: Estes & Lauriat.

Wallace, A. F. C. 1966. *Religion: an Anthropological View.* New York: Random House.

Weber, M. 1930. *The Protestant Ethic and the Spirit of Capitalism,* trans. T. Parsons. London: Allen & Unwin.

Wikan, U. 1980. *Life among the Poor in Cairo.* London: Tavistock Publications.

Wilmsen, E. M. 1989. *Land Filled with Flies.* Chicago: University of Chicago Press.

Wyman, L. C., W. W. Hill, and I. Osanai. 1942. *Navajo Eschatology.* (University of New Mexico Bulletin, Anthropological Series, vol. 4, no. 1.) Albuquerque: University of New Mexico Press.

Wyman, L. C., and C. Kluckhohn. 1938. *Navaho Classification of their Song Ceremonials.* (Memoirs of the American Anthropological Association, no. 50.) Menasha, WI: American Anthropological Association.

Yang, M. 1945. *Chinese Village.* New York: Columbia University Press.

INDEX